THE GLOBAL RULES OF ART

The Global Rules of Art

THE EMERGENCE AND DIVISIONS
OF A CULTURAL WORLD ECONOMY

LARISSA BUCHHOLZ

PRINCETON UNIVERSITY PRESS
PRINCETON & OXFORD

Published by Princeton University Press
41 William Street, Princeton, New Jersey 08540
99 Banbury Road, Oxford OX2 6JX

press.princeton.edu

All Rights Reserved

Library of Congress Control Number: 2022937851

ISBN 9780691172026
ISBN (paperback) 9780691245447
ISBN (e-book) 9780691239866

British Library Cataloging-in-Publication Data is available

Editorial: Meagan Levinson, Barbara Shi, and Erin Beranek
Jacket Design: Katie Osborne
Production: Lauren Reese
Publicity: Kate Hensley, Jodi Price, Charlotte Coyne

This book has been composed in Arno.

10 9 8 7 6 5 4 3 2 1

To Natalie Buchholz and Wilhelm Pfundner

CONTENTS

ILLUSTRATIONS

TABLES

An Unsettling Success

MY SCHOLARLY interest in global issues is partly the product of growing up in Dresden, a city cut off from the outside world during the Cold War era. In the 1980s, Dresden was part of the German Democratic Republic (GDR), the poor, eastern area of Germany, which, since 1961, had been separated by a wall from the wealthier, western part. Where I lived, unlike other areas in the GDR, we did not have access to foreign television. My hometown was so isolated that it was called the "valley of the unaware."[1]

When friends and I walked home from school, past the monotony of pre-fabricated, socialist high-rises, we played a question-and-answer game. "Given the opportunity," we asked each other, "what place would you most like to visit?" We went on imaginary travels, envisioning what it would be like to ascend the Eiffel Tower, embark on safaris in Africa, or explore the Amazon. But at the same time, we felt certain we would never even get to see West Germany. We all felt a sense of marginality, captives of the East's gray reality and its daily shortcomings.

In 1989, when the television announced that the borders were open, it felt surreal. Adults rushed us into the street, chattering with one another as if they were all seeking reassurance that it was really happening. Amid this joyous exhilaration, intermingled with more than a few tears, cheers, and drinks among the grown-ups, I sensed that something had happened on that cold November evening that would change my life forever.

After the Berlin Wall fell, I came to treasure every opportunity I had to visit countries beyond the former "Iron Curtain." I later took a gap year before university and traveled extensively throughout Asia, Australia, and Europe. As I emerged from a closed society and immersed myself in extended trips abroad—precisely at the historical moment that the internet was growing and "globalization" was becoming a buzzword—I noticed familiar patterns forming across cultures, albeit amid major postcolonial inequalities. I was stepping into a so-called global village of near boundless communication, an expanding consumer culture, and a thriving travel industry for backpackers who were exactly like me, people who had set out to see the authentic, exotic "other" only to realize how interconnected the world had actually become. Even the remotest Akha hill tribe village in Thailand had Coca-Cola for sale.

Stimulated by these travel experiences, I interned at the House of World Cultures in Berlin as a university student. Established the same year the Berlin Wall came down, it was a major German center for international cultural exchange. Shortly after I started working there, the September 11 attacks happened, and I instantly found myself in a hotbed of activity. Renowned social scientists and intellectuals were invited to try to make sense of the shocking events, and they debated the role different cultures play in ongoing global conflicts. Most refuted the ideas of the conservative political scientist Samuel P. Huntington, whose "clash of civilizations" thesis, which predicted a near inevitable cultural conflict between the West and Islamic civilization, had become quite popular. One platform where this debate unfolded was "Democracy Unrealized." It was a conference convened by the Nigerian-born curator and writer Okwui Enwezor as a prelude to Documenta 2002 in Kassel, a major international group show in the contemporary visual arts. September 11 had transformed Enwezor's program into an important discursive forum for engaging with the painful events. Many of the speakers opposed Huntington's cultural essentialisms as well as any reductionist dichotomies between the West and East or between good and evil. Instead, they tried to come to terms with cultural difference and integration in an age of globalization in more complex ways, paying special attention, of course, to the contemporary visual arts.

Through that event, the contemporary art world emerged in my eyes as a pioneering cosmopolitan laboratory for an alternative vision of worldwide cultural interrelationships. Theorists, artists, and curators talked about how the field had begun to welcome new kinds of exchanges and discourses after decades of artistic segregation and Western hegemony. They also discussed how formerly marginal players from Eastern and Southern world regions were now gaining recognition, prompting new ways of thinking about the arts in more globally connected terms. These discussions gave me the electrifying impression that a sea change was under way in this field. It was as if a new cultural cartography was about to be invented for the visual arts, one that would open not just territorial borders but also long-standing cultural ones. I once again felt like I was living through history in the making.

Observing this intense phase of international intellectual debate firsthand was deeply inspiring. I, too, wanted to join the community of thinkers who were exploring this more constructive side of global culture, one that looked beyond Huntington's scenarios of apocalyptic conflict. Perhaps because of my earlier sense of marginality in the GDR, I was particularly drawn to understanding how artists from historically peripheral locations had managed to break through old barriers and become central figures within a system that had not welcomed them previously. While the 2001 Documenta platform had highlighted single artists and works in this regard, it did not offer any broader explanation for these significant changes in the field. As someone who had just started studying sociology, I believed that the discipline's more collectivist and empirically grounded approach could uniquely contribute to the formation of a more complete picture that would be able to answer several pressing questions: How much had actually changed with regard to the recognition of artists from formerly marginalized countries? What were the broader social and cultural processes contributing to the breaking down of boundaries among segregated types of creative producers? What, after all, are the mechanisms that enable the development of more equality and diversity within a globalizing cultural space? Eventually, I decided to pursue the topic more closely from a sociological point of view, conducting research that explored the dynamics and consequences of globalization in the contemporary visual arts.

My initial findings were sobering. During extended empirical analyses in 2005, it became clear that despite all the talk of a new era of globalization, the hierarchies among the most recognized artists in the world seemed hardly to have changed since the 1970s; artists from regions outside the West continued to be highly marginalized into the new millennium. I struggled to make sense of this puzzling situation, which stood in stark contrast to what one would have expected. In the same year, I published the results with my academic mentor at the time, Ulf Wuggenig, in an international arts journal,[2] and in the spring of 2006, I presented the work at a symposium at the Museum of Modern Art in New York. There, I was surrounded by art historians, curators, and theorists who were as surprised about the findings as I had been originally. Later that year, I gave a talk at an international conference about Pierre Bourdieu at the University of Michigan. The critical impetus—identifying and explaining the ongoing marginalization of "non-Western" artists in a globalizing cultural realm—met with an engaged sociological audience. At that conference, I also learned that Alain Quemin, a French sociologist, had pursued similar questions and had just published his first English article on the topic. Though he had used a different theoretical approach, Quemin had reached a similar conclusion. Despite globalization, the contemporary visual arts remained strongly dominated by artists from a small number of Western countries, most notably the United States and Germany. Instead of a new world marked by cultural openness and exchange, Western cultural dominance seemed to be unfolding on an expanded global scale.[3]

Then, in 2007, something remarkable happened. Chinese contemporary artists like Zhang Xiaogang and Wang Guangyi rose to the highest echelons of the global art market, achieving multimillion-dollar sales at major auction houses, rivaling the economic success commanded by such Western market superstars as Jeff Koons and Damien Hirst. Unsettled by this sudden and unexpected turn of events, I realized I had to think differently. I soon found myself conducting interviews with gallerists and art-market experts in New York during a particularly hot summer, seeking to understand what had happened. Although these interviews ultimately could not answer my questions in a convincing way, they all underscored one important insight: success in the auction market did not necessarily correlate with what some gallery owners, curators, and art critics perceived as true artistic value and merit. There seemed to be a disjunction between commercial and artistic valuation.

This insight was a critical moment for my research. If the criteria for success in the global auction market were so different from what central gatekeepers considered to be artistic quality, then the dynamics underlying the recognition of artists from "non-Western" regions *must* work differently in contemporary art's commercial sphere. And I wanted to find out *how* they differed. In particular, I wanted to understand what had allowed these artists to break into this market and dramatically unsettle existing hierarchies in unexpected ways.

In this regard, Bourdieu's theory of the field of cultural production, which he elaborated in *The Rules of Art* (1992), seemed key. It centers on the opposition between specific artistic recognition and commercial success, between art and money, or more generally, between the sacred and the profane. To critically extend Bourdieu's influential framework, I decided to pursue the difference between market success in contrast to artistic prestige in my work on globalization. Hence, I revised my research approach again. Instead of focusing on the reproduction of hierarchies, I needed to explore possibilities for change—that is, the conditions that make the broader recognition of artists from historically peripheral countries possible. At the same time, however, I had to find out how and why these conditions were different in commercial and cultural cross-border circuits. In short, I wanted to account for the historical formation of a global art field and its dynamics of valuation, paying special attention to its internal divisions around art and money.

Little did I realize the challenge ahead of me. The study's geographic scope was almost too large for any serious art and subject-area specialist. Inevitably, nuances will be lost if one examines the historical emergence and multidimensional economy of valuation of an entire global art space. Doing so also required me to rely on sweeping, large-scale analyses while trying to stave off severe intellectual vertigo. The Italian literary scholar Franco Moretti once justified far-reaching quantitative analyses on the world literary system in time and space with the metaphor of "distant reading."[4] That is exactly how the research process felt to me at times.

Even more dauntingly, as my work progressed, it became clear that any attempt to write a book about global processes that used a theoretical framework with Western origins would be an intellectual minefield. Raewyn Connell is correct when she argues that sociologists who merely upscale Western theory to make wide-ranging claims about the nature of "global society" are being one-sidedly Northern-centric.[5] How could I avoid being a Northern, global, top-down theorist with my project? Indeed, when I joined the Harvard Society of Fellows as a junior fellow, my conversations with anthropologists and humanists made me painfully aware of how deeply my classifications were still steeped in Western bias. Just as I thought I was ready to complete my book manuscript, I had to revamp my methods and re-collect and reanalyze my data.

I also had to think more deeply about my conceptual methodology. To be sure, it did not make sense to simply discard Bourdieu's complex theory, which was suitable to my research problem. (In chapter 1 of this book, I expand on my rationale for using his approach.) But how could I extend his theory from a national to a global context without ending up with Northern upscaling and deductive reification? During the fellowship, this search turned me into an advocate of "analogical theorizing," a concept originally championed by Diane Vaughan.[6] In her method, which draws from Georg Simmel's formal sociology, analogical heuristics are used to identify basic equivalencies across cases that may involve different levels of analysis (for example, in her research on deviance among individuals and organizations on a subnational level). This establishes a basis that can then be used to identify how a new case differs from the original one in systematic ways; it thus provides one analytical strategy for reflexively altering theory. I realized that analogical theorizing also provided a fertile conceptual methodology for carefully extending and revising concepts across different scales in a global-level analysis.[7] Ultimately, I had to rethink my theoretical framework several times, all while remaining alert to the limitations stemming from my own geopositionality as an academic researcher in the privileged Northwest.[8]

Nevertheless, while working on this book, I also became convinced of the promise of going beyond the additive logic of single, specialized articles in journals or edited volumes and striving for a more integrative approach to the globalizing contemporary visual arts and the field's dynamics of value creation. We know that today, the most noted visual artists are becoming increasingly established on a worldwide level. But we still know relatively little concerning how an emerging global cultural system affects such processes. We know even less about the conditions that allow such systems to move toward greater equality and diversity among their leading creative producers. By developing a global field perspective, I have attempted to address such gaps and complement the array of insightful studies on specific countries and their rising art

worlds or those works on specific globalizing institutions—such as art biennials, museums, "global galleries," art fairs, or auction houses—with an integrative historical-theoretical perspective that traces how these entities connect
and diverge within a global context. I hope this book, however, will spark additional methodological and theoretical debates about the development of a
global (historical) sociology of culture.

Lastly, while changes in the commercial global art market drew me to this
study, I believe that one key contribution of this book is that it comparatively
showcases the globalizing circuits for artistic and intellectual exchange that
resist those same dynamics. With the dramatic growth of the auction market
for contemporary art in the new millennium, spectacular record prices in major
global cities have garnered ample public attention, and globalization in the arts
has widely come to be associated with the market's overarching triumph.

Concomitantly, an intellectually corrosive approach has gained momentum—a
market-centrism that gauges the contemporary visual arts primarily by their
economic output and allegiances. This perspective is not just an ideological
reality in the executive offices of cultural policy makers or certain museum
boards. It has also been fed and legitimated by a recent flood of publications
by economists and some sociologists. Several of these scholars have their professional homes in the growing institutions of higher education that were
founded by auction houses and that specialize in the "art industry." When "art
markets" or the "art industry" are studied, a great heterogeneity of institutions
and actors from the nonprofit sphere and the profit-driven market are thrown
into the same analytical pot without paying much attention to their diverging
interests and principles of evaluation. Instead, the "industry" metaphor is un-
hesitatingly extended to all of them. Within the rhetoric of market-centrism,
artistic innovation is directly compared with disruptive innovation at technology
companies, artistic careers are reduced to the establishment of marketable
brands, and curators and critics appear as little more than entrepreneurial
handmaidens of commercial interests. Any critique one might offer of the
market-driven rhetoric in such scholarly writings is decried as archaic, quasi-
theological, or merely anticommercial posturing.

In *The Global Rules of Art*, my goal is to counter and respond to this social
scientific way of thinking. While I do not deny that market forces have gained
power over the past few decades—and from a global perspective, this book
sheds added light on how they did so—it is important not to ignore or pre-
emptively sound the death knell of a coexisting noncommercial sphere in
global contemporary art either, one that has still been capable of articulating
and defending its own values. Scholarly market-centrism has unfortunately
lost sight of that noncommercial sphere's distinctive and evolving characteristics. It is precisely by adopting a comparative perspective on the globalizing

dynamics in cultural-institutional circuits that are dedicated to art as a relatively independent sphere of discourse and activity and those that strive to
enhance profits and market brands that one can more clearly see how the former have their own discrete momentum and how their transnational protago-
nists strive to resist the pulls and pressures of commerce.

This comparative perspective has also allowed me to see more sharply
where the real impulses for a more cosmopolitan, global vision of contemporary
art originated. Noncommercial art organizations and circuits provided the
necessary space for curatorial risk-taking beyond Western orthodoxies. They
empowered agents to undertake genuine artistic and discursive explorations,
and even to form symbolic revolutions, across borders—a dynamic that is
quite distinct from the fads and fashions of the market, the raucous celebrity
culture of certain art fairs, and the impatience of some deep-pocketed buyers
who shun an engagement with art to hop on the latest artistic "brand-wagon."
Without losing a critical bent, I am seeking to create space for more sociological inquiry into a relatively autonomous sphere of the globalization of culture,
the distinctive features of which become more visible when they are traced
against the backdrop of its growing global commercial counterpart. Instead of
joining the chorus of market-centrism or giving in to stultifying market fatal-
ism, this book spotlights the cross-border dynamics of institutions, artists, and
their mediators that have run against the zeitgeist of financial instrumentality.
Using a comparative perspective, it tells the story about an embattled but nevertheless resistant terrain of art production in a global context and about the
tireless work of its advocates. Now more than ever, given the onset of a worldwide
pandemic, their engagement and solidarity is absolutely critical for contemporary
art's cosmopolitan laboratory to persist and evolve further.[9]

THE GLOBAL RULES OF ART

1

A Global Field Approach
to Art and Culture

In place of the old local and national seclusion and self-sufficiency, we have intercourse in every direction, universal interdependence of nations. And as in material, so also in intellectual production. The intellectual creations of individual nations become common property.

—KARL MARX AND FRIEDRICH ENGELS,
THE COMMUNIST MANIFESTO, 1848

GLOBALIZATION IN THE ARTS is not a recent phenomenon. For centuries, cultural flows across borders have been omnipresent and fundamental for the development of the visual arts.[1] Beyond the mundane sale, exchange, or even plunder of artifacts, the circulation of artists and aesthetics between distant places has inspired numerous cross-cultural innovations.

If we merely look at the story of Western art, for example, during the Renaissance, artists across Europe flocked to Rome and Florence to familiarize themselves with the technique of central perspective being refined there, and they brought the essential technology of oil paint with them from the North to the South.[2] Later, the no-less-revolutionary movement toward abstract painting among the French Impressionists was inspired by Asian woodcuts of the Ukiyo-e School that had flourished in Japan between the seventeenth and nineteenth centuries.[3] Perhaps most famously, African tribal arts heavily influenced Picasso and Braque's invention of Cubism in early twentieth-century Paris.

More recently, the history of New York's postwar ascendance into an international art capital would be unthinkable without the forced migration of numerous European artists and intellectuals.[4] Their presence contributed to the growth of transatlantic networks that, in the 1960s, influenced the rise of "contemporary art," a type of visual art production that expanded beyond painting and sculpture to include transgressive practices like performance, conceptual art, land art, and Pop art, among others.[5] Such contemporary art practices came to circulate in an international field—that is, within a transatlantic space that connected North America and western Europe—and enabled more intensified cultural exchanges between the two continents.[6] Traveling exhibitions wandered from museums in Europe to the US and back, communicating and promoting major artistic developments beyond the boundaries of national fields.[7] Galleries on both sides of the Atlantic collaborated to foster the acceptance and sale of works by emerging contemporary artists.[8] And yet up until the 1980s, vast parts of the world did not frequently participate in this international field, and contemporary visual art from outside Western countries remained in a highly marginalized position, hardly considered at all. In fact, the body of work that emerged as the postwar canon of so-called international contemporary art consisted almost exclusively of American and western European artists, most of them white and male.

Over the following three decades, however, a new phase of globalization considerably transformed the contemporary art field. A whirlwind of changes—including the worldwide proliferation of international art biennials and museums, the far-reaching expansion of art fairs and auction houses, and the rise of global discourses and new internet platforms—combined to establish a *global art field* that now includes places in Oceania, Asia, Latin America, and Africa in qualitatively new ways. In contrast to previous eras, art scenes in these regions are no longer just gold mines for one-sided aesthetic appropriations. Nor are they simply distant sites for random cultural encounters.[9] Rather, this new, distinguished phase of globalization has witnessed the rise of an expanded institutional framework that allows for more sustained forms of global exchange and competition around shared artistic practices and stakes. Artists, intermediaries, aesthetic idioms, and histories of visual art from around the world have become entrenched within a common global field, one marked by expanding relations, extended communications, and the mutual quest for recognition and success on a broader worldwide stage.

The Global Rules of Art is an attempt to examine the complex dynamics that have led to the formation of this global field, illuminating its emergent structures, brokers, and some of its changing cultural practices.[10] From this deepened historical perspective, I also shed new light on a central debate among scholars of globalization—namely, if processes associated with globalization lead to increasing cultural homogeneity or diversity.[11] In the contemporary art field, we can think about the question of diversity versus homogeneity in terms of the aesthetic features of artists' works or their national backgrounds.[12] My study focuses on the latter aspect, exploring whether or not the latest wave of globalization has challenged the one-sided dominance of cultural producers from a handful of Western countries that characterized the earlier international field.[13] As the emergence of a global art field entailed extraordinary cross-border flows and the growing transcontinental mediation of art, have these dynamics led to the expanded dominance of artists from a few countries that are largely in the "West" and, in this sense, to cultural homogeneity?[14] Or have they enabled artistic creators from a more varied set of "non-Western" contexts—countries in eastern Europe, Asia, Latin America, or Africa—to attain greater global circulation and recognition, thereby increasing cultural diversity?[15]

This question—whether and why the most recognized artists have become more diverse while the art field's institutional context has globally expanded— dovetails with a second and even broader problem: namely, the making of global cultural canons. Ideas around "world art" have animated thinkers for decades. But after the new millennium, when global cultural circuits materialized, allowing artifacts to move across borders in unprecedented ways, it seems time to shift such ideas from being figments of the intellectual imagination to being questions that undergo actual empirical scrutiny. In other words, we can explore how the "intellectual creations of individual nations" could indeed— as Marx and Engels phrase it so colorfully in this chapter's epigraph—melt into worldwide "common property."

As a sociologist, I abstain from joining current debates among art historians and cultural theorists about how to properly define "global art," how to depict its distinctive aesthetic and historical features, or who can rightly claim to belong to it and why.[16] Rather than engaging in aesthetic judgement or valuation, I step back to understand the broader historical-institutional context in which valuations take shape, and how they play out. Like a second-order observer—in the sense used by Niklas Luhmann—my approach thus pursues a complementary perspective on questions surrounding global art and its canons.[17] It explores the contextual factors that give some valuations more weight than others in the globalizing art space, and it broadens that view to incorporate the wider social, cultural, and economic forces influencing how some artists rise to the top—and thus become part of the evolving "global canons" of contemporary art—while others do not.[18]

With this contextual focus on valuation, as an entry point into the questions how globalization affects canons and the diversity of their artists, this study joins a longstanding line of scholarship in cultural sociology that examines how new ideas, artifacts, and their creators become recognized and valued as important.[19] Within this extensive line of research, Bourdieu's fields theory has been particularly influential.[20] In his now-classic work *The Rules of Art*, Bourdieu discusses the ways an artist's recognition is not merely the product of their individual genius and their work's intrinsic aesthetic features. From a sociological perspective, that recognition is also shaped by the historical interplay of the structures, meanings, and specialized agents within a shared field of cultural production, which represents a relatively distinct social universe. Bourdieu furthermore suggests that cultural fields are internally divided between two main subfields, which are either oriented according to the judgments of cultural experts or according to commercial logics. Using the metaphor of the "rules of art," he emphasizes that the dynamics involved in the valuation of artists in these two subfields are far from random but instead follow distinctive patterns that sociological analysis can illuminate.

However, while we have by now a rich body of sociological contributions on the valuation of culture in general and on art fields in particular, most studies have tended to focus on cities or countries within North America or Europe. The rare exceptions that go beyond this confined radius and look in more transnational or global directions outside the West have primarily explored eras before the new millennium.[21] Thus, the current literature has paid less attention to how contexts and factors for cross-border valuation change under conditions involving more globally interconnected cultural mediation. So even as we have seen the obvious growth of global cultural circuits and increasing sources of artistic talent across the world, we still know comparatively little about the "global rules" governing why some of them have gained worldwide renown in times of accelerated globalization while others have not. We also know relatively little about the contextual forces that shape cultural canons at a global level and how those canons can expand and diversify. In a period in which the value of the most recognized creative producers is increasingly established across multiple continents, it is important to widen our analytical radius, advancing approaches that capture the construction of value and reputations at a global scale.

The contemporary visual arts seem to offer an ideal empirical site for exploring these issues. Unfettered from the need for literal translation, like novels or poetry, and tending to be unburdened from the necessity of local performance, like theater, the visual arts have grown into a particularly advanced globalized realm.[22] At the turn of the century, observers had already suggested that "[in] almost no other sphere of culture is the shrinking of North and South, of East and West so intense as in the fine arts."[23] As such, looking specifically at contemporary art will allow us to throw these less explored sociological topics of the effects of globalization on cross-border valuation, the making of global canons, and those canons' diversity into particularly sharp relief.

To engage with these issues, this book expands Bourdieu's influential theory of fields of cultural production from a national to a global scale. By advancing a global cultural fields approach and by drawing from abundant research on the globalization of the art field and its leading artists, my study shows how the contemporary visual arts have become a more artistically global affair. However—and this is the crux of the *dual* global cultural fields approach I will develop—within the same emerging global field, changes have unfolded differently at its commercial and expert-driven poles. In other words, I establish that there are systematic differences in the dynamics and conditions of the recognition of artists from "non-Western" countries and diversity in globalizing subfields that are oriented around a logic of artistic prestige and charisma on the one hand, and those that are ruled by a commercial logic on the other. The same Chinese artists whose works have achieved multimillion-dollar prices at an auction house like Sotheby's and who have joined the global ranks of the world's most economically successful artists are unlikely to gain worldwide cultural esteem to the same extent. Conversely, "global artists" from Latin America, Africa, or the Middle East who have made inroads into major shrines of consecration seldom reach the highest echelons of the global art market.

With this argument, *The Global Rules of Art* moves beyond dichotomic accounts of globalization in contemporary art that have either claimed Western reproduction and artistic homogeneity on a global scale or prognosticated radical change.[24] Instead, my study advances an alternative, more intermediate perspective: whereas there have been transformations that have created more diversity beyond the older Western "international" canon, I also demonstrate that these historical dynamics unfolded in uneven and diverging ways within the global commercial and expert-driven subfields. Hence, to approach the questions of diversity and valuation across borders, it is necessary to pay greater theoretical attention to the institutional diversity of globalizing cultural realms themselves.

Lastly, from this argumentative angle, this book also challenges recent interdisciplinary accounts of the contemporary visual arts that have posited a growing convergence between the expert-driven and commercial spheres for the shaping of artistic value and careers.[25] According to this view, a number of historical developments that accelerated in the new millennium—including the rising power of art fairs and auction houses, the growing institutionalization of art as an investment, as well as the growing influx of media and financial elites—have entailed that the art market has gained unprecedented authority in setting values, while noncommercial art experts and their criteria of evaluation have lost influence and independence. As a result, there would be a growing overlap in the types of artists who are prized in commercial and aesthetic terms and, thus, the end of any dualism between art and money.

Most of the scholarship that has formulated this market-convergence thesis, however, has relied on single, highly visible Western examples, especially Andy Warhol, Jeff Koons, and Damien Hirst. I revisit the problem of art versus money from a more global perspective and a broader base of evidence. By tracing hundreds of the most successful contemporary artists from different countries in the global exhibition space and auction market over several years, I reveal that the historical period most closely associated with the rise of a global art market has not in fact led to a growing convergence among artists who are successful in commercial or cultural terms. Rather, and perhaps counterintuitively, the overall pattern is one of increasing divergence. Contrary to accounts that associate globalization with the unmitigated growth of market forces for determining artistic prestige across borders, my study instead posits that the contemporary visual arts have become fundamentally structured around a dual cultural world economy.

This alternative position should not be misunderstood as a naive refutation of strong commodification trends in the contemporary art market. Ironically, as I point out later, it is precisely the radicalization of market criteria—with the growth of new types of institutions, buyers, and financial logics—that has decoupled judgments about the value of certain artists in the art market from judgments among cultural experts in historically new ways. The divide of art versus money also holds because the influence of money has become so strong and globalized, which has pulled the commercial and specific cultural spheres farther apart within the emerging global field.[26]

Ultimately, this book addresses a deeper and more enduring social difference—that of "status" versus "class," of symbolic valuation versus market valuation—showing how these divisions involve different and even inverse effects of globalization on the recognition of artists from diverse countries around the world. Uncovering such important differences, *The Global Rules of Art* offers the first substantially detailed, comparative explanation of how and why there can be divergent patterns of global change within the same social universe.[27] By examining the dual economy of an emerging global cultural field—and by charting its unique territories of circulation, interpretation, and valuation—I reveal the multifaceted forces shaping global artistic reputations and canons in a more interconnected world.[28]

From Cultural Imperialism to Global Art Worlds: Three Models of the Globalization of Culture

Sociological scholarship about the globalization of culture deals with a subject that is complex and elusive.[29] This complexity might explain why relatively few theoretical frameworks about globalization in spheres of cultural production exist, especially when compared with the broad variety of theories about the global economy or world politics.[30] So far, the most important models that have applications beyond singular cultural realms include the political-economy model of cultural imperialism, the cultural flows and networks model, and the global culture/art worlds model.[31] Each of these frameworks makes broader arguments about the emergence and structure of transnational or global realms of cultural production. Each one also implies a distinctive "scenario" concerning how accelerated globalization impacts the diversity of creative producers across borders.[32]

Because I am suggesting a conceptual framework that is an alternative to these pioneering models, it is important that I first review them and highlight how they connect with established arguments about globalization in the contemporary art world. Only then will it be clear how the book's theoretical approach allows us to synthesize and advance aspects of existing perspectives. I have tried to make this discussion accessible to readers who are not specialists in this area, and I have purged quite a few overly technical details. However, if you are less interested in this background and more interested in the book's historical account of the art field's multiple global transformations, feel free to skip this theoretical discussion and jump straight to the end of the chapter, where I offer an outline of the rest of the book.

The oldest theory on the globalization of culture, which emerged in the 1970s, is the *political-economy model of cultural imperialism*.[33] It argues that postwar sectors of media and cultural production have developed parallel to the overall capitalist world-system—that is, toward single global markets structured around the dominance of a small number of core countries over a vast periphery.[34] Politically motivated and profit-chasing actors from these core countries—particularly the US—push for the opening and deregulation of national cultural markets around the world. In the process, players from core countries benefit from strong competitive advantages in political, financial, and technological resources. Their expansion goes along with highly unidirectional cultural flows from the core to the periphery as well as strong dependencies on the sites of peripheral agents. Hence, this framework associates the globalization of culture with the one-sided expansion and concentration of power by mediating actors and institutions from (Western) core countries. This in turn has led to the worldwide dominance of their media and cultural producers and, ultimately, to cultural homogeneity.[35]

Although such expansionist arguments were originally applied to mass-cultural sectors, similar points have been made about contemporary art. Alain Quemin, for example, suggests that "a strong hierarchy of countries *controls* the organization of and participation in the international contemporary art world and market."[36] As he argues, "the art world has a clearly defined center comprising a small number of Western countries, among which the US and Germany are preeminent, and a vast periphery, comprising all other states."[37] Accordingly, visual artists from this small number of leading countries would overwhelmingly dominate the global arena.

The political-economy model of cultural imperialism productively shifted social-scientific perspectives about media and cultural production beyond the national level early on, and it correctly highlighted the important role macro-level inequalities play in our understanding of the dynamics of global cultures.[38] But it *only* focuses on material inequalities in globalizing cultural production, such as economic-technical resources, patterns of ownership, or political regulations. These kinds of disparities are then tightly coupled with the logic and structure of the capitalist world-system overall.

The model also problematically equates a country's political and economic-technological power with its global cultural influence—two attributes that, in reality, can diverge greatly.[39] Consider, for example, Japan. One of the biggest economies in the world, it has become a central player in the capitalist world-system in the postwar era. And yet within the contemporary art world, relatively few of its artists enjoy a vaunted reputation on the global stage.[40] In view of this and other asynchronies,[41] it seems safe to conclude with Ulf Hannerz that "center/periphery relationships of culture are not . . . a mere reflection of political and economic power."[42]

Seeking to overcome the imperialism model's limitations, Arjun Appadurai's *cultural flows and networks model* rejected the idea that cross-border dynamics in the media and arts are tightly determined by an overarching capitalist world-system.[43] He claims that processes associated with the globalization of culture since the 1980s have not led to the one-sided dominance of the US or a few core countries but instead to greater decentralization and diversification. In particular, the increasing availability of "capabilities to produce and disseminate" various cultural goods "throughout the world" has stimulated the growth of regional "scapes"[44] that offset Western hegemony.[45] From this regionalist angle, Appadurai rejects an all-encompassing center-periphery model as no longer adequate for capturing the more complex configuration of a "new global cultural economy."[46] So whereas the cultural imperialism model suggests the rise of an ever more integrated global system with a few (Western) centers of control, Appadurai, along with other scholars who have explicated this framework for contemporary art, paint a diametrically opposed picture, one of growing global diversification—and perhaps even entropy—due to the proliferation of more regional cultural networks and flows.[47]

Appadurai's model productively critiques the totalizing perspective of the political-economy model. However, its empirical scenario sets the global and the regional as exclusive entities when, in reality, they can coexist and be mutually influential. For example, as we shall see, the rise of regional art market centers like Hong Kong or Dubai in contemporary art did not override New York's powerful influence as a global art capital. I therefore must agree with Jan Nederveen Pieterse that it is most productive to circumvent any zero-sum conception and instead work toward an approach that accounts for the emergence of *global* meanings and structures in addition to regional ones.[48]

A third body of work, which I summarize as the *global culture/art worlds model*, addresses this gap in Appadurai's work.[49] Scholars that build on Howard Becker's sociological notion of an art world as "the network of people whose cooperative activity, organized via their joint knowledge of conventional means of doing things, produces the kind of art works that art world is noted for" suggest that global culture worlds differ according to their expanded scope of participants and activities.[50] They are defined as communities of creators, gatekeepers, organizations, and audiences from diverse continents who collaborate on the "creation, evaluation, dissemination and reception" of a certain type of art or media across borders.[51] Importantly, through such collaborations, global culture worlds develop shared conventions—that is, "shared understandings about what cultural products should be like . . . providing standards for evaluating and appreciating" them within a global context.[52]

A critical mechanism for the formation of global culture worlds is institutional infrastructures that connect people from around the world on a periodical basis. These include international trade fairs, international art biennials, and cosmopolitan art festivals. Diana Crane explains the importance of such events: "Global culture worlds require temporary settings such as intermediary trade fairs where cultural goods can be displayed to large numbers of creators, producers and sellers and where, most importantly, an unwritten consensus can be reached about the nature and direction of their activities."[53] Even in an age of enhanced communication technologies, direct personal encounters and frequent physical gatherings seem crucial for enabling the rise of global networks and shared cultural conventions in the arts or media production.[54]

When it comes to contemporary art, one of the earliest and strongest formulations of the idea of a global art world, which resonates with the sociological model outlined above, comes from the US-American philosopher Noël Carroll. He argues that the proliferation of international biennials for contemporary art since the late 1980s contributed to the rise of an interconnected art world on a global scale.[55] Significantly, this transnational/global art world has also developed a "common art culture" that turned contemporary art into an "internally coherent practice" around the globe.[56] The new cultural configuration encompasses the use of similar artistic idioms—such as video art, installation, or performance art. It moreover involves the rise of shared cultural presuppositions and sense-making strategies to engage with artworks in similar ways across continents, which "can be mobilized in Shanghai, Sydney, Rio or Cape-town."[57]

Carroll's argument about the emergence of a shared culture, which would feed into more cosmopolitan understandings of contemporary art, implies a scenario in which accelerated globalization enables a greater diversity of artists to circulate and become recognized on a global stage.[58]

In general, the global culture/art worlds model has made significant contributions in theorizing the global cultural arena as more than simply a one-sidedly Western-dominated playground or a looser assemblage of diverse local and regional clusters. Nevertheless, it still tends to conceptualize cross-continental relations and meanings in a way that is too unified and harmonious. While I agree with its emphasis on shared institutional circuits and understandings that allow people to interact in globalizing cultural realms, I think it is important not only to look at what participants have in common but also at what may still divide them. Cultural agents from around the world can use the same label of "contemporary art" or the same artistic idioms, for example; and yet, they may still ascribe different meanings and values to those terms.[59] Moreover, such differences can remain contested within entrenched global power dynamics. By not acknowledging the possibility of different cultural perspectives, persisting inequalities, and the clashes that may result from them, the global art world model risks projecting an overly unified perspective onto "globalized art."[60] This is precisely where I believe the alternative of a global field approach can be effective and valuable.

Toward a Global Cultural Fields Approach

Each of the two more global models just outlined offers important insights for theorizing the dynamics of globalizing cultures. They both, however, take overly one-sided and unitary approaches to global cultural production . While the political-economy model of cultural imperialism focuses on structural inequalities, the global art worlds approach privileges cultural meanings.[61] While the former emphasizes Western domination and related dependencies, the latter inverts that scenario by highlighting cosmopolitan interdependencies and collaborative consensus. Despite these stark differences, the models both imply that global cultures revolve largely around unifying commonalities, whether they are imposed through power or they emerge from more egalitarian interactions.

To move beyond these overly unitary either/or perspectives, I suggest working with the alternative of a global fields approach to contemporary art.[62] This framework provides a fruitful starting point for synthesizing the analytical dimensions that fall apart in existing theories. Moreover, it enables us to account for both commonality *and* difference in globalizing cultures, thus offering a better-calibrated lens for examining historical global transformations and artistic diversity across borders. But because a global cultural fields approach extends and revises Bourdieu's fields theory from a national to a transcontinental scale, I should first clarify some of his most fundamental concepts, especially for those readers who are not familiar with his work.[63]

Cultural Fields, Forms of Capital, Habitus

Similar to the art worlds model, Bourdieu's theory portrays realms of cultural production as relatively self-contained universes. However, he considers competition, rather than collaboration, to be a field's driving dynamic.[64] Consequently, the mediation and valuation of contemporary art cannot be thought of as a process that operates through consensus in a (global) art world "community"; it must be placed within a contested arena where several artists, intermediaries, and institutions are competing for specific symbolic or material rewards and trying to influence the criteria governing what good art is and who should be considered a worthy artist.

Fields are based on distinctive meanings insofar as participants are oriented around a common type of cultural production (such as contemporary art, literature, music, or fashion), and they share a collective belief in the field's particular stakes and core issues (what Bourdieu calls the "illusio").[65] But they are also fundamentally affected by distinctive structures—that is, inequalities in power resources. Bourdieu famously pluralizes Marx's notion of *economic capital*, suggesting that the basic forms of power extend to include *cultural capital* (cultural wealth and competencies), *social capital* (social ties), and *symbolic capital* (specific symbolic recognition and prestige).[66] The historically specific distribution of a field's most significant forms of capital defines its structure of dominant and dominated positions. In turn, this structure influences the field's dynamics.[67] Artists and intermediaries may play with multiple cards (i.e., capitals) to advocate for their agendas, but how they play the game also depends on where they find themselves in a field's hierarchy at any particular moment.

More specifically, Bourdieu suggests that cultural fields are structured around two main axes with different stakes and power sources. The primary axis revolves around the polarity and tension between what he calls a *relatively autonomous subfield of restricted production* and a *heteronomous subfield of large-scale production*.[68] For the latter subfield, the dominant stake and form of power is economic capital. The competitive valuation of cultural producers is shaped by profit-driven criteria and foregrounds their commercial success.[69] At the other end of the spectrum, at the relatively autonomous pole, economic rewards are secondary, and this subfield is instead oriented largely around specific symbolic capital (i.e., cultural legitimacy). The evaluation of creators revolves around field-specific aesthetic or intellectual criteria that are relatively independent from, or even opposed to, commercial or other "profane" considerations.[70]

A second structural axis runs through the autonomous subfield itself, setting up an opposition between *heterodoxy* and *orthodoxy*. The orthodoxy refers to the proverbial art establishment, those cultural agents who have reached dominant positions with high symbolic capital in the game. Heterodox factions, in turn, often consist of younger aspirants with low symbolic capital. To make a name for themselves and move the field forward, they are inclined to challenge the orthodoxy via "distinction" by advocating for innovative artistic approaches or mediation strategies (such as new curatorial strategies, discourses, outlets, or forms of criticism).[71] As such, inequalities in symbolic capital are a structural source for innovation at the pole of restricted production, fueling a kind of "permanent revolution" between newcomers and established players.[72]

Yet to fully understand the dynamics of art fields, shared meanings and structure are certainly not wholly determinative, however. It is also critical to look at the properties of individual players to make sense of their strategies (i.e., their *position-takings*) within their field positions in a given historical context. To theorize such a micro-level dimension, Bourdieu introduced the complex and much-debated concept of "habitus." In basic terms, it denotes the set of embodied dispositions that people bring to the game, the ways of thinking, seeing, feeling, classifying, and acting that have been inculcated by their own social upbringing and educational or professional trajectory.[73] For example, it makes a difference if a contemporary art curator was raised in an academic household and educated in a theory-heavy program or if they grew up in a wealthy family of entrepreneurs and began their education with interior design before studying in a traditional art history program. Even if these two exhibition makers started out in similar structural positions as newcomers in the art field, they would probably carry different habitus that predisposed them to champion different kinds of artists and curatorial strategies.

In sum, cultural fields represent relatively independent universes of cultural production and mediation. Broadly speaking, valuation emerges out of the interplay of field-specific meanings, unequal structures, and the habitus of the game's players within a broader historical context. It is a complex interaction characterized by an ongoing dynamic of competition (and related collaborations), whose directions, in turn, influence who gains recognition as an artist, who sells the most, and who can claim the power to symbolically consecrate artists to begin with.

From a National to a Global Cultural Field: Three Mechanisms and Multiscalar Configurations

Bourdieu originally developed his conception of cultural fields using the nation-state, namely France, as his primary unit of analysis.[74] As I have explicated in earlier work, this original national orientation does not mean that his idea of the field automatically falls prey to (implicit) methodological nationalism.[75] In fact, though Bourdieu did not elaborate a global field analysis himself, he referred to international or global fields in his later writings.[76] There is also a burgeoning—though still scarce—literature that has recently applied his work to the study of transnational or globalizing realms of cultural production and beyond.[77] The earliest contribution was Pascale Casanova's superb monograph about modern avant-garde writers in the world literary space.[78] Other scholars have illuminated the transnational patterns of book translations, the global diffusion and hybridization of rock music, the globalization of the performing arts in Central Asia, the emergence of a European field for trade with television programs or the institutional recognition of authors in the transnational literary field.[79] These contributions demonstrate how Bourdieu's approach can productively illuminate the examination of a variety of cross-border cultural spheres.

However, existing case studies have remained fragmented with regard to articulating the theoretical elements that need to be revised when one extends cultural fields theory beyond national boundaries. We have not yet seen the crystallization of a clearly identifiable "global cultural fields approach" that can readily serve as an alternative to established models in the globalization literature, while also providing an integrative basis for a cumulative research program on transnational or global cultural fields.[80] By synthesizing insights from existing scholarship and by building on findings from my own research on contemporary art, I develop a framework that delineates distinctive conceptual elements of a global, rather than national, cultural fields analysis.[81]

In a basic sense, a global cultural field materializes when agents from different national fields extend their rivalry over specific forms of capital and interpretative issues within a domain of cultural production across several continents. In contemporary art, for example, ambitious curators traveled more extensively to realize projects across multiple locations and to stay abreast of art production around the world. Leading galleries participated in art fairs on several continents to forge connections, compete for sales, and advance the success of their own artists. And aspiring contemporary artists exhibited their work in territorially expanded circuits within a larger pool of peers from different world regions than ever before. In short, a global cultural field emerges when the scope and stakes of exchange and competition in an arena of cultural production have become redefined in global terms, when field struggles no longer unfold within one country but across a wide variety of different countries.[82]

It is tempting to explain the rise of a global sphere of cultural production by using broader geopolitical, economic, or technological frameworks (like "the rise of the internet"). But if we think of contemporary art as a field, in Bourdieu's terms, we have to approach it as a universe that is relatively independent of the broader historical environment or any notions of technological determinism.[83] The key word is "relatively." External changes can and do affect the artistic realm, but they do so indirectly, becoming "refracted," like a prism, through the field's internal logics, structures, and historical state.[84] This idea of a *refraction effect* guards against seeing art's globalization as merely a passive reflection of wider political-economic or technological developments, a view that is still endorsed by several art theorists.[85]

The "internal" historical processes involved in the formation of a global cultural field are, of course, multifaceted and complex. They involve growing relationships among national and regional cultural fields with very different structures and traditions.[86] And yet I suggest that there are at least three field-internal mechanisms that both reflect and support the emergence of a global field within a cultural domain, while also interacting with facilitating broader historical conditions.[87]

The first refers to *global institutional circuits*, which refer to organizational infrastructures that support the transcontinental circulation of people, ideas, and artifacts. In contemporary art, two of the most influential circuits for the emergence of a global playing field have been the global biennial circuit at the autonomous pole and the global art fair circuit at the heteronomous, market-oriented pole. Over the past three decades, international art biennials and fairs have increasingly diffused across several continents. Moreover, they have come to form partly coordinated infrastructures for the circulation and valorization of contemporary art. Such circuits are important because they connect individual and organizational players from various national and regional fields on a more frequent, sustained basis. And while the global art worlds model underlines the significance of these institutions for the globalization process, a field perspective highlights how they lead not only to more cultural exchange across borders but also to extended competition.

Furthermore, the formation of a global field depends on the construction of distinctive meanings—that is, unique modes of perception, interpretation, and belief. In this regard, a second globalizing indicator and cultural mechanism is *field-specific global discourse*, ongoing discussions and publications about globalizing dynamics regarding a particular cultural realm and its practices. For example, the rise of new ways of writing and debating about globalization in the contemporary visual arts since the 1990s has gradually helped redefine the boundaries of "international contemporary art" beyond a narrow Western perspective or a merely additive approach involving various national artistic traditions. What has emerged is a more integrative, *global vision* of contemporary art through which artists, mediators, and institutions from around the world have become perceived as being part of a shared cultural space, even though differing understandings of "contemporary art" or "global art" persist and remain contested. Field-specific global discourse both expresses and constructs new schemes of perception and belief that reenvision a cultural practice as a common worldwide phenomenon, thus contributing to the global field's *cultural* foundation.[88]

Third, the formation of a global cultural field is bound up with the creation of *global institutions for consecration and evaluation* like the Nobel Prize in Literature or global art prizes and even artist rankings.[89] Such instances publicly contribute to the reformulation of the ultimate stakes of recognition in global terms. They are critical mechanisms for institutionalizing global principles of valuation and hierarchization within a cultural domain.

With these kinds of field-internal mechanisms, I am talking about much more than the diffusion of a particular cultural practice and its specialized institutions around the world. These three mechanisms are particularly important for the emergence of a global cultural field because they help progressively incorporate players from national or regional fields, which were previously more disparate, into a shared playing field.[90] By using the term "emergence," I also emphasize that a global field level is more than just the sum of various national arenas.[91] As the three mechanisms suggest, a global field develops its own institutional infrastructures, discourses, and stakes that cannot be reduced to the logics of singular national (or regional) fields.

Likewise, it would be wrong to assume that a global art field simply supersedes the relevance and diversity of preexisting national art fields. Instead, it embodies a relatively distinct dimension that cuts across and connects them at a historically unprecedented worldwide scope. A global field *partially* disembeds *and* reembeds artists, intermediaries, aesthetic idioms, and histories of contemporary art from a (sub)national or regional into a transcontinental dimension for exchange and competition. This also means that participants can belong to the (sub)national, regional, and global field levels simultaneously, within a nested configuration.

One might draw an analogy with sports. The World Cup in soccer constitutes just one (and one might say the highest) level at which the sport unfolds. But there are still regional and national competitions—for example, the UEFA Champions League, the DFB-Pokal—and these events follow their own protocols and logics, though they can feed into what happens at the World Cup as well. Similarly, a global cultural field constitutes just one field level within a multiscalar structure in which national, regional, and subnational field levels maintain, albeit to varying degrees, their relative independence in infrastructures and logics.[92] For example, while China has become more connected to the globalizing art field since the late 1990s, the Official Art Organizations (OAOs) in the country—that is, governmental artists associations and art academies—continue to exert considerable influence on the careers of visual artists domestically. And their work can look very different from that of Chinese artists who gained global visibility.[93]

Thus, a global cultural field can emerge out of a multiscalar configuration, whereby subnational, national, and regional field levels coexist relatively independently, although their dynamics also intersect and influence one another. Conceiving of a global art space in this way helps us move beyond a zero-sum conception of different scales in cultural production, as the regionalist scenario of Appadurai's flows and networks model implies. Instead, the field is one where regional and global circuits are simultaneously both in tension and partly intertwined with one another.

In sum, a global cultural field defines a space of cultural production in which agents (individual and organizational) have extended their competition over field-specific resources and interpretative issues to a transcontinental level. This space has developed its own infrastructures, discourses, and institutions for evaluation that operate relatively independently from (sub)national or regional field levels, without being completely independent of their influences.

Commonality and Difference in Globalizing Cultures

After having delineated defining characteristics and historical conditions for an emergent global cultural field, I would argue that using a global field lens offers a uniquely complex approach for examining dynamics of valuation across borders. It attends to structures, agents, and meanings and thus allows us to integrate analytical dimensions that the cultural imperialism and global art worlds models left unconnected.[94] More importantly, it allows us to theorize these dimensions in ways that overcome some of the prior models' overly unitary tendencies and thus to revisit the question of globalization and diversity in a new, more differentiating light.

Like the cultural imperialism model, fields theory pays attention to power structures, but it has two advantages. First, while the former is limited to the macro-level, when fields theory is extended to the global level, it differentiates between inequalities among individual players and those among macro entities (i.e., regions, countries, cities). The latter macro imbalances derive from the unequal distribution of field-specific forms of "macro capital," which constitute a "world structure" of more or less central and peripheral art fields with some semi-peripheral spaces in between.[95] In turn, cities with the highest concentration of field-relevant macro capital (e.g., the volume of prestigious art institutions) figure as the centers of the centers, so to speak. For example, Paris is the world capital in the geography of power for avant-garde literature, and New York is one of contemporary art's major capitals.

Distinguishing inequalities among a field's individual participants and the macro entities with which they are affiliated allows us to develop a more nuanced picture of the power dynamics marking globalizing cultural realms. It avoids treating macro entities, like countries, as homogeneous agents, which imperialism models have done at times when describing the US.[96] From a global field perspective, macro-level inequalities affect power dynamics among players at the meso-level, *without* being reducible to that level. A cultural agent's position within the macrostructure of countries and cities will have a "positive or negative *multiplier*" effect, but it will not fully determine their moves in a global culture game.[97]

Second, a global fields approach accounts for macrostructures in cultural production in a more multidimensional way. Extending Bourdieu's idea of multiple capitals, it is not only economic, technological, or political resources that are relevant but symbolic, cultural, and, as I suggest, institutional ones as well.[98] Casanova, for example, pioneered the concept of symbolic national capital, which refers to the worldwide prestige of a country's aesthetic production, such as the canonic works and artistic styles that it has originated.[99] Adding to Casanova's formulation, I differentiate an institutional dimension of macro capital that involves the volume of relevant institutions for cultural production and mediation, including flagship museums, exhibition spaces, art magazines, and galleries for contemporary art. When the topic of valuation is at stake, this institutional macro capital must be distinguished because it captures global inequalities between countries (or regions, cities, etc.) with regard to the cross-border circulation and consecration of cultural goods.[100] Since the types of macro capital that matter to the power structure of a globalizing field is an empirical question, the fields approach eschews the materially reductionist and totalizing outlook of the cultural imperialism model. Each globalizing field is structured around multiple and distinctive forms of macro inequality that cannot be reduced to the larger economic world-system in any uniform way. The center of the center in contemporary art (New York) is not congruent with that of the movie industry (Los Angeles), fashion (Paris), or theater (London).[101]

Additionally, while the imperialism framework myopically looks at structures, a global cultural fields approach remains sensitive to shared meanings among the field's participants as well. In contrast to the global art worlds model, however, it does so in a less unitary and more dynamic way. When we use a global field approach—with its stronger emphasis on competition and contestation—it is possible to relax any assumptions about cultural unity. What gives a global art field meaningful coherence is not the use of the same hermeneutical strategies in the interpretation of artworks or worldwide consensus on taste and aesthetic valuations. What unites participants most fundamentally is a shared vision of a cultural practice as a common global phenomenon—and thus a common symbolic battleground—as well as their belief in the value of the stakes involved in that practice. But such a vision of "global," rather than, say, Western, "international" contemporary art functions merely as a meaningful frame of reference. The interpretations of the term, how to evaluate it, or who the worthiest artists are within that field will perpetually remain open to debate.

For instance, as we shall see, in the global art field, the Venice Biennale represents a large-scale exhibition platform where more than eighty countries take part every two years. They share a belief in the institution's importance as a prestigious global instance for artistic visibility and consecration. Each national participant stages its own exhibition under the umbrella of the larger event, which also awards a series of global art prizes for national pavilions and artists who are chosen and declared as "the best." National participants at Venice traditionally exhibit artists from their own country or region, and they can feature quite diverse aesthetic perspectives on contemporary art that challenge the symbolically dominant—that is, Western—mainstream. Taiwan's past exhibition politics at Venice, for example, demonstrate how a relatively peripheral participant turned into a critical voice against the Western artistic mainstream. In 2005, Taiwan began staging group exhibitions that included artists from other countries in the Global South, seeking to create "cross-cultural alliances between suppressed and excluded groups" and to critique the "logic of cultural, political, and economic hegemony dominating the biennale" that was causing "Taiwan's own marginality."[102]

This example underscores how important it is to keep an eye on the integrative role of certain global institutions and the participants' shared beliefs and investments, while at the same time curtailing any assumptions about cultural convergence that could easily become too reifying, if not Eurocentric. A global art field does not merely revolve around transnational conversations, cosmopolitan networking, and consensual conventions. It also constitutes a space of competition and struggle in which cultural differences are put into critical relation with one another rather than being dissolved.[103] In other words, global fields theory's attention to contestation—within a meaningful, shared space—allows us to think about cultural commonality and difference simultaneously and dynamically. We can look at the ways Taiwan participated in a global institution that was dominated by Western players but also how it sought to subvert existing hierarchies through its heterodox exhibition strategies.

Finally, there is an even more fundamental way in which a global fields approach can uniquely capture the internal divisions of globalizing cultures. It builds on Bourdieu's proposition that fields of cultural production are structured around the tension between relatively autonomous and heteronomous subfields or "poles."[104] In the global art field, as table 1.1 lays out, the pole with greatest autonomy involves expert mediators who tend to be more oriented around field-specific artistic or intellectual values; they approach art primarily

TABLE 1.1. Two Main Poles of Mediation in the Contemporary Art Field

Relatively autonomous	Heteronomous market
Experts	Commercial agents
Curators, art critics, avant-garde gallerists, connoisseurs, etc.	Dealers, auction houses, speculators, investment funds, etc.
Symbolic capital	Economic capital
Specific cultural pole	Commercial pole
Artistic subfield	Commercial subfield

for the production of symbolic value (i.e., symbolic capital). At the opposite pole of heteronomy, by contrast, agents follow less specific, more "worldly" interests, especially when chasing material profits, that is, economic capital. In contemporary art, such a more heteronomous, market-oriented pole involves commercial dealers, profit-driven auction houses, speculative art buyers, and so on.

Existing global models have overlooked such divisions, and the book makes the case that we need to pay more attention to different logics of production and mediation in globalizing cultures.[105] Extending and revising the idea of a field's autonomy-heteronomy axis I examine how the historical formation of global infrastructures and discourses for contemporary art differ among specific cultural and commercial subfields. Moreover, I use this lens to discover different ways in which artists become valued on a worldwide stage *and* under what conditions such artists become more diverse.

To be sure, global cultural fields theory does not offer general predictions about the dynamics of artistic diversity because it is a framework that must be attuned to the historical specificities of each cultural realm. But advancing the distinction between relatively autonomous and heteronomous poles offers at least a *sensitizing* entry point for investigating how diversity is conditioned by internally varied field structures and meanings. The result is a comprehensive historical and theoretical account of how a divided cultural world economy has historically emerged and how it affects artistic reputations and diversities in remarkably different ways.[106]

The book's account of a global field's autonomy-heteronomy divisions is not simply an upscaling of Bourdieu's modernist Western theory. The divided cultural world economy I introduce is embedded in quite distinct institutions— global biennials, global art fairs, and global auctions—that Bourdieu did not consider. My study also reveals different logics of evaluation, looking at intellectual discursive logics rather than purely formalistic aesthetic principles; and it highlights financial speculative ones at the heteronomous, market-oriented pole. Moreover, I show how geographic factors are uniquely influential to valuation within a global, rather than national, cultural field—not just with regard to territorial location but also with regard to geographic meanings—and I explain why such meanings vary across the field's main poles.

Taken together, a global fields approach can capture a globalizing cultural realm as a kind of paradoxical entity that is both bounded and heterogeneous, one marked by power structures and meanings, commonalities and differences, exchanges and ongoing conflicts, and specific artistic and economic values—in short, as an entity of "institutionalized anomie."[107] As such, it offers a fertile theoretical framework for investigating the rise and dynamics of a global contemporary art space without exaggerating its level of unification or consolidation, staying attuned to ongoing frictions, new contestations, and the persisting heterogeneity of art practices around the world.

Overview

The Global Rules of Art examines globalization in the contemporary visual arts in three parts that foreground different yet complementary perspectives: (1) the macro-level global expansion of the art field; (2) the meso-level of the careers of worldwide leading artists and their diversity; and (3) the micro-level of the trajectories of individual artists, cultural brokers, and those who symbolically or materially appropriate art.

Comparative analyses run through each of these parts. Systematic studies concerning the globalization of art and culture are still rare, and when they have appeared, they are often based on the unit of the nation-state. This study pursues a more unusual comparative methodology, since it does not take countries as its main units for comparison, but the different cross-border subfields (or poles) of a globalizing field.

Empirically, the book draws on a vast array of quantitative and qualitative data as well as a mixed-methods research design (including hierarchical clustering, historical analysis, content and interpretative discourse analyses, and a biographical case study method), which I explain in the appendices. Given my data's global scope—and the risks of assuming a one-sided West-centrism—a high degree of reflexivity and methodological meticulousness was critical for approximating a solid empirical foundation for the book's arguments. Yet detailing all the methodological decisions I made to avoid the many pitfalls that came up along the way simply goes beyond the scope of this chapter. Here, I only add that the research was designed so that it draws from converging empirical sources across the book's three parts.[108] In this way, the book's chapters can mutually enlighten and inform one another, making it possible to forge connections between the macro-, meso-, and micro-levels, which is something I pursue further in the conclusion.

Part 1 (chapters 2 and 3) focuses on the macro-level of global transformations in the contemporary art field, especially those that have occurred since 1945. Drawing from archival research, numerous institutional histories, a discourse analysis of around eight hundred art publications, an examination of nearly thirty-nine thousand public and commercial art institutions across 155 countries, and a genealogy that covers the rise of global instances of consecration and evaluation, I argue that the twenty-first century has seen the emergence of a global art field in which the logic governing contemporary art's circulation and valuation has become increasingly redefined in global, rather than international, terms. I additionally demonstrate how the specific cultural and commercial subfields for cross-border mediation have followed divergent historical and territorial trajectories of institutional globalization.

Part 2 (chapters 4 and 5) engages with the consequences that these global transformations have had on the recognition of artists from different parts of the world and in this sense for the field's homogeneity or diversity. While the global art market has seen relatively rapid changes for artists from countries with growing wealth, especially China, the global exhibition space has tended to privilege artists from poorer world regions, especially African countries. Chapter 5 argues that these divergent patterns of diversity are not historically contingent. They are bound up in how the autonomous and heteronomous poles of the globalizing field affect the valuations of artists differently. By analyzing the trajectory patterns of nearly two hundred worldwide leading artists, I reveal a dualistic structure of symbolic and market recognition that is upheld not only by distinct types of institutions and evaluative logics but also by differing geographies of artistic migration and flows. Taken together, by uncovering key determinants for leading careers across continents, part 2 establishes that the emerging global art field is fundamentally structured around a dual cultural world economy. And it argues that this twinned configuration has had important ramifications for varying historical dynamics of diversity among globalizing artistic elites.

To illuminate how the global art field's distinctive forms of recognition unfold for artists from outside the traditional Western centers, part 3 (chapters 6 and 7) develops qualitative case studies of the biographies of two artists, Gabriel Orozco from Mexico and Yue Minjun from China. Orozco has reached worldwide symbolic recognition, while Yue temporarily became a superstar in the global auction market. The case studies ask how these artists, despite coming from historically peripheral countries in contemporary art, were able to arrive at dominant positions within the globalizing field. With abundant secondary source material and numerous interviews with artists, curators, critics, private collectors, and other art professionals in Europe, Asia, and North and Latin America, the chapters chart the two artists' careers, reconstructing how these "peripheral" artists navigated different gatekeepers, power dynamics, and discursive forces in their journey toward global success. Their stories illustrate the shifting dynamics for establishing artistic recognition and art prices through the lens of two lived experiences. At the same time, the comparative juxtaposition illuminates how Orozco's and Minjun's global trajectories at the autonomous and heteronomous poles were influenced by divergent micro-level factors, particularly regarding artistic habitus, criteria of interpretation and evaluation, and transnational networks.

The conclusion synthesizes key insights from the macro-, meso-, and micro-level analyses, providing an integrative picture of the emerging global art field and its divided economy. Similar to a Cubist painting, which portrays the same object from multiple perspectives, I return to the main puzzle at the center of this study and summarize how the internally differentiated cultural economy has influenced the recognition of artists from different world parts—and, in this sense, cultural diversity—in contradictory and complex ways. I also single out one specifically fascinating theoretical facet: the pronounced role that geography plays for field dynamics in a global context. I foreground how geographic situatedness, classifications, and meanings have become intertwined with the valuation of artists across borders in fundamental ways, which demands new understandings of artistic distinction and value beyond Bourdieu's mainly temporal parameters (e.g., new versus old, innovation versus tradition). The conclusion closes by discussing how the global field model could be extended to other spheres of art and culture, before an epilogue takes up more recent events involving the pandemic. In addition to developing critical knowledge about major transformations in contemporary art, this study advances a promising global fields approach that could be used for understanding the multifaceted and contradictory forces that affect the production of culture in our contemporary world.

PART I

The Emergence of a Global Field in the Contemporary Visual Arts

IN A 1978 manifesto presented at London's Institute of Contemporary Arts (ICA), the postcolonial theorist and artist Rasheed Araeen railed against what he considered to be the myth of art's "internationalism": "The myth of the internationalism of Western art has to be exploded. . . . Western art expresses exclusively the peculiarities of the West. . . . It is merely a transatlantic art. It only reflects the culture of Europe and North America. . . . The current 'Internationalism' of Western art is nothing more than a function of the political and economic power of the West, enforcing its values on other people."[1]

Araeen had started his artistic trajectory in the early 1960s when he was still living in Karachi, Pakistan. Through the arts club at his university and the hours he spent poring over art books and magazines in the United States Information Service's library, he became interested in contemporary art and began exploring avant-garde approaches.[2] Araeen's emerging practice did not match with what most of his contemporaries in Pakistan saw as proper art, however. While his peers were steeped in traditional figurative painting, Araeen created, for example, a sculpture out of "found metal scraps, drawing the motion of a moving hula-hoop or the geometric roofs of Hyderabad from above."[3]

Feeling like a misfit, Araeen moved to London in 1964. He was looking to join a more progressive, international art scene, but once he arrived, he faced numerous unanticipated obstacles. Galleries, out of a deep-seated Eurocentrism, refused to work with an artist from remote Pakistan, and curators tended to "consciously ignore" artists from "developing" countries as merely "ethnic" or derivative.[4] In response, Araeen developed a proposal for the British Arts Council, hoping to organize a major group show for diaspora artists from Asia and Africa to highlight their innovative contributions. His idea fell on deaf ears for more than a decade. Having traveled far from his home country to participate in the international conversation about contemporary art, Araeen felt out of place once again.

In the contemporary art field before the 1980s, Araeen's experience of marginalization was not out of the ordinary. The field prided itself on its internationalism, but its territorial scope, the concentration of its institutions, and their mediation practices remained profoundly West-centric. An "international cast" of gallerists, curators, and critics promoted artists across borders and onto the international stage, but these well-oiled networks operated primarily between the US and western Europe.[5] Their undisputed capital was New York City—which had "stolen" Paris's hegemonic position in the 1950s—and their channels of communication and competition stretched largely to only a handful of other European cities.[6] "Great international events," like the Venice Biennale or the Documenta in Germany, aspired to represent broader panoramas of contemporary art, but their organizers were exclusively Western and pursued exclusionary exhibition politics.

Not surprisingly, most of the artists and styles that gained prominence within this postwar power constellation were actually "transatlantic," as Araeen put it, including "major personalities" from the US, like "Rauschenberg, Johns, Stella," and "the great movements, . . . Pop art, minimal art, conceptual art," among others.[7] This does not mean contemporary art was nonexistent in different parts of the world. But cultural mediators in those regions were not as involved in art's international traffic, and they had comparatively fewer institutional resources for influencing trends across borders. Thus, artists from more peripheral regions, like Araeen, had to move to big Western centers, where most of them, with rare exceptions, encountered closed doors.[8]

Part 1 explores how this institutional configuration for the cross-border mediation of contemporary art has changed. Beginning in the late 1980s, a global art field emerged, which became minimally integrated around a shared set of artistic practices, discourses, and cultural and commercial circuits, reaching its full contours by 2010.[9] This expanding field has incorporated a broader range of previously disparate countries and regions into a common global space, but this new structure is not simply a flattened global "art world community." It is a place where power imbalances persist and where the field's major centers remain largely in the West. Despite these hierarchies, the global art field is a space where inequalities are no longer as pronounced as they once were and a space that is defined by more extended exchanges *and* competitive struggles. Cultural agents and institutions from a wider variety of world regions have not only become more involved in the field; they have also actively challenged one-sided Western perspectives on contemporary art. Through these contested processes, as part 1 details, the field's institutions and mediation practices have become gradually transformed into a global logic, rather than one that is largely West-centric and "international."

But how and why did this global field emerge? Existing scholarship, particularly the work of the Marxist art historian Julian Stallabrass, has interpreted contemporary art's globalization as a response to major "global events" in world politics and the world economy that erupted in 1989. As Stallabrass writes, "the reunification of Germany, the fragmentation of the Soviet Union, the rise of global trade agreements, the consolidation of trading blocs, and the transformation of China into a partially capitalist economy—changed the character of the art world profoundly."[10] In the slipstream of these broader transformations— so his historical argument goes—the "art world swiftly reconfigured itself" and assumed a more global dimension.[11]

However, just as the idea of a global art field helps us see new kinds of competition and struggle within a terrain that is still hierarchical, it also suggests seeing the field of contemporary art as a relatively independent universe that is not just the product of external forces. Consequently, we should not interpret art's globalization as a quasi-immediate reflection of wider political or economic developments. Instead, we must look more closely at how the field's principal actors and institutions—including biennials, museums, art critics, art fairs, and auctions—spurred global transformations *within* the contemporary art field without, however, losing sight of how such *internal* dynamics were also affected by *external* factors, albeit in indirect, *refracted* ways (cf. chapter 1). Additionally, we need to keep in mind that an art field does not form a homogeneous community but involves a great variety of mediating institutions and "specialized agents" that fundamentally differ in their approaches along the field's two main poles or subfields: the autonomous (i.e., specific cultural) and the heteronomous (i.e., market-oriented).[12] As we shall see, these subfields and their players have been susceptible to external historical forces in different ways while also drifting farther apart in the past thirty years of accelerated globalization.

Taking into account such a heterogeneous internal field structure, part 1's historical analysis puts into perspective the idea that the globalization of contemporary art can be reduced to a single watershed date, such as 1989, or even to a single wave.[13] Instead, what occurred were streams of relatively independent series of global transformations that took place at both the autonomous and the heteronomous poles, each with their own temporalities and preconditions and each variously impacted by external forces. It was as if multiple waves developed, but when they historically converged in the new millennium's first decade, they transformed into a roaring river, which only then—not in the late 1980s—produced an expanded art field that became more global in its logic but that also began to operate according to an increasingly divided dual economy of cross-border mediation and valuation.

2

The Genesis of a Global
Artistic Subfield

THREE GLOBAL TRANSFORMATIONS have affected key institutions for the mediation of contemporary art at the relatively autonomous pole: the worldwide proliferation of international art biennials and permanent exhibition spaces for contemporary art since the late 1980s; the rise of global discourses in art criticism since the early 1990s; and the foundation of new global institutions for artistic evaluation and consecration from the late 1980s to the middle of the first decade of the new millennium. The historical confluence of these developments in the early twenty-first century produced an expanded institutional and cultural infrastructure that enabled the genesis of a global artistic subfield. Agents from both central and peripheral regions around the world entered increasing exchanges and symbolic struggles, which gradually eroded the legitimacy of the old international order in contemporary art and led to the construction of a new kind of symbolic capital. This new capital—manifested in the ways contemporary art became exhibited, seen, discussed, and evaluated—demonstrates a fundamental shift toward a global logic in the field, which has become dynamically engaged with questions of cosmopolitanism, a decentering of dominant Western perspectives, and the contributions of artists, mediators, and institutions from more "peripheral" countries.

In focusing on these three transformations, I am not merely suggesting that a greater number of countries developed flourishing contemporary art scenes of their own. These developments were particularly influential for incorporating players and artifacts from national and regional art fields that were previously more disparate into a shared global framework.[1] What emerged in the millennium's first decade was a global subfield for the specific cultural mediation of contemporary art—with its own institutions, discourses, and stakes—that cannot, as the regionalist flows and networks model would suggest, simply be reduced to an aggregate of national or regional art circuits. Instead, it is an expanded playing field that is not as hierarchical as it was previously and in which ideas about what constitutes symbolic capital have become more cosmopolitan and global overall.

The Formation of a Global Exhibition Infrastructure

It is not enough to say that the history of the field is the history of the struggle for a monopoly of the imposition of legitimate categories of perception and appreciation; it is in the very struggle that the history of the field is made . . . between the dominants whose strategy is tied to continuity, identity and reproduction, and the dominated, the new entrants, whose interest is in discontinuity, rupture, difference and revolution.

—PIERRE BOURDIEU, *THE RULES OF ART* (1996)

Exhibitions are indisputably the central site for the public visibility and recognition of visual artists.[2] The proliferation of international biennials and permanent art institutions since the 1980s resulted in a worldwide exhibition infrastructure that provided a crucial foundation for the emergence of a global artistic subfield with a new logic.

The Rise of a Global Biennial Circuit and New Symbolic Struggles

The most influential development for the formation of a global artistic subfield has been the worldwide proliferation of international biennials for contemporary art, which began in the late 1980s.[3] The term "international art biennial" refers to a large-scale group exhibition that features artists from multiple countries and occurs at regular intervals—at least every two years.[4] Since biennials are temporary events, their institutional setup tends to be more flexible compared to permanent art institutions. As such, they can respond more nimbly to the latest trends, functioning like barometers that shape and reinforce the field's innovative artistic and curatorial tendencies. But the key question, of course, is how biennials were able to do this at the international and later increasingly global levels.

Culturally, by exhibiting artists from diverse backgrounds, biennials feed "world pictures"—that is, visions of visual art as a shared international phenomenon to begin with.[5] Their large-scale shows help construct cross-border aesthetic frames against which artistic styles or positions can be meaningfully compared and valued using international categories. But biennials also serve vital social purposes. They are events where artists, intermediaries, and art devotees from different countries periodically meet, cultivate their connections (or "social capital"), exchange information, and debate.[6] Such personal encounters can heavily influence the "choices of collectors and museums" over vast distances.[7]

Due to the attending critics, the proceedings of major biennials also "fill the international art magazines."[8] Thus, international art biennials can figure as crucial "field-configuring events" with far-reaching impacts on professional networks, aesthetic tastes, and artistic trends across multiple national fields.[9]

Until the late 1980s, however, most major biennials were in western Europe or North America, and their exhibitions privileged artists from those two regions. The onset of a biennial boom since that period—coupled with new exhibition politics by rising peripheral players from other world regions—increasingly challenged this exclusionary "international" situation within an emerging global biennial circuit for extended exchange and symbolic competition.

THE ESTABLISHMENT OF A CENTER AGENT
FOR INTERNATIONAL ARTISTIC CONSECRATION

The oldest-running art biennial was inaugurated in Venice in 1895. Following the spirit of nineteenth-century world exhibitions, the Venice Biennale created a unique platform where Western nations could present their achievements in the visual arts.[10] It aimed to showcase the "most notable activities of the modern spirit" and offer an overview of the "art of our time."[11] The first event included a considerable 516 works by 278 artists from fifteen countries.

From its inception, the Venice Biennale followed a survey-style exhibition format along with a national competitive setup. Artworks were grouped according to country, which resonated with prevalent nineteenth-century ideas about national styles and schools.[12] The show therefore represented visual art within an inter-national "comparative matrix" through which cultural hierarchies could be staged.[13] These hierarchies were manifested most basically in the unequal number of participating artists from different countries. Italians, for example, dominated throughout the biennial's first eleven editions.[14] Furthermore, the exhibition hall's topography shaped perceptions as well, with some countries receiving special exhibition rooms while others were cramped together. The halls' sequencing likewise suggested national hierarchies. In 1903, for example, visitors first passed art from Germany, France, and England before arriving at the Italian rooms, which could then be read as the apex of aesthetic developments at that time.[15]

Such imbalanced exhibition tactics by the Italian organizers soon led to frustrations among other participating countries. In 1907, Belgium moved out of the biennial's central exhibition hall, setting up its own national pavilion in a surrounding park. Hungary, Germany, and Britain soon followed in 1909 and then the French and Swedish in 1912 and the Russians in 1914.[16] With these pavilions, the national principle underlying the presentation of visual art

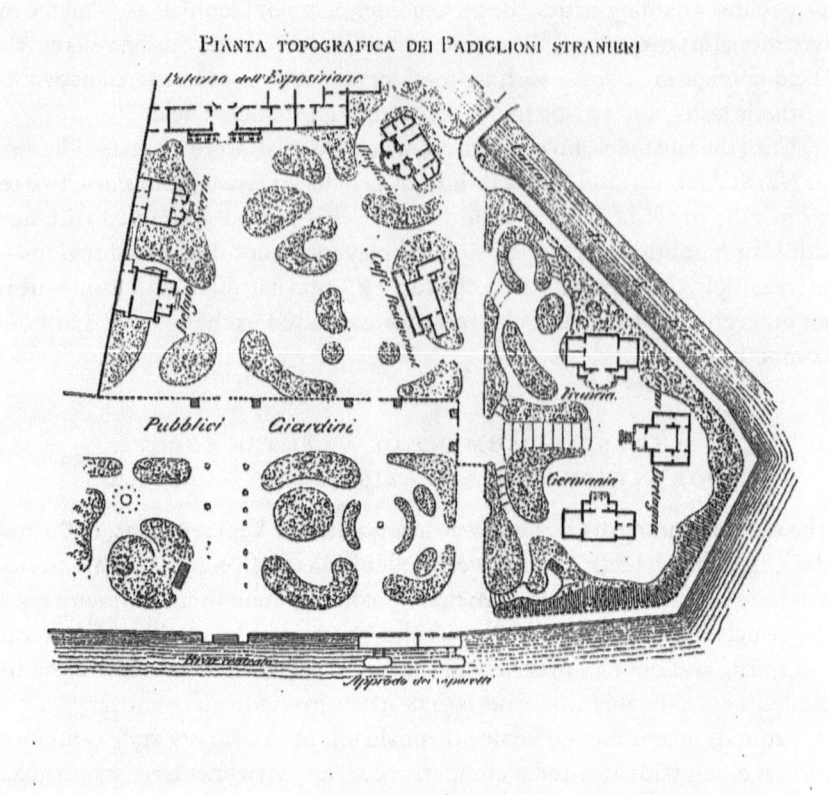

PIÁNTA TOPOGRAFICA DEI PADIGLIONI STRANIERI

FIGURE 2.1. Plan of the public gardens for the tenth Venice Biennale (1912),
showing the Belgian, Swedish, Hungarian, French, German, and British Pavilions.
(Copyright Archivio Storico della Biennale di Venezia—ASAC)

became literally cemented in the show's architecture. Participants from different countries could now orchestrate and finance their own exhibitions under
the umbrella of the larger event, as a means of peaceful cultural competition
(figure 2.1).

The biennial's competitive set up was reinforced by its prize system, which
named the best artist and pavilion and established Venice as a central agent
for international artistic consecration well into the twentieth century.[17] Its
prize selections exerted a strong signaling effect about the international state
of the visual arts and its respective cultural hierarchies. For example, when
Robert Rauschenberg was awarded the Grand Prix for painting at the 1964
event, the first American artist to win after years of European domination, it
symbolized a broader shift in the balance of cultural power toward the US.[18]

The Venice Biennale figured as the "ultimate" institution for "consecration" in the international art field, a central arbiter for defining, communicating, and reinforcing artistic values across borders.[19]

Given the Venice Biennale's international competitive structure, it is not surprising that it has been compared to the Olympic Games.[20] And yet, despite its universalistic rhetoric of offering an "overview of our time," the scope and orientation of the exhibition remained rather Western. European and North American countries made up a near absolute majority of the participants until the early 1980s. A deep-seated Eurocentrism also marked the biennial's very approach to contemporary art. As the Cuban curator Gerardo Mosquera explains, "Around the mid-1980s, segregation was an essential part of the visual art system. The periodic international art events already in place, from the Venice Bienniale to Documenta, were far from global. This was not only because the participating artists were mainly from Western backgrounds, but because the events' ideas of art were restricted to the Western mainstream, and their organisers were not interested in exploring what was going on elsewhere."[21]

THE GLOBAL PROLIFERATION OF
INTERNATIONAL ART BIENNIALS

Venice commanded a near monopoly of the biennial circuit up until the 1950s, but in the latter half of the century, a worldwide boom hit.[22] The first major biennial with international ambitions outside the West was founded in São Paulo, Brazil, in 1951, and over the next two decades, a handful of other important ones followed. Except for the 1973 Biennale of Sydney, most were still within Europe, however. But beginning in the 1980s, art biennials grew to such an extent that "biennialization" entered the lexicon in the 1990s (figure 2.2).[23]

What is more, the exponential surge of biennial foundations came along with growing global dispersion (figure 2.3).[24] Biennials spread throughout Latin America, made increased inroads into eastern Europe, began to mushroom in Asia, and gained a foothold in Africa. By 2017, 130 biennials with a broad geographic scope—regarding the background of their invited artists— had been founded, reaching across 117 cities in sixty-one countries. And by the first decade of the new millennium, the majority of these large-scale exhibitions were occurring outside the traditional centers of western Europe and North America (the "Northwest").[25]

This biennial boom was crucial for the emergence of a global artistic subfield. As I shall explain, it enabled extended cultural exchange and competition between "peripheral" and central players over symbolic capital or the very criteria that should define legitimate contemporary art practices and exhibition making.[26] A growing multitude of "biennials of resistance" increasingly

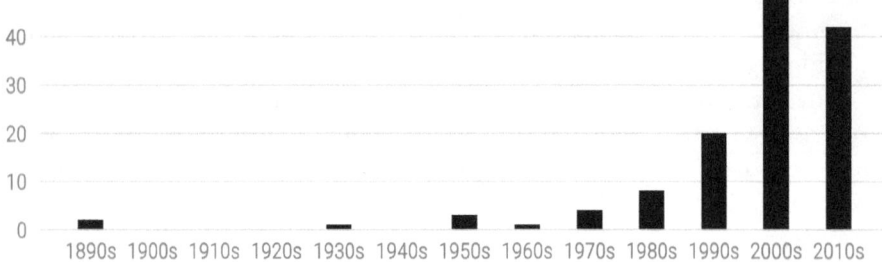

FIGURE 2.2. Increase in the establishment of international art biennials 1895–2017. (Biennial Foundation, ifa, e-flux, art catalogs, internet research, secondary sources; cf. appendix A)

1900

Northwest - 100%

1960

Northwest - 86%

Latin America - 14%

1980

Northwest - 67%

Latin America - 8%

Oceania - 8%

Eastern Europe - 17%

2000

Northwest - 51%

Latin America - 12%

Oceania - 2%

Eastern Europe - 7%

Asia - 21%

Africa - 7%

2017 Cumulative

Latin America - 8%

Oceania - 2%

Eastern Europe - 11%

Northwest - 40%

Asia - 32%

Africa - 7%

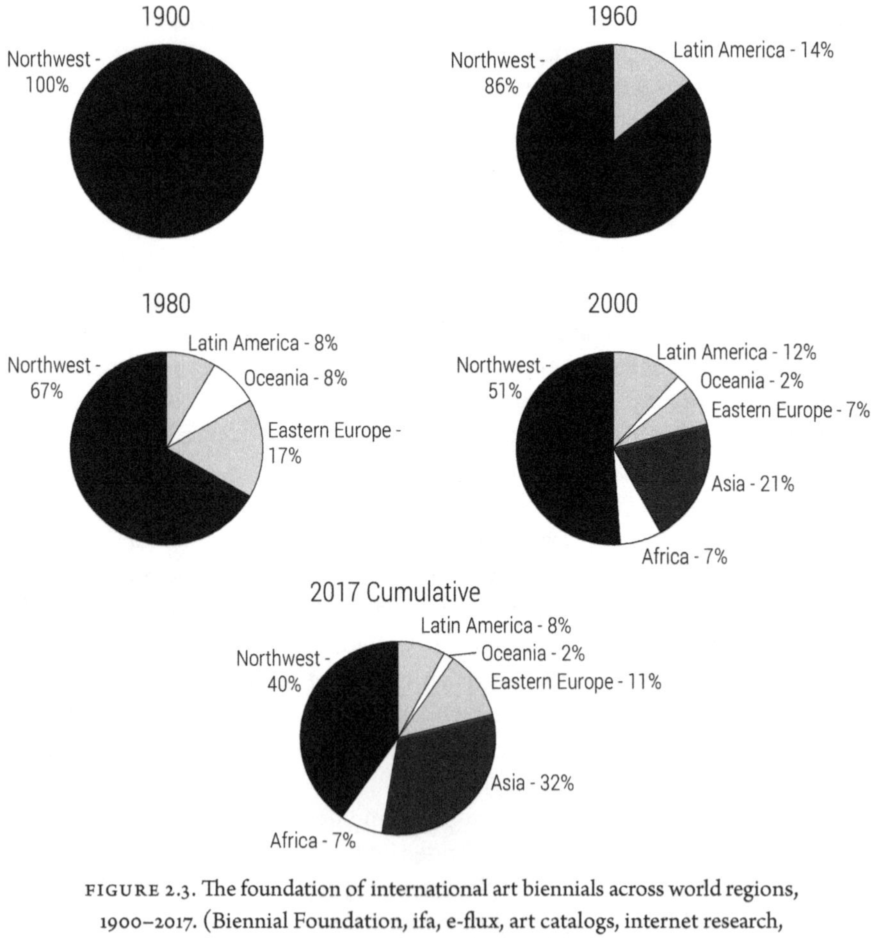

FIGURE 2.3. The foundation of international art biennials across world regions, 1900–2017. (Biennial Foundation, ifa, e-flux, art catalogs, internet research, secondary sources; cf. appendix A)

challenged Venice's hegemony, launching globally oriented formats that assailed the narrow values and hierarchies of West-centric art institutions.[27]

CHALLENGING A WESTERN MONOPOLY

To understand how biennialization contributed to the rise of an extended field of exchange and competition, it is instructive to attend to the motives behind the creation of these venues. Founding declarations reveal that biennials were often established with the ambition of helping an art scene gain traction in the international (and increasingly global) "attention space"—that is, to put a host city on the art world map and, at the same time, to increase the visibility and symbolic capital of the art of the country or region where they are located.[28] This was particularly true of geographic areas that did not contain a stable infrastructure of museums and other art institutions. In those contexts, a biennial often was the only available instrument to make the work of their artists visible across borders and to become an active participant in the international domain.[29] In short, biennials were not only about bringing the art of the world home. They were also about bringing a country's (or region's) art into the world under a self-directed aegis to heighten its recognition.

The spirited agenda of enhancing foreign symbolic capital appears as early as the inaugural Bienal de São Paulo in 1951.[30] In the foreword to its catalog, director Lourival Gomes Machado suggested a certain type of competition—he called it "conquering"—with the international field's established centers: "By definition the Bienal should fulfill two principal goals: to put modern art of Brazil not simply in proximity but in living contact with the art of the rest of the world . . . [and] to conquer for São Paulo the position of international artistic center."[31]

Later biennials in Sydney (1973), Istanbul (1987), Taipei (1992), Dakar (1992), Johannesburg (1995), Kwangju (1995), Benin (2010), India (2012), and many other locations would express similar ambitions.[32] The widespread goal of heightened worldwide visibility, however, often coexisted in complex ways with other political and more materialistic motivations that were specific to domestic-historical contexts. A biennial could also serve as a cultural vehicle supporting postcolonial nation building, as an instrument of Cold War politics by means of an international exhibition, as an event for the symbolic marking of political transitions, and as a means of bolstering tourism and urban development to cities now promoted as cultural capitals.[33] The latter, more economic motivations, however, rarely made it into the biennials' public self-presentations and exhibition catalogs. The quest for symbolic capital among biennials frequently necessitated the public suppression of worldly interests in "economic capital" to maintain, as Jeannine Tang points out, "a myth of neutral exhibition space" dedicated to art as a special sphere of activity.[34]

Nevertheless, the explosive growth of biennials cannot be reduced solely to a matter of "joining" the international art game. The new international biennials were not just looking to gain prestige (and other benefits) by replicating the central powers' methods and aesthetics. Beginning in the 1980s, "peripheral" players also increasingly challenged Western hegemony in contemporary art. La Bienal de La Habana—inaugurated in 1984 at the dawn of the boom—is the pioneering example of a "biennial of resistance," one that was looking to overturn West-centrism and replace it with a new vision.[35] While São Paulo had emulated Venice's nation-based setup and prize system and provided ample room for art from established Western countries, Havana developed a more antagonistic format that proved influential.[36] Sponsored by the Cuban communist state during the Cold War, the initiation of the Havana Biennial must be understood in the larger ideological context of anti-imperialism and decolonization.[37] Its inaugural mission was to provide artists from "third-world" countries—who had been excluded at Venice and within the international field more broadly—a forum for representation and dialogue, thus laying the foundation for an alternative, anti-Eurocentric internationalism.

In the Havana Biennial's first iteration, this mission largely concentrated on regional artists from Latin America and the Caribbean. But by the second exhibition, in 1986, the geographic range included Africa, Asia, and countries of the Islamic world. The resulting scope of more than twenty-four hundred works by 690 artists from fifty-seven countries—and only two artists who originated from countries in the Global North—was remarkable for the time.[38] Before the internet, hardly any information flowed between art scenes in the Global South. Through arduous research, a team member recalls, "we were starting a map of the world that had not existed until then."[39] The outcome was a "mammoth" biennial with "more than fifty exhibitions and events" that, as Gerardo Mosquera, the lead curator, described it, established "a gigantic 'Salon des Refusés.'"[40] It also served as a social forum to foster exchange and networks among cultural agents from the Global South, completely independent of the North.[41] As Mosquero emphasized, "never before had artists, curators, critics, and scholars from so many places—Beirut, Brazzaville, Buenos Aires, Jakarta, and Kingston, to name just a few—met 'horizontally.'"[42]

At the biennial's third iteration in 1989, this drive to support artistic crossover was also manifested in an altered exhibition format that departed further from Venice. Instead of using a panoramic survey—loosely assembling art by media and nationality—the team opted for a more unifying approach.[43] A focus on a shared theme, "Tradition and Contemporaneity," moderated by the curatorial team's decisions, brought art from diverse contexts into closer dialogue.[44] Within postcolonial societies, "tradition" had long been a rallying call against "imperialist incursions into local cultural development."[45] However, by the

1980s, it was clear that appeals to "tradition" also served conservative, nation-alistic agendas for postcolonial state building. By associating the term with "contemporaneity," the organizers opened up a more complex reconsideration between these two poles. To what extent was it possible to articulate tradition within a contemporary context, on the one hand, and to assert, on the other, mul-tiple genealogies of contemporary art beyond a uniform Western paradigm—each of them inflected by, and manifesting, different cultural roots?[46]

The 1989 Havana Biennial turned into a venue that deeply interrogated art's meanings outside the Northwest's dominant centers.[47] It juxtaposed a central exhibition with twenty-four smaller ones (cf. figure 2.4.), each dedicated to specific subthemes. The program's added workshops, discursive panels, and conference events marked another departure from Venice's format, which at the time focused exclusively on exhibitions. Over eleven days, the Havana Biennial brought together critics and scholars from multiple "third-world" countries and beyond. In line with the biennial's theme, they spoke about dynamics of postcolonial cultures, sparking lively discussions among the full audiences at the Museo Nacional.[48] The 1989 biennial also dispensed with art prizes, which were a central feature of Venice's format. The organizers wanted to emphasize a "spirit of solidarity," rather than competition, among artists; and given the curated heterogeneity of artistic practices across the Global South, the very idea of unitary judgment criteria seemed irrelevant.[49]

Taken alone, each of these changes to Venice's original biennial format had occurred at other exhibitions before.[50] The Cuban innovation was in how it articulated those changes into a single "symbolic model" that was at once anti-Eurocentric in mission, dialogical in its curatorial-thematic approach, and ac-companied by special discursive events for cultivating debate and theoretical publications.[51] Havana became a historic turning point in the process of bienni-alization because it synthesized a new counterformat to Venice that influenced a "majority of biennials" well into the new millennium.[52] With this new critical model, biennials were no longer just a tool by which marginal art scenes could reach the center of the art field.[53] The international art biennial became instead an artistic and social platform for mounting distinctive claims about contemporary art that could challenge West-centric perspectives, and it could enforce those claims through innovative curatorial strategies and discourse production.

In the second half of the 1990s, this critical biennial format became increas-ingly linked with rising discourses about globalization. The auxiliary discursive association provided a new rhetoric that called for an expanded *global* frame of reference. Rather than "reversing" a West-centric internationalism, as the Havana Biennial had initially intended, this new global frame constructed a broader cultural cartography that incorporated multiplying notions and values about contemporary art. Under this new model, the West was not excluded,

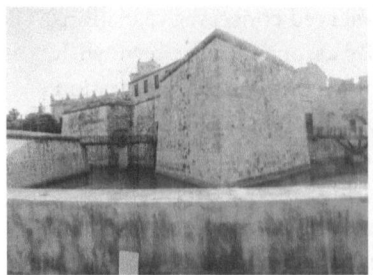
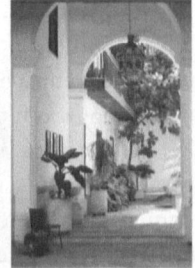
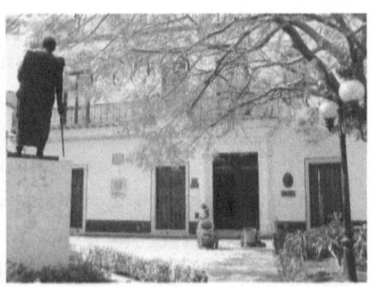
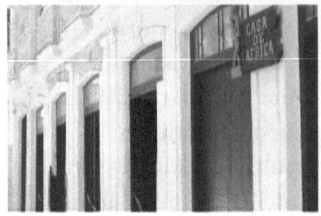
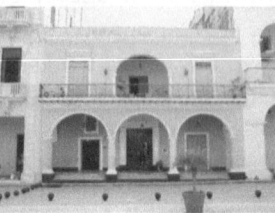
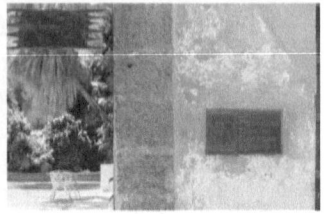

FIGURE 2.4. Photographs from *Making Art Global (Part 1): The Third Havana Biennial 1989* (Afterall Books, 2011) showing the 1989 Havana Biennial venues at the time of publication. *Top from left to right*: Castillo de la Fuerza, Casa de los Árabes, Casa de México. *Bottom from left to right*: Casa de África, Fototeca de Cuba, Centro Provincial de Artes Plásticas y Diseño.

as originally at Havana, but relegated to being one voice among many others and thus decentered.

The Kwangju International Biennale in South Korea provides a particularly clear example of how globalization discourses transformed Havana's anti-Eurocentric international model into a critical global model. Originally founded in 1995 as an explicit reaction to Venice, at its third iteration in 2000, the artistic director, Oh Kwang-su, made a remarkable statement:[54] "The Kwangju Biennale will strengthen the concentration and adaptability of art to pursue globalization rather than westernization, diversity instead of uniformity. . . . The West-centralized view of contemporary art is still disillusioned with the idea that the West still rules the world. It should be restructured in various alternatives. A truly globalized culture will be born as innumerous visions are presented and integrated in such ways as to incorporate the whole in an active and critical structure."[55] What appears here in sharp relief is how Oh invokes notions of "globalization" and a "globalized culture" against a "West-centralized view of contemporary art," which was decried as "uniform." The imagined alternative was a new global perspective that allowed for the coexistence of numerous alternative "visions" around contemporary art.

Oh's plea for a multifaceted global art culture that formed an "integrated" yet dynamic whole was mirrored in the biennial's exhibition concept, in which a multinational curatorial team developed a world map with five subexhibitions in a decidedly collaborative effort. Simultaneously, the Kwangju Biennale also included a special exhibition showcasing dominant strands of minimalist painting and sculpture in Korea and Japan—Korean *Dansaekhwa* and Japanese *Monoho*—during the 1970s and 1980s.[56] Thus, the biennial's overall globalist approach served as a framework for legitimizing these Asian art movements beyond nationalist and regionalist references and for bringing Eastern perspectives about contemporary art into the global discourse.[57]

The Kwangju Biennale typified many "peripheral" biennials' metamorphoses into "global exhibitions" beginning in the late 1990s.[58] Armed with a new global rhetoric and approach, upstart biennials reenvisioned contemporary art as a worldwide phenomenon. At the same time, they assertively positioned their work and their distinctive perspective on contemporary art within this larger circle of meaning. In this way, they turned into curatorial and discursive platforms within a growing field of symbolic competition over different positionings vis-à-vis a global vision of contemporary art, entailing a veritable multiplication of global narratives.[59] Since the 1980s, newfound biennials increasingly saw themselves as challenging the power and rules of the players at the field's center, but the way they did so shifted from what had originally been a more radical, anti-Western approach to a globalist one.

AN AMBIGUOUS SPACE: COLLABORATIVE COMPETITION

As much as biennialization was not meant to replicate the values of the field's dominant Western institutions, it was also not just a matter of an ascendant group of "peripheral" players assailing central agents. On the ground, the dynamics were much more complex. As the emerging global biennial infrastructure became increasingly coordinated, a give-and-take dynamic developed, in which agents collaborated even as they competed with one another.

This growing spirit of collaboration was supported by a series of conferences that took place at the dawn of the new millennium. The first, convened in 2000 by the curator René Block in Kassel, Germany, aimed to improve networking and "global dialogue" among biennial organizers from five continents. The more than forty participants included representatives from Western biennials but also those—like the organizers of Havana and Kwangju—who had set out to challenge them, a crucial sign that a *shared* space involving actors from both centers and "peripheries" was taking shape.[60] This congress was followed by several biannual iterations. And in 2009, a Biennial Foundation was established, followed by the founding of the International Biennial Association in 2014, which further institutionalized coordination and exchange.[61]

At the first conference in 2000, many of the participants met one another for the first time.[62] Over three days, they shared experiences and learned about the challenges other organizers had faced, including logistical issues, questions of funding, and biennials' relationships with local art scenes.[63] In addition to learning from one another, a seemingly mundane but crucial step occurred at the conference when biennial organizers coordinated their exhibitions' opening times. Representatives collaborated on a schedule that would allow them to better divide up the attention and visits from overseas gatekeepers, thus channeling their competition for symbolic capital.[64] Such attempts at creating a common calendar underline the importance of standardizing and coordinating times for the creation and sustenance of global relations.[65] But they also demonstrate that the rise of any field is inevitably intertwined with the creation of some common ground among its participants. Biennial organizers collaborated also to enhance the degree to which they could effectively compete with one another.

The complex coexistence of global competition and collaboration helps illuminate why "peripheral" locations—even as they sought to move beyond a West-centric view of contemporary art—frequently recruited curators from Western centers to work alongside a local curator or curatorial team to stage their biennial.[66] At first, such invitations may appear contradictory, since the involvement of these exhibition makers often entailed that they would bring a substantial number of artists from Western contexts. In Dakar and Taipei, for example, some critics argued that this approach would extend Western interests and cultural dominance on a global scale, implying a relapse of submission under old colonial power structures.[67] But portraying "peripheral" agents solely as passive recipients of Western dominance implies a problematic binary.[68]

A field perspective leads beyond this quasi-imperialistic interpretation and illuminates the full ambiguity of such maneuvers. "Peripheral" biennials often invited Western intermediaries to strategically increase their own visibility and legitimacy.[69] Established curators brought symbolic and social capital, which could augment a biennial's prestige in the eyes of the field's central players, thus maximizing the biennial's capacity to attract leading art experts as visitors and impact global discourses about contemporary art.[70]

While such moves affirmed the credentials of players from Western centers in the short run, they were not part of a zero-sum game based on a dichotomy of domination and resistance. Ultimately, partnering with established players could help "peripheral" biennials attain growing leverage in the long-term with regard to promoting the work of local or regional artists across borders. In line with this agenda, several "non-Western" biennials indeed maintained a considerable "home bias" in the millennium, and Western artists hardly became predominant there.[71] The Kwangju Biennale, for example, which had pursued this strategy in its first iterations, eventually assumed a "leading role in the global biennial business," contributing to "the rise of contemporary Asian art to global status."[72]

To be sure, the specific ways such collaborations played out on the ground could vary widely, and it remained ever important for "peripheral" biennials to guard against the foreign co-optation of difference. Yet the important point remains that foreign invitations should not be reduced to the dutiful adherence to Western positions. Nor are they mere expressions of a fancy cosmopolitan dialogue, as the global art world approach would suggest (cf. chapter 1). Framing biennials as part of an emerging global field of competition highlights the strategic aspects of such invitations. Biennials around the world were operating within a highly uneven structure in which they allied with established Western players to build up their own symbolic capital as a currency to promote their distinctive cultural agendas more effectively.

FEEDBACK EFFECTS ON DOMINANT WESTERN BIENNIALS

Given their foreign invitation strategies, biennials increasingly turned into a global circuit for the "intensified transnational engagement of artists, curators, museums, and cities," even enabling the rise of a new "transnational class of curators."[73] Growing exchanges among art biennials exposed exhibition makers and visiting professionals to a much wider range of art production around the world. And over time, these dynamics exerted feedback effects on the field's centers as well: the developing mass of biennials with anti-Eurocentric and increasingly global agendas "brought about a new critical pressure" for the latter to "renovate" and widen their scope and strategies.[74]

The 2002 Documenta 11 in Kassel made waves as an indicator of this new dynamic. The Documenta had been founded in post-Nazi Germany in 1955 as a panorama for showcasing innovative contemporary art, and it had quickly established itself as the second-most-prestigious large-scale exhibition event aside from Venice.[75] But it had gained a reputation as being more "'tone-setting' in the elaboration of international art."[76] In this spirit, the Documenta sent a clear signal to the art world when it unanimously chose the Nigerian-born Okwui Enwezor in October 1998 to curate the upcoming 2002 iteration. Enwezor had cofounded *Nka: Journal of Contemporary African Art* in 1994 and had curated, among other shows, the 1997 Johannesburg Biennale. He was known as someone who brought new postcolonial and global perspectives to contemporary art, with a particular emphasis on Africa. While the topic of globalization had already entered the seminal Documenta in 1997 under the leadership of the French Catherine David, Enwezor's appointment marked the first time a non-European artistic director would lead this established Western institution.

Enwezor turned the Documenta into an expanded global exhibition. Working with a team of curators from multiple continents, he reconceived the Documenta as a series of five global platforms.[77] Four consisted of interdisciplinary symposiums that took place in Europe, India, the Caribbean, and West Africa, which created interstitial intellectual spaces where scholars and artists from diverse world corners could debate major issues in contemporary art, culture, and politics. The biennial's final platform, the 2002 group exhibition in Kassel, was only one component of several events, thus symbolically decentering the status of the predominantly West-centric exhibition in Germany. Given Enwezor's global ambitions, it is not surprising that the share of Western artists who exhibited at the final platform dropped from nearly 90 percent in previous years to "a more respectable 60 percent," a change that initiated a lasting trend of decreasing Western dominance at this biennial.[78] But Enwezor's vision was about much more than just the simple inclusion of artists with origins from historically "peripheral" countries. The biennial's truly global characteristics lay in how he and his team changed the format of the Documenta to focus logistically and programmatically on transnational exchanges between formerly more segregated peripheries and centers in the international art field.

Just one year later, the 2003 Venice Biennale, a major rival of the Documenta, moved in a similar direction.[79] The artistic director, Francesco Bonami, invited a "global" curatorial team to contribute. His collaborators included cultural agents from Germany, France, Switzerland, Italy, the UK, and Sweden but also Argentina, China, Mexico, Thailand, and eastern Europe.[80] In ten subexhibitions, they created an unprecedented global map of art production in the biennial's theme-setting show. It was a collaborative artistic world-regionalism that echoed the format of Kwangju's 2000 event. As the participating Swiss star curator Hans Ulrich Obrist remembered a decade later, "China, the Middle East, Latin America—we started to discover their different modernities, their different pasts, which is something the art world has ignored until recently. I think Francesco Bonami . . . took into account this new condition."[81]

Nonetheless, some critics suggested that such changes at the Documenta and Venice amounted to nothing more than window dressing. Most of the invited "peripheral" curators and artists had resided in dominant Western capitals and thus were part of, and influenced by, those hegemonic artistic scenes.[82] The centers of the art world, the argument went, were merely making a cursory nod to multiculturalism and globalism while retaining their clear hold on power.

That criticism, however, downplays the cultural transformations that these events both signaled and catalyzed. Former bastions of West-centric internationalism began to deem it important to engage intermediaries and cultural producers who had originated from a wider variety of world regions. They may have been trying to demonstrate that they were "no longer as 'Eurocentric' as they used to be," but that indicates shifting *normative ground* concerning what biennials should be about.[83] Indeed, the orientation toward more diversity in recruitment could now serve as a symbolic currency for "biennial marketing."[84]

From a field perspective, it does not really matter if these biennials were merely globalism in West-centric disguise to acknowledge how important they were as symptoms and turning points for transformations toward a global logic within the field. After all, there can be no "neutral," quasi-universal artistic globalism. An emerging global field of struggle can only entail a proliferation of multiple perspectives around it, each informed by the distinctive positions, powers, and interests of its proponents. The crucial transformation was that a more global orientation turned into a source of symbolic capital at the field's centers, too. Though the major biennials were not truly "globalized," concerns about "globalization" did in fact become part of their discourses and practices, which marks a significant change in the competitive landscape.

FROM AN INTERNATIONAL TO A GLOBAL BIENNIAL PLATFORM

Important transformations also took place regarding the countries that participated at the Venice Biennale. As explained previously, the bulk of the Venice show consists of exhibition events or pavilions that are more independently organized by agents from different countries, publicly or privately. In 1984 still—the year of the first Havana Biennial—the number of national participations at Venice was a modest thirty-four; it had not changed much since the 1960s.[85] But during the global biennial boom, that number grew dramatically. In 2003, it had climbed to fifty-two, and in 2017, it reached eighty-five.[86] In the 1990s, after the end of the Cold War, eastern European countries enlarged their presence. In the millennium's first decade, Asian countries, including those from the Middle East, flocked in as new exhibitors. And in the following years, African countries, which doubled their participation from four to eight countries, accounted for the biggest jump.[87]

Thus, more and more countries began to congregate in Venice as the time-honored showground, presenting their distinctive perspectives on contemporary art and promoting their artists, just as they were doing in the biennial circuit at large. The worldwide proliferation of biennials had not diminished Venice's position as a major platform for artistic visibility and recognition across borders. On the contrary, as Monica Sassatelli argues, the biennial achieved a growing "global reputation," which "arguably owes much to the others that have mushroomed around it, reinforcing the genealogical role of the original and elevating it to the status of coveted ancestor."[88]

The modalities of participation among countries remained unequal, however—including different opportunities to exhibit in more centrally located national pavilions versus more remote exhibition spaces or so-called collateral events.[89] Nevertheless, with regard to the sheer number of exhibitors,

Western countries lost their former prevalence. While in 1984, they still made up nearly two-thirds of all contributors (59 percent), in 2017, their share shrank to one-fourth (26 percent).[90] With the overwhelming majority of national participants now coming from other parts of the world, the formerly Western institution had deprovincialized from within.

From an imperialist perspective on globalization, which stresses the reproduction of center powers, the expanded participation by countries from "peripheral" regions at Venice could be dismissed as a submissive gesture of deference by the culturally dominated.[91] But a country's involvement at the Venice Biennale does not mean that it is content with the event's prevailing representations and hierarchies. After all, national participants have considerable latitude to create exhibitions according to their own interests and cultural agendas.[92] If critical analysts do not keep such potentials for resistance in view, they run the risk of reproducing a hegemonic Northern view at the very same moment they decry it. Ultimately, the Venice Biennale itself became like a magnifying glass for the expanded scope and symbolic competition of the emerging global playing field in the new millennium.

In conclusion, biennials have not simply proliferated around the globe. They have grown into a global circuit that draws cultural agents, institutions, and cities from previously more disparate national and regional art fields into a common space of intensified exchange and struggle over symbolic capital, which in turn has engendered significant cultural transformations with regard to how contemporary art is debated and exhibited. A field perspective on these dynamics leads us beyond widespread "global art world" talk. Global relations and shared discourses are not merely created through friendly networks, dialogues, or even "community." They also come about through contestation and competition. At the same time, the relational field lens allows to avoid a simplified hierarchical picture that views globalization as a clash between antagonistic "colonizers" at the center and upstart players at the periphery. Instead, to grasp biennialization as part of an emerging global subfield implies a more complex scenario in which different perspectives and interests cross-pollinated with one another, creating a new space that is unequal but interdependent and one in which the idea of what constitutes symbolic capital has moved beyond older notions of Western internationalism into a new logic of global cosmopolitanism.

The Global Proliferation of Permanent Exhibition Institutions

Biennials have received the lion's share of attention in discussions about art's institutional globalization, but most of the foreign shows that an artist participates in during their career are typically not biennials. Hence, most of the exhibition institutions at the specific cultural pole that produce meaning and "exhibition value" as a form of symbolic capital must be situated within a wider, more permanent exhibition infrastructure that includes museums, public galleries, contemporary art centers, *Kunsthallen,* art associations, and university galleries.[93] Drawing on an unprecedented analysis of noncommercial exhibition spaces in more than one hundred countries reveals how they have dramatically proliferated too, forming a second dimension of an enlarging exhibition infrastructure in the globalizing artistic subfield.[94]

A GLOBAL EXPANSION

While "international biennials," by and large, tended to globalize in their approach in the new millennium, not all permanent noncommercial exhibition spaces engage in cross-border exchanges in their artistic programming. By 2017, for example, there were nearly thirty-seven thousand cultural institutions worldwide, but only around 10 percent of them had exhibitions that involved foreign contemporary artists (appendix A). And yet historically, a decade after the proliferation of biennials around the world, such more transnational art institutions underwent a tremendous geographic dispersion as well. In 1980, they were spread across forty-two countries (cf. the 1980 map in figure 2.5). But three decades later, the territorial scope of noncommercial institutions that exhibited contemporary artists from foreign countries had nearly tripled, appearing in a remarkable 118 countries on six continents.

The biggest additions came from countries in Asia, Latin America, Oceania, and, to a lesser extent, Africa. Particularly since the 1990s, after the onset of the biennial boom, regions outside the Northwest experienced a large increase (figure 2.6).

So, while biennials were historical forerunners for institutional globalization at the specific cultural pole, more permanent exhibition spaces soon followed their lead and often in similar locations. Biennialization foreshadowed, and partially influenced, a much larger eruption in exhibition institutions dedicated to showcasing artists from foreign backgrounds and, consequently, a dramatic morphological explosion in the overall audience for contemporary art around the globe.

Transnational exhibition institutions are, however, not as integrated as the biennial circuit on a global level. Some collaborate with one another through traveling exhibitions, some share a jet-setting "transnational class of museum directors, administrators, curators, and educators," and some draw from "global museum assemblages" (that is, similar "repertoires of ways to display, look at, and organize objects and educate others about them").[95] Despite such cross-border connections and the fact that an openness toward foreign artists makes such institutions susceptible to cultural forces beyond their national fields, it would be inaccurate to say that they directly exchange or compete with one another in the same way that international biennials do overall.

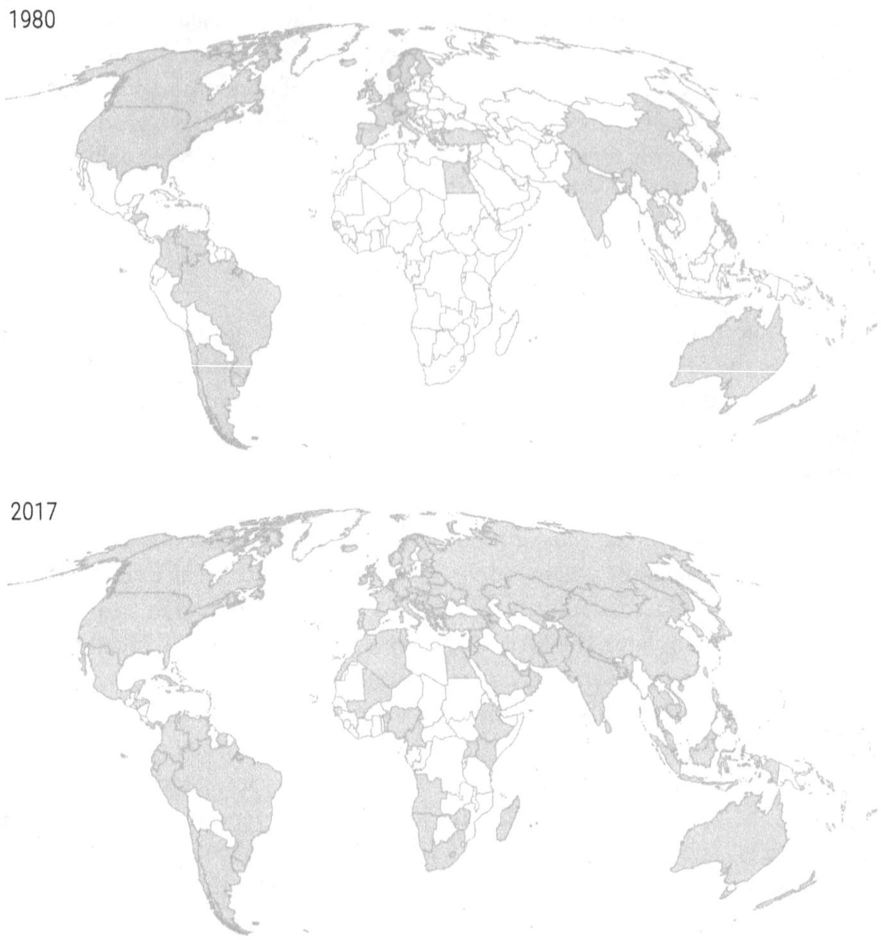

1980

2017

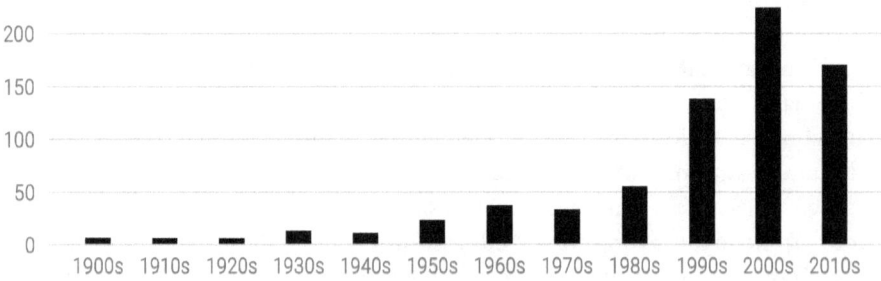

FIGURE 2.5. The geographic expansion of transnational exhibition institutions for contemporary art. (ArtFacts.Net, filtered and expanded through extensive research; appendix A)

FIGURE 2.6. Increase in the establishment of transnational exhibition institutions outside the Northwest, 1900–2017. (ArtFacts.Net, complemented through extensive research; appendix A)

Regardless, the increasing number of such transnational exhibition spaces was another important, albeit often less explored, institutional development for the globalization of the contemporary art field. Since the new millennium, artists could increasingly show their work at permanent institutions in every part of the world. As such, their growth contributed to a global shift in the scope of artistic careers and the accumulation of symbolic capital (see chapter 5). Together, the proliferation of both biennials and transnational exhibition institutions established a new global infrastructure for the circulation and valorization of contemporary art at the specific cultural pole, reaching far beyond the geographic boundaries of the older international field.

PERSISTING INEQUALITIES IN INSTITUTIONAL CAPITAL: EXHIBITION CENTERS AND PERIPHERIES

Despite these dynamics of geographic expansion, however, major inequalities in the volume of institutional capital among countries and cities persist. Most transnational exhibition institutions remain clustered in North America and western Europe, as we can see by the map's dark shadings in figure 2.7.

The United States stands out as *the* global exhibition center. With around 1,100 noncommercial exhibition institutions that also showcase foreign contemporary artists, it accounts for nearly 30 percent of the worldwide total. The US benefits not only from its sheer size but also from a federal arts structure that includes numerous museums and noncommercial galleries at universities around the country. Of course, the heart of artistic life beats in urban centers, and in this, New York stands as contemporary art's biggest art capital. With approximately 220 noncommercial exhibition institutions, the city commands the highest volume in the country *and* globally. The US is followed largely by western European countries with strong art historical traditions, including Germany, the United Kingdom, France, Italy, Austria, Spain, the Netherlands, and Switzerland, and another North American outpost, Canada. Among these, Germany is home to the second-biggest art capital, Berlin, which, after reunification, has amassed more than 190 noncommercial art institutions that include foreign contemporary artists in their exhibition programs.

It is after the top ten that countries beyond the Euro-American axis are on the rise in the world-structure of exhibitions, including Japan, Australia, Israel, and an impressively strong South Korea. China follows in twenty-first position, yet compared to its population and its general boom in national museums in recent years, it appears relatively weak and more aligned with the semiperiphery with regard to its volume of transnational exhibition institutions for contemporary art.[96] Finally, as indicated by the map's lighter shades, we see that

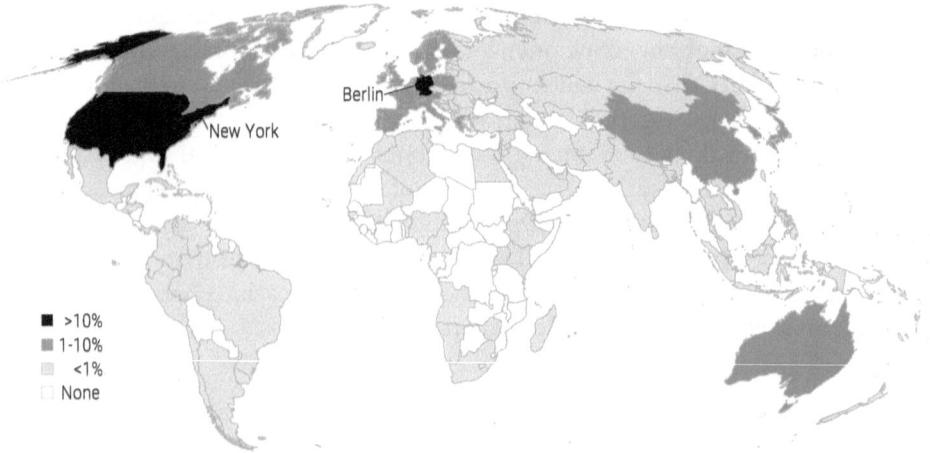

FIGURE 2.7. Global inequalities in the distribution of transnational exhibition institutions for contemporary art. (ArtFacts.Net, filtered and refined through extensive research; appendix A)

the majority of countries still constitute more peripheral exhibition zones, with five or fewer transnational exhibition spaces.

Thus, despite the massive worldwide proliferation of permanent exhibition institutions for foreign contemporary art since the 1990s, a few Western countries and cities still hold great institutional power for cross-border mediation and valuation. The idea that a center-periphery structure has become a matter of the past, as Arjun Appadurai has previously argued, does not apply when one considers these persisting inequalities in crucial resources, where institutions at the center retain supremacy.

It would be wrong to see these distributions as merely a reproduction of older international power structures, however, as suggested by sociologists who have argued in line with the imperialism model.[97] For one, these maps reveal that beyond the West's former prevalence, more art institutions than ever are participating in contemporary art's extended circulation. The hierarchies are no longer as unbalanced as they used to be, and a configuration previously marked more by dependencies has taken on more asymmetric interdependencies.[98]

What is more, since the turn of the new millennium, major museums and other permanent institutions in Western centers—not just biennials—have increasingly globalized their strategies as well, as we shall see in the next section. Artists and curators from countries beyond the Northwest have become more involved in exhibitions there, and new global discourses and debates have arisen. Consequently, permanent institutions in locations of centralized power have moved further away from an exclusionary Western paradigm and curatorial practices. The West may still dominate with regard to the field's institutional centers of mediation. Yet just as it was with biennials, the very logic of the elite game and its type of symbolic capital are no longer simply "international" and West-centric but increasingly global, too.

The Transformation of Discourses at Western Centers: The Contested Emergence of a Global Vision

As pivotal as the worldwide proliferation of exhibition institutions has been, the global art field did not arise quasi-mechanically out of a shared infrastructure. It had to come to life in the subjective representations of its participants, who needed to develop new interpretations and shared meanings rendering such global transformations intelligible.[99] In this regard, another central historical force underlying the field's globalization since the 1990s has been the rise of *field-specific global art discourses*. By this, I mean texts that engage with the relationship between contemporary art—its cultural practices, aesthetic values, institutions, and histories—and processes of globalization. Tracing the dynamics of such discourse not only reveals how a field evolves with regard to how field-internal agents describe it. Even more so, the way that people talk about a field influences its logics and operations.[100] The rise of global art discourses was both a symptom *and* a mechanism of the field's cultural transformations.

We have already seen how discursive dynamics impacted biennials when they adopted a global rhetoric that challenged international hierarchies and boundaries in contemporary art. This section additionally explores the rise of global discourse for other players as well, focusing on publications at *Artforum International*, a major journal for art criticism and debate in New York. Founded in 1962, *Artforum International* became one of the field's central agents for the production of critical discourse, attaining a dominant position among internationally oriented art magazines. As the sociologist Sarah Thornton has pointed out, more than forty years after the magazine's founding, "*Artforum* is to art what *Vogue* is to fashion and *Rolling Stone* is to rock and roll. . . . A front cover, feature, or sometimes even a review can have a tremendous impact on an artist's career."[101] As she further explains, the journal's prestige is rooted in its "perceived integrity" and distance from the art market in the eyes of art experts from multiple countries, as well as its "strategic ties" with academics, especially art historians, who serve as regular contributors alongside professional art critics and cultural journalists.[102]

One Western-based art journal, of course, can hardly be representative of art journals worldwide. Nevertheless, it allows us to explore how global changes have impacted not just "peripheral" players (like upstart biennials) but also a major agent for discourse production at the field's center. Additionally, through the *indirect* lens of the magazine's publications—which, in addition to biennial shows or artistic features, cover the exhibition politics of major museums and permanent art spaces—we can see how several of these latter institutions, and their mediators too, became more involved with global debates and strategies over time. Likewise, given that this powerful journal reached a more global circulation in the new millennium—by 2017, it was distributed in eighty-two countries across six continents—we can assume that it exerted effects on the evolution of meanings as the field expanded and changed.[103] So, although *Artforum*'s history provides a far-from-exhaustive picture of the field's overall discursive dynamics, it can offer us a window into the rise of hegemonic global discourses in Western centers, which potentially had feedback effects in more "peripheral" art contexts in turn.[104]

The Threefold Contested Rise of Global Art Discourse

If one begins with a "distant reading," tracking how often the words "global" or "globalization" appeared in *Artforum International*, an incipient increase over the second half of 1990s is clearly visible (figure 2.8).[105]

Then, in the new millennium, the frequency with which these terms appeared surged, albeit to different degrees. Parallel with the historical rise of a global exhibition infrastructure, "global talk" became more frequent at this powerful art journal in the field's center.

While existing contributions on art's globalization have already pointed to the rise of global discourse in contemporary art, they have often done so by jumping quickly from a variety of events in 1989 to a more recent period, presupposing that a distinct historical moment occurred that marked a "before" and "after" point in art's globalization.[106] But if one adopts a closer interpretative look to decipher changes in discursive meanings and struggles over time, it becomes evident that the rise of global discourses—like the globalization of biennials—is full of transitions and mutations, which once again point to the field's ever-evolving nature.

More specifically, by engaging in a "close reading" of around eight hundred text passages from a thirty-year period (1987–2017), the case of *Artforum International* suggests that the rise of global art discourse unfolded in three analytically distinct—but, historically, not fully disjunctive—stages (table 2.1).[107]

Following an initial period that was heavily influenced by broader multicultural politics and that manifested itself in growing normative attacks on a Western vision in the arts in the early 1990s, a second discursive stage in the later 1990s was informed by biennialization and the formation of an expanding

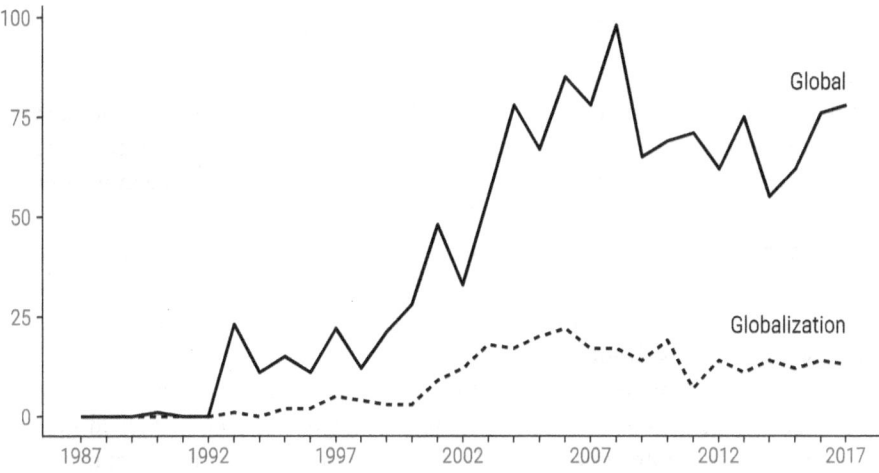

FIGURE 2.8. The rising frequency of the words "global" and "globalization" at *Artforum International*, 1987–2017. (*Artforum International*; appendix A)

TABLE 2.1. Three Stages in the Evolution of Global Art Discourse at *Artforum International*.

Stage 1: Challenging a Western vision	Stage 2: An expanding global context	Stage 3: The emergence of a global vision
Multicultural politics as external influence	Biennialization as internal influence	The broadening and internalization of global meanings
Western binary	Dialectic of global and local	The "third space" of a global aesthetics
Western vision	Reflexivity	Emerging global vision
Segregation	Interplay of shared "global" artistic frameworks and locally specific elements	Growing integration without aesthetic homogenization
"Global" as normative category for critique of West-centric order	"Global" as increasingly "real" but negotiated category	"Global" as accepted, "taken for granted" category, a foundation for new debates and stakes

global context. The third stage involved the emergence of a *global vision* in the new millennium. The phenomenological notion of "vision" insinuates that global assumptions became operative in the art field not just through ideas in people's heads but also by becoming part of embodied dispositions. What occurred was the rise of a new paradigm for *seeing* the world of contemporary art, which, in the form of incorporated schemes and tacit beliefs, became a cultural bedrock for novel stakes and debates.[108]

THE POLITICS OF MULTICULTURALISM:
ATTACKS ON THE WEST-CENTRIC GAZE

The first phase of global art discourse emerged at the beginning of the 1990s and was unleashed by broader multicultural politics in the immigration hubs of the Global North. Multiculturalism had emerged as a wider social movement in the wake of rising identity politics over the previous decade.[109] Despite many variants, at its core was a critique of how Western societies marginalized the cultures of minorities.[110] Activists demanded that excluded expressions from minority groups should become part of official cultural canons and that public institutions should more accurately mirror demographic diversity.[111]

By the end of the 1980s, multicultural debates increasingly exerted an influence on the international art field as well. In *Artforum*, there emerged more extensive critical interrogations of Eurocentric views at dominant art institutions.[112] Much like the Havana Biennial around that time, the rising global discourse in the West attacked the boundaries of a narrow West-centric gaze, seeking to shake up the principles of vision and division underpinning hegemonic institutional practices and aesthetic discourses, which were now being decried as complicit with postcolonial power constellations.

At *Artforum* global art discourse first appeared in an essay about an international exhibition that was engaged with multicultural questions, the *Magiciens de la Terre* at the Centre Georges Pompidou and Grande Halle de la Villette in Paris (May 18–August 14, 1989). The French curator Jean-Hubert Martin—in his midthirties at the time—had the ambition to create a contemporary exhibition that would showcase artists from five continents. He invited fifty artists from "non-Western," "third-world" contexts along with fifty artists from the West, seeking to display them on the same level. His heterodox show provoked fierce international criticism.[113] Martin's contract with the institution was not extended, and he even complained about a backlash that lasted for half a dozen years, during which he felt "marginalized in the milieu of art."[114]

Reviewing these negative reactions in *Artforum*'s March 1990 issue, the art historian Thomas McEvilley discussed how orthodox art critics attacked *Magiciens de la Terre* for selecting artists on the basis of an external social criterion—their ethnicity—rather than on autonomous aesthetic standards, and how more leftist critics bemoaned that the curatorial setup fell prey to neoprimitivist impulses. The work that Martin had selected implied a problematic binary division between the traditional, "craftlike," "ritualistic" contributions of non-Western artists and the "cool, intellectual and conceptual" works by Westerners.[115] Despite that and other issues, McEvilley advocated for evaluating the show on the basis not of its curation but of its critical impulse and the way it significantly contributed to a shake-up of Western orthodoxies. Note how McEvilley—who was conversant in Indian culture and philology—linked his own heterodox defense of the exhibition's ambition with the notion of a "new global sense of civilization":

> All the criticism of the show . . . fails to confront the monumental fact that this was the first major exhibition consciously to attempt to discover a post-colonialist way to exhibit first- and third-world objects together. . . . *"Magiciens"* opened the door of the long-insular and hermetic Western art world to third-world artists. . . . Western culture as it enters the 1990s is . . . seeking a new definition of history that will not involve ideas of hierarchy, or of mainstream and periphery, and a new, global sense of civilization to replace the linear Eurocentric model that lay at the heart of Modernism.[116]

These words, penned by the most frequent global voice at the journal during this first stage, proved prophetic. In hindsight, *Magiciens de la Terre* is widely considered a symbolic landmark show.[117] Taking place in the same year as the Havana Biennial's third edition, the Paris exhibition demonstrated that the battle against a West-centric art paradigm was not just being fought on the terrain of biennials; it was also erupting from within permanent institutions in the centers, driven by younger heterodox mediators as well as diasporic agents.[118] McEvilley's own review in turn exemplifies how, at this time, the global was still primarily framed as a normative critique of exclusionary Western practices rather than a belief in a global art space that actually existed.

Such normative debates were reaching other major exhibitions in the early 1990s, most prominently the 1993 edition of the Venice Biennale. The overarching theme, "Cultural Nomadism," opened this international platform up for the first time to issues of multiculturalism instead of sticking with a more conventional—that is, strictly aesthetic—focus. The show attracted massive criticism, not least for this departure from institutional tradition. Yet two *Artforum* contributors, including McEvilley, defended it that same year, arguing that the show marked an important historical shift beyond Eurocentric ideas of artistic quality.[119] One review associated the biennial with the idea of an "emerging global culture."[120]

At the time, *Artforum* also featured museological publications and artistic projects that questioned the long-held idea that museums represented universal cultural values.[121] The institutional construct became historically contextualized within colonial societies' imperial quest to stage their cultural superiority. Such museological debates spilled over to Western contemporary art museums, some of whose practices were denounced as Eurocentric because they either ignored living visual artists from "non-Western" backgrounds or represented

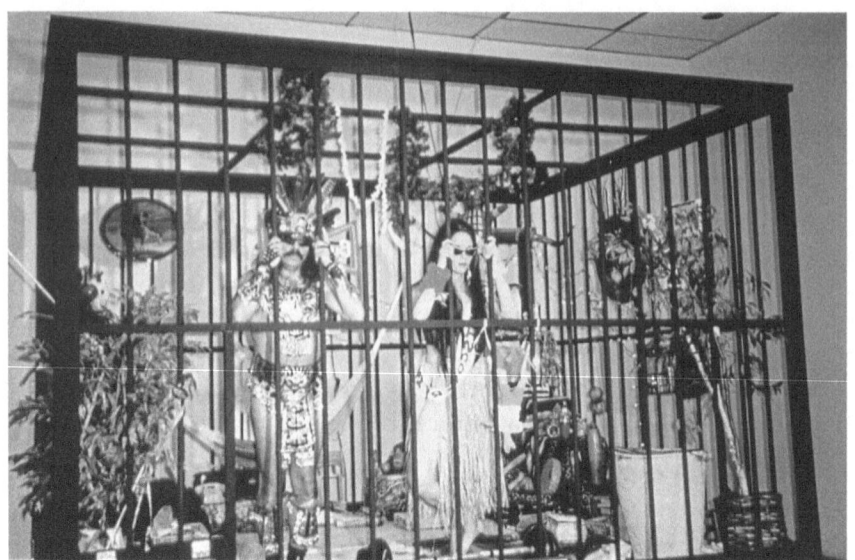

FIGURE 2.9. Coco Fusco and Guillermo Gómez-Peña performing *The Year of the White Bear*, 1992, at the Australian Museum, Sydney, as part of the 1992–93 Biennale of Sydney from the Biennale of Sydney Archive 1992–93. (National Art Archive, Art Gallery of New South Wales. Gift of Biennale of Sydney 2015. Photo: Unknown)

their work in problematically denigrating ways. For example, a 1987 traveling show, *Hispanic Art in the United States: Thirty Contemporary Painters and Sculptors*, which originated at the Houston Museum of Fine Arts, was noted for showcasing the art in an overly exoticizing fashion. As an essay in *Artforum* highlighted, in a time of "complex, multicultural environments" and a more global sense of humanity, museums are called upon to overcome old hierarchical binaries and become "places for interrogation of cultural diversity."[122]

Although the journal's global discourse in the early 1990s primarily centered on institutions and their exclusionary practices, artistic practices also became cast in this new discursive light. For example, at the Sydney Biennale in 1992, Guillermo Gómez-Peña and Coco Fusco performed *The Year of the White Bear*, in which the artists "exhibited themselves as caged Amerindian savages" (figure 2.9).[123] In the eyes of one of *Artforum*'s contributing critics from Australia, their performance figured as a caustic comment on the quincentenary celebrations of Christopher Columbus's landing in the Americas. The artists' work denounced modes of "museum spectacle" that failed to properly engage with the artists' in-between identities as Hispanic Americans.[124]

Reviews in the spirit of multicultural global discourse tended to foreground contemporary art as a symbolic medium for interrogating broader cultural power dynamics and questions of identity in colonial or postcolonial constellations. During this stage, the art the magazine discussed figured primarily as a vehicle for external representational politics that questioned Western notions of culture and related Eurocentric hierarchies. In this context, the global provided a normative topos, which, by connoting inclusion and cultural diversity, served as an alternative to exclusionary, one-sided Western dominance. In short, in the early 1990s, global concepts were invoked largely in aspirational terms. They were a way to call for a more inclusive understanding of contemporary art and culture.

AN EXPANDING CONTEXT FOR CULTURAL EXCHANGE AND HYBRIDIZATION: THE RISE OF GLOBAL REFLEXIVITY

The next stage in the evolution of global art discourse occurred in the second half of the 1990s and involved the rise of global reflexivity. This stage saw increasing debates about global transformations, particularly in the wake of the worldwide biennial boom. The category of the global was no longer just about normative aspirations but began to refer to dynamics that one could empirically observe. Simultaneously, discussions turned from primarily focusing on what was happening in Western capitals to a geographically widened perspective, reflecting the growing sense that the "situation" was not "just North American and European."[125] Notwithstanding, there was still a reluctance to speak of something like a common global art world. Instead, the emphasis was placed on process, on a dynamic that was in the making in "an *increasingly* global art scene" or "an *emergent* global art village," though there was not yet a belief in something like a shared global space itself.[126]

In institutional terms, most of the global discourse during these years focused on biennials. At a historical moment of explosive biennialization, when one could see the ascendance of "peripheral" players challenging hegemonic centers, *Artforum* witnessed a corresponding rise in the number of reviews by Western curators or critics who attended the exhibitions. The tenor of their writings diverged strikingly from the journal's earlier reviews about more peripheral, "non-Western" biennials. In 1993, for example, such biennials had been portrayed as remote, discrete events that worked for their "own cultural audiences . . . and cultural functions of their own."[127] Just four years later, however, agents in the centers stopped viewing biennials outside the transatlantic axis as an institutional "other" from the distant "third world." Instead, they interpreted them as events that shared "numerous characteristics" with more established international art shows in the West, and these biennials were now seen as "joining" a shared "field of large international contemporary art exhibitions".[128]

Reviews also paid attention to the unique political and cultural contexts in which such biennials were embedded, recognizing that the exhibitions were not simply replicating the methods and aesthetics of the center powers. An essay about the 1997 Johannesburg and Gwangju Biennales by the American art historian Mary Anne Staniszewski, for example, noted how they staged special exhibitions on South African or Korean contemporary art and thus "transcend the generic, international group show by presenting new work that speaks to the diversity of the global."[129] In her eyes, such "distinctive" offerings made these biennials "among the most important of this year's exhibitions."[130] Staniszweski's statements convey, in an exemplary way, a reflexive attention to local specificity, which, however, becomes legible *and* valued in relation to the assumption of a growing global commonality. This is what I mean by the rise of global reflexivity: there was a new kind of interpretative work that went beyond reviewing "other" "non-Western" biennials in their alterity. In a time when agents from Western capitals began to visit biennials around the world more frequently and to see them as part of the same "field," one now appreciated how these exhibitions—precisely through their distinctiveness—were contributing to a shared contemporary art space.[131]

Furthermore, new discussions of a "globalist mentality" and a new nomadism among artists and curators associated the "local" with an emerging sense of the "global".[132] A "travelogue" by a senior curator at the New Museum in New York in 1997, for instance, listed Barcelona, Los Angeles, Las Palmas, Germany, Santa Fe, and Johannesburg among the numerous places he had visited in one year of the "never-ending biennial."[133] The curator, Dan Cameron, underlined how extended travel and increasingly nomadic lifestyles would inform new kinds of cross-cultural reflexivity. Exhibition makers and artists, comparing their notes about art within different contexts, would gain an enlarged frame of reference for contemporary art around the world, which in turn would feed back into how they perceived their "proverbial backyard"— casting the specificity of Western art contexts in a new, globally reflexive light.[134]

The new reflexivity became apparent in a shift in aesthetic discussions, too. Whereas earlier multicultural-global discourse had focused on a critique of the lack of representation by "peripheral" artists, what emerged in the second half of the 1990s was a more aesthetic reflectiveness concerning how they could not be assimilated into older Western paradigms of contemporary art. The relationship between "Western" and "non-Western" art and culture was reformulated, moving away from issues around "inclusion" and "cultural diversity" to focus more heavily on concerns around artistic difference, hybridization, and aesthetic translation between traditions and contexts. Although artists from outside Western centers might draw on similar aesthetic styles—such as "the constructivist tradition," "the tradition of conceptual art," or the "international lingua franca" of installation art—critics were now paying greater attention to how they articulated them with artistic elements from their own differing cultural backgrounds. Art from semiperipheral countries also came to be valued for its complex "negotiation between global and local cultural values."[135] In this regard, artists could create hybrid expressions that at times contradicted established Western understandings of the same styles, implying aesthetic challenges and subversions that critics, curators, and audiences needed to attend to and fully appreciate.

For example, in a 1997 *Artforum* review about the Brazilian artist Cildo Meireles, the Argentinian curator Carlos Basualdo situated Meireles's work within the broader tradition of conceptual art. But Basualdo's discussion also emphasized how Meireles's approach deviated from a Western understanding of conceptual practices as being primarily about the "dematerialization of the art object."[136] Meireles instead placed a strong emphasis on his installations' material and sensual properties. In *Volátil* (1980–94), for instance, viewers enter a dark room that is lit by a candle and full of the odor of natural gas, and they walk barefoot across a floor covered with small granules of material (figure 2.10). For Basualdo, the distinctive focus on sensual materiality must be interpreted within the context of the Neo-Concretists from the 1970s in Meireles's country of origin, Brazil. This artistic movement had embraced ideas about embodied perception from French phenomenology and created a style that critiqued the oppressive nature of the country's military dictatorship. Meireles's material focus thus gains specific meaning within the context of a critical, artistic-political stance in Brazil. Yet because it was formulated using a nonlocal aesthetic idiom, the work, according to Basualdo, acts simultaneously as a hybrid critical commentary on the "passive, depoliticized nature of North American Conceptual art."[137]

Basualdo's review exemplifies the more self-referential problematization of artistic translation and hybridity in this era of rising global reflexivity. In the early 1990s, global discourses engaged with artworks primarily as symbolic media for interrogating external cultural power relations in thematic terms. The decade's second half then saw a shift toward more field-specific, aesthetic analyses, where the rhetoric of the global figured as a contextual foil for specialized "autonomous" interpretations of artistic commonality and difference. Critics began to situate the meaning of works by artists from different world parts at the interstices between *shared* artistic frameworks and *locally specific* elements. And it was in that "third space" where the possibility of "global art" as a new "paradigm" began to be located at the end of the 1990s.[138]

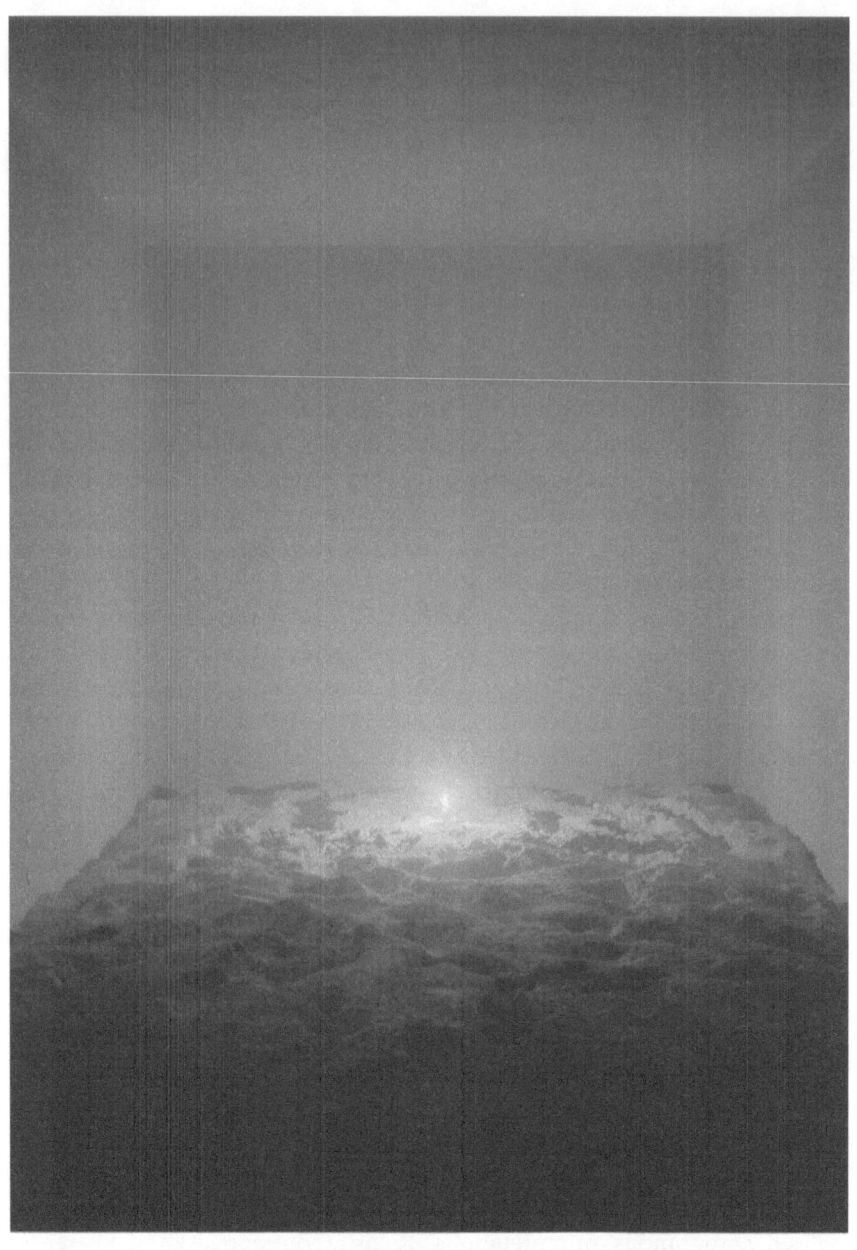

FIGURE 2.10. Cildo Meireles, *Volátil* [Volatile], 1980/94, wood, talc, candle, essence, dimensions variable. (Copyright Cildo Meireles; courtesy of Galerie Lelong & Co., New York)

THE EMERGENCE OF A GLOBAL VISION

The third stage of global discourse began at the turn of the new millennium but reached its full contours from around 2006. In this phase, discussions about empirical global transformations extended to museums, art schools, the art market, art collectors, aesthetic categories, and increasingly, art history. But beyond this broadening move, there was a deeper internalization of global meanings, which I interpret as the emergence of a global vision. The "global" did not just represent a normative topos or a geographic expansion in scale and artistic mixing across borders. More than that, the global began to establish itself as an immanent logic that redefined the game of contemporary art from within. This emerging global vision should not be seen as a new master narrative. It merely formed a novel cultural bedrock that set the stage for new modes of interpretation, new debates and competitions, and ultimately, new understandings of what constitutes symbolic capital.

On the institutional side, the emergence of a global vision was indicated by the drastic increase in more integrative categories—including "global biennial circuit," "global art world," "global art market," "global gallery network," and "global community"—that no longer referred to single institutions but to entire spaces. In contrast to the previous period, these categories appeared more frequently and were invoked less skeptically, without temporal qualifiers like "emerging" or "increasing." *Artforum* contributors now seemed to believe that they had become part of, and were operating within, a global art space with its own presumptive facticity.[139]

Regarding art biennials, the move toward a more integrative global vision might not be surprising. During the second stage, reviews had already noted that despite persisting diversity, biennials were developing some shared characteristics across continents. However, since 2003—a time when the first biennial conferences had occurred and more institutionalized coordination among their organizers had emerged—these views went one step further. Biennials began to be seen as part of an integrated global circuit to such a degree that some critics even began warning about homogenizing tendencies.

Perhaps even more revealing for the emergence of a global vision, however, was the evolution of the phrase "global art world." In an influential 2003 *Artforum* essay, the art historian and critic Pamela Lee advocated for a deeper accounting of how the "art world has internalized the conditions of the global as its daily habitus" and for "rethink[ing] the 'art world' as itself a mode of immanent global production" in "its audiences and range of influence, its norms and procedures."[140] When the concept of the "global art world" initially gained traction, it nevertheless remained largely associated with biennials. In 2006, the curator and critic Lisette Lagnado, for example, noted that "the international biennial may be taken as an emblem—if not a symptom—of today's global art world."[141]

In the millennium's second decade, however, the idea of a "global art world" loosened its links with biennials and more frequently came to designate broader institutional configurations. Around this time, as Lee had foreshadowed, the idea became also more closely associated with shared artistic practices and meanings. In 2013, for instance, a critical review by a New York–based art historian about the artist Luigi Ghirri, highlighted how Ghirri's "innovative vision" would impact the "global art world" as it continues to "investigate . . . the real through photography."[142] The critic framed Ghirri's contributions in relation to artistic idioms assumed to be part of a shared global space. Another essay in the same year, by the American art historian David Joselit, went even further, asking about the proper strategies for exhibitions that were addressing the "*history* of a global art world."[143] Thus, experts who were positioned at the field's center began to imagine the contemporary visual arts as a global space of shared cultural meanings, practices, and perhaps even common historical narratives.

Nevertheless, it is important to keep in mind that a burgeoning global vision did not entail a consensual appeasement. It merely constituted a new "global" cultural frame of reference for new debates and forms of competition, which included permanent art institutions, curators, critics, and art historians, etc. For example, the rise of a global vision was expressed in perceptions that museums had become part of an environment of "increasingly fierce global competition."[144] In 2008, an essay highlighted the Tate Modern in London and the Guggenheim and Louvre Abu Dhabi as exemplary cases of a broader situation in which "countless" cultural institutions would find themselves at a "critical point of redefinition" where they had to rethink their strategies "to make their mark on the global map."[145]

Such increasingly global competitive strategies manifested themselves, among other ways, through changing exhibition programs. As the journal's publications highlighted, leading art institutions in Western centers appointed new curators from outside the Western mainstream and engaged in new exhibition politics.[146] As far back as 1999, an *Artforum* article lauded New York's Museum of Modern Art (MoMA)—a longtime bastion of European and US-American modernism—for appointing the curator Paulo Herkenhoff from Brazil as a significant departure for the museum, since he would bring "Latin American roots and global perspective" to the institution.[147] Ten years later, another contribution credited MoMA for approximating a "newly global purview" in its exhibitions.[148] More broadly, the journal reported how Western curators in their thirties and forties at the New Museum New York, the Palais de Tokyo in Paris, or the Whitechapel gallery in London underlined at the time of their appointments that they aimed to pursue more global perspectives. Thus, in the new millennium, elite institutions and rising curators embraced an expanded global vision in curating as forward-looking and innovative and, in this sense, as a new basis for symbolic capital.

To be sure, what a proper "global perspective" would look like remained a matter of ongoing professional debate. In 2007, for example, reviews of that year's Venice Biennale by younger, midcareer curators with positions in London, Chicago, and New York criticized Robert Storr's work as the artistic director for an overly universalizing perspective that paid insufficient attention to the "historical and cultural specificity" of art from different world contexts.[149] Storr, a former senior curator at MoMA who was in his late fifties, defended his professional honor by referencing his own global commitments:

> I painted murals in Mexico in the early 1970s, participated in several conferences there, . . . contributed a section to Paulo Herkenhoff's 1998 Sao Paulo Biennial . . . and have made focused curatorial trips to Argentina (twice), Chile, Colombia, Cuba, Uruguay, and Venezuela. Moreover, I was told by curators I met in Senegal at Dak'Art 2006 that I am also the first director of the Biennale to travel to Africa expressly to look for art for the Venice exhibition. I will skip mention of my two trips to China, two to India . . . and much else along the way. Indeed, for thirty years I have been an outspoken advocate of greater cosmopolitanism in the art world, have repeatedly made the effort to build the necessary bridges, and have crossed them myself.[150]

Storr's defense underlines how an approach that goes beyond Western art worlds became linked with legitimacy at the elite level of exhibition makers. This link had not yet existed in the early 1990s; but in the new millennium, the normative ground had shifted, and a global vision had turned into an immanent yardstick for symbolic capital in the upper tier of the game.

In the third stage, global discourse also saw the proliferation of more integrative global artistic categories, exemplified by such terms as "global idiom," "global style," "global Conceptualism," "global neo-dada," "global realism," "global feminisms," "global pop," or "global contemporary art." This discursive development and the classification struggles that came along with it signal a remarkable departure from the second phase. While the late 1990s saw a growing aesthetic reflexivity of similarity and difference, the global nevertheless remained a vague background category for looking at "local" cases in relational terms. In this subsequent phase, by contrast, specialists sought to reevaluate artists and practices from around the world as part of new global categories and genealogies that would influence the way "contemporary art" itself should be envisioned. With such discursive moves, the global penetrated the grammar of aesthetic taxonomies and the (re)evaluations of artists and styles. At stake was not just the critique of a Western gaze but the construction of a *common* symbolic framework, beyond an outmoded Euro-American perspective, for contemporary art.

In this regard, the 1999 exhibition at the Queens Museum of Art *Global Conceptualism: Points of Origin 1950s–1980s* was particularly pioneering and influential on the evolution of global aesthetic discourses at *Artforum* (figure 2.11).[151] The exhibition's curatorial team—Jane Faver, Luis Camnitzer, and Rachel Weiss—had launched an innovative survey of conceptual practices from multiple continents with the goal of overcoming a one-sided Western historical perspective on conceptual art that described the art movement as originating in New York and London before diffusing around the world. The exhibition demonstrated how conceptual practices had developed simultaneously in different regions, including Asia, Africa, and Latin America, thus debunking the myth of the movement's Anglo-Saxon origins. Subsequent exhibitions in France and the US followed in these footsteps, further exploring conceptual art from a global perspective and garnering critical attention in *Artforum* as well.

Another prominent case of a global category in the journal was "Global Pop," which highlights how global rewritings were not simply about aesthetic homogenization. In 2013, the curator Jessica Morgan—who had been one of the fiercest critics of Storr in 2007—argued for a notion of "Global Pop" that captures the multiplicity of this style worldwide. Note how the author uses below the word of "iterations," as opposed to "adaptations," to stress that there was no single Western origin of Pop that would have "disseminated from founding hubs in New York and London to other parts of the world." Her wording further exemplifies how integrative global categories of art styles aimed to create an interpretative framework for common diversity.[152]

> Just as "Pop style" encompassed various strategies of composition and process, so there was not one universal Pop art but rather hundreds of iterations around the globe that shared a populist concern. Numerous movements and artists developed a Pop strategy: Among the former were Nouveau Realisme, neo-Dada, Otra and Nueva Figuracion, and Saqqakhaneh or Spiritual Pop; the latter included the collective Equipo Cronica, as well as such singular figures as Oyvind Fahlstrom, Keiichi Tanaami, and Erro. These tendencies differed from one another due to their varying origins, in countries such as Argentina, Brazil, France, Iceland, Iran, Japan, and Spain, and were necessarily informed by their respective traditions and sociopolitical situations.[153]

And once again, the rise of a global vision did not simply mean a new consensus. In 2016, a review article in *Artforum* about two exhibitions on "Global Pop"—at the Walker Art Center in Minneapolis and the Tate Modern London (which Jessica Morgan curated)—critically debated the shows' diverging approaches. While one went with national classifications in mapping worldwide variants of Pop, the other abandoned them in favor of shared themes; while one included US-American artists, the other discarded them altogether; while

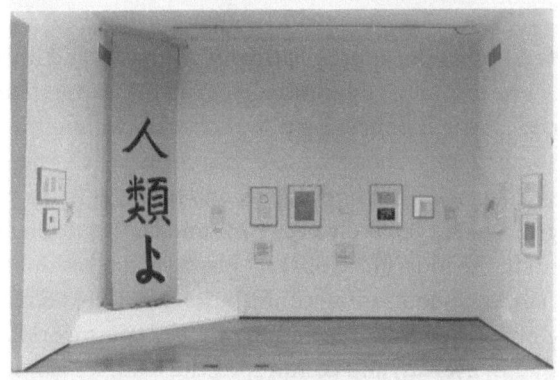

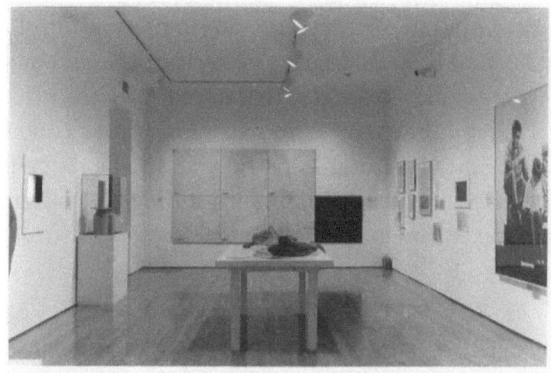

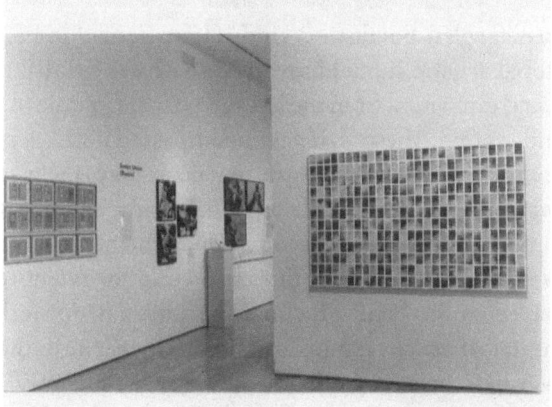

FIGURE 2.11. Images that depict views of exhibitions rooms from *Global Conceptualism: Points of Origin, 1950s–1980s* (April 28, 1999–August 29, 1999), Queens Museum, New York. *Top*, "Japan" installation organized by Reiko Tomii. *Center*, "Latin America" installation organized by Mari Carmen Ramírez. *Bottom*, "Russia" installation organized by Margarita Tupitsyn. (All photos courtesy Queens Museum, New York)

one interpreted Pop as the appropriation of commodified images, the other included "visceral modes of figuration," suggesting a more erotic, "very hot version of Pop."[154] Such persisting differences underline that an emerging global vision was merely operating as a shared frame of reference for novel disputes about categories, methodologies, and histories in the construction of a new paradigm, which eventually became framed with another integrative yet contested term in the journal: "global art history."

To appreciate such continuing contestations, it seems fertile to decouple the idea of a global vision from the notion of a "global art world" and its flattening overtones of consensus and community. Instead, we can see it as an integral part of an emerging global artistic subfield for both exchange and ongoing struggle that operates with a new logic of symbolic capital. As the evolution of discourse at *Artforum* reveals, by the new millennium, art experts at the field's center could no longer stick to old, West-centric narratives and modes of operation if they wanted to make innovative contributions to the field. This marks a clear cultural shift—also in the field's centers—from no longer just international but global understandings of contemporary art, its institutional contexts, and its mediation practices.

The Globalization of Institutions for Consecration and Evaluation

A third, partly entangled, but distinct kind of transformation affecting the emergence of a global artistic subfield involved the rise of global institutions for consecration and evaluation from the late 1980s to the middle of the first decade of the new millennium. These changes encompassed both art prizes and artist rankings, and they contributed to institutionalize new principles for classifying and evaluating contemporary artists in global terms, and thus to redefine the ultimate parameters for symbolic recognition in the field.

As we saw in the first section of this chapter, in the twentieth century, the awards conferred by the Venice Biennale became a major form of consecration, a barometer of artistic values and hierarchies within the international field.[155] However, Venice long remained heavily West-centric, which was reflected in the artists who received its prizes. For decades, the recipients came overwhelmingly from Europe or the US. This exclusionary situation began to change in the early 1990s. During biennialization and a period that saw an expanding number of countries flock to the Venice Biennale as exhibitors, the scope of artistic comparison and competition for Venice's prizes expanded. The broadening of biennial participants became reflected in changes among award recipients. Between the early 1990s and 2017, the share of prizes and honorable mentions won by artists with origins outside the prevalent Euro-American axis grew to 35 percent, a seven-fold increase over prior iterations, when it was only around 5 percent.[156] Within an increasingly globalized arena of symbolic competition, the Venice Biennale's prize system metamorphosed into a more global institution for consecration.

Venice was not singular. Amid a more general proliferation of new art prizes since the 1980s, at least one newer institution, the Praemium Imperiale, would claim a status as a global art prize, and it was created outside the traditional Western centers in 1988.[157] Founded in Japan, it deliberately aspired toward cosmopolitanism from the beginning, aiming to move beyond transatlantic discourses of "international contemporary art." And indeed, the institution's awards in the categories of painting and sculpture eventually assumed such universal legitimacy that they informally gained the reputation as something akin to the Nobel Prize for the visual arts. Hence, with Venice and the Praemium Imperiale, the field began globalizing with regard to its consecratory prizes, whose scope and meaning assumed global dimensions.

New online artist rankings also played a role for globalizing evaluative practices in the art field, contributing, despite their contested status, to the institutionalization of global principles of evaluation and hierarchization. Artist rankings are by no means new, and there is a long historical tradition of comparisons and rankings on a limited scale in both the visual arts and literature.[158] The first international ranking system for contemporary art took shape with the Kunstkompass, which was founded in 1970 in Germany. The economist and art journalist Willi Bongard set out to introduce a systematic way of annually determining the top one hundred contemporary artists in the international field. The quantitative method he created, partly inspired by measurement methods in science, radically departed from what the field had seen before. Experts were asked to score art institutions and magazines so that Bongard could single out the most prestigious ones on the basis of reputation points. He then ranked the artists who had the most visibility in those venues, subjecting them to a highly rationalized system of international hierarchical comparison.[159]

As the creation of the Kunstkompass marked a drastic shift in the international evaluation of visual art, it is not surprising that its initial appearance in the magazine *Capital* provoked harsh criticism.[160] Artists in particular claimed that the idea of assessing artistic merit using numbers and ranks was degrading and scandalous.[161] Criticisms of the ranking system never fully subsided, but international players in the art field, including the megacurator Harald Szeemann and renowned artist Joseph Beuys, soon recognized it, increasing its legitimacy.[162]

In hindsight, it has become clear that the introduction of this ranking fed into greater international integration in the art field since the 1970s.[163] Before the digital age, when information beyond one's own country was still difficult to access, the Kunstkompass provided a comprehensive source of orientation and comparison about the exhibition status of artists and related aesthetic trends, contributing to bridge more fragmented national art fields.[164]

And yet, like other institutions in the postwar international art field, the Kunstkompass operated with a West-centric scope. The first ranking considered exhibitions in thirteen countries that were overwhelmingly in the Northwest. Only two countries outside this radius, Japan and Brazil, were included, with one institution each. In 2003, the still fairly West-centric setup of the Kunstkompass was challenged by the rise of a competitor. Marek Claassen (another German economist) introduced a multilingual online platform, ArtFacts.Net, that began tracking the visibility of artists in the expanding global exhibition infrastructure.[165] ArtFacts' rankings drew from a vastly bigger geographic scope. By 2008, it had amassed a digital archive of 130,000 exhibitions in 140 countries on six continents, including 125,437 contemporary artists worldwide, in its assessments.[166] The site's global inclusivity of both art institutions and artists soon earned ArtFacts the reputation of being more "democratic," which also gave it a competitive edge over Kunstkompass.[167] ArtFacts even overtook the latter's place at the magazine *Capital* in 2008, where the Kunstkompass had been published for the previous thirty-eight years.

Nevertheless, like the Kunstkompass, the ArtFacts ranking provoked "tumultuous" responses, and it received strong critical reactions when it was launched in 2003.[168] Merely attempting to measure artistic recognition in quantitative terms was still considered to be inappropriate, subjecting art to an industrial logic.[169] Despite the controversies, within just two years, ArtFacts had managed to attract around ten thousand visitors and ninety thousand visits per day.[170] A 2005 *New York Times* article, which portrayed the ranking in positive terms, further broadened its audience across borders.[171] And by 2012, ArtFacts' clients reportedly included art institutions in sixty-two countries on six continents and a collection of private clients—the majority of whom were artists—from seventy-five countries.[172] Not only was ArtFacts more global in the range of information it offered, but it also commanded an increasingly global audience. Undoubtedly, the fact that it was an internet forum facilitated this broad range of reception; the technology made it easily accessible and searchable by almost anyone in the world. Correspondingly, ArtFacts has assumed a paradoxical status in the globalizing field: while its public legitimacy has been contested, it has quietly come to be used regularly by professional and private clients on multiple continents.

Precisely because of this extensive level of global reception, the ranking can be credited with discursive power in shaping new understandings that contribute to the symbolic construction of the global field. ArtFacts fulfills, first, an orientation function, all the more valuable because of the massive morphological expansion of art institutions and participants in the new global context. As the German art critic and theorist Isabelle Graw has argued, "These rankings satisfy the desire for clearly defined hierarchies in a global art world that is perceived as increasingly confusing."[173]

Yet the ArtFacts rankings also play a performative role. The French sociologists Luc Boltanski and Arnaud Esquerre have suggested that such rankings have turned into "indispensable tools" that *influence* "the evaluation of works, artists" in the contemporary visual arts themselves.[174] They not only offer a digital map of the aesthetic choices of intermediaries and related hierarchies around the world but can affect their choices regarding selection and promotion. In this performative capacity, I would argue further that these rankings also have contributed to institutionalize the very idea of conceiving of artistic recognition—and thus artistic value—within extended global parameters. In a period when global discourses had gained a greater taken-for-granted legitimacy among both "peripheral" and central players and as global art prizes had come into existence, online platforms further solidified the idea of the global as a new reference category that signified the field's highest stakes. While "international artist" had previously been the ultimate level of recognition a cultural producer could attain, now the highest level of success was to be assessed at a global level.[175] Thus, ArtFacts established a global institution of hierarchization and evaluation that also played a role in redefining—in contested but nevertheless discursively powerful ways—ideas of symbolic capital beyond the art field's old international scope.

Conclusion

The globalization of the artistic subfield was not simply the result of the multiplication of cultural practices and institutions around the world. More than just a matter of geographic dispersal and proliferation, the process entailed the creation of an expanded space with a new logic. This chapter has traced the emergence of this space, examining the rise of a global exhibition infrastructure, global discourses, and global institutions for consecration and (e)valuation. The confluence of these transformations in the new millennium created a shared global institutional and cultural framework that enabled intensified exchanges and competition between "central" and "peripheral" players from formerly more segregated world parts. New dialogues, collaborations, and struggles erupted, and over time, these dynamics undermined the legitimacy of a West-centric "international" artistic order, morphing into a transformed global art game with its own logic and understandings of symbolic capital. This new global logic is expressed in the value that has been placed on decentering Western perspectives, new norms of cosmopolitanism, and the ongoing—and contested—construction of a global paradigm for contemporary art that aims to attend more readily to the histories, practices, and contributions of artists, mediators, and institutions from almost every single continent.

Of course, this global subfield did not develop in a historical vacuum. Its emergence, as mentioned in part 1's introduction, was certainly facilitated by major external political, economic, and technological developments. But such external historical dynamics primarily constituted facilitating background conditions. Over time, their effects were refracted and then further developed by field-internal configurations and concerns. That is clear in the exhibition politics among biennials and their call for more multifaceted "global" understandings of contemporary art specifically, in the invention of new global aesthetic categories like global conceptualism, and in the construction of new online tools for properly assessing artistic recognition in relation to a global exhibition infrastructure. The subsequent debates in the evolving global field were not really about how the art world was replicating the globalized elements of politics or economics. More accurately, they were asking questions about field-specific art matters and practices: What should "global art" look like? What does it entail? What values does it espouse?

Let us not mistake the global artistic subfield for a flattened global art world "community." It is still marked by major power imbalances, though the new configuration does not adhere to the tenets of a thesis involving one-sided Western dominance. The chapter's account of the rise of a global subfield at the relatively autonomous pole instead points to a more transformational, intermediate perspective, one that transcends common dichotomies of radical change or reproduction. While inequalities continue to exist, they are no longer as unequal as they were in the past. Relationships between central and (semi-)peripheral players have become more akin to asymmetric *inter*dependencies. The idea of a global art field, therefore, goes beyond cultural imperialism and its picture of globalization as an unstoppable, one-sided expansion into peripheral regions. When various agents from both the "centers" and the "peripheries" became entangled in the same force field, they all transformed, ultimately facilitating the construction of a new global logic in the field's cross-border game, including in the dominant Western centers themselves.

3

From an International
Avant-Garde Market to a
Global Commercial Subfield

LIKE THE GLOBALIZATION process that has occurred at the cultural pole, the market for contemporary art has undergone an enormous geographical expansion over the past thirty years too.[1] Fancy galleries and glamorous art fairs have sprung up in cities worldwide, and auctions now occur on six continents.[2] Economists have also reported a growing number of contemporary art buyers from eastern Europe, Asia, the Middle East, and Latin America.[3]

By itself, this obvious geographical expansion is insufficient to say the art market has become "global," however. While it is true that market institutions for contemporary art have diffused around the world and collecting has become more geographically widespread, that does not necessarily mean that market mediation itself has assumed a global dimension. Most newer markets may still function primarily at national or regional scales without much exchange between them, let alone a worldwide reach.[4] An artist whose work gets sold in a rising market location like China to a collector from the same country may not get much commercial exposure beyond it. So, if we want to explore whether the context and logic for the mediation of contemporary art at the market pole have assumed global parameters too, the crucial question is not if art markets have multiplied around the world. The more important question is whether we can see increasing integration *between* these markets—so that works by artists may circulate on an expanded scale and their economic value might gain traction on a worldwide stage.

Economists have addressed this question by examining the degree of geographical extension in the art trade, and other scholars, who ascribe to the global art worlds model, have traced territorially expanding networks or collaborations.[5] A field perspective, with its emphasis on power structures and competition, complements these approaches. It presupposes that market integration across borders not only occurs *directly* at the level of economic transactions or personal ties but also emerges *indirectly* through the rise of shared stakes of competition, related global infrastructures and symbolic forces. For example, what happens at a dominant auction house in a global city like New York can affect market trends in London and Cologne, but increasingly, it can also impact prices in Hong Kong, Brazil, and South Africa. And this may occur without direct interactions, based on the field forces that impinge on players within a shared space of art market pursuit. As we shall see, this emphasis on unequal and competitive market relations at a distance becomes even more relevant in the age of the internet, when people can more readily observe and react to market dynamics across larger distances.

Moreover, a field approach also differs from some economistic accounts because it highlights that art markets are not merely about players who are striving for commercial profits. They also are driven by brokers who are more oriented toward advancing specific cultural goals in their market promotion of artists and who operate more closely to the values of the relatively autonomous artistic subfield. Attending to this internal differentiation of the art market along the field's principal autonomy-heteronomy axis allows us to explore how globalization affects relationships among distinct types of market intermediaries and their diverse strategies of mediation at the emerging global level.

Based on the field approach and a broad variety of original sources, this chapter advances two interrelated arguments about the art market's globalization. First, I argue that a series of dramatic changes in the twenty-first century have led to the rise of a global commercial subfield. Within a broader context involving the liberalization of national economies, increasing global wealth polarization, and advances in digitalization, the emergence of this subfield was enabled by at least three market related developments: the formation of a global art fair circuit, the extension of a worldwide interdependent auction infrastructure, and the launch of new internet agencies that evaluate global price trends and artists' sales success. The historical convergence of these transformations in the first two decades of the millennium established an expanded global framework for a shared arena of market exchange and competition that involves artists, intermediaries, and collectors from countries around the world. Correspondingly, the ultimate stakes involved in the mediation and economic valorization of contemporary art have become redefined in global terms, too. Some of the highest prices across borders and the careers of economic art super stars are meanwhile shaped within a globally expanded market game.

Second, the same dynamics that allowed the contemporary art market to assume new global dimensions have entailed heightened levels of commercialization and financialization in the expanded subfield. The nature of the art market shifted from an international avant-garde affair in the 1990s toward a more radically heteronomous game populated by big corporate and financially oriented players. Insightful sociological studies have already revealed important aspects of the growing commodification of the art market, especially in view of single institutions like auction houses, art fairs, and art investment funds.[6] We also know about changes that have occurred on the consumer side, such as the rise of megacollectors and Asian art investors.[7] This chapter examines a broad variety of different art market intermediaries including those who are more autonomous and motivated primarily by cultural goals as well as those that lean toward profit-chasing methods. From this more holistic field perspective, it demonstrates how globalization processes have led to greater commodification by changing their *overall* structural relations and rules of competition, which have caused more autonomously oriented players to lose influence.

The chapter develops these arguments in four sections. The first looks at the international art market of the 1990s, suggesting that it was still dominated by avant-garde galleries oriented more readily around art rather than money. The second section investigates the rise of a global art fair circuit, highlighting how art fairs not only extended galleries' geographic reach in unprecedented ways but also intensified the economic pressures they felt, transforming their rules of the game. The third section traces the massive global growth of commercial auction houses for contemporary art in the twenty-first century. I first chart the "grobalization" ventures of Christie's and Sotheby's[8] with a historical account of their competitive institutional expansion and explain how it has linked various national and regional art markets into a global auction circuit for the high-end valorization of contemporary art. The section then explores the second tier of "beta" auction houses, showing how they similarly expanded into a worldwide interdependent space that has enabled a broader set of artworks to circulate and gain value across multiple markets. The chapter's fourth section sheds light on the rise of online price databases. It discusses how they have contributed to global integration at the level of information flows but also how—like movements in the global stock market—they have installed a more heteronomous, financial logic in the global evaluation of artists and their careers.

The conclusion encapsulates how all of these developments operated in tandem to enable the emergence of a global subfield for art market exchange and competition, a process that fed into the growth of large-scale enterprises and greater heteronomization. I also highlight how global transformations at the heteronomous pole have been different from those at the relatively autonomous, cultural pole. Ultimately, while a global field for the valuation of contemporary art materialized by the end of the twenty-first century's first decade, the specific dynamics involved have pushed both sides of the autonomy-heteronomy axis farther apart, creating a stronger polarity between the artistic and the commercial global subfields. In short, the global art field has become structured around a dual cultural world economy.

Galleries in the International Art Market of the 1990s

Until the 1990s, the international market for contemporary art largely revolved around centers in North America and Europe.[9] Most major sales took place at galleries in the West's urban hubs. Among them, New York—with its ability to set market standards and influence trends—occupied a dominant position in the international art trade.[10] Underpinning the market's international dimensions were gallery networks that connected the United States with European cities like London, Paris, Cologne, Amsterdam, Vienna, and Zurich. Gallerists developed partnerships to promote emerging artists and boost their sales in multiple countries.[11] Some dealers formalized their cross-border operations by establishing gallery branches that served different markets on their own. This strategy required substantial resources, however, especially in the pre-internet age. Thus, it was not very common in the 1990s, and the scale of these satellite operations was largely limited to the US-European axis.[12] While New York was the heart of the international art market in the 1990s, informal gallery networks were still its most significant vessels for contemporary art's transatlantic promotion and trade.

Economists who have written about galleries in the international art market have tended to employ pyramid models, distinguishing between the top-tier players and those below them.[13] But a unitary hierarchy like this overlooks the substantial heterogeneity among galleries in their strategies for market mediation. Pyramid models also ignore how the field's principal conflict between art and money affects players in the market itself. In this respect, the primary structural division, which economists have largely overlooked, consists of the opposition between artist-centered, "avant-garde" galleries and sales-oriented dealers.[14] By looking at developments in New York, which has been the gallery game's international capital since the 1950s, we can follow the story of their evolving historical relations.[15] It begins with the dominance of avant-garde gallerists that was then destabilized by the rise of a new type of commercial gallery in the 1980s that was radically oriented around sales and branding. Then, in the 1990s, before globalization's acceleration, the avant-garde galleries gained power again.

Avant-garde galleries adhere to the greatest autonomous principles in the market. Their decisions about which artists to represent are mainly oriented at artistic criteria rather than straightforward economic ones.[16] For market promotion, the avant-garde gallerist first tends to bring an emerging artist to the attention of critics, curators, and scholars, seeking to increase that artist's recognition among cultural experts.[17] Then, once an artist's work attains a certain level of symbolic recognition, it can be translated into economic capital by passing the "expert's judgement to the collectors," gradually increasing an artist's prices and sales.[18] In this market strategy, the heightening of symbolic capital serves as the fundamental basis for an artist's worth in the market, which in turn can raise the gallery's own reputation and symbolic capital.

The avant-garde approach to market mediation is risky, however. There is no guarantee that more experimental art will eventually find a paying audience and that the gallerist will see a return on their investments. It is thus not surprising that these types of galleries tend to operate with an anticommercial ideology, often portraying themselves as working for the "eternity of art" rather than for mere commercial gains.[19] Profane commercial motivations are disdained, a stance that is symbolized by avant-garde gallerists' refusal to publish any prices for artworks. Such economic qualifiers remain hidden from the public in their special white cubes.[20] For these gallerists, the central concern should be the quasi-sacred value of art as art.[21]

Ever since the rise of the modern art market at the end of the nineteenth century, more heteronomous sales-oriented galleries have coexisted alongside such avant-garde players.[22] For such heteronomous galleries, their decisions about which artists to represent are primarily informed by economic considerations about the market's established positions and prevailing tastes.[23] Their rosters tend to include an eclectic mix of deceased, consecrated masters as well as those living artists who have already received positive critical attention. The strategy is less about building new markets and more about exploiting existing ones, with the goal of achieving the highest prices possible.[24] As such, these galleries operate in what art professionals tend to call the "secondary art market." By contrast, nurturing artistic careers and first-time sales in the service of also artistic goals is the main mode of avant-garde galleries, which are often classified as being part of a "primary market."

The distinction between the primary and secondary market must be seen as a spectrum, however, and galleries frequently operate between them.[25] Avant-garde galleries, for example, might support their mediation of emerging artists by selling profitable works from established names or by handling an artist's estate.[26] Similarly, consecrated avant-garde galleries, those that have been successful in the symbolic promotion of their artists, enter a phase of commercial success in which they inevitably engage in the secondary market.[27]

Along this age-old spectrum, in the late 1970s, a third position, the "radically sales-oriented" gallery, surfaced and gained prominence during the next decade's international market boom.[28] Occupying the most heteronomous position, this type differed from avant-garde galleries not only in its stronger orientation toward economically lucrative deals but also in the way it conceptualized and aggressively promoted market value. Instead of relying primarily on symbolic capital as a basis for market mediation, the radically sales-oriented gallery embraced a new logic of branding and celebrity. It deliberately mobilized mass media and advertising and often staged spectacular openings to create publicity for its artists and mold the gallery into a recognizable brand.[29] This conception of value moved away from the avant-garde ideals of art for art's sake and connoisseurship and instead framed contemporary art as a lifestyle luxury good, a commodity capable of bestowing glamour and social status on its consumers.

An early example of this new breed was Mary Boone, a New York dealer who first made headlines when she appeared on the cover of *New York* magazine in 1982. In her interview, she told colorful stories about the artists she represented and her own persona as a dealer. This approach represented a clear breach of the norms for avant-garde gallerists. For example, as Paula Cooper remembered quite critically, "[Boone] was in every magazine, painting her toenails. P.R. really began then."[30] Boone's first commercial coup was with the painter Julian Schnabel, who achieved spectacular economic success at her gallery despite not receiving prior symbolic recognition.[31] Within three years, prices for his work soared from $3,000 to $40,000, and Schnabel became an art world star. As another gallerist recognized in hindsight, Boone and Schnabel "totally changed how to deal with the media," establishing the artist and dealer as "a personal public persona, a fashion-oriented stylistic promotion."[32]

Since the early 1980s, several radically sales-oriented dealers rose to become "branded dealers" as an elite commercial counterpart to consecrated avant-garde gallerists.[33] They could accumulate economic capital because they profited from heightened demand by a growing class of nouveau-riche media moguls, advertising gurus, stockbrokers, and hedge-fund managers. Previously, the contemporary art market had largely been a niche for old money and cultured elites.[34] But in the 1980s, in an environment stoked by a heated stock market, upwardly mobile social and business elites expanded as a buyer pool.[35] This new audience had a more positive attitude toward mass media and luxury consumption and saw publicity as a valid attribute of artistic value.[36] Consequently, the radically sales-oriented galleries that catered to them gained commercial momentum quickly. Nevertheless, these dealers remained in stiff antagonism with avant-garde players, who reproached them for their use of vulgar, or even illegitimate, marketing tactics and for the way they hyped the newest fads without contributing anything innovative to the field.

Then, in 1987, the stock market plummeted.[37] Sales-driven gallerists lost their primary economic foundation, and the art market went into recession, a contraction exacerbated by other international economic developments and the onset of the First Gulf War. As a result, during the 1990s, the "art market's superstar culture of the 1980s" shifted to a "more prudent, inward-looking culture" in which the anticommercial norms of avant-garde galleries regained the upper hand.[38] New York galleries again sought to conceal or heavily justify any sales-related activities in order to uphold their reputation.[39] Players who deviated too readily in a money-driven direction, like the American dealer Larry Gagosian—who was notorious for calling potential buyers ten to fifteen times a day to stimulate sales—were "accused by ... colleagues of degrading the business" and "bringing the habits of a souk rug seller to a refined trade."[40]

Thus, in the 1990s, the avant-garde approach, and its anticommercial ideology, had reasserted itself as the dominant path to legitimacy within an international art market capital that was structured around contested relations among three main gallery positions. Yet the overall scope of the art market was still transatlantic. It was not globalized or interconnected at a worldwide scale. As the twenty-first century began, this situation changed with the global rise of art fairs. They both extended the market and propelled it back in more commercial directions.

The Global Fair Circuit and the Commercialization of the Gallery Trade

Between 2000 and 2010, the international avant-garde market underwent several changes that drastically altered its scope and nature, resulting in a global subfield dominated by commercial agents and logics. One key development in this regard involved the worldwide proliferation of international art fairs (ICAFs).[41] They operate as market platforms where galleries from various countries meet and set up small trade booths for a limited number of days to present and sell art to international audiences. The founding of the first ICAFs dates back to the 1970s in Europe, and up until the 1990s, their locations were largely in the Northwest. Traditionally, art fairs played only a secondary role for exchanges in the international art market, which were primarily driven by informal gallery networks. Their subordinate position was such that in 1995, the French sociologist Raymonde Moulin still noted that ICAFs were "invariably less important for promoting contemporary art than the understandings between galleries, which help to forge ties across borders."[42] Yet one decade later, this situation shifted radically. Art fairs became more powerful and pushed gallery practices in more global *and* commercial directions.

The Rise of the International Art Fair

The history of fairs that showcase contemporary art began in Cologne in 1967, when two art dealers, Hein Stünke and Rudolf Zwirner, joined forces in the hopes of boosting the German art market.[43] At that time, the country's gallery scene was ailing, and it lacked a central metropolis like New York or Paris that would support galleries to attract and cultivate collectors' interest.[44] Launching an art fair was a grassroots attempt to compensate for the fragmentation within Germany's federal structure, creating a centralized market platform that could heighten consumers' attention in the frame of a special event.[45]

The first Cologne fair, which involved eighteen galleries, was an immediate and remarkable success, generating a turnover of about one million German marks in five days.[46] However, it was reserved solely for German dealers. Soon after, in 1970, another fair in Basel opened its doors to any gallery regardless of national background.[47] Initiated by local Swiss gallerists—Trudl Bruckner, Ernst Beyeler, and Balz Hilt—the Basel fair quickly expanded, and by 1975, it was playing host to nearly three hundred galleries. Despite this size, the fair had not yet achieved its now-familiar position as a major global event. Dealers primarily brought second-rate works they had been unable to sell, and even by the exhibitors' own estimations, Art Basel was largely regional, that is, European in scope.[48] Swiss and German galleries regularly made up most of the fair's participants throughout the 1970s and 1980s, while gallerists from the internationally leading US market constituted only about 3 to 5 percent.

This more provincial status changed over the course of the 1990s, however. After the art market slowdown caused by the 1989 recession, galleries from international art capitals reconsidered the role fairs could play as tools "to cope with the social turbulence."[49] Both autonomous and heteronomous galleries from New York, Paris, and London—which had previously enjoyed denser foot traffic than their colleagues in smaller towns like Basel—revised their strategies to survive. They began flocking to art fairs in larger numbers, hoping to expand their audience and make up for weak prospects at home.[50] With the ensuing "dramatic increase" in high-profile galleries from major art hubs, Basel's annual event began to shed its largely regional reputation.[51] By the end of the 1990s, US galleries had even become one of the fair's largest exhibiting groups, second only to Germany. New leadership supported such changes in participants. In 1991, Lorenzo Rudolph, a public relations manager from a financial services firm, took over and aggressively promoted Art Basel as an exclusive, distinctively branded social event. By establishing new PR strategies, including a VIP relations program, the organizers aimed to attract more deep-pocketed international collectors.[52] The strategy was effective, and by the end of the decade, the Art Basel fair, which began as a regional professional trade show, had become a prestigious international market platform.

The Proliferation of International Art Fairs in the Twenty-First Century

Art Basel was the most prominent ICAF in the late 1990s. Only a handful of other international art fairs existed overall, and they were largely Western. In the following two decades, however, the number of new establishments on a global scale sharply increased. The economist Stefano Baia Curioni has suggested that the millennial fair boom closely parallels the growth of international contemporary art biennials (ICABs; cf. chapter 2).[53] But art fairs proliferated in unique ways, and as we shall see, those differences are related to the fairs' increasingly commercial underpinnings.

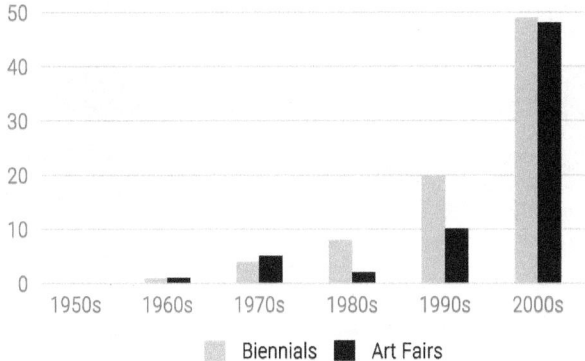

FIGURE 3.1. The proliferation of international contemporary art fairs compared to international contemporary art biennials, 1950–2017 (appendix B).

For one, ICAFs and ICABs became prominent at different times. As a historical comparison of their establishment dates shows (figure 3.1), the number of ICAFs did not increase significantly until the new millennium's first decade, ten years after the biennial boom. By 1999, around nineteen large-scale ICAFs existed, largely in Western locations like Basel, Cologne, Paris, Chicago, Madrid, and New York.

Just ten years later, however, ICAFs as a group had grown exponentially, and the events had become more geographically diffuse, spreading to more locations beyond the West, including Zona Maco in Mexico City in 2002, the India Art Fair in 2008, and FNB Art Joburg in Johannesburg in 2008. By 2017, there were 126 operating ICAFs that were dispersed across six continents overall. However, in comparison to ICABs, ICAFs remained more heavily concentrated within western Europe and North America (about 72 percent), while ICABs were much less centralized in the Northwest (about 40 percent). Certain world regions, particularly eastern Europe and Africa, also made up a far more marginal share of ICAFs than ICABs (figure 3.2). In view of such historical and geographical discrepancies, it seems hardly possible to uphold that the global proliferation of art fairs and biennials has moved in lockstep.

Far from random, these divergent dynamics are influenced by the art market's greater dependency on favorable external economic conditions, such as levels of private wealth. Because art purchases tend to come from consumers' "stores of wealth rather than current income," an affluent upper class is a necessary precondition for flourishing sales.[54] In this light, the ICAF boom occurred in the first years of the new millennium—and not earlier, alongside biennials— because the dramatic increase in global wealth during this period provided a facilitating background condition for the expansion of art market activities

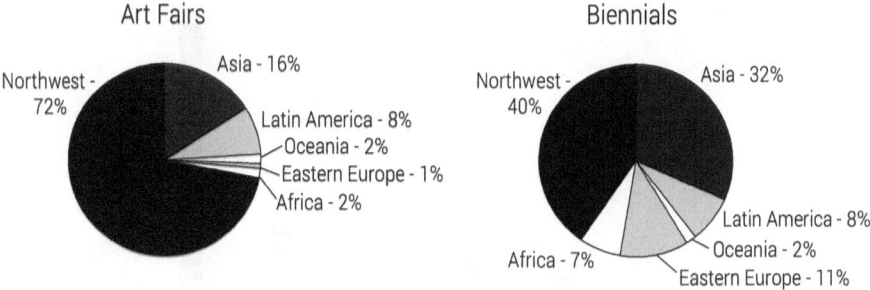

FIGURE 3.2. The dispersion of ICAFs and ICABs across world regions in 2017 (appendix B).
Note: Values may sum to more than 100% due to rounding.

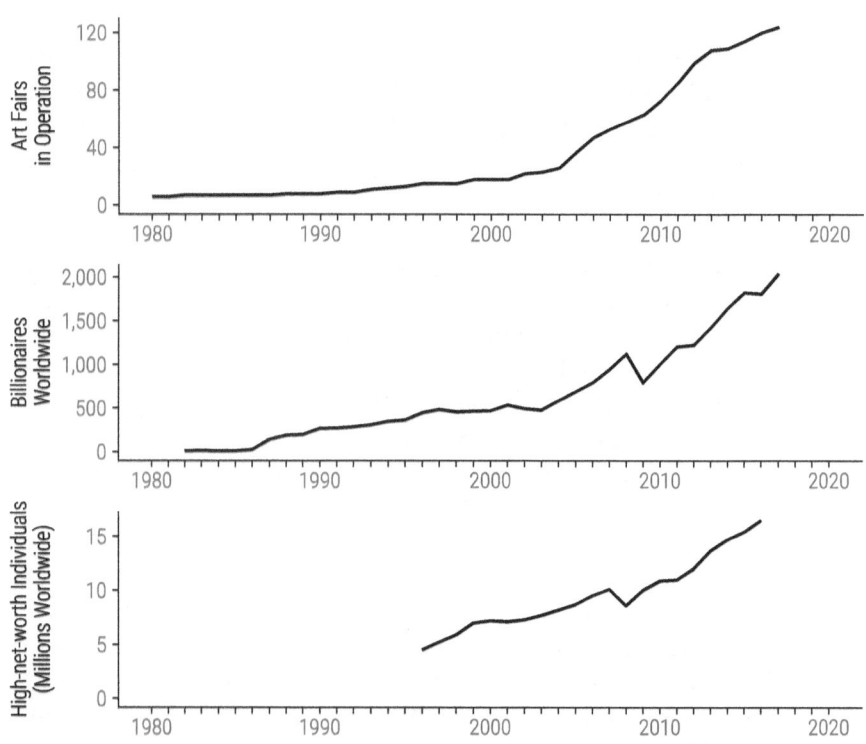

FIGURE 3.3. The growth of operating ICAFs and global wealth. (ArtFacts.Net
and extensive research on ICAFs; appendix B); data on billionaires by *Forbes*,
hypertextbook.com, and businesswire.com; data on high-net-worth individuals
derived from *Credit Suisse Global Wealth Reports*)

across the globe. This *indirect* ICAF-wealth relationship is conveyed in figure 3.3, which suggests a near parallel movement in the growth of operating ICAFs and the increase of wealthy billionaires and high-net-worth individuals (although the 2008 financial crisis did not affect the number of operating ICAFs to the same extent as it impacted wealth levels).[55]

Given the influence of broader macroeconomic developments, it also becomes clear why the world's richest countries, or those that experienced the steepest increases in wealth, saw the biggest surge in new ICAFs after 2000. This particularly applies to the US (+41), Germany (+11), the UK (+11), and China (including Hong Kong, +8), while poorer regions, especially countries in Africa, remained more peripheral than they were on the biennial circuit. Such findings underscore why a field perspective, which distinguishes between the more autonomous and heteronomous poles among mediating art institutions, can more fully attend to the heterogeneous processes involved in the art field's globalization.

However, the dramatic increase in the number of ICAFs was not a simple reflection of the broader global economy. At least four developments *within* the art market were key to propelling the fair boom during a favorable macroeconomic period. The first of these involved the expansionist strategies of corporate art fairs. Several ICAFs, including Art Basel, became owned by professional trade fair firms, which meant they were not simply platforms self-organized by galleries but were controlled by corporate players with their own business agendas. As gallerists grew increasingly interested in art fairs and as external economic opportunities increased, these firms began to expand their fair properties in new, wealthy areas to boost revenues.[56]

Art Basel itself is the most prominent among such expanding corporatist fairs. The fair grew for the first time in 2002 with a new branch in Miami, a move that was inspired by the initiative of US-based collectors and pushed to success by "calculated entrepreneurialism."[57] The city promised a "high density of great collectors," and given its "proximity to Latin America," it could serve as an interface between the latter and North America, benefiting from two market regions at once.[58] In 2013, the Basel MCH corporation additionally took over a fair in Hong Kong to take advantage of the rising Asian art market, especially its growing base of Chinese collectors.[59] With both cross-continental expansions, Art Basel established itself as a profitable "global art fair brand."[60] Other ICAF enterprises naturally attempted to keep up by venturing their own entrepreneurial extensions, and this new competition was one field-internal dynamic animating the expansionist art fair boom in the twenty-first century's first decade.

Various governments also jumped on the train and drove the ICAF boom. After the earliest fairs had proven successful and gained international prominence, governments saw them as a tool for potentially boosting a city's creative economy and positioning it as an art market capital.[61] The cultural government organization of the United Arab Emirates (UAE), for example, supported Art Dubai in 2007 with such ambitions.[62] Officials made sure to place the fair within the Dubai International Financial Centre, a tax-friendly zone with a favorable legislative framework to create economic incentives for international dealers and buyers.

Two kinds of "grassroots" dynamics fed into the ICAF boom too. On the one hand, in growing economies like Mexico, Brazil, and India, new fairs also grew out of local initiatives to boost their own developing markets. The India Art Fair in Delhi, for example, was launched in 2008 as a "private initiative" to help "to mobilize the collector base and offer artists and dealers new outlets to promote homegrown visual arts."[63] In regions where infrastructures for contemporary art markets were still developing, a fair offered a less intimidating opportunity for novices to "familiarize themselves with the works of art," and galleries could court potential buyers through personal interactions, panel discussions, and parties.[64]

On the other hand, upstart galleries in the West, which had trouble breaking into more established fairs like Art Basel as exhibitors, increasingly began to set up smaller satellite events around bigger fairs. In this way, they could take advantage of the attention and visitors that the main fairs attracted. While the motivation behind these satellite fairs was often paired with a sense of artistic idealism among its founders—and not just commercial interest— many of these smaller fairs soon got absorbed by corporate fair chains and then branched out across several countries themselves. A similar dynamic of corporatization occurred with those "grassroots" fairs in the "non-Western" markets mentioned earlier; once they attained a certain level of success, they also tended to move into bigger corporate hands.[65]

Overall, it seems safe to say that among the four subfield-internal dynamics that propelled the expansion of ICAFs in the new millennium, the dominant motives revolved around economic capital controlled primarily by corporate players within a favorable climate of growing global wealth. This contrasts sharply with the development and proliferation of biennials, whose history, as chapter 2 described, is characterized more by cultural goals and a predominant quest for symbolic capital.[66]

A Global Fair Circuit

Once ICAFs multiplied, they supported an expanded infrastructure in which market players could disperse themselves across a wider range of countries. Gallerists no longer just participated in established Western events; they also transported their artworks to far-flung locations in Hong Kong, Shanghai, Istanbul, Delhi, and São Paulo.[67] In 2012, for example, the galleries that had attended Art Basel participated that same year in another sixty-eight fairs in Europe, North America, Latin America, and Asia.[68] Furthermore, a study of the fair participations of over nine thousand galleries between 2000 and 2010 revealed that galleries had extended their travels across larger physical *and* cultural (that is, linguistic) distances, a sure sign of "increasing globalization in the activity . . . in the art market."[69] As a gallerist from Berlin tellingly described the heightened mobility, "There is an international fairs' circus. The galleries travel; they are invited; the collectors are invited and travel with them. They get their golden or black VIP card and travel around the world."[70] The growth of a worldwide fair infrastructure led to more global circulation among gallerists, artworks, and audiences and, ultimately, a veritable global fair circuit.

However, not all fairs have the same prestige or offer the same attractions for galleries in this global circuit. Overall, it is highly stratified, and only about five out of more than one hundred ICAFs have attained a status as preeminent global fairs. Three of these belong to the Art Basel corporation: the original fair in Switzerland and its branches in Miami and Hong Kong.[71] The other two are part of the Frieze Art Fair chain, which opened a London branch in 2003 and a New York branch in 2012 and, like Art Basel, came under the control of a larger corporation.[72]

These five corporate fairs have reached their preeminent status because of their large size and their ability to attract elite stakeholders, including leading galleries, major representatives from the world's museums, and ultra-high-net-worth individuals. The dealers who participated, however, remained predominantly Western.[73] The main reason for these fairs' *global* reputation lies not so much in the variety of their exhibitors but more in the geographically diverse audiences they have cultivated. Art Basel, for example, "invested a lot of time and energy" to expand its visitor base worldwide, capitalizing on its VIP-relations program and established prominence with increasing success.[74] In 2006, the fair's former director Sam Keller could already announce, "Art Basel has always been international. But this year we've had several delegations from China, collectors from Russia and Dubai. And for the first time we've also seen Indian buyers."[75] Art Basel turned into a "dynamic intermingling of big business and new money."[76] In turn, for galleries and their artists, it grew into a key forum for accessing an increasingly worldwide, elite audience.

By comparison, fairs that have emerged in "non-Western" regions have been often perceived as "specialized regional fairs."[77] This is partly because their organizers regularly brand them with narrower geo-aesthetic identities to compete in the increasingly crowded global fair circuit.[78] The emphasis is on asserting a regionality-infused "individuality" by creating an image as a preeminent Latin American, Middle Eastern, or South Asian fair that can offer participants unique access to a region's growing art production and its roster of collectors.

Such distinction strategies lure both foreign collectors who are curious about new discoveries and galleries looking to expand into new markets.[79] Interestingly, with such strategies, some of these so-called regional fairs—one thinks of Zona Maco in Mexico—can draw a more diverse set of participating galleries than the top fairs do.[80] In this sense, regional fairs are not outside the global fair circuit at all. Instead, they are an integral part of it, a channel through which global players and market exchanges operate, further integrating markets for contemporary art.

Changing Rules of Gallery Competition

Several scholars, whose arguments resonate with a global art worlds approach, emphasize that the fair circuit affected galleries' mediation strategies primarily by expanding their networks of exchange and collaboration. Through a globalizing fair infrastructure, they benefit from unparalleled opportunities to reach collectors from a wide variety of countries and forge personal contacts with other galleries, curators, or museum directors from around the world. In this view, ICAFs are fundamental networking machines that aid galleries not just in sales, but also in placing artists in collections and exhibitions worldwide. Moreover, as sites for "encounter and dialogue," ICAFs contribute to greater cosmopolitan awareness in the art market, which also helps the "promotion of new talents" from "non-Western" regions and the development of shared conventions around pricing and self-presentations across borders.[81] In short, by connecting "art dealers, professionals and collectors from distant regions" into a "small-world network," ICAFs would figure as "the ultimate enabler for a newly global art world."[82]

However, as important as these network dynamics are, focusing on them exclusively can overlook how ICAFs have altered and intensified competition among galleries and thereby pushed mediation strategies in more commercial directions. Put simply, seen through a field lens, ICAFs have not simply extended the gallery game; they have qualitatively changed it on an increasingly competitive global stage.

One element of the new rules of global competition pertains to the heightened material requirements galleries need to succeed in a market environment where ICAFs have assumed a central role. A visit to one of the top fairs alone could cost a gallery more than $300,000.[83] Traveling long distances adds to a gallery's financial burden, and prospects become riskier when sales in less familiar markets do not meet expectations.[84] Only those galleries in the securest financial positions can shoulder that type of risk on an extended basis. As one consecrated avant-garde gallerist from New York commented, "Today the demand for the gallerists themselves are much higher. . . . You do need money to

participate in all of it, in the game, so to speak. So, for the classic idea of building up young artists . . . you've got to really work the business now. In the past,
I think you could really do it with very little overhead. That's changed. The
overhead for every gallery has gotten much higher than ever before."[85]

Such heightened material requirements have led to major inequalities with
regard to who benefits the most from the new fair circuit. The bigger, more economically established galleries can afford to participate in the most lucrative
ICAFs, and some of them attend up to fifteen per year. Inversely, emerging avant-
garde galleries that operate in the less commercially profitable primary market
tend to be less present. Moreover, top galleries that tend to be most involved in
the global fair circuit also saw the greatest growth in revenues. But the rest of the
market, especially smaller, artistically oriented galleries, struggled. For example, a
survey of six thousand dealers in 2012 by Clare McAndrew revealed that galleries
with sales below €500,000 (about US$660,000) faced a loss in their average
turnover by 17 percent year over year, while those on the opposite end of the
spectrum, whose sales topped €10 million (about US$13.2 million) were able to
increase their gross revenue by spectacular 55 percent in the same period.[86] This
trend persisted. By 2017, only the biggest, most established galleries experienced
strong sales increases, while smaller galleries faced negative growth.[87] Evidently,
the rise of the global art fair circuit is associated with greater structural polarization in the gallery market to the detriment of less established, less commercial
avant-garde players. Not only does it require substantial economic resources
to join, but it is also the type of context that propagates economic advantages to
those agents who already have those resources.

The new rules of competition involve novel kinds of symbolic inequalities
as well. Participation at the most prestigious art fairs has become a key for
galleries to gain status and symbolic power for promoting their artists across
borders. Consequently, the top ICAFs and their selection committees have
become something like the gatekeepers of the gatekeepers. Acceptance can
now establish a gallery's prestige, sanctioning it as part of the "global establishment of art dealers."[88] A gallery owner from Cape Town explained the
ICAF effect on his business: "I come from South Africa, and people don't
necessarily know my gallery. . . . When I say I exhibit at the Basel and Frieze
fairs, it tells them about us."[89] Spots at top ICAFs are extremely competitive,
however. At Art Basel each year, about eight hundred galleries apply, and only
three hundred are accepted.[90] The bigger fairs tend to favor galleries with
established reputations and entrenched market power, which helps to reinforce the fairs' own status as prestigious market platforms.[91] The ICAF boom
thus led to new modalities of *symbolic* market competition, which have again
pushed smaller, more autonomously oriented galleries to the sidelines in the
global game.

Ultimately, it is no coincidence that the same period that saw an explosive growth in the importance of ICAFs was accompanied by the rise of a new type of global megagallery, an institution that did not exist in the 1990s. These galleries are in line with sales-oriented or radically sales-oriented strategies, and they have grown into large corporate conglomerates with branches spanning an unprecedented range of global cities. One of the most notorious megagalleries in this new market environment is owned by the American Larry Gagosian. His Gagosian Gallery benefited immensely from the expanding ICAF circuit and accumulated the resources to create an empire of nearly twenty locations across three continents. As the previous section explained, in the international avant-garde market, Gagosian was "criticized for his aggressive market practices."[92] But as the art critic and theorist Isabelle Graw observed around a decade later, "today he is universally respected and admired."[93] This drastic shift in the reputation of a radically sales-oriented dealer is a prime example of shifts in the dominant principles of market legitimacy as the subfield globalized.

A Global Countercircuit to Biennials

Gallerists who frequently participate in the global fair circuit are not automatically all commercial players, however.[94] Often, consecrated avant-garde galleries, for example, use their fair sales from already-established artists to continue supporting innovative contemporary artists. And of course, a small number of emerging avant-garde galleries always gain admission to the most prestigious ICAFs, which allows the fairs to include some fresh faces in what otherwise might be a predictable gathering of the market establishment. Less established galleries also can attend the smaller satellite fairs and thus benefit indirectly from the collective effervescence that the bigger ones create.

Notwithstanding, the ICAF circuit imposes a range of constraints on *all* participants that make it a difficult setting for pursuing an avant-garde approach toward market mediation. For one, the high costs of fair attendance demand that galleries prudently showcase artworks that will have sufficient market appeal. This is simply to help them secure enough in sales to cover the high expenses. And while the globalization of fairs has expanded the range of attendees, this change has also created unique cultural constraints. For many potential buyers, fairs are their first foray into the art field before they become more knowledgeable about contemporary art and then also visit biennials.[95] The tastes of these newcomers tend to be oriented around recognized brand names and traditional media rather than the latest avant-garde work.[96] Such commercial and cultural constraints have real effects on galleries' mediation strategies and, ultimately, the kind of art that appears at ICAFs, which tends to be "moderate in size" and "in tune with dominant market trends."[97] Indeed, a 2017 study of sixty-eight major art fairs found that the two most conservative, object-based media—painting and sculpture—were clearly dominant.[98]

While such observations are unsurprising for any art world insider, they suggest that fairs differ from biennials in their prevailing aesthetics. While the global biennial circuit has tended to favor nontraditional and less easily commodifiable artistic media, including "video, film, photography, installation pieces (often multimedia in nature), conceptual art and performance art," the fair circuit's unique demands tend to push exhibitors in more market-friendly, artistically conservative directions.[99] Art fairs are not just different from biennials. They force gallerists—who can also act as cultural tastemakers for more challenging, unwieldly artistic work—to drastically adapt their strategies for success.

Beyond these constraints, changes in the setup and culture of ICAFs have in turn created a favorable context for mediation strategies that align with publicity and branding. To appeal to a growing number of newly wealthy elites, large-scale international fairs, attempting to create an aura of celebrity and glamour, have become more streamlined into "lifestyle" events.[100] In such an institutional atmosphere, contemporary art has become foregrounded as a luxury commodity rather than an object of critical engagement and aesthetic connoisseurship.[101]

This value structure has affected how participating galleries position themselves. As ICAFs grew into glamorous events, gallerists adopted more spectacular PR strategies to help their artists stand out.[102] Jack Bankowsky, the former editor of *Artforum*, has even suggested the rise of a new genre of "artfair art," where dealers and artists have begun to launch "attention-grabbing . . . special projects" to engage in a "PR game" that is "fully complicit with the entrepreneurs who operate the fair."[103] In the prior 1990s international market dominated by avant-garde galleries, sensational strategies of publicity and branding were frowned upon; now, ICAFs fuel them.

In conclusion, although ICAFs have been frequently likened to biennials and were assumed to be a parallel or even converging phenomenon in the art field's globalization, they actually constitute a commercial countercircuit that differs from the biennial circuit in its geographies, the kind of art it showcases, and the heteronomous logics of value it fosters.[104] To be sure, like biennials, ICAFs have helped integrate national and regional art fields into a global circuit of exchange and competition that involves mediators, artists, and audiences from multiple continents. Geographically, however, fairs have remained more heavily concentrated in the world's richest countries. What is more, the global fair circuit has created new rules for galleries, submitting them to immense financial pressures and a highly selective global gatekeeper system that favors dealers and artists with established market reputations. It has also led participating gallerists to exhibit art that foregrounds and reinforces a lifestyle culture of glamour and branding. The same institutional transformations that allowed the gallery market to assume a global dimension commercialized it. This idea runs counter to those who see the big fairs as privileged global events for market elites to personally connect with curators and art critics as part of one big "art world" family.[105] If one looks beyond opening events and personal interactions at fairs, and more deeply into how the global fair circuit has affected the structure of competition among galleries, it becomes clear that this new infrastructure has created deeper structural rifts between market-oriented agents and their culturally oriented counterparts.

The Worldwide Expansion of Commercial Auction Houses: The Rise of a Global Logic of Auction Valuation

ICAFs were not the only institution in the globalizing market subfield that put avant-garde players under increasing pressure. Auction houses—both the major players, Sotheby's and Christie's, and several beta auction houses— assumed an enlarged presence too. The preeminent houses expanded and globalized their business as the new millennium got under way, and their growth across multiple countries sparked a highly commercial cross-border auction circuit for contemporary art. In the process, Sotheby's and Christie's made unprecedented profits by attracting big money from buyers around the world. And they gained greater symbolic power over galleries in defining and communicating market values at an expanded global level.

Before we follow this drastic historical shift, it is important to understand the contested and more marginal position auction houses had still occupied until the 1990s. While auctions for contemporary art had existed since the 1970s, they had been a relatively small service at major houses, which tended to focus on sales of Impressionist or modern art. Moreover, they were highly controversial within the international art market, especially among more autonomous galleries and their supporters. This clash was structurally rooted in the fact that auction houses pursue highly commercial strategies and conceptions of value that are anathema to an avant-garde approach privileging artistic values.

Auction houses are notorious for their focus on short-term profits, and they often cherry-pick single artworks that promise high sales revenues rather than making a sustained commitment to representing an artist's entire body of work, as galleries tend to do.[106] On the basis of the consignments that auction specialists can secure from private collectors or art dealers, they quickly readjust their selections each season, constantly looking for the most promising commercial trophies or trends. Avant-garde gallerists resent this mercenary and volatile orientation, and they have reproached auction houses as the "parasites of the art market," companies that reduce the business of art to its crassest economic core.[107]

The leading international houses—Sotheby's and Christie's—have also bolstered heteronomous conceptions of value. Even in their earliest days, they linked contemporary art with conspicuous luxury consumption. Through staging glamorous evening auctions, they sought to attract new moneyed buyers and branded their auctions as major news events.[108] Requiring an invitation and a dress code, art auctions became framed as status symbols for the wealthy, sure signs of "social distinction."[109] What is more, the process of competitive bidding at the event itself turned the acquisition of contemporary art into an open status contest that contrasted sharply with galleries' private approach to sales.[110] Auction sales are effectively a public stage for conspicuous consumption, a forum that can shower the most outrageous bidders with broader attention and media publicity.[111] It is exactly the type of status-seeking, more instrumental process that avant-garde galleries scorn.

Yet while an open profit orientation or an appeal to status-based luxury consumption might align auction houses with branded dealers, the key *qualitative* difference between auction houses and galleries for contemporary art is that the former post prices publicly and use them in their marketing efforts. While avant-garde galleries seek to suppress art's commercial aspects by keeping prices confidential and by emphasizing an artist's symbolic capital, auction houses foreground economic capital and turn it into a public measure for the (e)valuation of artists.[112] The best artist is not just someone who has prestigious exhibitions or glowing art reviews but someone whose work can attract the highest auction prices. In the international art market up until the 1990s, the semiannual evening sales at Sotheby's and Christie's in New York and London even became something of an economic "barometer of value" for artists and their works, albeit one that avant-garde galleries continuously contested.[113]

As prices and price fluctuations became publicly available as metrics through auctions, another heteronomous conception of value could gain ground, namely, conceiving of contemporary art as a financial asset for speculation. In recounting the first major auction of contemporary art—the sale of the Pop art collection by the taxi-fleet owner Robert Scull and his wife, Ethel, at New York's Sotheby's Parke-Bernet in 1973—the art historian Barbara Rose tells how, from the time of auctions' appearance, they encouraged a financial outlook: "This auction had very high prices for the first time for contemporary art. . . . Suddenly there was the realization because of the prices that these works of art by living artists got that you could make money by buying low and selling high."[114]

A Double Expansion

Since the advent of contemporary art auctions in the 1970s, they undoubtedly added significant heteronomous energy to an avant-garde market that had long been opposed to mercantile luxury commerce and financial speculation. Nevertheless, up until the 1990s, international auctions for contemporary art remained fairly limited in number and only "performed a secondary role" in the market behind the more widespread influence of galleries.[115] Beginning in the twenty-first century, however, auction houses began to expand more aggressively into the contemporary art segment. As the most coveted pieces of Impressionist and modern art became rarer commodities and as a younger clientele expanded, contemporary art promised a seemingly infinite supply of works that could be marketed to new audiences.[116] Indeed, in just ten years, auctions for contemporary art dramatically increased. Between 1998 and 2008, their annual sales volume swelled from about $48 million to more than $1.3 billion.[117] This growth continued into the next decade. From 2004 to 2014, the value of postwar and contemporary art auctions ballooned over 600 percent, rising to an annual sales volume of around $7 billion.[118]

Importantly, this exponential growth of auction sales in the art market was bolstered by forces of globalization. Before the twenty-first century, the main contemporary sales by Sotheby's and Christie's occurred in New York and London, and they were largely populated by Western international audiences. As the new century got under way, both houses adopted increasingly global strategies or this segment. And with the simultaneous explosion of other international auction houses, a global infrastructure for contemporary art auctions soon emerged. Sociologists who have examined globalization in the auction market have tended to focus on sales data across various cities and countries, but they have not systematically traced this market's underlying institutional extension.[119]

The Competitive Global Expansion of Sotheby's and Christie's

As indicated, Sotheby's and Christie's primary operations in the contemporary art segment were long limited to the Western hemisphere. That situation changed between 2000 and 2010, a decade that also saw the growth of global wealth and international art fairs. Both enterprises increasingly used a broader network of sales locations and representative offices to stimulate demand for their contemporary art sales globally.[120]

While Sotheby's and Christie's use a limited number of sales venues for their regular auctions, they employ a broad army of representative offices to attract new collectors, buyers, and consignors worldwide. These representatives can build close relationships with dealers and clients on the ground more steadily than can an auction specialist from one of the central offices who has to fly in and out for short visits. Cultivating relationships in a more hands-on manner builds trust (i.e., social capital), and this type of high touch experience is vital for recruiting wealthy consignors and buyers. Representative offices also provide added value as foreign "intelligence outposts" that closely observe the cultural nuances of national or regional art markets to inform the houses' global business strategy.[121]

Given the crucial promotional role that these smaller offices play, it is surprising that they have largely been neglected in empirical research on globalization in the auction market. Tracing their worldwide proliferation together with Sotheby's and Christie's sales venues offers insights into the formation of a partially integrated global auction market infrastructure. Obviously, the two major houses function themselves as integrated enterprises, but they also contribute to the opening up of national art markets and establish models for other auction houses and galleries regarding their own price levels and business practices.[122] Once Sotheby's and Christie's more aggressively entered the contemporary art segment in the new millennium, they could quickly capitalize on their global network of outposts and develop transcontinental strategies that boosted their position vis-à-vis galleries.

When charting the territorial moves of these elite players empirically (figure 3.4), it becomes evident that they both followed rising economies and wealth, which toward the end of the twentieth century, were largely the result of expanding neoliberal economic policies around the globe.[123] And yet, while the houses' extending networks seem to mirror the economic booms that marked postwar economies, their expansion should not, as the Marxist cultural imperialism model would suggest, be taken as a simple reflection of the broader political economy. External macroeconomic forces certainly had an influence on the houses' decisions and movements, just as they did for art fairs. But it is once again crucial to think about the specific ways those external forces were filtered (or "refracted") through meso-level relations within the art market. In this regard, a key field-internal motor was, and continues to be, the fierce competition for market leadership between Sotheby's and Christie's. When one house moved to a site that appeared promising, the rival house soon made sure to follow, a relational dynamic that is, as figure 3.4 shows, apparent in the houses' near-parallel movements to newer market regions over the course of six decades.

The expanding battle for market dominance across continents unfolded in three main phases, for which figure 3.5 provides a detailed historical overview. A first phase of *transatlantic expansion* lasted from the mid-1950s to the 1970s, when Sotheby's and Christie's moved into the wealthy United States and the booming postwar economies of continental western Europe. Sotheby's took

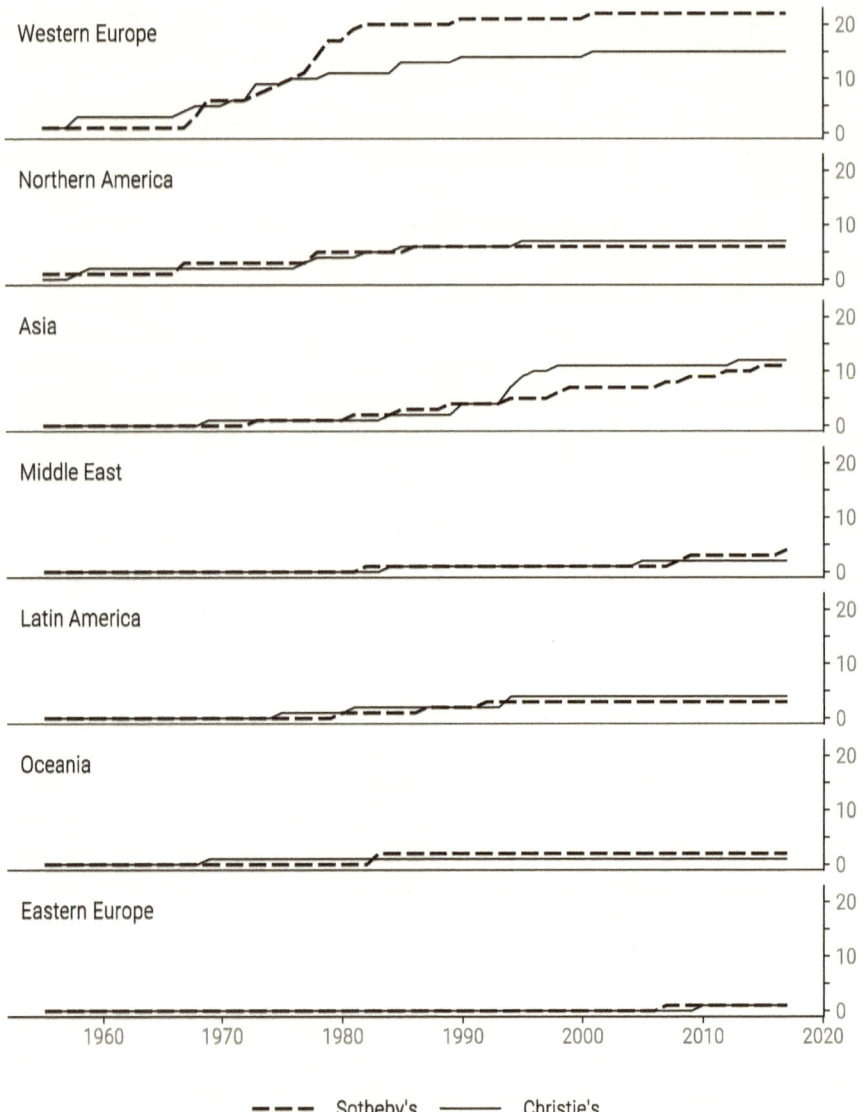

FIGURE 3.4. The expansion of Sotheby's and Christie's sales venues and operating representative offices across seven world regions, 1955–2017.

the first step, creating a foreign office in New York in 1955. Although the city's international status in the art market was already rising, this move was also triggered by lucrative legal changes: in 1954, the US Revenue Code made art donations deductible for up to 30 percent, and the UK loosened monetary restrictions so that foreign buyers could pay in their own currency.[124]

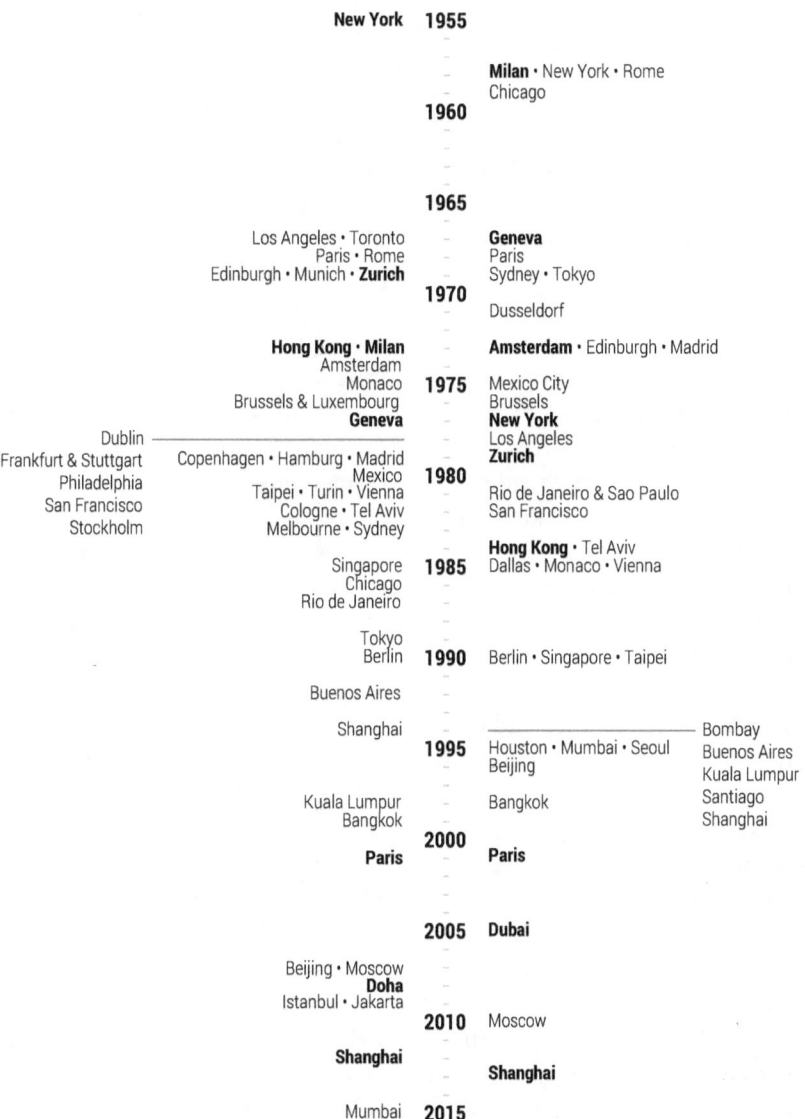

Sotheby's		Christie's	
	New York 1955		
	1960	**Milan** · New York · Rome Chicago	
	1965		
Los Angeles · Toronto Paris · Rome Edinburgh · Munich · **Zurich**	1970	**Geneva** Paris Sydney · Tokyo Dusseldorf	
Hong Kong · Milan Amsterdam Monaco Brussels & Luxembourg **Geneva**	1975	**Amsterdam** · Edinburgh · Madrid Mexico City Brussels **New York** Los Angeles **Zurich**	
Dublin Frankfurt & Stuttgart Philadelphia San Francisco Stockholm	Copenhagen · Hamburg · Madrid Mexico Taipei · Turin · Vienna Cologne · Tel Aviv Melbourne · Sydney	1980	Rio de Janeiro & Sao Paulo San Francisco
	Singapore Chicago Rio de Janeiro	1985	**Hong Kong** · Tel Aviv Dallas · Monaco · Vienna
	Tokyo Berlin	1990	Berlin · Singapore · Taipei
	Buenos Aires		
	Shanghai	1995	Houston · Mumbai · Seoul Beijing	Bombay Buenos Aires Kuala Lumpur
	Kuala Lumpur Bangkok	2000	Bangkok	Santiago Shanghai
	Paris		**Paris**
	2005	**Dubai**	
	Beijing · Moscow **Doha** Istanbul · Jakarta	2010	Moscow
	Shanghai		**Shanghai**
	Mumbai 2015		
	Dubai		

FIGURE 3.5. Timeline of the global expansion of Sotheby's and Christie's for sales venues and operating representative offices, 1955–2017. Sales locations are marked in bold and may appear twice in those cases when they first began as representative offices. Note that this chart does not include locations with consultancies only, which represent a far less institutionalized, volatile form of foreign representation. (Data compiled through extensive research on websites, from individual offices, the Christie's London historical archive, and information from the Sotheby's press office)

Christie's soon followed to the US as well, opening a New York office in 1958. And by the end of the 1970s, New York ascended to be the premier location for the two houses' international auctions.[125] Back in 1958, Christie's also expanded to continental Europe, establishing offices in Milan and Rome at a time when the Italian economy was experiencing record growth. In the following three decades, both houses continued to expand in Europe and North America. Their combat for the lucrative Swiss market seemed almost choreographed. After Christie's opened in Geneva in 1967 and began sales there the subsequent year, Sotheby's set up a competing office in Zurich in 1969. In 1977, the moves were reversed. Sotheby's opened a Geneva office, and two years later, Christie's opened its own office in Zurich.[126]

Although most of the houses' expansions during this time revolved around a transatlantic axis, four of their forty-one new locations fell outside this territory. In 1969, Christie's inaugurated a branch in Australia, a former British colony. Both houses also made their first forays into Asia. Christie's opened its Tokyo office in 1969, looking for consignments that could satisfy the West's ongoing Japonisme and seeking out new clients in a soaring economy that had witnessed a postwar miracle. By the 1980s, the power of Japanese buyers had grown so much that they were setting the tone in the international auction market, albeit for modern and Impressionist sales rather than for contemporary art.[127] Sotheby's also moved into Asia by expanding to Hong Kong, Asia's first emerging tiger economy, and held its inaugural sale there in 1973. The move was relatively more conservative, however; at that time, the port city was still a British colony and was occupied by wealthy Englishmen.

A second phase of *global ascendance* began in the 1980s but really gained steam in the 1990s, an era marked by the neoliberal opening of national markets. Sotheby's and Christie's grew into global players during this time, competitively chasing each other in Latin America and Asia, two regions that together made up about 70 percent of the houses' new satellites. The stiffest competition took place in Asia. By the late 1980s, both houses had established offices in booming Tokyo and Hong Kong. They then set their sights on three other Asian tiger economies—Taiwan, Singapore, and South Korea—and at the end of the 1990s, they expanded into Malaysia and Thailand, the two national economies most likely to boom next. In 1994, three years after India underwent economic liberalization, Christie's opened an office there. That same year, seeking to reach potential buyers and to find property to sell, it became the first Western auction house to break into mainland China, with a representative office in Shanghai. Not wanting to miss out on the growing Chinese economy, Sotheby's established a Shanghai office almost simultaneously. By the end of the 1990s, the two houses had undergone the largest geographic expansion in their history, transforming themselves into global commercial empires.

A third phase, *global dominance*, began in 2000 and was marked by the houses' intensifying battle over rapidly growing wealth in the Middle East, Russia, India, and, above all, China. In 2006, Christie's opened its first branch in Dubai. The tax-friendly United Arab Emirates had recently announced its ambition to establish itself as a global center for art and culture, including grand plans for Guggenheim and Louvre satellites, and the country's massive wealth began to gravitate toward art purchases. Two years later, Sotheby's opened a branch in Qatar, a country with extensive wealth and cultural ambitions like the UAE. After Sotheby's launched a formal office in Moscow in 2007, Christie's promptly expanded to Russia as well.[128] In 2013, Christie's held its first major auction in Mumbai, a city that had already solidified its status as an art capital on the Indian subcontinent.[129] Not surprisingly, Sotheby's followed with its own Mumbai office just two years later.

Mainland China, which by this time had transformed itself into the world's fastest growing economy, remained the biggest prize. Up until 2005, the People's Republic of China (PRC) had barred foreign auction houses from conducting sales on the mainland, and even after those restrictions were lifted, Sotheby's and Christie's encountered numerous obstacles in their attempts to obtain licenses. Sotheby's was eventually required to invest $1.2 million in a joint venture with Beijing GeHua Art Company; in September 2012, Sotheby's became the first foreign house to enter the lucrative Chinese market.[130] Just a few months later, Christie's managed to get an independent license for sales in Shanghai.[131] When both houses held their first regular auctions in mainland China in the fall of 2013, the competition over the world's third-largest national auction market was officially underway.

Eventually, by the twenty-first century's second decade, both houses had expanded their commercial reach through head-to-head competition from a mainly transatlantic to a global scale, pursuing emerging markets as they spread around the world. As of 2017, Sotheby's was operating sales branches in ten major cities and had local auction offices in thirty-nine cities on five continents. Meanwhile, Christie's had ten sales venues and boasted an additional army of offices in thirty cities on five continents. The two houses had become the art market's biggest global players.

From an International to a Global Logic of Auction Valuation

Just because the houses expanded their geographic reach, however, does not necessarily mean that their contemporary art auctions developed a more global dimension. Olav Velthuis, for example, has highlighted in 2015 that the share of auction exports remained heavily concentrated on the UK and the US. He suggests that such transactional data show that the idea of a more cosmopolitan, globally integrated auction market is a "myth."[132] Others have pointed out that rising "non-Western" auction locations, such as Hong Kong and Dubai, have functioned more readily as regional hubs for Asia and the Middle East.[133] In this view, rather than forming an integrated global network, the empires that Christie's and Sotheby's have built are actually a loose patchwork of regional markets where local specialists cater to discrete, independent audiences.

With a multiscalar field perspective, however, we do not have to think of global and regional scales as being mutually exclusive. Instead, the various national and regional auction locations are *partially* integrated into a global market level that is dominated by New York and London as capitals with expanded power. Beyond an assessment that focuses primarily on the distribution of economic trade numbers, a field account directs attention to the globalization of market practices and symbolic field forces, ultimately arguing that the logic governing the high-end auction valuation for contemporary art became redefined from international to global terms in the new millennium.

For one, the two houses' expansion in scope allowed them to transform their contemporary art auctions in New York and London into global bidding events. Because of their extended institutional network and broadened promotional activities—which included traveling exhibitions in collaboration with representative offices or flying especially valuable artworks to ultra-high-net-worth individuals around the world for a private showing—both houses attracted a new, more globally diverse set of participants for sales in these Western capitals.[134] This influx was facilitated by the possibility of phone or internet bids from abroad, which could make up as "many as half the bids" at major contemporary art auctions in these capitals.[135] More collectors from rising markets—including eastern Europe, the Middle East, and the Far East—competed with Western collectors for the most popular work, which in turn influenced the prices and market careers of contemporary artists.[136]

At a 2007 auction at Sotheby's London, for example, a member of Qatar's royal Al-Thani family purchased Damien Hirst's cabinet *Lullaby Spring* (2002) for $19.2 million, catapulting the artist's market status to new heights and setting a world record at the time for a living European artist.[137] Ten years later, Yusaku Maezawa, the Japanese entrepreneur, acquired Jean-Michel Basquiat's *Untitled* (1982) for an extraordinary $110.5 million at an evening auction at Sotheby's in New York. Tellingly, an art market report linked this "eye-watering auction record" for "a canvas coveted by collectors *around the world*" with New York's "capacity to attract buyers and have them compete with each other."[138] To be sure, not all contemporary sales in London and New York became more globally diverse with regard to their bidders. Yet compared to the 1990s, they were no longer as confined to a Western audience as they once were. Supported through an enlarged infrastructure and mediation strategies, the pool of potential buyers expanded, and the logic of competitive bidding assumed a more global dimension in principle, contributing to unprecedented price records for certain contemporary artists.

Auction sales in New York and London also transformed into more global events through the houses' symbolic rise to "global brands."[139] An extensive geographic reach—that is, globality—can significantly bolster the status and prestige of a commercial brand.[140] Such an effect contributed to the houses' growing symbolic power across borders together with their immense communicative reach in the world mass media. There really is only one other commercial enterprise—namely, the stock exchange—that can match the global scope at which Christie's and Sotheby's operate with regard to their media publicity.[141]

As a result of their symbolic power and global communicative reach, major contemporary art sales by Christie's and Sotheby's in London and New York turned into something akin to global instances for market consecration. On the one hand, the mere inclusion of artworks in such an auction could bestow "final legitimacy on an artist" at the global market level.[142] On the other hand, as auction results were reported broadly, Christie's and Sotheby's could exert a "major influence" in setting reference prices around the world that put galleries' own pricing and promotion strategies under pressure.[143] Hence, if the two houses' contemporary art auctions had already attained a status as "barometers of value" in the international market of the 1990s—albeit heavily contested from galleries—beginning in the millennium, they began to function as global barometers of market values.[144]

Lastly, the houses' extended organizational network enabled them to orchestrate new transcontinental valuation chains, which highlight the interplay of regional and global market levels in the auction circuit. To increase consumer appeal and prices, both Sotheby's and Christie's began to transport works or collections by certain artists between sales venues in Hong Kong or Dubai and more global venues in London or New York. Success in one location could lead to success in another, and it proved to be an effective strategy for driving up price levels.[145]

For example, Sotheby's was able to boost auction values for Chinese contemporary art by first offering it in Hong Kong and then leveraging the regional market success in other locations. Specifically, building on initial positive auction results for "Chinese contemporary art" in Hong Kong in 2004,[146] the house then introduced a special sale in New York in 2006 to establish a "global presence in this exciting and fast developing field."[147] The prior success in the regional auction hub created a foundation on which specialists could promote the relatively new genre in New York, emphasizing the fact that a "dramatic increase in client demand" had occurred elsewhere.[148] New York's global status in turn helped to extend the pool of bidders from four continents, leading to a major record sale, which then boosted sales in Hong Kong.[149] While such globally coordinated strategies affirm the symbolic power of London and New York as global art market capitals, they also embed those sites within a broader set of regional hubs beyond the West, creating interdependent relations for increasing market values.

Hence, in the first two decades of the twenty-first century, Sotheby's and Christie's had clearly expanded and redefined their strategies in the contemporary art segment in global terms. The continuing allure of glamorous evening auctions, the houses' ability to mobilize global and regional networks, their status as global brands, and the extensive media publicity they could create became major advantages over galleries in the globalizing game.[150] Nevertheless, the auction houses' global competitive edge did not just mean that they could attract lucrative works and buyers from every corner of the world. Crucially, they also increased their *symbolic* power to establish market values for contemporary artists and to communicate them in highly visible ways at great distances, which ran counter to avant-garde galleries' traditionally opaque price strategies. As consecrators of market value, Sotheby's and Christie's determine *who* becomes perceived as successful at a global level. And they substantially shape the cross-border discourse about *what* constitutes value in contemporary art. As such, they have broadened and further cemented the heteronomous notion of using monetary value and sales success as a yardstick for an artist's importance in the global commercial subfield. This power to dictate the value of contemporary art can increase in emerging markets. In the absence of extensive cultural and gallery infrastructures for contemporary art, novices in such contexts tend to favor the auction process because they perceive it as "more transparent."[151] For such buyers, auction sales function as "judgement devices" because they convey the apparent certainty of public "objective" figures, which enhances the houses' symbolic influence.[152]

The Growth of Beta Auction Houses

Focusing solely on the rise of Sotheby's and Christie's, however, only provides a partial understanding of the development of a global auction commerce for contemporary art in the twenty-first century. A full picture must also include the so-called beta-level auction houses.[153] After Christie's and Sotheby's, these houses constitute a secondary tier in the auction industry—hence their label "beta," which was given to them by the economist Ian Robertson. These houses represent a sizable proportion of overall sales, and they have a "foothold in the international trade" in at least three ways: their self-presentations and services are oriented toward foreign buyers; their auctions include work from foreign contemporary artists; and their sales are reported in world-spanning market price databases for a global clientele of collectors and investors.[154] Some of these houses also operate branches in multiple countries, though not to the same extent as Christie's and Sotheby's. Phillips, for example, an auction house specializing in contemporary art, operates sales locations in New York and London, and in 2015, it expanded to Hong Kong as well. Other beta houses in the West include Bonhams in the UK and US, Artcurial and Drouot in France, Lempertz and Villa Grisebach in Germany, Kornfeld and Koller in Switzerland, Dorotheum in Austria, and Bukowskis in Sweden.[155]

In the twenty-first century, beta auction houses underwent a massive expansion as well. Figure 3.6 provides a first historical overview of the foundation of beta auction houses whose sales programs include contemporary art from foreign countries (cf. appendix B). The graph underlines that the largest growth coincides with the same period in which ICAFs grew at unprecedented rates, the first decade of the new millennium. Figure 3.7 details their founding dynamics along the same three stages of expansion that Christie's and Sotheby's experienced. This additionally underscores the new millennium's historical weight. It is the era with the highest rate (about 50 percent) of new beta houses in the postwar era.

The multiplication of beta auction houses enlarged the geographic scope of auctions that offer works by foreign contemporary artists (figure 3.8). While the sales venues of Christie's and Sotheby's reach up to nine countries in Europe, North America, and Asia (which does not include the broader spread of their representative offices), together, beta auction houses stretch across thirty-eight countries and six continents. So while Christie's and Sotheby's were clearly the elite players in creating a more globally integrated auction circuit, this second tier of auction houses further extended the territorial scale for contemporary art's cross-border commodification.

Unlike Sotheby's and Christie's, these transnational beta houses form a globally interdependent, rather than a directly integrated, competitive infrastructure for auction valuation. Because they sell works from contemporary artists who originate beyond the national fields in which the houses are situated, they are interdependent insofar as they are susceptible to transnational or global market forces. Specifically, with the rise of online auction databases, which I discuss in the next section, it has become easier for mediators to observe market trends in other countries, which can affect the kinds of contemporary art they sell on their own turf. Such interdependent responsiveness can amplify market trends across borders.[156] For example, after the widely publicized record sale of Chinese contemporary art at Sotheby's New York in 2006, beta houses in Paris, Los Angeles, San Francisco, Cologne, Zurich, Naples, Seoul, Singapore, Tokyo, and Beijing began auctioning works by such artists too. By echoing, reinforcing, and countering moves made by the majors, beta houses can measurably influence auction values or even booms across continents for certain artists or genres.

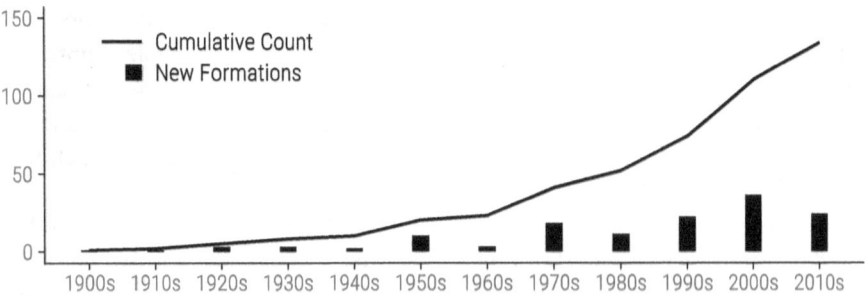

FIGURE 3.6. The historical growth of beta auction houses, 1900–2017 (cf. appendix B)

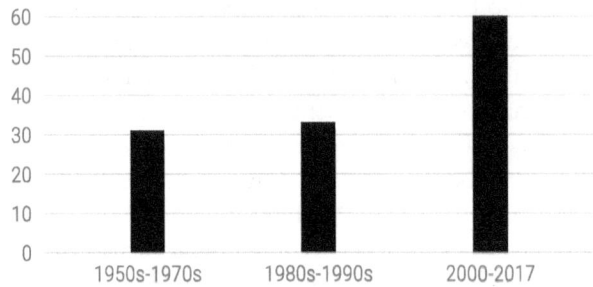

FIGURE 3.7. Foundations of beta auction houses across three
periods. (Note that beta auction houses that were founded
before the 1950s are not represented in this graph)

This mediation can flow in the reverse direction as well. Given that beta houses can reach audiences beyond their national context with regard to their status and visibility, they also serve as a preliminary stage where artists' works first gain exposure to foreign auction markets, an initial stop before they are potentially taken up by beta houses in other countries or by Christie's and Sotheby's. Thus, beta houses can function as a test market for certain kinds of art, making it more readily available to a global marketplace.[157] This role is all the more foundational considering how rare it is for artists' work to be taken up in the value-adding but risk-averse high-end commercial sphere of Christie's and Sotheby's. As the economist Don Thompson has estimated, "Only one artist in two hundred—and that is two hundred established artists—will reach a point where her work is ever offered at Christie's or Sotheby's auctions."[158] In this hypercompetitive context, beta houses can serve as the proving ground for the value of artists before their work eventually ascends to the highest auction echelons.

Overall, the massive expansion of beta auction houses in the new millennium created another institutional backbone for the emergence of a globally extended market subfield. While Christie's and Sotheby's dominate the global

Sotheby's & Christie's

Beta-Auction Houses

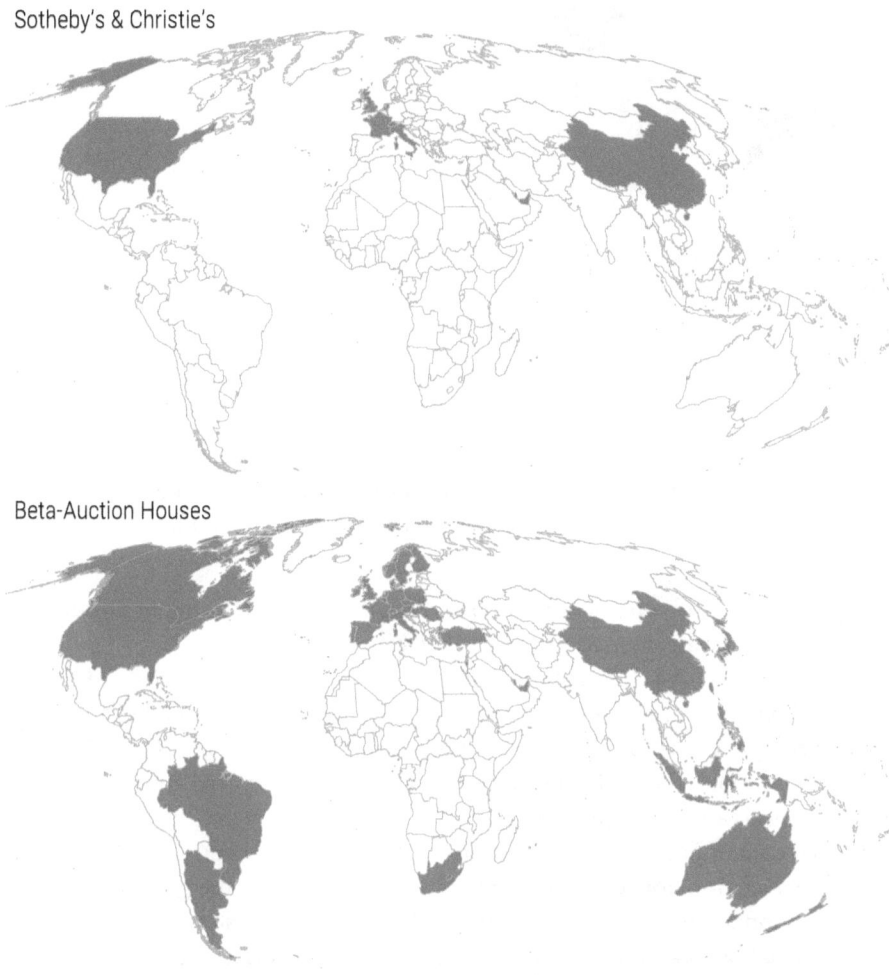

FIGURE 3.8. The geographic scope of sales venues by alpha and beta auction houses in 2017.

market, beta houses enhance it as players that serve as the first step in cross-border auction trajectories or that enforce certain market trends, diffusing them back into various countries around the world. As such, they operate like relay stations between national, regional, and global field levels for the extended commercialization of contemporary art.

GLOBAL DISPARITIES

And yet, despite the greater geographic extension of both alpha and beta auction houses since beginning of the new millennium, significant disparities remain in their dispersion around the world. The distribution of this type of institutional

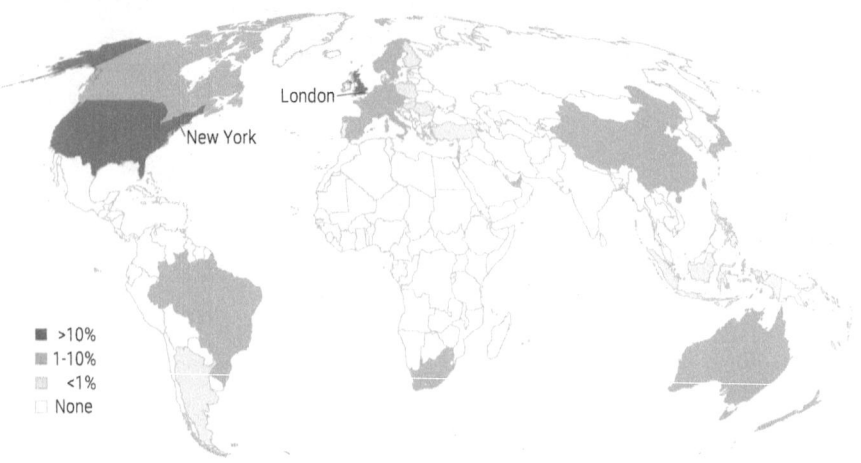

FIGURE 3.9. Global inequalities in the distribution of alpha and beta auction
houses offering foreign contemporary artworks (appendix B).

market capital still centers on a handful of countries, which, as figure 3.9's dark-
est shades indicate, remain primarily Western.

Beta houses have clustered most densely around the few countries and capitals that are key locations for Christie's and Sotheby's as well: the US and the
UK, with New York and London serving as the biggest magnets. Outside this
transatlantic axis, Hong Kong has been on the rise; the special administrative
region holds around 70 percent of China's auction houses that include sales of
foreign contemporary artists. In addition to the major players, it attracted several beta auction houses in the millennium, which turned the port city into a
new regional-global market hub poised between the West and locations in
South and Southeast Asia.[159] Corresponding to the territorial nodes of Christie's
and Sotheby's, these concentrations underline that the global auction market
is characterized by an institutional center-periphery structure. A small number
of locations still command the lion's share of resources and power for the cross-
border mediation of contemporary art at commercial auctions.

However, this auction-based, center-periphery configuration differs from
the institutional macrostructure of the global exhibition space in ways that
once again highlight the art market's stronger dependency on the external
economy. For example, this market has a much smaller global reach overall,
encompassing only 38 countries, while noncommercial exhibition institutions
encompass 118, more than three times as many. Stark differences like this suggest a much higher barrier of entry into the commercial game of contemporary
art, not least because of the wealthy "high-net-worth-individual" buyers whom
auction houses need to attract in order to remain viable.[160]

Furthermore, the world's major auction capitals—New York, London, and Hong Kong—happen to be centers of global financial power, and as Julian Stallabrass points out, this indicates that the auction market for contemporary art also functions as a "minor speculative market in which art works are used for a variety of instrumental purposes, including investment, tax avoidance, and money laundering."[161] However, at the more autonomous pole of public exhibition institutions such territorial connections with financial markets loosen. As we saw in chapter 2, apart from New York's central position, Berlin plays a much larger role as a cultural capital, and Hong Kong vanishes entirely as a central location. Therefore, the global field's most heteronomous market zone is structured around macro inequalities that are influenced more by a location's levels of external wealth, commercially favorable regulations, and links with financial markets. This difference once again highlights the importance of using a field lens, one that distinguishes between autonomous and heteronomous conditions of institutional globalization and avoids overly totalizing assessments.

New Online Devices for the Global Market Evaluation of Contemporary Art

A third major development that marked the international avant-garde market's transformation into a commercial global subfield was the rise of online price databases, which centralize and publish information on worldwide auction results. The appearance of these ostensibly neutral digital platforms has drastically redefined practices of market (e)valuation of contemporary art in ways that have once again fueled both a more global and a more radically heteronomous market game. For the first time, these instruments established global tools and categories for assessing the relative market success of artists from all corners of the world. As such, they influenced the discursive construction of a more global vision of the art market and related principles of hierarchization. Simultaneously, they bolstered the heteronomous approach of using economic value as an independent metric for assessing an artist's worth. Because these databases made it possible to track the economic trajectories of artists or single works in systematic ways—as if they were assets in the global stock market—they intensified financialization trends in this new global subfield, increasingly attracting investors and speculators and solidifying art's categorization as a financial asset. Beyond simply changing the kinds of consumers who bought art, these databases helped discursively shape how market participants conceptualized contemporary art within a global market.

The first online price database of its kind was launched in 1996 by Artnet, an enterprise based in Berlin and New York.[162] Just one year after Artnet's initial appearance, a French competitor, Artprice, established a second database of this kind. In the ensuing competition for subscribers, both enterprises strove to accumulate auction information at an ever more comprehensive, worldwide level. By 2010, Artnet had cataloged sales results for more than 500 auction houses and 182,000 artists from a broad variety of styles and nationalities.[163] Meanwhile, Artprice had expanded its online coverage even further, including around 405,000 artists and more than 2,400 houses.[164] For a fee, subscribers could search these databases for a wide range of auction estimates and past prices for artistic works, along with digital images and descriptions of media, size, and creation date. Both firms also introduced new econometric services, including artist rankings, financial indices, and regular art market reports that allowed subscribers to monitor trends in sales and value.

As the new millennium got under way, the technological consolidation and expanding geographic coverage of Artnet and Artprice radically increased the transparency of auction dynamics in numerous national art markets. It became feasible to instantly access sales information worldwide, something that had never been possible in the more confidential international avant-garde market.[165] In the former configuration, any related details—the price of a specific artwork or an artist's typical price level—had remained embedded in personal, and often more localized, networks. And even though auction houses themselves had publicized prices, before the rise of Artnet and Artprice, it was still difficult to track them in a systematic way, particularly at a global scale.

Against this background, the introduction of computerized databases—which centralized sales figures from an extensive number of houses—was nothing less than a quantum leap. Now, art professionals and lay buyers could rapidly and seamlessly follow the vacillations and trends of auctions, and users could chart and compare the market success of contemporary artists across markets worldwide. Never had auction information been available so rapidly in such an accessible way and with such a global scope. Thus, these platforms not only increased market transparency but also heightened global integration at the level of information flow.

More than that, these platforms established global tools for the market evaluation of contemporary artists. In 2007, for example, Artprice launched a worldwide auction ranking. An annual list of the five hundred leading contemporary artists, based on their sales volume, pitted both living and dead artists from across six continents against each other.[166] By numerically arraying various visual artists—who are nested in diverse local histories, contexts, and biographies—into a radically homogenizing economic framework, the ranking both presupposed and indirectly asserted the idea that there was now a shared global market space.

Simultaneously, the ranking helped institutionalize new global categories for classifying and evaluating the highest levels of market success. By 2010, Artprice had assumed a broad communicative reach, which reportedly included 1.3 million clients, 4.5 million subscribers to its email newsletter, and "90% of the world press."[167] With this type of reach, it is clear that Artprice could exert discursive power in redefining the highest categories of economic evaluation from "international" to global levels. Even if players at the more autonomous pole decried the rankings as the product of hypercommercialization, the global hierarchies that these online providers created began informing the way market participants—art advisers, journalists, art collectors, and investors—reported art market trends.

In addition to globalizing information flows and evaluative practices, these online providers simultaneously pushed the terms of valuation in the market in more heteronomous directions in three ways. First, by making sales data much more accessible, they allowed market prices to play an increased role in the judgment of the worth of artists and their works in the globalizing game.[168] In the prior international avant-garde market—which held considerably fewer auctions of contemporary art and did not offer widely available price overviews—the most accessible formal clues for many lay buyers still had been an artist's exhibition record and coverage from art critics. Thus, collectors could assess an artist's public record of "symbolic capital" to orient themselves and estimate the value of the artist's works. It is often overlooked how drastically the contemporary art market differed in this regard from other cultural markets. In the publishing, movie, and music industries, sales data had been publicly available on a broad scale for decades, so the category of "best seller" or "box-office hit" has long been accessible as an alternative measure of success. When Artnet and Artprice allowed broad audiences to rapidly check auction records, even the complete absence of sales figures could now tell a story about an artist's standing, or lack thereof, in the globalizing market. This dealt yet another blow to symbolic capital's long-standing reign as the main public currency for market valuation in the contemporary art field.

Second, the Artprice rankings instilled an overt commercial logic of artistic hierarchy into the global market subfield. Subtly, but importantly, it did not base an artist's economic status on price levels per artwork—the more established and status-infused signal of market value—but on an artist's sheer sales volume.[169] In this, the rankings inaugurated something like a global best-seller list of contemporary art, an "external principle of hierarchization" that resembles performance measures in the broader economic field or cultural industries (for example, in rankings like the *Forbes* 100 list or best sellers in the global book market).[170] Given such a commercial turn, it is not surprising that avant-garde gallerists have "frowned upon" the rankings.[171] Not only did the institutionalization of these worldwide measures for sales success globalize forms of comparison and hierarchy in the contemporary art market. Concomitantly, it opened this formerly high-cultural enclave to a commercial principle of evaluation that had long characterized popular cultural industries.

Finally, the rise of online databases facilitated the growth of financial practices and audiences. As I mentioned previously, the idea that contemporary art could be a profitable investment had emerged as early as the Robert and Ethel Scull sale in New York in 1973. Yet before the twenty-first century, only a small circle of adventurous investors were active in the contemporary art segment, a niche that had remained heavily contested by most members of the art world.[172] In the 1990s, for example, in order for avant-garde gallerists in New York to protect the works of their artists from speculation, they shared blacklists of investment-driven buyers who were looking to buy art at a low cost and resell it for a profit.[173] Just a decade later, however, the globalizing auction market offered an alternative playground where financial agents could bypass the rules of the more autonomous zones of the gallery market. For these players, Artnet and Artprice provided the tools for computing price developments—that is, to calculate the statistical probability of increases in the financial value of certain artworks or artistic positions, like assets in the global stock market.

Hence, online price databases offered an expanded means for treating contemporary art as a rationally calculable investment, raising its popularity as an asset class and being part of a new wave of financialization in the new millennium.[174] The rise of art pricing services encouraged international banks to increasingly endorse art as an investment; they acknowledged art collections as components of "financial investment portfolios, and offered art advisory services."[175] Art investment vehicles also grew, and individual financial elites or lay investors from both Western and Eastern world regions flocked to contemporary art in greater numbers.[176]

In sum, by establishing economic value as a broadly accessible measure of an artist's worth, by launching global best-seller lists, and by enabling the extended financial assessment of art, these online data firms have further undermined the primacy that avant-garde galleries place on specific artistic value and expert judgment within the growing global commercial subfield, contributing to turn it into a worldwide playground for investors and speculators.

Conclusion: A More Heteronomous and Global Market Game

Over the span of two decades—an astonishingly short period of time—the contemporary art market has undergone the most drastic changes in its history. An international art market that was relatively small and Western-centric has rapidly expanded into a multibillion-dollar global industry. This chapter has traced this dramatic historical shift along two related, but analytically distinct, trajectories: the push toward greater globalization and the associated move away from a more autonomously oriented, avant-garde market toward an enlarged subfield governed by commercial and financial forces.

Against the broader backdrop of global neoliberalism, rising world economies, unprecedented wealth polarization, and the internet's rapid advance, three transformations were particularly influential for the emergence of the global commercial subfield: the rise of a global art fair circuit, the formation of a worldwide interdependent infrastructure for contemporary art auctions, and the launch of online firms for global auction data. When these developments converged in the twenty-first century's early years, they established a global institutional and symbolic infrastructure that incorporated locations that were previously not as involved in the international art market into a shared space for market exchange and competition. In the process, the highest stakes for the competitive valorization of contemporary art became redefined in global terms, involving artists, brokers, art collectors, and buyers on multiple continents, not just from within the Euro-American axis. To be sure, this global market represents the top tier of the game and is not as fully integrated as national art markets are, not least because of import duties and persisting cultural differences.[177] Nevertheless, a global level for the market valorization of contemporary art has undeniably materialized. And as subsequent chapters will further show, the highest auction prices and the cross-border careers of art superstars must be understood in light of this expanded subfield and its unique features.

One macro-level feature is that this global commercial subfield embodies a highly hierarchical terrain that remains largely centered around Western capitals, where both market institutions and power are most heavily concentrated. Inequalities of this kind can be, and have been, interpreted as evidence for a lack of globalization, but the information analyzed here shows that the forces impacting the concentration of market power have been *integral* to globalizing dynamics.[178] The creation of new global market infrastructures and the competitive strategies of players who already commanded substantial amounts of capital were key factors that transformed New York and London from international to global market hot spots. They became locations that could attract more buyers (and sellers) from around the world while functioning as barometers of value at a greater geographic scope than before. In other words, the continuing centrality of certain Western cities and market institutions is not just a reproduction of their attributes from the international era. Their extended influence was *dynamically* produced within a globalizing space of unequal market competition through which they themselves changed from within.

Correspondingly, a field perspective on the contemporary art economy counters arguments that suggest growing regionalization would offset any global center-periphery structure.[179] It is certainly true that the multiplication of art fairs and auction venues has supported the consolidation of more regional commercial centers for contemporary art in various parts of the world. Yet, as much as these developments may have followed their own regional dynamics, they have not been insulated from globally oriented players and events occurring in major capitals. Regional centers also offer extended nodes through which globally oriented mediators operate in their capital accumulation strategies. They can function as intermediate stations between the global and national market field levels. Rather than seeing global centers and regionalization as mutually exclusive processes, the commercial global subfield must be understood as a complex nested configuration in which global, regional, and national market levels and their respective centers can operate relatively independently of one another but in which they *also* interact and shape market processes interdependently.

Furthermore, this chapter has traced how the same transformations that allowed the contemporary art market to assume a global field dimension led to its greater commercialization and financialization. The expanded subfield is no longer primarily governed by avant-garde gallerists, who are more closely oriented toward specific artistic values, symbolic capital, and connoisseurship. It is instead a space more readily dominated by heteronomous, market-driven agents and corporate entities. This shift in the balance of power has significantly impacted the prevailing conceptions of market value and the currencies of contemporary art's valorization. As art fairs proliferated, as auction houses expanded their reach, and as commercial data firms became more popular, the market for contemporary art gained broader appeal as a financial asset and became a bigger playground for new money and lifestyle luxury consumption. Branding through mass media exposure, building an artist's celebrity, and sheer auction sales success became more widely influential for evaluating an artist's worth within the global market game.

Comparatively, the story of the global field's emergence at the heteronomous pole makes it distinct from the specific cultural pole. It was affected more heavily by field-external economic forces, which had several important ramifications. For one, while the rise of the global artistic subfield historically began toward the end of the 1980s, the globalization of the art market really only gained momentum two decades later, in a period when wealth, and thus the number of potential art consumers, became more globally dispersed. Likewise, compared to the former, the art market's institutional macrostructure remains more confined to the world's wealthiest countries, and the art market's major capitals still closely overlap with centers of global economic and financial power. By contrast, art institutions at the cultural pole have proliferated more widely across countries in Latin America, eastern Europe, and Africa. Finally, the competitive dynamics driving the art market's globalization were largely about the accumulation of economic capital. They were shaped by a kind of oligopolistic competition, in which a small number of centralized, profit-chasing actors looked to increase their power within a context of growing global infrastructures and monetary opportunities. A different dynamic marked the globalizing artistic subfield, which was characterized more by collaborative competition for symbolic capital. Particularly at biennials, agents from the peripheries could have a stronger relational impact in shaping an emerging global logic for new mediation practices and debates.

These divergences in turn underscore that global transformations at the specific cultural pole have been *less* affected by external economic forces. A political-economy perspective—which several art and cultural theorists still embrace and which might rely on a reading of globalization that states that neoliberal economic policies spread around the globe and then the contemporary art field followed suit—overlooks the complexity of these historical developments. To accurately understand the art field's globalization process, we must avoid a totalizing approach and instead adopt a framework that is able to account for the historical particularities of the more autonomous, artistically oriented zones in their own right. Ultimately, the dynamics of the art field's institutional globalization have been uneven, and they have coincided with greater polarization along the autonomy-heteronomy axis. The specific cultural and commercial global subfields have drifted farther apart in their infrastructures, geographies, and currencies of symbolic and economic valuation.

PART II

Dynamics of Artistic Recognition in the Globalizing Field

NUMEROUS INSTITUTIONAL transformations have occurred as the art field has globalized over the past three decades. But what have those changes meant for artists themselves? Has the expanded space of cross-border circulation and exchange actually brought artists from "non-Western" countries to higher levels of recognition and created more diverse global canons?[1] Or have artists from the field's traditional centers simply cemented their dominance at an even larger scale, extending the homogeneity that defined previous periods?

Intellectuals, artists, and curators have long debated such questions of representational inequality and diversity. Early on, some exhibition makers hailed the end of an era dominated by Euro-American art, suggesting that visual artists from diverse world regions enjoyed greater opportunities to be part of cross-border cultural networks and present their work at the world's most prominent institutions.[2] Even Rasheed Araeen revised his caustic assessment from the late 1970s (cf. introduction to part 1), noting that by the turn of the millennium, the field had grown increasingly open: "Young, post-colonial artists from Africa or Asia" were no longer as segregated from their "white/European contemporaries. Both of them display and circulate within the same space and same art market, recognised and legitimated by the same institutions."[3]

More skeptical voices, however, have rejected the idea of globalization's growing inclusivity as euphemistic, if not illusionary.[4] To Olu Oguibe, a diaspora artist and scholar from Nigeria, the rise of a "global culture game" had led to neither equal visibility nor accessibility by the new millennium.[5] Though the art world opened some "rationed slots" at important exhibitions and museums, behind that façade, Oguibe suggests the field's most powerful agents still cynically preside over an essentially closed, Eurocentric—if not racist—system, which pays lip service to inclusion without enacting any authentic broader changes. He identifies a pattern:

> Every ten years over a designated period, there are huge African, Asian or Latin American exhibitions after which the pained rhetoric of institutions becomes, *Well, but we just had an African or Asian or Latin American show!* Having staged the routine decade shows, museums and galleries feel no further obligation to touch any art or artist from these provenances. . . . Ultimately, things degenerate to a game of numbers: *We had five Africans in the Biennale, seven Chinese, two Southeast Asians, and even two Australian Aborigines. We do our best to ensure that this year's exhibition was representative.* What is masked in such a seemingly liberal gesture is that Western artists are seldom subjected to the same game of numbers, unless of course, they too belong outside the mainstream: folk artists, . . . Native Americans, self-taught artists, prison artists.[6]

Sociologists have tended to share this critical suspicion.[7] Alain Quemin, for example, drawing from a trove of quantitative data, has consistently argued that recognition at the field's highest levels has overwhelmingly accrued to art producers from Euro-American contexts. In his view, a substantial global shift toward artistic diversity has not occurred. What seems to be happening instead is the extended reproduction of Western hegemony on a worldwide scale.

Building on the global field perspective I developed in part 1, the two chapters in part 2 will carve out some middle ground between this diversity-homogeneity binary. Unique, extensive evidence of hundreds of contemporary artists and their shifting transnational successes shows that transformations beyond West-centric artistic canons have, in fact, occurred, though they have played out unevenly and according to different timelines. The commercial pole underwent rapid changes in the twenty-first century's first decade—precisely when the auction market's institutional globalization was in full swing. Yet its "inclusion" of artists beyond the transatlantic axis concentrated on figures from a few Asian countries with rising wealth—especially China—rather than encompassing a broader range of diversity. The cultural pole's elite levels, by contrast, have expanded in much more cosmopolitan ways, opening up to artists from a wider variety of countries. This increased diversity, however, took longer to surface. It became visible only in the new millennium's second decade and it primarily involved younger artists.

My central contention in part 2 is that the divergent dynamics we see in the global art field are intertwined with the different, sometimes opposing logics that dominate how the field's specific cultural and commercial poles construct artistic value across borders. In other words, it was the field's dual world economy that substantially influenced artistic recognition beyond established Western countries, and ultimately the diversity of contemporary art's emerging global canons.

To develop this argument, chapter 4 first lays out some conceptual groundwork about the social construction of value and careers in contemporary art, which will then help explain my alternative theoretical approach for understanding these issues in a global context. Against this backdrop, chapter 5 presents a collection of data on shifting patterns of artistic recognition and transcontinental careers in the field's emerging dual world economy.

4

Cross-Border Valuation between Art Experts and the Market

FROM BOURDIEU'S CONVERSION MODEL
TO A DUAL CULTURAL WORLD ECONOMY

QUESTIONS OF ARTISTIC recognition in a time of accelerated globalization involve a fundamental theoretical problem at the heart of the sociology of culture—namely, the construction of artistic value. By now, it is a sociological truism that the worth of art derives not merely from its intrinsic aesthetic qualities and the inspired genius who created it. Challenging charismatic notions of the singular artist, which emerged in the Romantic period and became institutionalized with the advent of a modern art system, numerous scholars have demonstrated how the valuation of an artist's work (and that artist's related reputation) is shaped by the interaction of a variety of contextual factors. Some highlight the importance of the extent and nature of critical discourse in constructing artistic value.[1] Others elaborate on these insights, underlining how discourse interacts with mediation networks or historically specific market exigencies.[2] An additional line of research has brought attention to macrolevel conditions of valuation, such as changes in the economic or political climate, or institutional structures of cultural markets that are specific to a nation-state.[3] There have also been contributions pointing to crucial microlevel aspects, such as the promotional activities of "reputational entrepreneurs," including, of course, artists themselves.[4]

Within this line of scholarship, Bourdieu's field's approach has offered a particularly influential model for studying valuation in artistic realms (cf. chapter 1).[5] It considers and connects meso-, macro- and micro-levels of analysis and allows us to study them with reference to both field-internal and field-external developments.[6] Moreover, it offers a framework that can attend to diverse logics of evaluation characterizing a cultural field's different poles of production.

And yet Bourdieu's proposition about a polarity between "art" and "money" (i.e., autonomy and heteronomy) in such fields has been widely critiqued, directly or indirectly, as being outdated for the brave new world of contemporary art. Indeed, over the past twenty years, interdisciplinary contributions have increasingly argued for an alternative view that posits a growing convergence in modes of valuation among aesthetic experts and commercial brokers.[7] In these accounts, the market and the museum have never been closer with regard to the logics of evaluation that govern them.

In this chapter, I first compare Bourdieu's original framework and this latter "market convergence model," exploring the implications of both approaches for examining artistic careers and globalization's effects on the recognition of artists along the art-money spectrum. Refined by these insights, I then propose an alternative model—a dual cultural world economy—that extends and synthesizes these previous approaches for examining global dynamics of recognition in a more differentiated light.

Bourdieu's Anticommercial Conversion Model

Bourdieu developed what I call an *anticommercial conversion model* of careers that involves a complex, even paradoxical, configuration of art experts and the market. Broadly speaking, his model suggests a two-stage pattern for artistic recognition. Success in the art market ("economic capital") depends on the prior approval of aesthetic experts ("specific symbolic capital"). But in order to gain this symbolic capital, the artist must appear pure—that is, aloof from commercial interests and activities—in the eyes of experts. This is in line with Bourdieu's assumption that their judgment criteria are governed by a normative antagonism to the market, a default stance of relative autonomous anticommercialism.

This two-stage process begins when artists accumulate symbolic recognition from peers and intermediaries at the relatively autonomous pole. Here, it is particularly valuable to gain the recognition of distinguished mediators. Along with symbolic capital, they possess cultural capital, the "categories of perception and appreciation" that can endow "meaning and value" to an artwork "by reference to the entire tradition" of a field.[8] These capital-rich gatekeepers—art critics, curators, museum directors, avant-garde gallerists—must believe in the distinctive value of a particular artist's work. Only then can the artwork enter, as Bourdieu calls it, a "cycle of consecration" in which value gradually increases through the mutual transfer of symbolic capital.[9] Ultimately, what generates value in this subfield is the interplay of multiple "specialized agents" and art institutions whose own position defines their level of authority.

Bourdieu's theory suggests that ever since art's rise as a relatively independent, specialized sphere of activity in the late nineteenth century, the dominant criteria for artistic evaluation within this cycle of consecration have been rooted in a logic of *art for art's sake*. Art becomes relatively free from patronage, the state, or the market; it is a practice that demands to be seen and appreciated for its own intrinsic aesthetic sake.[10] According to this logic, evaluative criteria are both more self-referential and more focused on values that are specific to the field itself. To gain recognition, an artist must look original, creating work that is experimental and new relative to an art field's internal debates and field-specific histories. Innovation thus becomes a major marker of "distinction." It is the foundation of building symbolic capital, both for the artist and the people who spot and promote cutting-edge art early on.[11] This more self-referential logic of distinction might help explain to a layperson why an artist like Marcel Duchamp—who shrewdly signed and submitted a urinal to an exhibition in 1917—could attain his iconic status as one of the twentieth century's greatest artists.

Another related criterion in Bourdieu's model is an artist's distance (i.e., autonomy) toward "money, 'the commercial.'"[12] In this view, consecration cycles are underpinned by a "charismatic ideology" that rejects any compromise with profane worldly forces, including commercial ones.[13] This refusal is necessary for an artist to gain recognition as an exceptional, authentic creator, and the artist expresses it through work that resists easy absorption by an established market.[14] With this anticommercial norm, any "instant success" in the market looks even suspicious, and it can damage an artist's reputation as a "mark of intellectual inferiority."[15] As Bourdieu famously asserts, the artistic subfield is "the economic world reversed; that is, the fundamental law of . . . disinterestedness."[16] Hence, "The artist cannot triumph on the symbolic terrain except by losing on the economic terrain (at least in the short run)."[17]

Innovative artists need not live in poverty, however. In fact, over time, they can secondly convert their symbolic capital into increasing market sales and prices, and, as we saw in chapter 3, avant-garde galleries play a key role in this process of value "conversion." But if an artist makes it too obvious that they are cashing in, they run the risk of being seen as a banal and profane market-pleaser.[18] Bourdieu's view thus suggests a paradoxical opposition of art and money underpinning valuation processes. Economic capital requires symbolic capital. But the norm of autonomous "disinterestedness" dictates that commercial success can only happen after a delay, and it comes with the risk of being labeled as a sellout.

A last important characteristic of Bourdieu's model pertains to temporality. For Bourdieu, valuation in relative autonomous art fields unfolds in "long production cycles" for two reasons.[19] First, innovative art, by definition, does not appeal to established broader tastes but needs to create its own market, which, as the myths surrounding artists like Vincent van Gogh radically exemplify, can take time.[20] As Bourdieu explains, there is a "time-lag that is necessary for works to impose the norms of perceptions that they bring along.... The partisans of art for art's sake, compelled to produce their own market, are destined to deferred economic gratification."[21]

Second, valuation in relative autonomous art fields takes time because it tends to unfold in generational rhythms. As Bourdieu states, the "initiative for change can be traced back almost by definition, to new (meaning younger) entrants."[22] The sociological logic behind this idea goes back to the "heterodoxy-orthodoxy" opposition I outlined in chapter 1. Newer cultural agents tend to have less symbolic capital, and in a competitive arena, where the accumulation of this capital is associated with innovation, they are more predisposed to engage in "subversive" strategies that challenge the existing artistic order.[23] Almost naturally, then, younger mediators (and their artists) tend to form a heterodox faction that drives change. Older mediators (and their artists) in dominant positions, in turn, tend to form the field's "orthodoxy" or status quo, which they helped establish and to which they owe their positions. In this constellation, younger mediators need time to build up recognition before they can fully impose their innovative choices and, under favorable circumstances, become a field's prevailing orthodoxy. Therefore, in Bourdieu's model, changes in symbolic valuation tend to occur in slower, drawn-out, generational cycles.

These arguments about valuation between art experts and the market carry interesting implications for thinking about dynamics of artistic diversity across borders. Globally, if the artistic elite were to change in its composition, the expert-driven pole would instigate it because that is where artists must first find success. But such transformations would only develop gradually, along generational cycles. Then, after further delay, the art market would reflect that change. In short, in Bourdieu's model, increasing artistic diversity would originate with symbolic valuation and evolve in long production cycles.

The Market-Convergence Model

Bourdieu's theory only considered galleries as market mediators. But as we have seen in chapter 3, since the 1970s, new players have appeared, disrupting the modern system of the expert-driven art market.[24] And by 2010, a formerly avant-garde market had become something entirely different.

Given such historical changes, several scholars have posited that a new market-driven regime in the contemporary art world would render Bourdieu's conversion model, and the idea of an ideological opposition between "art" and "money," outdated. This alternative model is not based on a homogeneous theoretical orientation. Its main ideas were introduced by the pioneering sociologist Raymonde Moulin and then radicalized in the twenty-first century by several interdisciplinary studies on the visual arts.[25]

At its core, this model argues that commercial agents have assumed an outsized role in influencing artistic careers. The construction of economic value no longer depends as heavily on an artist's prior symbolic recognition but is instead determined by the sheer power of market dynamics: "the value of an artist's work is less determined by a slowly evolving consensus of experts, critics, and curators, and more by market forces of supply and demand."[26] With regard to career chronology, this suggests that artists can rise to market heights much more quickly because they do not first have to endure a long cycle of consecration involving public art institutions and traditional gatekeepers.[27]

This shift in valorization at the market pole is also driven by the changing profile of elite art buyers. The market's accelerated transformations, as chapter 3 discussed, have generated an influx of new, deep-pocketed consumers whose tastes are not necessarily oriented around the aesthetic standards of professional experts.[28] In this "new economy of enrichment," financial elites, corporate players, and celebrities follow more popular art tastes; they embrace financial criteria, market fashions, and the sheer publicity artists in the media.[29] The increasing presence of these types of art buyers (and the money they have injected into the game) have drastically changed how the top tier of market valuation functions and which audiences it caters to. As Diana Crane summarizes, "unlike art markets in the past," the global art market is "driven by the eclectic and often superficial tastes of a new cohort of exceedingly wealthy collectors."[30] As a result, at the global market's upper echelons, experts from the cultural pole have lost their grip when it comes to affecting economic value and shaping artistic careers.

Finally, this alternative model also holds that the market has profoundly influenced art specialists' own sense of artistic value. Isabelle Graw, for example, observes a growing "propensity" among art critics "to let commercial success dictate one's own aesthetic approval."[31] In contrast to the past, "rather than positing a threat to artistic repute, success in the market and in the media is actually capable of generating such prestige."[32] Expert valuations also increasingly follow a logic of celebrity that resembles that of the commercial film or fashion industries.[33] The crucial upshot is an inversion of Bourdieu's original theory: economic capital positively fuels symbolic capital, or, as Crane poignantly asserts, "prices now determine reputations."[34]

The artist whose career was paradigmatic in this shift toward the commercial is, of course, Andy Warhol. A self-declared "business artist"[35] who notoriously played with celebrity culture and commerce, Warhol's expert recognition rose in the slipstream of his market fame.[36] Other famous examples, whom I will discuss later, include Jeff Koons, Damien Hirst, and Takashi Murakami, who have profitably followed in Warhol's footsteps.[37]

Ultimately, the market-convergence model suggests a dissolution of the ideological "(legitimate) art versus money" antagonism that resides at the center of Bourdieu's theory. Taking its place is a stronger ideological convergence between the art market and the sphere of expert judgment, which shapes how artistic careers are forged in a new global "art industry."[38]

This complete reevaluation of industry drivers has created an alternative template for considering any changes to the world's dominant artists. In this new framework, more diversity would originate in the art market before radiating out and influencing expert tastes. Though the art theorist Lotte Philipsen is not a representative of this model per se, she seems to embrace such a globalization scenario, writing that the "global art market is more capable of . . . a New Internationalism. . . . Non-Western contemporary art is given access to the framework of the market on the same terms as Western art" because "capitalism" has grown into a "global system that is culturally and geographically neutral."[39] What counts, after all, in the global art industry is money, wherever and however it can be earned, and the ideological lure of high prices and sales would then feed back into the evaluations of art experts. Yet the model also implies a different temporality of change. Because it suggests that the market dictates the making and breaking of artistic careers within a globalizing context, we can assume that any changes in the types of artists who reach the top would unfold relatively quickly, driven by the sheer "forces of supply and demand."[40]

A Dual Cultural World Economy

Scholars of the market-convergence model have insightfully revised Bourdieu's older conversion theory, making significant connections between global transformations in the art market and shifts in economic valorization for contemporary artists. The model, however, tends to generalize observations about the commercial realm—particularly the auction market—to the entire field. Likewise, claims that aesthetic experts have embraced more commercial- and media-friendly evaluative criteria are not often supported by much empirical evidence. Both Graw and Crane, for example, cite only a few anecdotal quotes from critics to make their case.

Given such omissions, a market-convergence approach risks portraying millennial developments in a way that is too totalizing and deterministic. The

TABLE 4.1. Artistic Careers and Diversity between Expert Valuation and the Market: Three Models

	Bourdieu's conversion model	Market-convergence model	Dual economy model
Artistic careers	Artistic consecration leads to market success.	Market success leads to artistic consecration.	Artistic consecration and market success are more decoupled.
Direction of change	Artistic evaluation shapes market forces.	Market forces shape artistic evaluation.	Market forces and artistic evaluation diverge.
Temporality of change	*Longue durée*	Volatility	Parallel tracks of development (both short and long term)
Globalization and artistic diversity	Diversity in artistic consecration would influence diversity in the market after a time lag.	Diversity in the market would affect diversity in artistic consecration in the short run.	Global transformations entail changes but with different time horizons and patterns.

market gets framed as the main driver of (global) change, while nonmarket art institutions and their intermediaries appear as passive agents swept up by the market's overpowering dynamics. The alternative view that I suggest argues for a more differentiated dynamic, one where cultural experts—though they are not immune to the market's whims and economic pressures—have played a more active and resistant role in the valuation game across borders overall. In contrast to both Bourdieu's conversion schema and a "triumph of market" scenario, a dual cultural world economy model accounts for major commercial changes in the global art market but remains attuned to tendencies of resilience and resistance. As such, it permits us to explore more heterogeneity in (e)valuation patterns in the global field and, by extension, dynamics of artistic diversity.[41]

Specifically, my primary contention is that the contemporary art field's globalization coincided with the rise of commercial forces but that this process did not merge the formerly divided world of "high art" and "the market" into a single monolithic "global art industry." Instead, the previous dominance of expert evaluation has given way to the growing *bifurcation* of expert and market selection systems, each with diverging global infrastructures, stakes, *and* methods of shaping artistic careers.[42] Table 4.1 briefly summarizes how a dual cultural world economy framework differs from the other two theoretical approaches.

Like Bourdieu, the idea of a dual cultural world economy presumes that previously, the market for contemporary art—even though it was always ideologically kept at arm's length—was largely an avant-garde forum of "restricted production," aligned closely with the pole of symbolic capital. The massive transformations that created the global commercial subfield in the twenty-first century have loosened that bond, however. With the rise of worldwide art fair conglomerates, megagalleries, large-scale auction empires, and online sales databases, the contemporary art field, just like other cultural industries, now has an extended pole of large-scale production. This has ultimately created a starker internal segmentation—ideologically *and* structurally—between the expert-driven symbolic sphere (à la Bourdieu) and the commercial one (à la Crane and Graw).

Within the art market, these developments have put tremendous pressure on formerly dominant avant-garde galleries, as I discussed in chapter 3. And yet the fact that the market-centric pole has developed its "own norms and its own canonization strategies" does not mean that the conventional methods avant-garde players use to support innovative, upcoming artists have disappeared.[43] But they have become harder to pursue in a profit-driven competitive environment. Consequently, Bourdieu's traditional market "conversion" path has become less commonplace in the art market game, coexisting alongside logics that create hyped celebrity stars and artists whose rise is driven by a range of other heteronomous factors, including financial speculation.[44] Treating the art market as a more structurally decoupled subfield would accommodate also for the rise of new buyers with "cultural missions."[45] For example, as I found during interviews in Beijing (cf. appendix D), Chinese consumers have used major auction sales as a global stage for asserting the market value of "their" artists for nationalistic reasons. Tactics like these underline how cross-border market valuation has become a more motley, heterogeneous terrain than ever before.

But even as the art market has globalized and commercialized, the pole of symbolic capital has also undergone major transformations in becoming more global (cf. chapter 2), developing its own global institutional circuits and stakes for contemporary art. And these elements, as we will see, have remained relatively resistant to commercial logics.[46] Of course, art institutions and aesthetic mediators depend on revenue and material support. But this does not mean they have relinquished their specific cultural agendas and criteria for choosing and supporting artists altogether. A dual cultural world economy carves out critical space for a relatively autonomous global subfield, suggesting that the situation is more contested than a totalizing notion of a "global art industry" would imply. Though the pole of symbolic capital no longer ideologically dominates the market side as it once did, it has not completely lost its relatively independent logics involved in the shaping of artists' positions and careers. Rather than being discarded, it needs to be updated to capture the nuances of the global field more accurately.

Against this backdrop, the model of a dual cultural world economy offers an alternative perspective on the making of successful artists along the spectrum of "art" and "money," suggesting that the attainment of symbolic and economic capital often diverges in their careers. Contemporary artists may win acclaim from expert mediators, *or* they may sell their work for highest auction prices. But these two phenomena will converge less often over time.

This growing chasm also affects dynamics of artistic diversity. In a more divided economy of valuation, each subspace is marked by its own "specific law of change."[47] At the cultural pole, if innovation continues to be a dominant criterion for symbolic capital—although what that means for *contemporary* artists in the new millennium remains to be specified—changes to the diversity of the world's most valued artists would unfold more slowly than they do in the market-driven zone.[48]

Thus, if artists from more diverse countries increasingly entered biennial circuits at the end of the 1980s, we should expect a time lag before some of them reached the top of the global artistic subfield. Additionally, in line with Bourdieu's idea that change in autonomous subfields is mediated by generational divisions, we can assume that shifting biennial politics and global discourses particularly influenced younger intermediaries, who would be more predisposed to challenge a Western artistic orthodoxy. And if aspiring intermediaries tend to orient their choices around artists in a similar age range and if they need time to accumulate field-specific recognition before fully asserting their heterodox approaches, transformations to a West-centric artistic order would unfold according to the *longue durée* of generational progressions.[49] In other words, the younger the artists, the *more* change we should see.

According to a dual cultural world economy model, we should not observe slower generational rhythms in the global art market, however. Here, more straightforward commercial dynamics would prevail. Note that this assumption aligns with a market-convergence approach, but the dual economy model avoids generalizing it for the entire field. In particular, the rise of new consumers, including "rich collectors from Asia, the Arab region, Russia and Latin America," could unleash relatively rapid but also more volatile changes among the artists with the greatest economic success across borders.[50] At the same time, because this framework presumes that evaluation in the art market has become more decoupled from expert recognition, it implies that new consumer money, and the tastes that come along with it, can have quicker effects on unraveling the global market's established Western hierarchies.

Ultimately, the model of a dual cultural world economy, which attends to the global art field's internal structural differentiation, seeks to more accurately capture the heterogeneity of artistic careers and diverse canons across borders.

Due to its multidimensional frame of reference, it allows us to appreciate how the symbolic status of artists and the aesthetic canons of global art are produced according to cross-border "rules" that cannot merely be reduced to the dictates of a more "industrial" market regime. But it also allows us to see how the latter's strategies for promoting global market stars have "released" commercial agents, to a greater extent, from the specialized judgment and symbolic authority of aesthetic experts.

5

Diversity and Careers in a
Dual Cultural World Economy

TO EXPLORE how globalization has affected the recognition of contemporary artists from around the world with regard to symbolic and market recognition, I draw on data from Artprice and ArtFacts.Net. These online platforms provide rankings that map the relative success of tens of thousands of artists in these two dimensions (see chapters 2 and 3). They offer exceptionally comprehensive sources, a living record of the field's top performers.

Artprice focuses on artists' economic success in the global auction market, based on their annual sales volume. It is a genuinely global enterprise, assembling data from more than two thousand auction houses on six continents.[1] The ArtFacts ranking, by contrast, tracks the visibility and recognition of artists in the global exhibition space. On the basis of a vast digital archive of exhibitions from virtually all corners of the world, it ranks more than one hundred thousand artists. Yet whereas Artprice uses a straightforward monetary logic, ArtFacts follows a more intricate approach. The ranking's assessments operate with a complex multidimensional index that assigns artists "exhibition points."[2] The *New York Times*, paraphrasing the explanation of an ArtFacts associate, describes the process like this:

> To rank these international artists, the staff of Artfacts.net starts by looking at exhibition announcements, newsletters and Web sites. Then the point toting begins.
>
> Solo shows are worth more than group shows. . . . Public museums count more than galleries. And different museums have different weights. Those in cities like Paris or New York count for more. Small museums and university museums count for almost nothing. . . .
>
> And how is a famous gallery or museum defined? Circularly. An institution with famous artists is famous, and a famous artist is one who shows in a famous institution.[3]

Although ArtFacts is not entirely free of limitations, it offers a fitting indicator for symbolic capital because it attempts to represent the evaluation of cultural mediators who do not have straightforward commercial orientations.[4] It deliberately excludes information on sales as well as exhibitions at art fairs or auctions. The ranking aims to capture the "curator's point of view," unveiling the artists who are most favored by exhibition makers on a global scale.[5] As of 2017, the database encompassed more than 750,000 exhibitions and around thirty-seven thousand cultural institutions across more than hundred countries. With such a uniquely wide scope, ArtFacts allows us to empirically explore the shifting global canons of contemporary art according to cultural mediators, distinguishing artists with charismatic consecration from those who lack the symbolic recognition that would enable them to make decisive moves in the globalizing culture game.[6]

Globalizing Canons? Diverging Dynamics of Artistic Diversity

I think the point about the market is that it is short term. You can have a very hot market and artists can become famous very quickly, but the question we have to ask is, "Will they be around in one hundred years?"

—LISA DENNISON, SOTHEBY'S EVP, CHAIRMAN, AMERICAS[7]

Let us first look at the effects globalization has had on the art market. Figure 5.1 charts developments among the hundred best-selling artists according to their relative share in "economic capital" from 1997 to 2017.[8] I derive the distinction between artistic producers from the "Rest" and the "West" from Stuart Hall's critical discussion in which he generalizes Edward Said's notion of Orientalism to a world level.[9] This classification does not specify the national backgrounds of the artists who are involved yet, but the data already reveal dramatic disruptions with regard to previously West-centric hierarchies.

In 1997, before the market's accelerated globalization, sales success was heavily concentrated around artists from Western countries. They accounted for no less than 87 percent of the top tier's sales volume (versus 13 percent of their "non-Western" colleagues from the "Rest" of the world). Yet just a decade later—precisely at the time the global market had come into its own—their sales volume plunged to 48 percent. Simultaneously, the share in "economic capital" of artists from outside the "West" rose from 13 percent to a remarkable 52 percent. That trend did not hold, though, and in 2017, their relative sales sank again to 32.7 percent. Hence, the redistribution of commercial success in favor of the "Rest" followed a relatively rapid but still volatile pattern. Instead

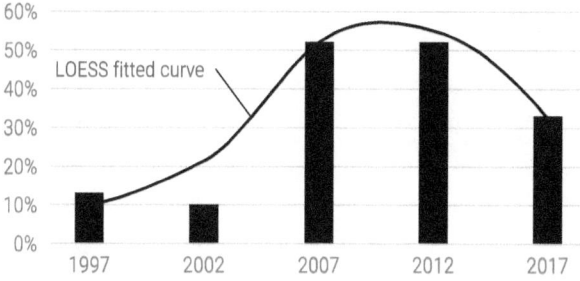

FIGURE 5.1. The share of "economic capital" among the top one hundred contemporary artists from the "Rest" versus the "West" in the global auction market, 1997–2017. (Artprice.com)

of a slow and linear increase—as Bourdieu's theory implies—there is an inverted U-shaped curve, indicating the swings in supply and demand that typify the heteronomous market game.

To explore shifts in artistic diversity more specifically, table 5.1 details the artists' countries of origin and their respective shares in "economic capital." If we follow the range of countries, summarized at the bottom of the table, it becomes clear that the overall national diversity of the commercial elite hardly changed during the considered period. Between 1997 and 2017, it merely increased from twenty to twenty-three. The lists also reveal that among the most successful "non-Western" artists in the globalizing art market, the biggest winners came from Asia, especially China. In 2007, twenty Chinese contemporary artists ascended the global auction market, securing an impressive 43.8 percent market share. Their US-American colleagues, who sold less than half that, settled for second.[10] The extraordinary speed of this change is underlined by the fact that just ten years earlier, China had only one artist in the market's top hundred, giving the country a mere 4.1 percent share overall.

Yet with the market's volatility, China later fell to third place in 2017, with a 14.8 percent share of "economic capital," while US-American artists reclaimed their leading position. Artists from Latin America and Africa were also part of the market's top segment at this time, but Asia nevertheless remained at the forefront, accounting for a collective 22.5 percent turnover among the global commercial elite. Apart from China, there was also demand for artists from Japan—including the Pop painter of children Yoshitomo Nara and the splashy works of the artist-entrepreneur Takashi Murakami—and, to a lesser degree, for painters from India, Iran, Indonesia, and the Philippines.

Undoubtedly, the commercial success of artists from Asia was facilitated by the growing wealth of their countries, especially China. But a political-economy

TABLE 5.1. National Diversity and Market Share among the Top One Hundred Contemporary Artists in the Global Auction Market, 1997–2017

1997		2002		2007		2012		2017	
USA	40.0	USA	39.4	China	43.8	China	41.6	USA	24.7
Germany	14.6	Germany	16.5	USA	19.0	USA	24.6	UK	21.8
Italy	11.1	UK	13.5	UK	16.6	UK	8.5	China	14.8
UK	7.4	Spain	8.4	Germany	6.6	Germany	6.9	Germany	10.9
Spain	5.5	Italy	7.3	Japan	3.4	Japan	3.9	Italy	6.6
China	4.1	Japan	4.3	Italy	2.8	India	2.3	Japan	5.8
Cuba	3.8	Netherlands	1.6	India	2.8	Brazil	2.1	Panama	3.1
Ireland	3.2	France	1.6	Spain	1.4	Italy	1.9	South Africa	2.6
France	2.9	China	1.2	South Africa	0.7	Spain	1.4	Romania	2.3
Argentina	2.5	Ireland	1.0	South Korea	0.5	Ireland	1.1	Nigeria	1.1
Austria	1.3	Iran	0.8	Denmark	0.5	South Africa	0.9	Ireland	1.0
Netherlands	0.7	Australia	0.7	Ireland	0.4	Canada	0.8	Spain	0.9
Panama	0.6	New Zealand	0.7	Switzerland	0.3	Switzerland	0.8	India	0.8
Venezuela	0.5	Brazil	0.7	France	0.3	Taiwan	0.4	Switzerland	0.7
Barbados	0.5	Cuba	0.6	Iran	0.3	France	0.4	France	0.5
Brazil	0.4	Austria	0.4	Indonesia	0.2	Cuba	0.4	Brazil	0.4
Japan	0.3	Argentina	0.4	Cuba	0.2	Iraq	0.4	Iran	0.4
Canada	0.2	India	0.3	Brazil	0.2	Serbia	0.4	Indonesia	0.4
Czech Republic	0.2	Canada	0.2			Philippines	0.4	Philippines	0.3
Switzerland	0.2	Lebanon	0.2			Indonesia	0.3	Ghana	0.3
		Chile	0.2			Puerto Rico	0.3	Belgium	0.2
						South Korea	0.2	Uruguay	0.2
								Colombia	0.2
20 countries		21 countries		18 countries		22 countries		23 countries	

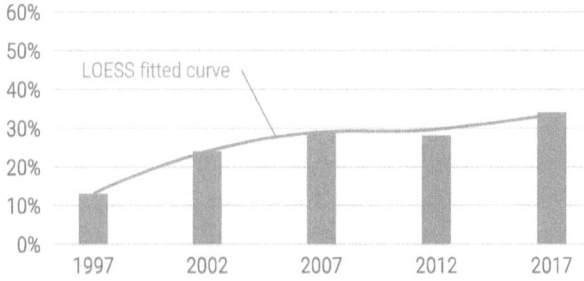

FIGURE 5.2. The share of symbolic capital among the top
one hundred artists from the "Rest" versus the "West" in the
global exhibition space, 1997–2017 (ArtFacts.Net).

rationale can only partially explain the striking rise. As we have seen in chapter 3, as the new millennium got under way, Asia experienced the most dramatic institutional integration into the commercial global subfield, particularly with Hong Kong's ascent as a new art market capital connecting Asia with global players and circuits. The field's transformed institutional power structure was a significant mediating factor for these changes among artists, apart from other historical influences that I address in chapter 7 on the commercial rise of Yue Minjun. For now, it suffices to conclude that the global auction market's relatively rapid dynamics primarily involved a shift in success toward contemporary artists from China and some other Asian countries. That shift, however, remained concentrated to a relatively small number of "non-Western" countries. It did not signal a broader diversification of artists from the "Rest" of the world.

The cultural pole also witnessed important changes in the redistribution of symbolic capital, though they developed according to their own timeline (figure 5.2). As we saw in part 1, the 1990s involved increasing global transformations among biennials, major art museums, and critical discourses. These field-internal changes are reflected in the growing recognition of "non-Western" artists. Between 1997 and 2017, their share in symbolic capital ballooned from 13 percent to 33.7 percent. This means that the cultural pole ended up with a share of artists from the "Rest" that is similar to the commercial pole's (32.7 percent). But it is noteworthy that it took twice as long to reach that level. The overall change was much more gradual but also steadier, following a near-linear progression that aligns with Bourdieu's idea of longer consecration cycles.

Diverging further from the market, the cultural pole asserts itself in the arc of diversity among its elite artists. Table 5.2 summarizes the national backgrounds of the leading hundred artists in the global exhibition space, which

TABLE 5.2. National Diversity and Shares of Symbolic Capital among the Top One Hundred Contemporary Visual Artists in the Global Exhibition Space, 1997–2017

1997		2002		2007		2012		2017	
USA	37.2	USA	25.6	USA	25.4	USA	29.8	USA	18.0
Germany	11.5	Germany	14.0	Germany	13.6	Germany	14.6	Germany	10.0
UK	10.1	UK	11.5	UK	10.7	UK	10.8	UK	9.6
Italy	6.1	Switzerland	4.4	Switzerland	5.1	Austria	3.5	France	6.0
France	5.1	Japan	3.7	South Africa	4.4	South Africa	3.3	Austria	4.5
Belgium	3.0	South Africa	3.3	Austria	3.9	Poland	3.2	Morocco	4.3
Austria	2.8	Canada	3.2	France	2.6	Israel	3.0	Belgium	3.9
Ireland (Rep.)	2.4	Austria	3.1	Mexico	2.6	France	2.7	Switzerland	3.3
China	2.4	Belgium	2.5	Canada	2.3	Belgium	2.0	Denmark	2.5
Japan	2.1	France	2.4	China	2.2	Switzerland	2.0	Poland	2.4
Switzerland	2.0	Italy	2.3	Belgium	2.0	Lebanon	1.8	South Africa	2.4
Netherlands	1.8	Ireland	2.1	Denmark	2.0	Cuba	1.7	Italy	2.3
Portugal	1.6	Mexico	1.4	Cuba	2.0	China	1.6	Nigeria	2.3
Canada	1.4	Brazil	1.4	Poland	1.8	Albania	1.6	Russia	2.1
Australia	1.4	South Korea	1.4	Lebanon	1.7	Canada	1.6	Lebanon	2.0
Spain	1.3	Lebanon	1.3	Lithuania	1.5	Italy	1.5	Ireland (Rep.)	2.0
South Africa	1.3	Australia	1.2	Netherlands	1.5	Ireland	1.5	Canada	1.9
Mexico	1.0	Iran	1.2	Serbia	1.4	Morocco	1.4	Cuba	1.6
Lebanon	1.0	Ivory Coast	1.1	Israel	1.3	Serbia	1.2	Colombia	1.2

Thailand	0.8	Lithuania	1.1	Brazil	1.1	Chile	1.1	China	1.2
Brazil	0.8	Albania	1.1	Romania	1.1	Vietnam	1.0	Albania	1.1
Russia	0.8	Serbia	1.1	Japan	1.0	Japan	0.9	Thailand	1.0
Armenia	0.7	Spain	1.1	Spain	0.9	Iran	0.9	Kenya	1.0
Serbia	0.7	Bulgaria	1.0	Italy	0.8	Denmark	0.9	Algeria	0.9
Denmark	0.7	Finland	1.0	Algeria	0.8	Mexico	0.8	Iran	0.9
		Netherlands	0.9	Iran	0.8	Thailand	0.8	India	0.8
		Denmark	0.9	Albania	0.8	Netherlands	0.7	Serbia	0.8
		Vietnam	0.9	Chile	0.7	Croatia	0.7	South Korea	0.8
		Portugal	0.9	Kenya	0.7	Algeria	0.7	Chile	0.8
		China	0.8	Bulgaria	0.7	Brazil	0.7	Mexico	0.8
		Cameroon	0.8	Argentina	0.7	Slovenia	0.7	Vietnam	0.8
		Cuba	0.7	Australia	0.7	Spain	0.7	Croatia	0.8
		Turkey	0.7	India	0.7	Bulgaria	0.6	Portugal	0.8
				Croatia	0.7			Ethiopia	0.8
				Sweden	0.7			Brazil	0.8
								Sweden	0.8
								Spain	0.7
								DR Congo	0.7
								Israel	0.7
								Argentina	0.7
25 countries		33 countries		35 countries		33 countries		40 countries	

Source: ArtFacts.Net.

are listed along with their shares of symbolic capital. The increasing number in the countries of origin at the bottom immediately suggests that globalization had a stronger impact on diversity. In 1997, both poles' upper echelons featured artists from about twenty countries. Two decades later, the art market remained fairly stagnant (with twenty-three), while the elite level of the global exhibition space nearly doubled in national diversity, encompassing artists from forty countries across five continents.

Strikingly, at the cultural pole, Chinese artists experienced an inverse trajectory to the global auction market. In the same period in which they asserted themselves as commercial leaders, their symbolic capital declined from a 2.4 percent share in 1997 to a mere 1.2 percent share in 2017. Instead, artists born in Africa—that is, Morocco, South Africa, Nigeria, Kenya, Algeria, Ethiopia, and the Democratic Republic of the Congo—garnered the most curatorial attention among the leading "non-Western" artists, ahead of their colleagues from eastern Europe and Latin America. It is yet another significant disjuncture. Not only does the pole of expert valuation follow a different temporality of change and end up being more cosmopolitan, but its cultural experts have also favored artists from different kinds of continents.

We might interpret this preference for artists from Africa with reference to the fact that "members of the cutting-edge have historically identified with marginalized groups, perhaps due to their homologously dominated position" in the broader social space.[11] But we must also think about specific histories involved in the artistic subfield's globalization. Since 1989, widely received exhibitions increased the transnational visibility of African artists and bolstered postcolonial discourses in contemporary art. One thinks of *Magiciens de la Terre* in Paris in 1989; *The Other Story* in London 1989, curated by Rasheed Araeen; and Documenta 11 in 2002, spearheaded by Okwui Enwezor, among others (see chapter 2). Many of the leading artists with an African background in 2017 address postcolonial issues in their work, exploring issues of race and identity, exclusion and integration, and the predicaments of related geopolitics. Thus, at the cultural pole, to ascend to the global artistic elite, it seems that speaking to intellectual discourses that are prevalent among curators and critics is more important than coming from a country with a rising economy. This is a very different dynamic than at the commercial pole, especially with regard to several artists from China.

Lastly, the overall slower rhythms of global transformations in symbolic capital were distinctly mediated by generational dynamics. That becomes clearer if we compare the leading artists among different age groups. As table 5.3 conveys, the younger the generation, the more diverse and de-Westernized the world's most symbolically recognized artists are. This is precisely in line with the generational dynamics of more autonomous subfields.[12] A growing diversity

TABLE 5.3. National Diversity and Shares of Symbolic Capital among the Top One Hundred Contemporary Visual Artists of Three Age Groups in 2017

1945–1954		1955–1964		1965–1974	
USA	37.91	USA	21.49	Germany	12.03
Germany	13.85	Germany	14.04	UK	11.1
UK	7.49	UK	8.09	USA	9.35
Canada	3.95	Belgium	6.02	France	5.3
Austria	3.20	France	5.23	South Korea	5.1
France	2.94	Switzerland	4.80	Morocco	4.74
Japan	2.21	Austria	3.52	Nigeria	3.48
Switzerland	2.12	Spain	3.37	Denmark	3.3
South Africa	2.09	Mexico	2.53	Mexico	3.29
India	2.07	Ghana	2.22	Israel	3.24
Lebanon	2.04	India	2.11	Italy	2.68
Ireland (Rep.)	2.01	South Africa	1.87	Spain	2.64
Greece	1.79	China	1.82	Cuba	2.63
Argentina	1.52	Australia	1.74	Russia	2.61
Serbia	1.48	Netherlands	1.72	Lebanon	2.50
Croatia	1.39	Brazil	1.71	Netherlands	1.73
Brazil	1.37	Thailand	1.49	Poland	1.72
Italy	1.28	Iran	1.43	Austria	1.6
Mali	1.23	Portugal	1.38	Albania	1.58
Egypt	0.87	Finland	1.36	Brazil	1.57
Poland	0.87	Ireland (Rep.)	1.29	Belgium	1.18
Romania	0.87	Chile	1.27	Portugal	1.17
Portugal	0.83	Italy	1.01	Ethiopia	1.16
Spain	0.80	South Korea	0.99	Zambia	1.14
Tanzania	0.75	Vietnam	0.96	Bulgaria	1.05
Lithuania	0.70	Egypt	0.82	Canada	1.02
Albania	0.61	Canada	0.71	Romania	1.01
Turkey	0.61	Denmark	0.69	Iran	0.95
Belgium	0.60	Pakistan	0.69	Guatemala	0.92
Sweden	0.55	Colombia	0.69	Bangladesh	0.90
		Israel	0.67	Japan	0.89
		Greece	0.65	Slovakia	0.83
		Argentina	0.55	Cambodia	0.78
		Poland	0.54	Turkey	0.76
		Romania	0.53	Kenya	0.74
				Cameroon	0.73
				Philippines	0.73
				India	0.72
				Norway	0.58
				Greece	0.55
30 countries		35 countries		40 countries	

Source: ArtFacts.Net.

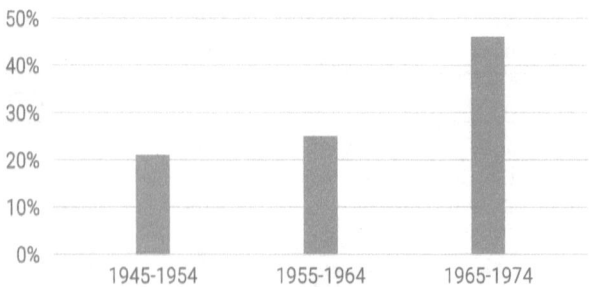

FIGURE 5.3. The share of symbolic capital of "non-Western"
artists among the top one hundred contemporary artists of
three age groups in 2017. (ArtFacts.Net)

among the national backgrounds—from thirty to thirty-five to forty countries
among the youngest cohort—parallels a remarkable upsurge in the collective
symbolic capital of artists from "non-Western" countries. Indeed, as figure 5.3
further illustrates, their share more than doubled among the most recent generation of curatorially championed artists, reaching nearly 46 percent, roughly
equal to their Western peers.

Generational trends toward de-Westernization are also echoed in the dramatic decline of US-American contemporary artists. While those born between
1945 and 1954 held a central position, their collective symbolic capital shrank to
just a quarter of its former share in the youngest age group (37.9 to 9.4 percent).
And although the three most central countries—Germany, the UK, and the
US—still belong to the Western hemisphere, they possess less symbolic capital
(32.5 percent) overall than their "non-Western" colleagues do. Without claiming
a radical change, we can thus speak of a global transformation of Western artistic
dominance that is uniquely mediated by generational cycles.[13]

By contrast, such generational dynamics are not relevant in the global auction market. As figure 5.4 shows, the share of artists from "non-Western" countries in the three age groups follows a nonlinear pattern, while the overall diversity of the artists' national backgrounds remains relatively unaffected across
three generations. These figures underline again how the global field's commercial and cultural poles differ in their patterns of change among worldwide
leading artists.

Any argument that the exhibition landscape has been less open to global
newcomers and more static than the market wilts in the face of these findings.[14]
While the cultural pole's top echelons change more slowly, it has ultimately
diversified more broadly, especially among its youngest cohort. The emergence of
a global artistic subfield since the late 1980s went along with a growing inclination
among curators to engage in "heterodox"—that is, more global—choices of artists

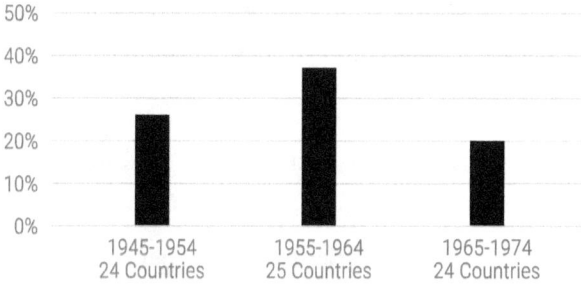

FIGURE 5.4. The market share of "non-Western" artists among
the top one hundred contemporary artists of three age groups
in 2017. (Artprice.com)

vis-à-vis an older Western artistic orthodoxy. But the younger aspirants who
are more likely to enact innovative strategies typically need time to develop
field-specific recognition before they can fully establish their "heretical" agendas. Thus, transformations of a West-centric artistic order become more visible
when one pays attention to the transgenerational rhythms underlying the globalization of the artistic subfield.

The divergences in the diversity of elite artists at the cultural and market-
driven poles are striking and question existing theories. Contrary to Bourdieu's idea of conversion, the developments in the global art market did not
just reflect previous changes in the global exhibition space. Relatively rapid,
volatile dynamics favored Asian artists (especially those from China), and they
appear to be decoupled from the slower, more varied patterns of change at the
cultural pole. The latter's leading artists ended up becoming more cosmopolitan, while the relative status of Chinese artists declined over the same period.
Such discrepancies also run counter to assumptions of the market-convergence
model. The global art market was hardly an overarching, tone-setting force,
and aesthetic experts have operated relatively independently of major market
trends in their selections of artists.

The model of a dual cultural world economy can most readily accommodate these divergences of transformations marking the aesthetic and commercial canons of global contemporary art. However, we should still be cautious
about fully embracing the idea that the cross-border valuation of artists is
mediated by a dual economy. So far, we have traced global changes only according to artists' countries of origin. Such aggregated data might still conceal
a high degree of overlap among *individual* artists, especially for those countries
that still tend to have a strong presence at both poles, like the US, Germany,
and the UK. The findings also tell us nothing about the artists' typical trajectories between "art" and "money" beyond these snapshot years. For a fuller

understanding, we must look more closely at the ways artists traverse these two economies of valorization throughout their careers.

Transcontinental Artistic Careers between Symbolic and Economic Capital

To chart transcontinental trajectories between expert valuation and the market, we should focus on those artists who emerged at the top hundred tier of the global exhibition space and global auction market in 2017.[15]

Visualize the individual careers of these 179 artists as a two-dimensional movement of successive positions.[16] We count the artists' annual positions with regard to, on the one hand, symbolic recognition (based on their exhibition activity according to ArtFacts) and, on the other, their market status (their annual turnover in the global auction space as registered by Artprice).[17] Mapping their careers between 1997 and 2017 in this way involves no fewer than 7,160 positions. It is a massive amount of data, and to identify the most typical trajectory patterns, hierarchical cluster analysis had to come into play (cf. appendix C).

As figure 5.5 illustrates, a cluster analysis reveals four main ideal types of successful careers in the globalizing field, which I designate as: (1) "Autonomous: Mid-Garde"; (2) "Semi-Autonomous: Consecrated Elite"; (3) "Semi-Heteronomous: Winner-Take-All"; and (4) "Heteronomous: Commercial Stars." The autonomous Mid-Garde in the upper left encompasses the second largest and most diverse group: sixty-one artists from thirty-one countries and five continents. With a median birth year of 1970, these artists typically got their careers under way by the mid- to late 1990s, which is reflected in their tendency toward weak exhibition records—and no market presence—in 1997. Over the next twenty years, however, their profiles rose among curators in the global exhibition space. And yet the auction market hardly followed suit. By 2017, when most of these artists had reached midcareer status, their sales in the commercial subfield remained low. Put simply, the most cosmopolitan group of artists—which achieved critical prominence during the years of the biennial boom and rising global discourses—shows the largest discrepancy between higher symbolic capital and lower economic success. As their transcontinental trajectories developed with the greatest distance from the commercial market, we can characterize their trajectory as *autonomous*.

The second career type, on the upper right side, includes thirty-three older artists from fifteen countries on five continents. Their trajectory pattern reaches the highest symbolic prestige among all the groups. They also show steady auction sales, though lower than those of the winner-take-all artists and commercial stars. The median birth year of this smaller group is 1955, meaning

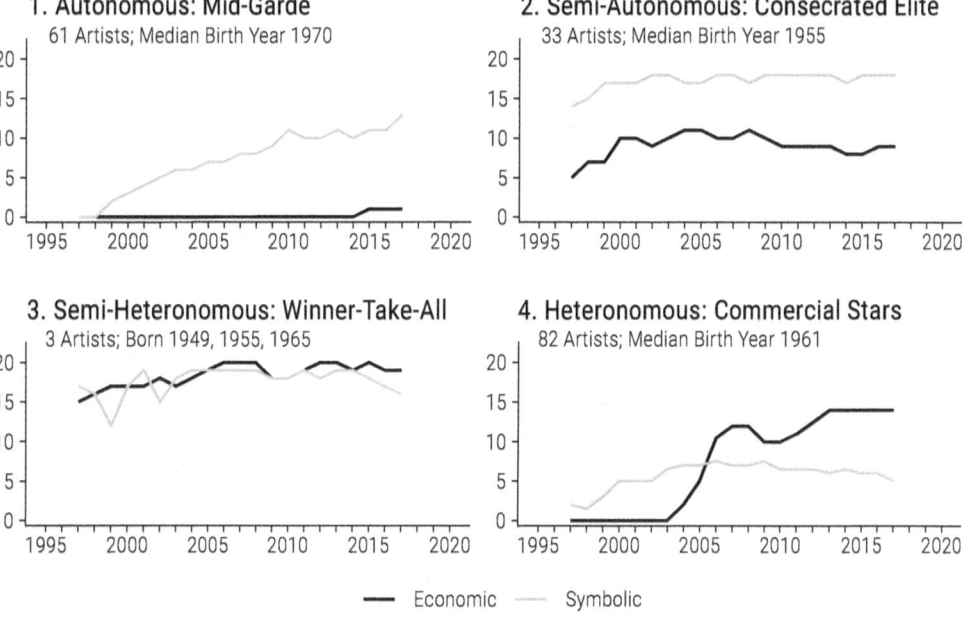

FIGURE 5.5. Four ideal-typical career patterns among globally leading contemporary artists. (ArtFacts.Net; Artprice.com)

these artists typically garnered their initial critical acclaim in the international field of the late 1970s and 1980s. So it is not surprising that they were already active in high-level exhibitions by 1997 and that they sustained that presence over the next decade as institutions for contemporary art multiplied around the world. This career pattern aligns with Bourdieu's conversion model, though overall, their level of curatorial appreciation dwarfed their success in the auction market. We can call them the *semiautonomous* consecrated elite.

The winner-take-all trajectory, which combines exceptional commercial performance with a high level of symbolic recognition, is the third career type. This cluster includes only three artists from the US and UK: Richard Prince (b. 1949), Jeff Koons (b. 1955), and Damien Hirst (b. 1965). In 1997, these artists enjoyed relatively stronger exhibition records than commercial sales, but the market caught up soon enough. Particularly in the new millennium's first decade—right as auction houses expanded further into the contemporary art market—their commercial status skyrocketed. And although their sales declined temporarily after the 2008 financial crisis, these three men largely consolidated their position as the global auction game's megastars. They were not merely market darlings, however. They also maintained a strong foothold at prestigious art institutions. In fact, although trends in their success with curators in the global exhibition space slightly declined between 2014 and 2017, their level of symbolic capital is not wildly different from that of the consecrated elite; in fact, it is the second highest among the four groups. This career type so closely mirrors the market-convergence model that these artists have regularly functioned as its main illustrative examples. Some studies have suggested that their exorbitant commercial success was not just integral to their symbolic consecration but in fact fueled it.[18] Later, I return to the artistic strategies of these three white men. For now, it is important simply to highlight that rather than representing a new major pathway toward success in the global arena, Prince, Hirst, and Koons are actually rare cases. As their pattern of success hews more closely to the commercial pole, they can be designated as *semiheteronomous*.

Commercial stars make up the fourth and largest cluster—eighty-two artists from twenty-two countries on five continents. After the winner-take-all group, they have the most commercial success in the global auction market. But they also have the lowest amount of symbolic capital. With a median birth year of 1961, they tend to be about a decade older than those in the Mid-Garde. Between 1997 and 2007, they experienced a sluggish increase in exhibitions and hardly registered any auction sales before 2003, quite like their Mid-Garde colleagues. But then their auction sales took off. This is especially evident between 2005 and 2008, a period that has been associated with a bubble in the global auction market.[19] Following a spike, this career path tended to involve a relatively high amount of economic turnover until 2017, with a slump during the financial crisis. Interestingly, after 2007, these artists' elevated status in the global auction market went hand in hand with a gradual decline in their symbolic capital, suggesting that their heightened commercial success actually exerted negative feedback effects among cultural experts. This pattern recalls Bourdieu's notion that these agents tend to disdain overly commercial artists. It also contradicts the market-convergence model, which predicts a positive correlation between the two subfields. Nevertheless, it is clear that this career type does not follow Bourdieu's slow and steady market "conversion" pattern either. Their "economic capital" far outweighs their prior symbolic recognition, which becomes especially evident if we compare this group with the consecrated elite. In contrast to the latter, commercial stars, *despite* their lower symbolic capital, end up in a higher market position. As these artists represent the most commercial type of career pattern, they can be considered *heteronomous*.

The four typical trajectory patterns among elite artists demonstrate that the global field is divided into relatively independent spheres of expert and market valuation. The two major subfields—the artistic and the commercial—not only favor artists from different types of national backgrounds but also shape different kinds of transcontinental careers. In this dual economy, Bourdieu's conversion model applies only to the consecrated elite, which is a small group (18 percent of all top artists). The much more frequent career pattern of the commercial star (46 percent), by contrast, involves relatively quick commercial success that far outpaces an artist's previous levels of symbolic recognition. Thus, the global market sets its own values that are distinct from expert tastes. Contrary to the market-convergence model, however, this commercialization does not mean that market success always has positive consequences for symbolic capital. For heteronomous careers, higher sales accompanied a decline in symbolic recognition. Clearly, the idea that "prices now determine reputations" does not reflect a *typical* career pattern. The large group of autonomous artists (34 percent), who received higher curatorial esteem without ever gaining much commercial exposure, further testifies to this gulf between expert evaluation and market signals.

The picture of a divided pattern of success between "art" and "money"— except for the rare winner-take-all types (1.7 percent)—only solidifies further after examining the records of more than 71,832 exhibitions and 10,288 auctions results which we gathered across the *entire* careers of all artists until 2017. Comparing the volume of group and solo exhibitions (figure 5.6), for example, confirms important differences between the two larger groups of autonomous and heteronomous artists. Even though commercial stars tend to be a decade older than the Mid-Garde on the left, they have about 30 percent fewer group and solo shows.

Even more salient, however, is the divide in the *type* of solo exhibitions, which are the most important consecration platforms for contemporary artists (figure 5.7). The two autonomous career types have around two-thirds of their solo exhibitions at public/noncommercial art institutions (59 and 56 percent, respectively) and one-third at galleries as market institutions.[20] For the heteronomous groups, these shares are exactly the opposite. So it is not just the sheer number of exhibitions but more specifically the degree of *noncommercial* exhibitions that distinguishes more autonomous careers from heteronomous ones. In other words, it is about a higher volume *and* a higher "purity" of symbolic capital.

Figures 5.8 and 5.9 round out the picture by detailing the volume of the sales turnover and maximum value of auctioned works for artists' overall careers on the global market side. The figures corroborate that the most autonomous elite artists fare the weakest in the market, with the smallest median turnover and the lowest median price level of $23,000. In stark contrast, the semiheteronomous winner-take-all artists are the most exceptional commercial performers, commanding a staggering median turnover of $554 million across their careers and the highest maximum price level. And while heteronomous artists reach only a fraction of this—which is also due to their shorter time in the auction market—they command the second-highest prices overall. At $2.6 million,

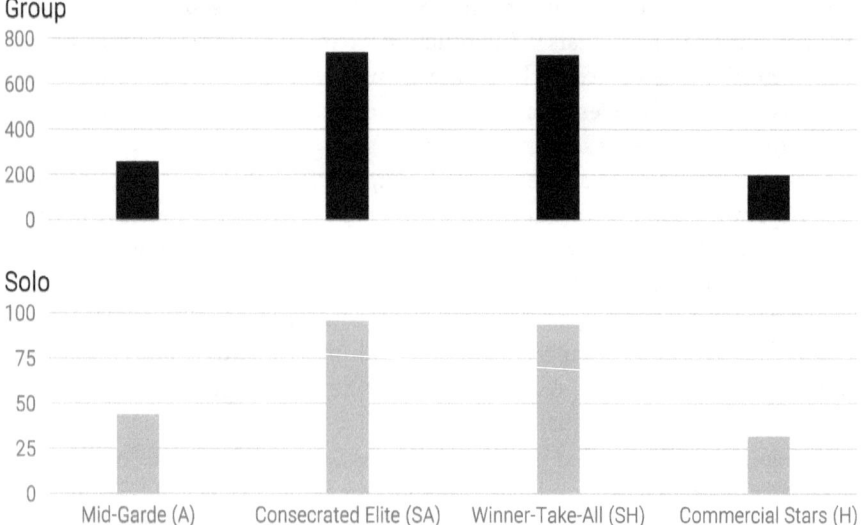

FIGURE 5.6. Median volume of group (black) and solo shows (gray) until 2017.
(ArtFacts.Net, supplemented by extensive research regarding artist CVs published in
art catalogs and on gallery websites, as well as other internet sources)

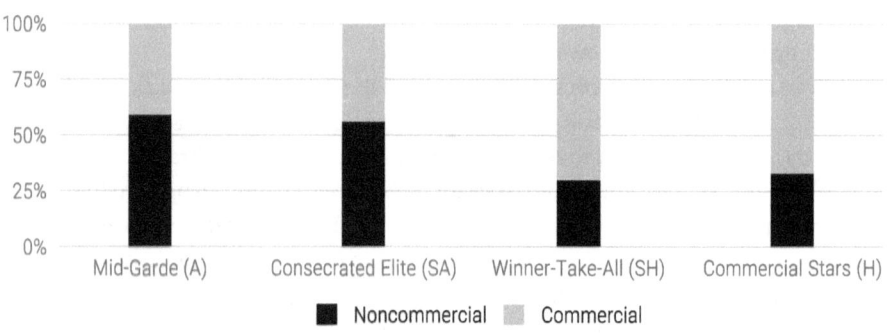

FIGURE 5.7. Median share of solo shows at public/noncommercial art institutions
versus market venues (galleries) until 2017. (ArtFacts.Net, supplemented by
extensive research regarding artist CVs published in art catalogs and on gallery websites,
as well as other internet sources)

their median maximum price is around five times higher than the $450,000 of
the much more critically recognized semiautonomous elite. For a large group
of globally leading artists, price, just like auction turnover, does *not* closely
reflect symbolic capital. The dual economy model holds true yet again.

The four groups confirm a pattern marking the careers of the world's top artists. There is a principal division between those who have reached higher

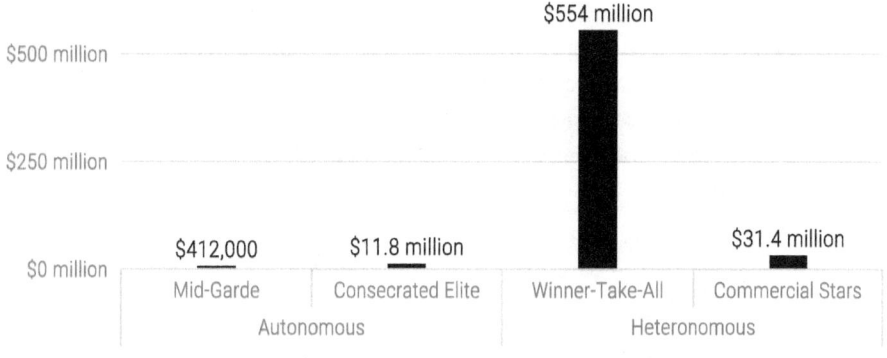

FIGURE 5.8. Median auction turnover until 2017. (Artprice.com)

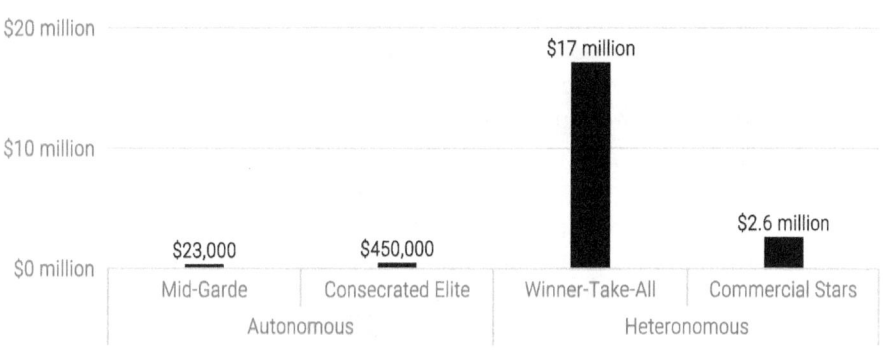

FIGURE 5.9. Median maximum prices until 2017. (Artprice.com; results were cross-checked with sales data from Artnet)

symbolic capital than "economic capital" (ninety-four) and those whose market success outshines their symbolic valuation (eighty-two). Only three artists could achieve convergent victories in both dimensions. These analyses span two decades. They cannot be brushed aside as merely a cross-section of a cyclical boom or bust period in the market. Rather than painting a picture of a transitory constellation, they testify to the globalizing field's dual economy, in which the valorization of contemporary art and the making of related careers have become both ideologically *and* structurally segmented around a divide of "art" and "money."

The Cultural Divides of Global Art

Naturally, looking at artists in view of their symbolic and market success can only offer an initial, cursory understanding of how careers are shaped in the globalizing art field. Other, more specifically cultural factors matter a great deal. On a deeper level, the divisions among critically recognized artists and market stars are intimately bound up with differing modes of cultural production and evaluation that propel their cross-border careers. When we attend to additional biographical characteristics among the artists and the work they create, it becomes clear that deep cultural and aesthetic cleavages mark the global field's top segments.

Sociocultural Divisions

One of the most profound biographical attributes that an artist brings to the game—and one that Bourdieu ignores—is gender. Figure 5.10 sketches out distributions that are unfailingly clear about where men win out.[21] The three artists in the semiheteronomous winner-take-all category are *all* male. Nearly 90 percent of the heteronomous stars are too. As we saw in part 1, the "heteronomous" pole is more closely aligned with the values of mainstream society, and that principle certainly holds here. As it is in societies more broadly, success at the top of the global commercial market favors male producers.

Those dynamics shift significantly, however, among the other two groups. Women make up about 40 percent of the semiautonomous consecrated elite, and the female artists of the autonomous Mid-Garde are almost on equal footing with men with regard to their representation in the field's upper echelons. This suggests that mediators at the specific cultural pole tend to be more open to traditionally marginalized female producers; aesthetic experts make their own "heretical" field-specific choices vis-à-vis external societal hierarchies.[22] In other words, gender disparities reveal that careers at the autonomous and heteronomous poles are either subversive of or closely aligned with broader sociocultural orthodoxies.

Similar imbalances appear in the artists' biographical countries of origin. It is already clear that the most autonomous artists are the most diverse with regard to their national backgrounds (in proportion to their cluster size). But figure 5.11 also validates that they tend to come more often from countries at the outer peripheries of the economic world-system. Around 30 percent of the artists in the autonomous Mid-Garde originate from the poorest, most marginal countries, as opposed to the 14 percent of heteronomous artists who do. As we have seen, that higher proportion reflects the elevated curatorial recognition that artists from Africa have received. More broadly, though, these figures reinforce the idea that the evaluation of artists at the cultural pole is shaped fairly independently from external social or economic hierarchies. The global exhibition space just seems to be more welcoming toward heterodox gender or national diversity than the global market is.

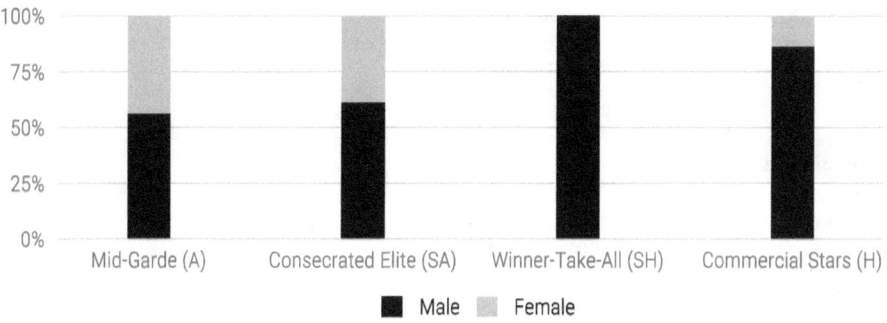

FIGURE 5.10. The distribution of gender among four types of global elite careers.
(data based on internet research on each artist's biography)

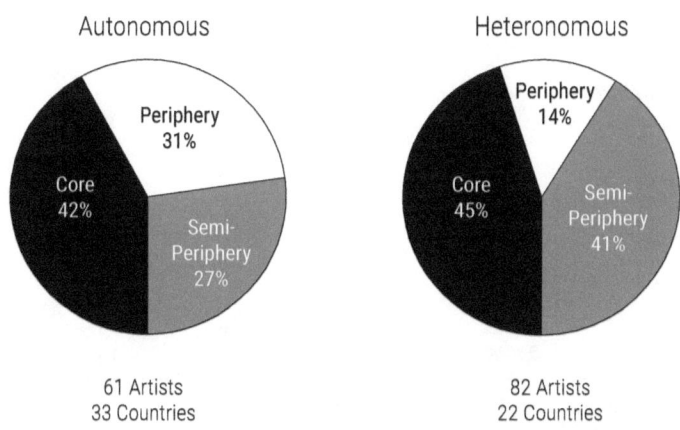

FIGURE 5.11. Artists' countries of origin, according to the hierarchies
of the capitalist world-system.

A Global Aesthetic Cleavage

These biographical variables, however, still do not address the issue that field
participants care most about: the art itself. Table 5.4 summarizes the media
that the artists under consideration have engaged in during their careers.[23] The
first row reveals a sizable gap between two media—installation and painting—
that predominate among the most autonomous or heteronomous artists, respectively.[24] Installation is a much more frequent medium for the autonomous
Mid-Garde: 78 percent of them engage with it, compared to the 15 percent of
commercial stars who do. The latter still clearly favor painting; 86 percent work
in that medium, compared to only 18 percent of autonomous Mid-Garde

TABLE 5.4. Prevailing Artistic Media

	Autonomous		Heteronomous		Absolute difference
	Mid-Garde	Consecrated	Winner	Commercial	
Strongly different					
Installation	78	58	33	15	63
Painting	18	30	100	86	68
Different					
Video art	48	18	0	3	45
Photography	44	67	67	6	38
Film	29	27	0	4	25
Performance	22	21	0	1	21
Drawing	22	21	33	9	13
Concept art	19	30	0	6	13
Text works	5	27	0	0	5
Animation	5	3	0	1	4
Sound art	2	15	0	0	2
Marginally different					
Sculpture	37	36	100	35	1
Textile	2	6	0	0	2
Light sculpture	2	3	0	0	2
Digital art	2	0	0	0	2
Mixed media	5	15	0	6	2
Land art	0	3	0	0	0
Ceramic	0	3	0	3	3
Graffiti	0	0	0	3	3
Print	6	9	0	15	9

Sources: Artists' websites, multiple internet sources, and art critical reviews.

Note: For paintings, the Mid-Garde and Consecrated clusters are similar to each other but are statistically different from the Winner and Commercial clusters that are also similar to each other. For installations, all groups, Mid-Garde, Consecrated, Winner, and Commercial, are statistically different from one another. For video art, Mid-Garde is the only group that is statistically different from the other three groups. For photography, Mid-Garde and Winner clusters are similar to each other but statistically different from the Consecrated and Commercial clusters which are also similar to each other. For film and for performances, the Mid-Garde and Consecrated clusters are similar to each other but are statistically different from the Winner and Commercial clusters which are also similar to each other. For concept art, the Winner and Commercial clusters are similar to one another but are statistically different from the Mid-Garde and Consecrated clusters which are also statistically different from each other. The Mid-Garde, Consecrated, Winner, and Commercial clusters are all similar to each other for all other mediums not specifically mentioned. "Statistically different" was determined at the 0.05 significance level.

artists. It is a nearly chiastic pattern. The second tier reveals further artistic differences—albeit not as stark—with regard to autonomous artists' stronger embrace of video art, photography, film, performance, and conceptual art. The final grouping aggregates artistic media that are either distributed relatively equally among the four career types or whose variance is insignificant.[25]

For insiders, it comes as no surprise that painting is prevalent among the global market's leading artists. The medium's long history means that it is more traditional and thus accessible, naturally making it "the most saleable form of art."[26] Of course, painted artworks can vary tremendously in their aesthetic and innovative features, so it is important to note that the prevalent painting styles among the commercial stars tend to involve popular, conventional forms and techniques. They are often figurative and realistic—including styles like Neo-Pop (including Superflat), Neo-Expressionism, Neo-Realism, Artificial Realism, and Cynical Realism—rather than abstract or formally experimental. The perfect aesthetic recipe for success at the commercial pole, then, seems to involve a mix of a traditional medium with realistic styles that have broad appeal.

It is striking, however, that painting is *not* a preferred medium among the most symbolically recognized autonomous producers, for whom it ranks eighth. This finding underlines that we cannot say that museum curators, for example, champion different artists than the auction market does because they cannot afford to follow the latter with regard to their acquisitions—that they would just be priced out, so to speak.[27] Rather, and contrary to the market-convergence model's predictions, the tendency to reward those artists who gravitate toward installation confirms that cultural mediators make independent decisions in their choices of artworks that do not necessarily mirror dominant market trends.

Installation is an artistic practice that, by and large, defies easy commodification. Strictly speaking, it is not a medium at all. Instead, it involves mixing several media, including video, performance, objects, and even painting in ways that are frequently site specific and context dependent.[28] Like conceptual and postconceptual art, it often engages with intellectual discourses like feminism, race, postcolonialism, identity, and consumer culture.[29] Installations also tend to reject a traditional focus on form by constructing spatial environments—which can sometimes be quite large—and by favoring immersive sensory experiences that foreground the "feeling of a body moving through a particular space surrounded by huge video projections or work that has weight, fragrance, vibration, or temperature."[30]

With installation's often more ephemeral, site-specific character and its emphasis on critical intellectual discourse over object-centered aesthetics, it goes beyond traditional understandings of art; and as an artistic practice, it is less conducive to transposable market exchange. The sheer size of some installations exacerbates this issue. Compared to painting, it embodies a "medium" that is clearly harder to commodify.

While installation is not a great fit for the commercial pole, it is critical in this context that the medium's history is closely intertwined with the emergence of the global artistic subfield, especially the biennial circuit. Though this contemporary art practice originated in the 1960s, it really came to greater promi-nence in the 1990s.[31] Installations' tendency toward transitory, heavily contextual-ized experiences echoed the way biennials were structured as temporary, situated exhibition events.[32] Julian Stallabrass even suggests that biennial curators invited site-specific installations to heighten attention from the art world public. One simply had to go to a biennial to experience these works, which could thus function as "powerful magnets" for increasing attendance.[33] In short, it is no coincidence that for the autonomous Mid-Garde, who made their careers in this globalizing context, installation is the most prevalent artistic practice.

Video art, the second-most-chosen medium among the autonomous elite, is not straightforwardly commercial either.[34] Like installation, it has been a "preferred idiomatic" medium in the global biennial circuit.[35] Hans Belting has compellingly argued that the medium is uniquely suitable to function as a shared visual language for "global art" because it is relatively young and does "not depend on the genealogy of Western art history" and long-standing Eu-rocentric exclusions.[36] As such, it can more easily facilitate a contemporary "global dialogue" for artists from across the world.[37] The fact that the autono-mous Mid-Garde is also the most diverse in view of its artists' backgrounds supports this argument for the global artistic subfield.

These aesthetic cleavages across the autonomous-heteronomous spectrum add crucial perspective to the market-convergence model's proclamations of an overarching "global art industry." Leading curators and art institutions in the global artistic subfield tend to follow aesthetic criteria that are not only different but often opposed to global market trends. Bourdieu's arguments concerning an anticommercial ideology that reigns in the "restricted" sphere of high cultural experts still seems valid in light of these patterns. But it is also clear that Bourdieu's original model must be revised to account for the twenty-first century's global aesthetic divides. The prevailing media among leading artists at the cultural pole tend to be associated with discursive rather than strictly formalist innovation, which makes Bourdieu's emphasis on a modern-ist *l'art pour l'art* logic outdated (see chapter 6). Simultaneously, these media are characterized by an ability to enter transcontinental artistic exchange and circuits. The relevant aesthetic capital for making a global (rather than na-tional) career at the relatively autonomous pole has an inherent global dimen-sion itself. On the other hand, the artistic position-takings of commercial art stars put Bourdieu's notion of "conversion" into perspective. The fact that the global art market rewards male artists who engage in object-centered media and accessible styles underlines that contemporary art's internal split occurs not despite but *because of* the radicalization of heteronomous logics—away from a stronger orientation around the judgment of aesthetic experts.

Lastly, these divisions are reflected in different volumes of "cultural capi-tal."[38] Given the innovative media and discursivity that autonomous creators

TABLE 5.5. Overall Years of Arts Education

	Autonomous		Heteronomous	
	Mid-Garde	Consecrated	Winner	Commercial
Median	6	6	4	4
Mean	6	5.7	3.7	4.3
Standard Deviation	2.2	2.1	0.6	2.0
N	61	33	3	82

Note: There are significant differences at the .05 level between autonomous and heteronomous career types for this variable. Clusters 1 and 2 are the same. Clusters 3 and 4 are the same.

gravitate toward in their artistic practices, it is not surprising that they have spent around a third more time at art schools than their commercial counterparts have (see table 5.5). The median and mean length of schooling is six years for autonomous artists and four for heteronomous artists. And while one Mid-Garde artist had fourteen years of formal art education, the commercial stars include two artists who were self-taught. These differences in cultural capital further highlight a principal cleavage in modes of artistic production and mediation. They speak to the idea that successful autonomous artists tend to engage in conversations that are more deeply embedded *internally* in the art field, both through the media they work in and because of the additional time they have spent at art school, a space that would give them time to think about and engage with field-specific discussions and innovations. More indirectly, these data reveal that curators more readily value creators with high amounts of cultural capital than mediators and audiences in the global auction market do.

Thus, to achieve recognition in the globalizing artistic subfield, artists have to command relatively higher volumes of cultural capital and embrace nontraditional artistic practices that resist easy commodification and accord with its distinctive global circuits. Yet the very forms of capital that give autonomous artists an advantage among experts disqualify them from attaining major success in the global market. The opposite is true as well. A model involving a dual world economy seems best suited for capturing this internal polarization in the prevailing "subcultures" of aesthetic creation and evaluation in global art.[39]

The Exception to the Rule: Winner-Take-All Stars in the Lineage of Andy Warhol

DAMIEN HIRST: I don't agree with the old van Gogh thing that artists are supposed to suffer for their art, but a lot of people still believe that's the way it should be. I think it's tragic that great artists die penniless. I think Warhol made it ok for artists to deal with money and not be seen as a sellout. How's your relationship with money now that you're selling for mega bucks?

RICHARD PRINCE: Warhol made a lot of things possible. . . . I've been rich and I've been poor. I'd rather be rich.[40]

But if the global art field is marked by a cultural divide, how have a minority of winner-take-all stars been able to bridge the gap? What is it about their art that allows them to occupy a seemingly untenable position amid countervailing forces? From a dual economy perspective, it is only logical that these three artists—Richard Prince, Jeff Koons, and Damien Hirst—deliberately subvert the polarity between art and money in their practices in the tradition of Andy Warhol. Their bridging capacity is aesthetically mediated.

As is well known, it was part of Warhol's heretical practice that he questioned the idea of the traditional avant-garde artist's distance from the market and celebrity culture. He created artistic distinction precisely by bringing the poles of high art and commerce into a controversial yet innovative tension, which eventually earned him both critical recognition and market success.[41] Hirst, Prince, and Koons all follow Warhol's idea of the "business artist," though they have radicalized it by further exploring the boundaries of consumer and celebrity culture, kitsch, pornography, finance, and unabashed commercial self-branding.[42] In other words, their extended play with commerce and cultural industries is a foundational element of what makes their art distinctive within the field's charged schisms. It also makes their exorbitant commercial success an inherent part of their artistic reputations.

The American Richard Prince, the oldest among the three, made his name in the late 1970s by appropriating and decontextualizing pictures from consumer and popular culture as fine art. He famously rephotographed images from cigarette advertisements and, following Warhol's exploration of celebrity culture, copied promotional head shots of movie stars. Prince's techniques of appropriating and manipulating generic images from the mass media earned him critical recognition as a pioneer of the "Pictures Generation" and an artist who uniquely fetishizes his motives by using "an aesthetic procedure that intensifies the glow of the original image" from consumer culture.[43] But since the late 1990s, his provocative lack of distance toward consumerism and celebrity has become more pronounced. In 2007, he also entered a commercial collaboration with the luxury brand Louis Vuitton, submitting to tendencies of artistic "corporatization" that had been pushed by the Japanese Pop artist Takashi Murakami just five years earlier.[44]

Jeff Koons, the "Wall Street broker-cum-celebrity artist," also made his career through a provocative engagement with commodity culture.[45] His emblematic *Banality* series from the 1980s appropriated the aesthetics of porcelain kitsch figurines in enlarged sculptures, the most famous of them being one of the Pop star Michael Jackson and his chimpanzee (*Michael Jackson and Bubbles*, 1988). In a subsequent series from the 1990s, the "superstar of kitsch" moved on to create large sculptures and paintings of balloon dogs, Easter eggs, diamonds, and Valentine hearts, oversizing them into shiny steel art objects in dazzling colors.[46] Critics have debated how much critical irony Koons brings to such works, but contrary to the old norms of avant-garde art, Koons openly declares that he is not trying to disrupt popular taste and is simply aiming to make art that allows people to "feel good."[47]

Damien Hirst, the youngest among these three artists, began his career in the 1990s with a series of preserved animals in glass vitrines filled with formaldehyde. The shock value of these works turned him into an instant art celebrity, yet what aligns him most with this line of artists is how he has pushed his business activities. Like Warhol and Koons, Hirst established a company in which assistants churn out art products according to instructions, which he then furnishes with his brand name. One of his notorious works—*For the Love of God*, 2007—directly plays with questions about art's economic value. Consisting of a human skull covered with 8,601 diamonds and embellished in the middle with a 52.4-carat pink diamond in the shape of a pear, in material terms, it is the most expensive contemporary work of art ever made.[48] Priced at $100 million, the work ended up in an "investment consortium" that involves Hirst (who maintains a 24 percent speculative stake in it), his dealer, and an anonymous third party. For the cultural theorist Mark Taylor, this "deal" marks Hirst as an artist who drives the financialization of art to the extreme.[49]

The provocations that these three artists have launched against the ideological oppositions of art and money, which Warhol had pioneered, have caused controversy. But these same debates have also garnered them critical relevance. All three men have received extensive attention from leading art journals and theorists, and they have been featured in major solo shows at prestigious museums.

At the same time, these artists' commercial moves created "highly accessible art" that is of "simple character . . . and faux-expressive," turning it into "populist art."[50] It is a type of art that appeals to "time poor" super-rich collectors from the financial, fashion, and luxury worlds, those looking for "quick, easy, showy, branded art" that mirrors, rather than questions, the broader cultures of their life-worlds.[51] And it is no coincidence that the market careers of these artists were propelled by radically sales-oriented dealers and conspicuous auction sales that serve this exact same audience. Charles Saatchi pushed Hirst's work early on, and Prince benefited from hedge-fund investors who worked together to increase prices for his work.[52] With such alliances, these artists have become true outliers in their combination of relatively high symbolic recognition *and* megacommercial success. Contrary to market-convergence apologists, however, they are deviant cases. They occupy an extreme position that very few can reach and cleverly master, an exception to the general rule. And perhaps most importantly, it is the very dual structure of the field that has created the foundation from which their artistic strategies gained distinctive meaning and symbolic value to begin with.

Geographies of Circulation and Migration

Another fundamental factor influencing artistic careers across borders is geography. Bourdieu did not consider this dimension in his cultural fields theory, but once the inquiry assumes a transcontinental scope, territorial factors—including circulation patterns of artworks and the migration of their producers—can indeed become "destiny" with regard to who enters global art canons.[53] But how geographic contingencies affect careers in the globalizing field varies between symbolic capital and market success.

As we saw in part 1, the contemporary art field underwent massive transformations over the past thirty years, developing expanded global infrastructures and logics. Those changes are apparent in the careers of its leading artists, which spread across an ever-widening range of countries and continents. In terms of symbolic recognition, the role of globality becomes clear when we compare the four career types with regard to their foreign exhibition activity (figure 5.12) and their geographic scope (figure 5.13). Both the Mid-Garde and the Consecrated Elite hold more than two-thirds of their group and public solo exhibitions in foreign countries. For market darlings at the heteronomous pole, however, the situation is almost the opposite: their exhibitions tend to cluster on their own national turf. Perhaps this reflects what a recent study called a "strong home bias" among contemporary artists' exhibitions, but these differentiations suggest that artists with high critical recognition tend to elude that local pull more than their commercially oriented colleagues do.[54]

If we further consider the spatial scope of exhibitions, the four major career types all engage with art institutions beyond the regional level, showing their work on more than one continent. Yet autonomous types of artists with higher symbolic capital have had more globally dispersed exhibitions. In the aggregate, group shows involving the Mid-Garde and the Consecrated Elite reach an impressive median value of five continents. Many of these artists likewise have been invited to solo shows on three or four continents, meaning they have transcended the "international" field's older, transatlantic scope in this key form of artistic consecration. It is noteworthy that the geographic scope of circulation among these two career types is almost equal, although artists

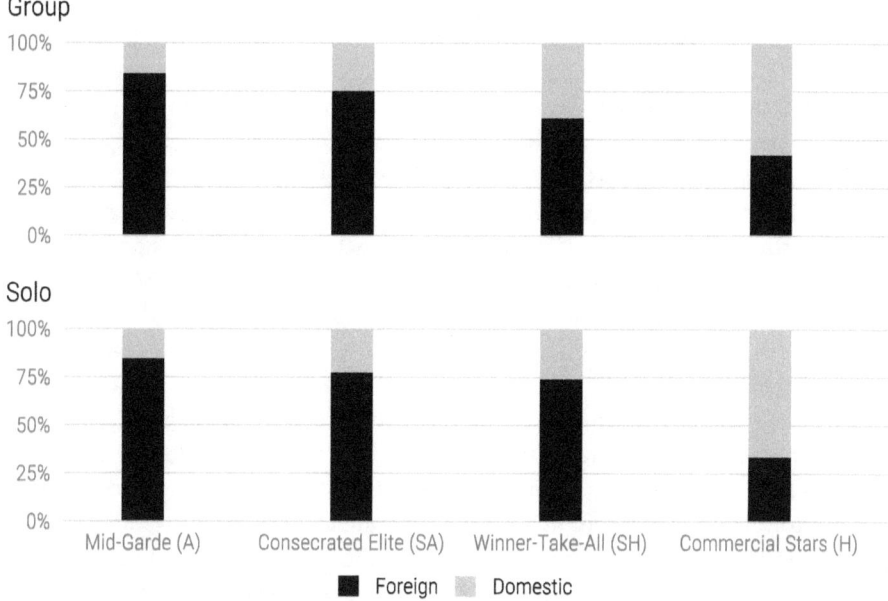

FIGURE 5.12. *Top,* share of foreign group shows (median); *bottom,* share of foreign public/noncommercial solo shows (median) as of 2017.

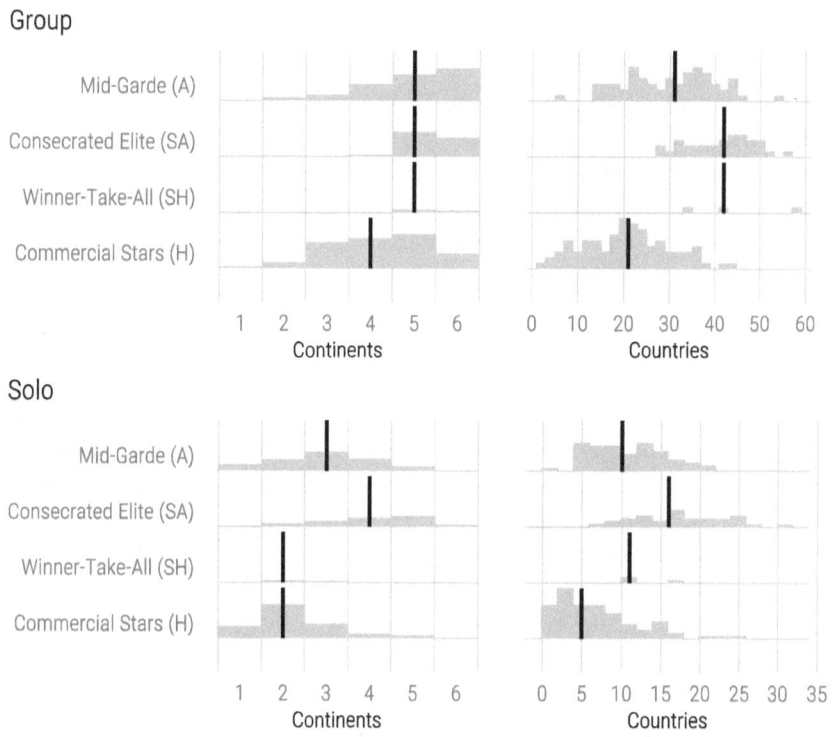

FIGURE 5.13. The spatial distribution of group and public/noncommercial solo exhibitions (from top to bottom) as of 2017. The black vertical lines symbolize median values.

in the Mid-Garde tend to be around fifteen years younger and have fewer exhibitions under their belt. Given that this generation had their foreign debuts around the turn of the new millennium—a time when the global expansion of the artistic subfield was in full swing (chapter 2)—it makes sense that they would be able to gain a broad exhibition presence at an earlier career stage.

The three winner-take-all artists can only match this type of geographical dispersal with their group exhibitions. When it comes to public/noncommercial solo shows until 2017, Koons and Prince have only exhibited in Europe and North America, while Hirst, like the Mid-Garde artists, has reached at least three continents. Commercial stars tend to be the most territorially confined once again, with a median of four continents for group exhibitions and two for solo shows. Overall, what distinguishes the Mid-Garde and Consecrated Elite at the relative autonomous pole is that they more regularly show their work beyond their countries of origin and have a wider transcontinental reach. In simplest terms, higher specific symbolic capital tends to go along with the most far-reaching cultural circulation across borders—that is, the most globality in the artistic subfield.

Even as an expanded geographic scope has become a hallmark of the most critically recognized artists, these careers often still depend on being firmly present in a few institutional centers in the Northwest. In the autonomous and semiautonomous career categories, more than 90 percent of the artists had most of their public/noncommercial solo shows in North America and Western Europe, whereby few countries stand out as exhibition centers with consistently high concentrations, especially the US and Germany (see table 5.6). And semiheteronomous producers even exhibited all most often in the US. Only the artists in the heteronomous group are not as heavily associated with these places. Around 16 percent of them had the largest volume of their solo exhibitions in China, their home country. As we have seen earlier, this corresponds with the fact that commercial artists with lower critical recognition are more confined to the domestic terrain for their exhibitions in general.[55] Given these distributions, the overall pattern is clear and echoed by the data regarding group exhibitions (table 5.7). Careers with higher symbolic capital and more globality are still heavily dominated by a few Western centers. Worldwide critical recognition is forged by geographies that simultaneously show signs of broader transcontinental extension and concentration.

The US and Germany dominate global career-making, not least because they are awash in field-specific forms of macro capital, including the highest volume of transnational art institutions in the world (see chapter 2).[56] With such high concentrations of exhibition resources and expertise, it is critical to note that the US and Germany function as truly cosmopolitan art centers within the globalizing field. In fact, the lion's share of autonomous artists who

TABLE 5.6. Countries Where Artists Had the Majority of Their Public/Noncommercial Solo Exhibitions (until 2017)

Autonomous		Semiautonomous		Semiheteronomous	Heteronomous	
Mid-Garde (%)		Consecrated (%)		Winner-Takes-All (%)	Commercial (%)	
USA	23	USA	53	USA 100	USA	40
Germany	22	Germany	28		China	16
France	13	UK	11		Germany	10
Other (17)	42	Other (3)	8		Other (17)	34

TABLE 5.7. Countries Where Artists Had the Majority of Their Group Exhibitions (until 2017)

Autonomous		Semiautonomous		Semiheteronomous		Heteronomous	
Mid-Garde (%)		Consecrated (%)		Winner-Takes-All (%)		Commercial (%)	
USA	24	USA	64	USA	67	USA	49
Germany	24	Germany	24	UK	33	China	22
France	24	UK	6			Germany	10
Other (10)	28	Other (2)	6			Other (9)	19

Note: The numbers in parentheses after "Other" refer to the number of other countries in each cluster.

have most of their exhibitions there are *not* US-American or German.[57] New York and Berlin in particular serve as global consecration hubs for artists from all world regions.

The weight of these Western centers for the making of symbolic capital in the globalizing field is underlined by the fact that successful autonomous artists also tend to live and work in them—or did at one time. In most cases, corporeal integration into one of these territorially demarcated networks of artists, critics, curators, and gallerists has been necessary for careers with high recognition at an expanded global scale.[58] The US and Germany, and especially the cultural capitals of New York and Berlin, figure as the biggest migration magnets for artists from around the world (see figure 5.14). France and the UK, particularly their urban centers, likewise exert a considerable pull, though their immigration flows are much less diverse and are more patterned around older colonial ties with countries in Africa and Asia.

Thus, for symbolic valuation in the global field, the worldwide proliferation of biennials and exhibition institutions and the expanded mobility of artists and mediators have not fully overthrown a geography of power in which a few institutional centers stand out.[59] Nor has digitization, and its promise of unprecedented communication across the globe, brought about a deterritorialization

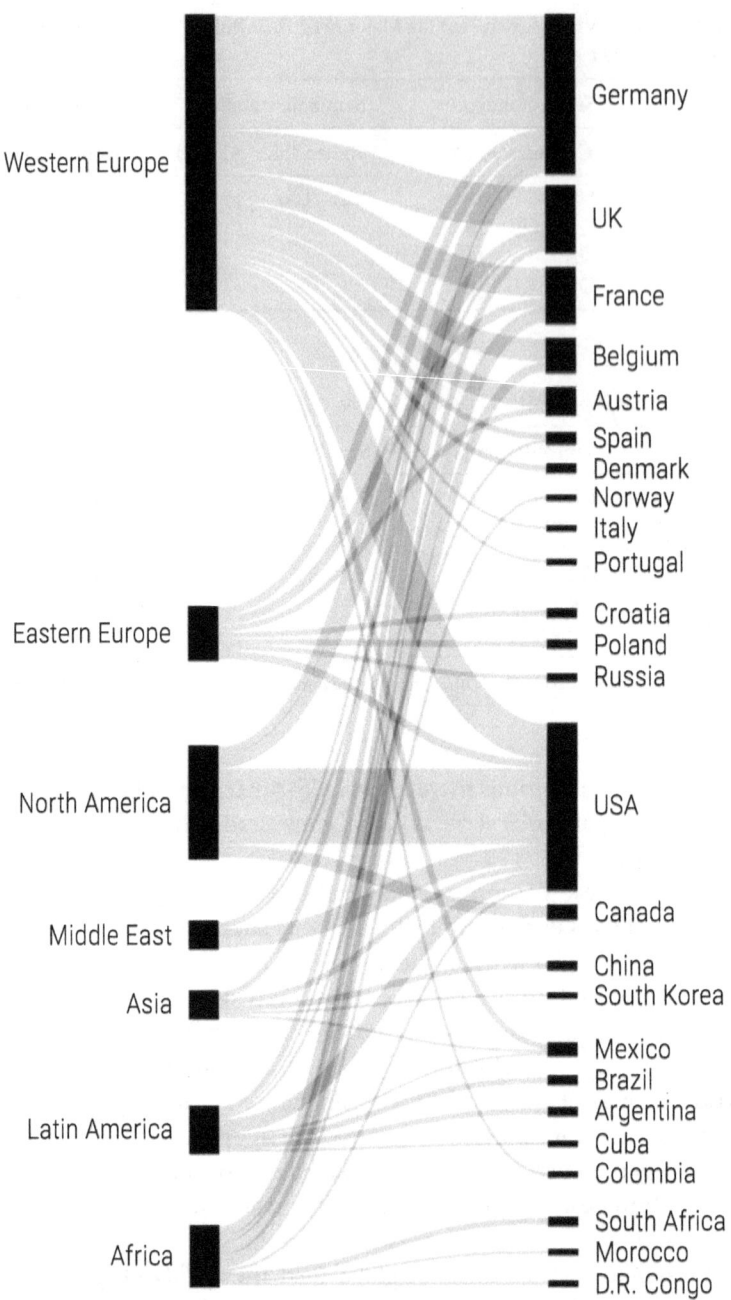

FIGURE 5.14. Migration flows among top autonomous global artists (mid-garde and consecrated elite). This graph matches the region of the artist's country of birth with their (multiple) countries of residence as of 2017.

with regard to the production and mediation of aesthetic canons at a global level.

Going beyond any crude center-periphery notions, however, we need to recognize that in the course of the artistic subfield's globalization, these metropolitan centers are no longer as West-centric as they used to be. With the growing visibility of diasporic artists and curators from around the world and with the rise of global discourses and the increasing opening up of art institutions to these producers—signaled, among other things, by the rising diversity among autonomous elite artists—they have themselves become more globalized and decentered *from within*. Ultimately, the role that these global art centers played, and the logics they employed, *transformed* as they moved from the older international order into an expanded field of exchange and struggle (see chapter 2).

Moving to geographies of valuation at the commercial pole, globality has become a prominent career feature of leading contemporary artists as well, but it also varies across the different career types. The winner-take-all megastars—who, of all artists, enjoy the greatest market success—also tend to have the largest geographical reach with regard to sales (figure 5.15). Until 2017, works by both Hirst and Koons have appeared in auctions on six continents, and Prince's work has reached at least three. Their territorial scope aligns with a majority share of auctions in foreign countries, at around 60 percent (figure 5.16). These numbers differ starkly from the autonomous Mid-Garde. Given the latter group's lower commercial appeal, it makes sense that their works have more limited market circulation, with a median of only three countries and largely within traditional European and North American strongholds. The older semiautonomous elite, by comparison, could achieve a broader territorial scope with their sales. With a median of three continents, most of them have expanded beyond the established Northwest into other market regions, particularly Asia. Forty-five percent have even appeared in auctions on at least four continents.[60] We might relate this to their longer history and volume of sales in the market, as well as the fact that they boast the highest proportion of auctions on foreign territory (70 percent). Meanwhile, works by commercial artists at the heteronomous pole, despite being younger and newer to the market than the consecrated artists, tend to go up for auction on three continents, with around a quarter of them reaching four or more.[61] One commercial outlier, Takashi Murakami—the Japanese business artist with an incredible 5,332 auction lots over two decades—hits six, on par with the winner-take-all business artists.

Previous sociological contributions have highlighted the continuing weight of local ties and sales in the contemporary art market, and Arjun Appadurai's regionalist flow and networks model emphasizes the importance of regional circuits (see chapter 1).[62] But the geographic patterns laid out here point to

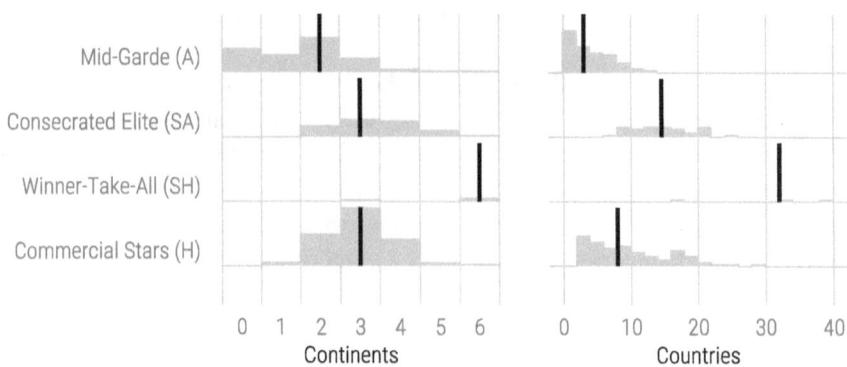

FIGURE 5.15. The spatial distribution of auction sales as of 2017. The black vertical lines symbolize median values.

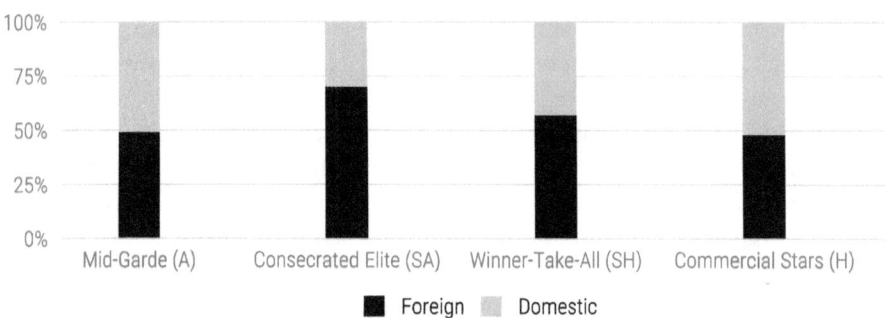

FIGURE 5.16. The share of foreign auction sales as of 2017 (median).

globalization's significant impact on the scope of commercial circulation beyond single world regions. Yet higher globality in sales still primarily accrues to those artists who have been around longer in the auction market and who command a larger market share to begin with. In other words, a higher volume of "economic capital" is associated with a broader territorial reach, a clear sign of the rise of a more global logic in the art market's top tier (see chapter 3). Correspondingly, the circulation of artworks by the autonomous Mid-Garde tends be the most confined in the global commercial subfield, an inversion of their relatively high globality in the exhibition sphere.

Nevertheless, while artists with a strong market presence have a high degree of globality, the majority of sales among elite artists still cluster around a few centers as well. As tables 5.8 and 5.9 demonstrate, the US and the UK are the leading duopoly in the market for all career types, though they share different proportions. These two countries, and especially their auction capitals of New

TABLE 5.8. Countries Where Artists Had the Most Auction Sales (until 2017)

Autonomous		Semi-Autonomous		Semi-Heteronomous		Heteronomous	
Mid-Garde (%)		Consecrated (%)		Winner-Takes-All (%)		Commercial (%)	
UK	33	USA	55	USA	67	USA	41
USA	26	UK	30	UK	33	UK	19
France	15	Germany	9			Hong Kong	13
Other (6)	26	Other (2)	6			Other (8)	27

Note: Cities for autonomous artists only pertain to the 76% who had an auction debut. The numbers in parentheses after "Other" refer to the number of other countries in each cluster.

TABLE 5.9. Cities Where Artists Had Their Highest Prices (until 2017)

Autonomous		Semi-Autonomous		Semi-Heteronomous		Heteronomous	
Mid-Garde(%)		Consecrated (%)		Winner-Takes-All (%)		Commercial (%)	
London	41	New York	42	New York	67	New York	34
New York	24	London	36	London	33	London	30
Paris	17	Paris	12			Hong Kong	15
Other (7)	18	Other (2)	10			Other (6)	21

Note: Cities for autonomous artists only pertain to the 76% who had an auction debut. The numbers in parentheses after "Other" refer to the number of other countries in each cluster.

York and London, are the nerve centers for sales and the highest prices of works by most artists, which aligns with their field-specific resources as well. As we saw in chapter 3, as the locations of Sotheby's and Christie's flagship venues, they also commanded the highest density of beta auction houses worldwide and enjoyed tax- and trade-friendly regulations. In other words, their centrality coincides with their relative wealth of institutional macro capital in the global commercial subfield. Their pattern of geographic dominance has been relativized among the most heteronomous artists through the rise of an alternative market center in Asia: Hong Kong. The Chinese special administrative region has assumed the role of a third central location for the commercial career type. But while the US and the UK serve as major platforms for works by artists from around the world, Hong Kong has a stronger regional focus. It is the chief location for art sales by heteronomous stars from Asia, particularly China, and it serves them as an important gateway to other market venues around the world.[63] Of the artists who have had their highest sales and prices in Hong Kong, 80 percent have been featured in auctions on at least three other continents. Thus, Hong Kong stands as a regional center with transcontinental relevance, a regional-global market hub for the making of commercial stars. This power position aligns with a strong concentration of art market related resources as well (see chapter 3) but does not translate beyond the market. In fact, the Asian hot spot does not play a role at all for exhibition careers, while Germany, a global cultural hub for the latter, significantly loses relevance in this commercial cartography of power in turn. Territorial hierarchies at the two poles do not necessarily coincide, given their divergent forms of macro capitals.

What is more, within this commercial geography of power, migration rates among heteronomous career types are much lower than those of autonomous artists (see figure 5.17). Around 60 percent of cultural producers from outside central market locations continue to reside in their home countries, even though their careers involve sales abroad, which contrasts with the 15 percent among both autonomous elites who stayed and the overwhelming majority of 85 percent who left.[64]

The biggest exception in this pattern are artists from Africa, who *all* had to migrate from their country of birth to make it to the top. But the overall implication is clear: for artists who are not born in global market centers, reaching the top tier has far less to do with *direct* bodily presence within them.[65] Although commercial valorization is dominated by a few geographic centers that play an outsized role in brokering deals, they exert less of a gravitational pull on artists' actual *lives*. As we will see in part 3, such strikingly different migration dynamics need to be understood in relation to mediation practices and cultural dynamics on the ground. Because auction transactions operate most of the time at arm's length—that is, without the artist's direct involvement—art producers can become global market stars without ever leaving their home country. Moreover, culturally, emphasis on an artists' home country can function like an "authentic" geo-aesthetic asset in the global marketplace, which could be a liability in the global artistic subfield. For autonomous artists, in contrast, the continuing requirement of physical proximity to a few cultural metropolises seems partially mediated by the need to develop strong ties and discursive affinities with the gatekeepers residing there (see chapter 6). Thus, a macro structural perspective alone is certainly not sufficient to make sense of the different geographic patterns among elite careers. Yet for now, they too testify to the divergent, even contradictory dynamics of valuation in the global art field.

Conclusion

Up until the 1980s, the art field was a highly West-centric affair. As the postwar canon of contemporary art took shape, artists from most parts of the world ironically found themselves marginalized by a field that regularly touted its own progressive, "international" character. Critics and sociologists remain

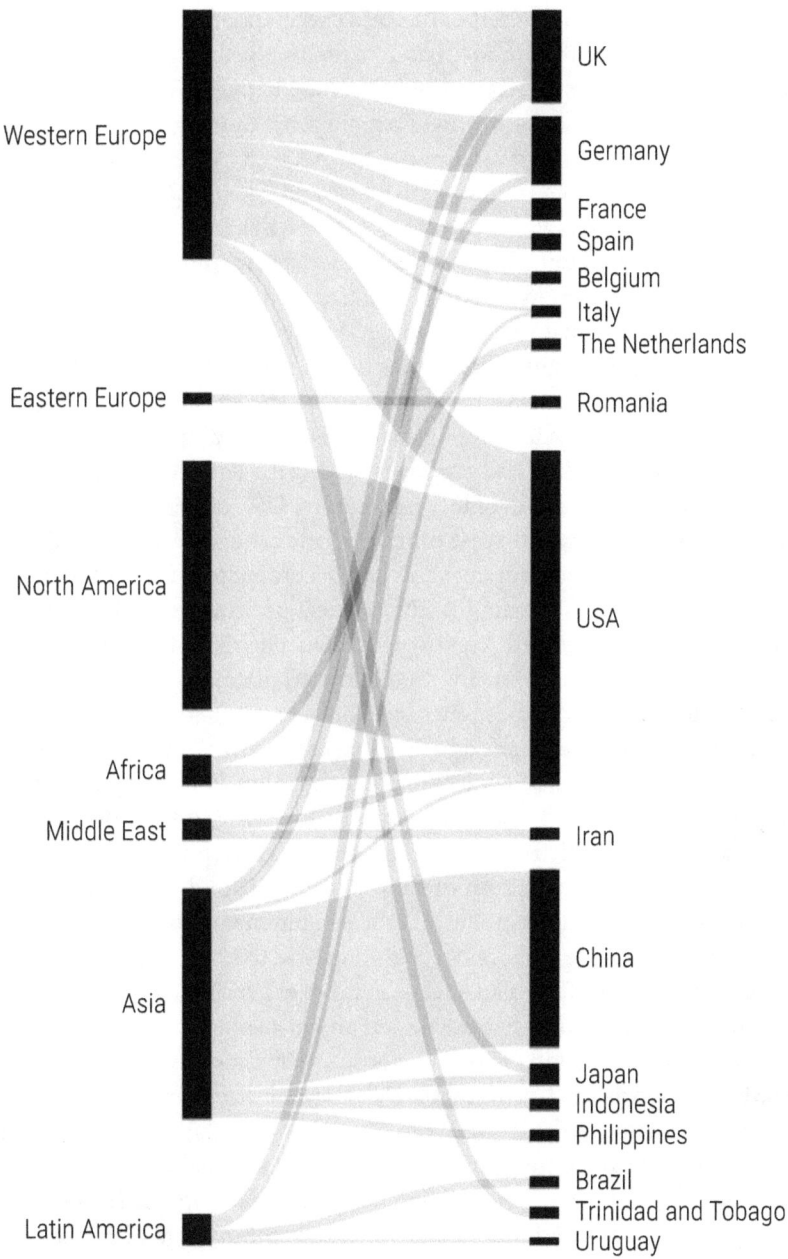

FIGURE 5.17. Migration flows among top heteronomous global artists (winner-take-all and commercial). The graph matches the region of the artist's country of birth with their (multiple) countries of residence as of 2017.

sharply polarized about whether the field's accelerated institutional globalization over the past three decades has actually changed this originally discriminatory situation in a significant way. Some have hailed an era of radical change marked by greater diversity. Others remain more tentative.

One of my primary goals in part 2 has been to carve out some potential middle ground between these "globalists" and "skeptics."[66] If we break up a monolithic approach and attend to the global field's internal heterogeneity around "art" and "money," we can clearly see divergent patterns and logics at work. The global auction market is characterized by comparatively rapid and volatile changes. In that subfield, though the commercial recognition of artists from Asia has grown substantially, they have not entirely supplanted the dominance of US-American artists over time. At the specific cultural pole, however, slower generational cycles have ultimately led to more cosmopolitan diversity among its leading artists, and especially among the younger generations, there has been a striking decline of formerly central US-American artists. In short, "transformations" beyond West-centric artistic canons *have* occurred, though they have clearly played out unevenly and according to different timelines.[67]

These divergences are not just the product of contingent historical forces. They are influenced by the discrete logics dominating each of the global field's two poles. The trajectories of nearly two hundred practitioners has shown that global elite artists tend to be more successful in one subfield than the other. For the cosmopolitan Mid-Garde and the Consecrated Elite, higher symbolic capital goes along with a relatively lower market position. For commercial stars, the opposite is true. Only a scant minority, the three winner-take-all business artists, have been equally triumphant in both. What is more, as table 5.10 summarizes, this dualistic pattern of valuation corresponds to other significant variations in the forms of capital and the geographies of these career types.

Artists with higher symbolic recognition tend to bring more cultural capital to the global game. They also engage in more experimental, discourse-driven artistic practices and defy traditional, object-centered aesthetics and easy marketability—the kind of art that, not surprisingly, shows up regularly at the market-driven pole. Contrary to arguments put forward by the market-convergence model, these two types of aesthetic capital demonstrate that intermediaries from contemporary art's different subfields embrace opposing evaluative criteria. To get the attention of leading curators, artists must engage relevant discourses and media that are at the cutting edge of global circuits. But that makes it much less likely that their work will find a sympathetic audience with auction experts, who most often pursue art that will easily and profitably appeal to established tastes of deep-pocketed buyers.

Valuation is also deeply intertwined with varying geographies of circulation and migration. Within an expanded field, a high degree of globality has become

TABLE 5.10. Forms of Capital and Geographies of Circulation among Four Types of Elite Careers in the Globalizing Art Field

	Autonomous	Semi-Autonomous	Semi-Heteronomous	Heteronomous
Gender	Male/female	Male/female	Male	Male
Cultural capital	High	High	Medium	Medium
Aesthetic capital				
Type of Media	Innovative	Innovative	Traditional/Innovative	Traditional
Position-taking*	Installation	Photography	Painting	Painting
Focus	Discursive	Discursive	Entrepreneurial	Representational
Symbolic capital**				
Volume	Medium	High	High	Low
Purity	High	High	Low	Low
Globality	High	High	Medium	Low
"Economic capital"				
Turnover	Low	Medium	High	High
Price level	Low	Medium	High	High
Globality	Low	Medium	High	Medium
Exhibition geography				
Countries	USA, Germany, France	USA, Germany	USA, UK	USA, China, Germany
Cities	New York, Berlin, Paris	New York, Berlin	New York, London	New York, Beijing, Berlin
Spatial configuration	Centralization and dispersion	Centralization and dispersion	Home bias	Home bias
Commercial geography				
Countries	UK, USA, France	USA, UK	USA, UK	USA, UK, China (Hong Kong)
Cities	London, New York, Paris	New York, London	New York, London	New York, London, Hong Kong
Spatial configuration	Transatlantic	Centralization and dispersion	Centralization and dispersion	(Regional) Centralization and dispersion

* The entry reflects the dominant medium among the artists per cluster.

** "Purity" denotes the distance to the market in view of the relative share of public/noncommercial solo exhibitions versus solo shows in market venues; "globality" designates the extension of exhibitions across continents.

a hallmark of elite careers. Yet it fluctuates among the autonomous and heteronomous types, along with their volumes of symbolic and "economic capital." At the same time, and seemingly paradoxically, an artist's success often depends on being associated with a few geographic centers that concentrate the most relevant resources for the cross-border mediation of contemporary art. And these tend to differ for the two poles. While the US, and especially New York, figures as *the* global hub for all four career types, for symbolic valuation, Germany—particularly Berlin—has emerged as a second cultural center. In the global commercial subfield, though, the US is followed by the UK, where London's financial and institutional prowess made it a favored global auction center. We have, so to speak, a division of labor among duopolies. At the two outer poles, they are flanked by Hong Kong, which is a more regionally anchored market center that has played a significant role for launching the global commercial ascent of Chinese contemporary artists (see chapter 7). France, especially Paris, in turn, represents a supporting cultural hub for the rising Mid-Garde.

It goes without saying that since my interest is in factors that influence global art canons, these results speak only to the top tier. This does not mean to deny that other types of producers circulate at more regional scales or bypass these centers altogether. But the findings clearly show that the careers of leading artists are significantly influenced by a few metropolises and associated field-specific territorial hierarchies, even if their works have come to crisscross the globe in more extended and diverse ways.[68] At the cultural pole, the weight that central locations exert is further underlined by the fact that most globally recognized artists had to be physically immersed in them as residents, something that is not as important on the commercial side. So contrary to arguments that have proclaimed the end of center-periphery inequalities in contemporary art or those that align with Appadurai's model and speak to the disruptive role of regionalities in a new global cultural economy, the dominance of a few geographic centers to shape values and global art canons cannot be denied.

Nevertheless, from a historical perspective (see part 1), I have also emphasized that these centers operate within an expanded field of exchange and competition and are no longer as West-centric as they once were with regard to their intermediaries, cultural practices of mediation, and ultimately, the diversity of the artists they promote. Over time, they have become more cosmopolitan and decentered from *within*. Going beyond any dichotomic views of the reproduction or radical change of institutional center-periphery dynamics, my global field perspective assumes a multidimensional geography of power and suggests that it has *transformed*.

In the globalizing art game, economic and symbolic capital have operated along divergent tracks. Successful careers in these dimensions have been shaped by different logics of artistic evaluation and mediated by diverging geographies of valorization. The field's dual world economy substantially influenced the dynamics of artistic recognition beyond established Western countries—and in this sense the diversity of contemporary art's emerging global canons. A model that accounts for such a divided economy allows us to better capture the complex and multifaceted changes that have affected transformations of West-centric artistic orders, moving the field from its "international" past to its "global" conditions today.

PART III

Creative Lives

FROM THE "PERIPHERY"
TO GLOBAL RECOGNITION

IN LIGHT of the broader picture that part 2 has provided, the question remains regarding how artists from formerly "peripheral" countries were able to navigate their individual careers and attain global recognition after decades of discrimination and exclusion. What strategies did they use? What transnational networks did they engage with? What were the aspects of their art that allowed it to diffuse across multiple continents? And to what extent were they able to overthrow traditional artistic hierarchies between the "center" and the "periphery" and affect the "rules" of the globalizing game? As Gerardo Mosquera presciently stated, "The fact that a certain number of artists are coming from every corner of the world . . . only means, in itself, a (not so dramatic) quantitative internationalization. But number is not the issue. The question for these new subjects is agency: the challenge of mutating a hegemonic and restrictive situation towards active and enriching plurality."[1]

The following two chapters address these questions by engaging with the creative lives and transcontinental careers of Gabriel Orozco from Mexico and Yue Minjun from China. I am not interested in looking at these artists as "representatives" of their home countries; after all, national artistic traditions are far too heterogeneous to be captured by the careers of two individuals. Instead, I am more interested in them as cases of distinct types of global recognition.[2] While Orozco gained worldwide renown with regard to symbolic consecration, Yue temporarily became a commercial star in the global auction market. Thus, following their careers gives us an opportunity to compare how artists— who were close in age and who both originated outside Euro-American centers—navigated the various gatekeepers, power dynamics, and discourses at the different poles of the globalizing field.

To understand how Orozco and Yue individually positioned themselves across borders, we can draw on Bourdieu's complex idea of "habitus." As chapter 1 explained, this concept refers to an agent's incorporated "system of generative schemas" and dispositions that inform their "thoughts," "perceptions," and "actions."[3] Habitus is shaped by both primary socialization in certain "social class" settings and secondary socialization in small groups, educational institutions, or larger fields.[4] As "embodied history"—that is, something "internalized as a second nature"—habitus affects a person's choices within given historical contexts in ways that are not necessarily "deliberate" but are "nonetheless systematic."[5] For Bourdieu, "strategies" are thus not necessarily "strategic," in the sense of being *consciously* calculated. For example, though Yue attained great success in the auction market, his artistic choices were not originally geared toward purely commercial goals. Yet his habitus—shaped by his family background and involvement in an unofficial artistic community in China—predisposed him to eschew official state dogma and embrace a kind of aesthetic simplicity in his paintings. This eventually led him to develop a catchy realist aesthetic that resembled Pop art, which gave him an advantage over some of his peers in the global market. Put simply, when seen through the perspective of habitus, certain forms of practice lead to certain outcomes without a "conscious aiming . . . to attain them."[6] Making this distinction is absolutely critical if we want to avoid a crude, rationalistic sociologism that would be inappropriate for the artistic domain.[7]

Within a global context, however, these strategies may become even more complex because they can simultaneously be oriented around (sub)national, regional, or global levels. They can also have different meanings within each of these arenas.[8] This can lead to situations in which artists might pursue double or even "schizophrenic" strategies with their multiple relations.[9] For instance, as we shall see, Orozco's turn toward neoconceptual artistic traditions at the end of the 1980s was not just informed by his interest in certain developments in the international field but also by his distaste toward Neomexicanismo, a commercial painting movement that was part of his national field. In short, within multiscalar global fields, participants' practices are overdetermined by a set of diverse and nested games. The trick is trying to keep all of them in view.

To get a nuanced picture of these artists' careers, we must furthermore chart the intermediaries who supported them by showcasing their art, ascribing meaning and value to their work in "transgressive global circulation processes," or by arranging sales.[10] Some of these agents operated as cosmopolitan *global mediators* (e.g., "the global curator"), while others functioned more readily as *hybrid brokers*, connecting and translating between specific artistic traditions and markets.[11] Still others played a role as *nationally situated supporters*. Regardless of their roles and positions within intersecting fields, we can look at their practices through the lens of habitus, too. And as we shall see, one of the most crucial "magnetic" forces that connect artists with supporting intermediaries, especially in the early stages of their careers, involves the degree to which their habitus and aesthetic sensibilities do or do not have affinities.

Finally, it is important to keep in mind how all of these micro- and meso-level dynamics are embedded in larger macro-level environments, which I explored in the book's first part. The more "peripheral" an artist is when they enter the playing field, the more barriers and resistance they are likely to face. Consequently, their ultimate recognition will also depend on the supporting indirect influence of broader macro-societal changes.[12] In short, to explain Orozco's and Yue's symbolic and commercial transnational careers, we have to connect the micro-level of their artistic strategies and related evaluations, the meso-level of their sociocultural relations within and across fields, and the macro-level of larger structures and historical dynamics.[13] By attending to these multileveled historical entanglements, the case studies will deepen our understanding of the global field's institutional transformations (part 1) and circulation patterns (part 2), drawing connections between grand-scale developments and the richness and diversity that define people's experiences on the ground.

6

Becoming a Global Artist at the Relatively Autonomous Pole

THE CASE OF GABRIEL OROZCO

Orozco practically invented today's genre of globe-trotting artist. But Orozco's at-home-everywhere-and-nowhere persona is less a stylish pose than an extension of his artistic project: a fusion of post-Minimalism's concern for site-specificity and Conceptual art's reliance on the portable photographic document.

—MARGARET SUNDELL

IN 1993, Gabriel Orozco, a young artist from Mexico, received the unique opportunity to present his work at the Venice Biennale, one of the world's most prestigious group shows. A few months before the exhibition opened, he met with the gallerist Marian Goodman for breakfast in New York. She would soon be representing him, and she asked about the work he was planning to showcase. "It is a very important show for you, Gabriel," she reminded him. To Goodman's surprise, the youthful artist responded, "Yeah, I have the work right here." He opened his backpack and revealed an empty white shoebox. Goodman was immediately taken aback, and in a quiet yet determined way, she encouraged Orozco to go a different route. "Oh, Gabriel," she told him, "you still have time to think of something else."[1]

Orozco decided to stick with his idea, however. But as the Venice Biennale's opening drew closer, the exhibition's curator, Francisco Bonami, also grew nervous about the piece. He asked Orozco if they could at least glue the shoebox to the floor so that it would not get kicked by accident. But the artist declined; his submission should simply be a loosely placed box.

Orozco's contribution—which might look to many laypeople like a proverbial art world prank—reportedly went on to attract "more attention than anything else at the biennial."[2] It also became a critical stepping-stone in Orozco's
extraordinary career, which soon spanned six continents and ultimately cul-
minated in his consecration as a "global artist."

Orozco was not the first Mexican artist to make headlines on the international
stage, of course. In the 1930s, for example, Diego Rivera was more famous than
any artist from the US.[3] The neighboring countries also had a history of rich
artistic exchange. But once the Cold War set in, the Mexican art field became
more sequestered from metropolitan art circles in the US and western Europe,
and it was increasingly construed as artistically "peripheral" or even "non-
Western."[4] This was the historical context when Orozco entered the international field, which leads to a puzzle: How was he able to surmount such obstacles and become a globally dominant artist, especially with work as
seemingly basic as an empty shoebox?

This chapter reveals how Orozco's worldwide recognition was initially catalyzed by intermediaries in US-European art centers who promoted his work
because it allowed them to reconcile two somewhat contradictory demands
at an early juncture in the art field's globalization process. On the one hand,
the broader rise of multicultural politics and the expansion of biennials
increasingly sparked interest and pressure among art institutions and experts
in the Global North to venture beyond the traditional Eurocentric canon.
On the other, however, these gatekeepers were in a position where they needed
to exhibit work that was compatible and distinctive in relation to the prevailing
artistic issues marking the international field's autonomous pole, which was
still dominated by Western art histories and the inertia of long specialized
Western tastes.

Many "non-Western" artists who worked within a multicultural paradigm
did not meet these latter preconditions because their art relied more heavily
on thematizing their ethnic identity (critically and affirmatively). Orozco, by
contrast, refused to make his Mexican background an overt focus of his work.
He became well versed in "international" contemporary art by traveling
widely, and he expanded Western conceptual art traditions in innovative ways.
His cultural capital and autonomous habitus predisposed him toward bold
strategies during his first exhibitions in Western art centers, which maximized
his initial visibility as a rebel from abroad and helped jump-start his global
career. Importantly, Orozco's rejection of ethnic allusions in his art and his
increasingly cosmopolitan tendency toward conducting site-specific work in
the countries where he exhibited enabled him to keep his transnational recognition afloat when debates around multiculturalism waned. It also allowed
critics to increasingly value his work in universal terms. This process began

with discourses describing Orozco's "artistic nomadism" and peaked in the new millennium with his being labeled as a "global artist." Thus, a decisive paradox resides at the root of Orozco's career. While intermediaries supported his work during an era of rising multiculturalism because he was Mexican, they also promoted it because it did not appear *too* Mexican and was reflexively and distinctively engaged with relatively autonomous art histories and debates in Western centers.

In broader theoretical terms, Orozco's case underscores the role that power inequalities play for cultural valuation dynamics across borders, and it reveals how the influence of an artist's support network operates within multiscalar global hierarchies. Furthermore, for Orozco, the principles of autonomy and distinction crucially functioned as important criteria of artistic evaluation, but they were associated with newer discursive, rather than strictly formalist, aesthetic criteria. This runs counter to Bourdieu's framework. More importantly, though, Orozco's career highlights how "universality" mattered as another evaluative principle for cross-border valuation and how it assumed specific meanings during a period of accelerated globalization. In the past, as the writings of art historians have suggested, the value of universality was reserved for dominant Western traditions, while art from the "rest of the world," including Mexico, often became denigrated as parochial.[5] But Orozco's ability to maneuver around his "peripheral" status resulted in an alternative, cosmopolitan universality, one in which he did not deny his Mexican background but gradually universalized it through practices that traversed both aesthetic and geographic borders. His distinctive cosmopolitan artistic language allowed him to subvert boundaries and create an alternate path toward universal legitimation. He could avoid becoming pigeonholed as a "non-Western" artist or, conversely, becoming assimilated into dominant Western traditions through a simple negation of his Mexican origin. And all this took place at a moment when such differences mattered for exhibition and discursive politics in the globalizing field.

This chapter fleshes out these arguments in two main sections. The first descriptively reconstructs three main phases in Orozco's career that led to his consecration as an elite global artist: his education in Mexico; his move to New York and his transition into becoming a "nomadic" artist in the 1990s; and his increasingly global legitimation. I then shift to a field-theoretical analysis of the multilayered influences that made Orozco's worldwide career possible, including the macro-level of multiculturalism, the micro-level of his artistic habitus, and his evolving relations with cultural agents across national and globalizing fields. Finally, I discuss how Orozco's case extends existing theory, offering us insights into how symbolic consecration takes shape in a global, rather than just a national, context.

Gabriel Orozco's Global Trajectory

From Mexican Painter to Conceptually Driven Artist:
The Early Years

BORN TO ART

Gabriel Orozco was born in 1962 in Xalapa, Veracruz, and he grew up in an intensely cultural environment of artists and intellectuals. His father was a renowned muralist painter and art professor, and his mother played classical piano. When Orozco was six years old, his family moved to the more artistically vibrant Mexico City; his father had begun collaborating with David Siqueiros, a founding figure of Muralism, one of the most internationally recognized Mexican art movements of the twentieth century. Muralism, known for its large-scale realistic paintings in or on public buildings, combined pre-Columbian and European traditions to convey social and politically progressive messages. Orozco's father—the nephew of the prominent muralist José Clemente Orozco—felt deeply committed to continuing this tradition, and he encouraged his son's artistic practice (as well as his leftist leanings) from an early age. As Orozco remembers, "I grew up with art. I was painting when I was a kid. I remember during the 1968 Olympics, I liked to paint all the athletes, Picasso style, which was very easy for me."[6]

When Orozco was nineteen, he entered the Escuela Nacional de Artes Plásticas in Mexico City, where he pursued formal art education until 1984. At that time, both the school and the country's official art institutions focused on painting, graphics, and sculpture that emphasized Mexico's artistic heritage. International contemporary art practices, especially conceptual art, were not considered. Before the internet, the main source for information about the latest developments in the international art scene was foreign art journals, which were only accessible through libraries after a considerable delay.[7] It was in this more insular and traditional context that Orozco received his training as a painter.

While Orozco initially identified with the Muralists, he increasingly painted work that eschewed the movement's overt political style and sought instead to create abstract renderings of "baroque nothingness."[8] Some of his large paintings in the early 1980s depicted "nothing but gilded adornments of gothic fashions."[9] Soon, he also took inspiration from the Flemish school of painting and created a series of works on raw pinewood that "featured details of fine robes, fabric, carpets, and even graphic marks taken from works of artists such as Jan Vermeer and Adriaen Brouwer."[10] But even as Orozco's orientation drew from international influences at this time, it was still rather traditional overall.

In Orozco's final two years at the Escuela Nacional, he started showing his work at group exhibitions in Mexico. The first one occurred within the context of the Salon National de Artes Plásticas at the Instituto Nacional de Bellas Artes in Aguascalientes in 1983, and it was followed by a group exhibition in 1984 at the Museo Universitario del Chopo in Mexico City. While the former institution was more conservative, the latter museum, which launched in 1975, was more open toward contemporary influences, although they were of national or regional origin.

AN INTERNATIONAL EXPERIENCE

Orozco grew increasingly frustrated with the national art scene's insular tendencies, and in 1986, he moved to Madrid (Mexico's onetime colonial capital) to take a one-year residency at the Circulo de Bellas Artes.[11] He originally intended to use this stay to refine his traditional training in painting, but he slowly began reorienting his artistic interests around contemporary conceptual practices. At the Circulo de Bellas Artes, Orozco studied with two Fluxus artists, Nacho Criado and Mitsuo Miura, among others, and was able to absorb a lot of new information about international contemporary art. As he explains, "The year coincided with a boom in Spanish art. There was a great deal of activity, and it was one of the periods when Spain was best informed, when large numbers of books were translated."[12] He regularly went to the bookshop at the Museo Reina Sofia, where he immersed himself in material that had been inaccessible in Mexico.[13] During this time, he also traveled around Europe, becoming acquainted with the art and ideas of Robert Smithson, Gordon Matta-Clark, Piero Manzoni, and John Cage, among others, and he developed an increasing interest in English sculpture and Arte Povera.[14]

These new influences significantly affected Orozco's evolving approach. During walks in Madrid, he began to find or devise art-like objects out of things in city streets, focusing more and more on sculptural and conceptual elements in his work and moving away from more traditional practices, particularly painting. As he recalls,

On my way to the Bellas Artes from Atocha I created a lot of things. There was a timber yard nearby where I found bits of planks which I arranged on the pavement to see how they looked, rearranging carpentry scraps. Walking around the Retiro I would also take old branches and assemble them by tying them together. My walk to the Bellas Artes was a process in itself, finding things, making and undoing. I did not use a camera and wasn't thinking about photography in any way yet, but was rather concentrating on the phenomenon, on the found objects and how to assemble them. . . . It was an individual reconstruction, a period of profound change, in which I was evolving and was part of a process existentially and artistically.[15]

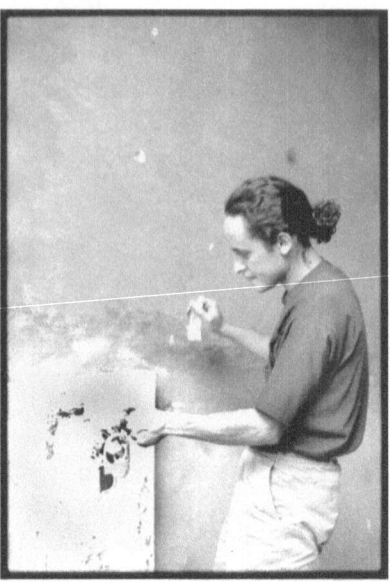

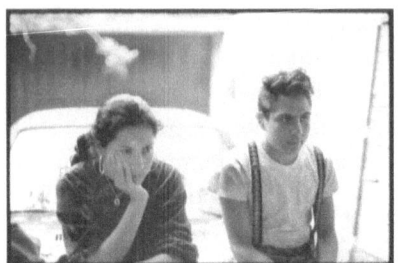

FIGURE 6.1. Laureana Toledo
and Dr. Lakra, 1991, Fridays Workshop.
(Photo: Laureana Toledo Archive)

FIGURE 6.2. Gabriel Orozco, 1991,
Fridays Workshop. (Photo: Laureana
Toledo Archive)

When Orozco returned to Mexico in 1987, he gathered like-minded artists and intellectuals to set up a workshop.[16] Every Friday for the next four years, they met informally at Orozco's house to practice together, discuss national and international artistic developments, and critique each other's work (figs. 6.1 and 6.2).[17] With the influence of this "collaborative circle," Orozco deepened his interest in more conceptual practices that fell outside Mexico's official artistic mainstream.[18]

The alternative, oppositional thrust of this small group and the evolving Mexican art scene was enriched by the influx of contemporary artists from other parts of the world in the late 1980s, including Jimmie Durham and Thomas Glassford from the US, Melanie Smith from the UK, and Francis Alÿs from Belgium.[19] But perhaps the most influential figure for Orozco within "unofficial" circles was Guillermo Santamarina, the independent curator. Santamarina had previously spent time in Europe and New York, and during numerous encounters and smaller curated shows, he was an inspiring figure for a new generation of artists within Mexico. He argued that if they were interested in making twentieth-century art, they had to stop painting and instead become more familiar with conceptual international traditions.[20] Orozco's own collaboration with Santamarina reached a high point in 1989 when they cocurated the group exhibition *A propósito. 14 obras entorno a Joseph Beuys* with Flavia Gonzalez and Sylvia Gruner.[21] The show, designed as a tribute to Beuys, the deceased German performance, installation, and graphic artist, took place in an abandoned convent far from Mexico City's mainstream institutions.[22] But it still generated attention for the way it radically departed from the country's dominant art styles. One of Mexico's major art critics, Raquel Tibol, reviewed it favorably. After that show, Orozco stopped painting for several years and instead pursued investigative photography and more experimental practices, including making assemblages like "a sleeping bag stuffed with banana leaves, or a group of lit flashlights placed on several ceramic tiles."[23] This shift aligned his practice with neoconceptual trends taking place in the international capitals of contemporary art at the time, creating a crucial aesthetic bridge to connect with them.

From International Breakthrough to "Nomadic Artist," 1990–99

INTERNATIONAL TIES

In 1990, after a few years of regular showings in Mexico (as well as at the Mexican Cultural Center in Paris in 1987), Orozco began exhibiting in the United States. At that time, most group shows that included his work either specialized in Latin American or Latinx-Hispanic art or were exhibitions that had a similar focus. Thus, when Orozco entered the center of the international art field, most mediators were apt to identify him as a Latin American or, more specifically, a Mexican artist.

Two of these shows took place in 1990 in New York and were mediated by Carla Stellweg. She had founded the first gallery for contemporary Latin American and Latinx art in New York in 1989 and had become familiar with Orozco's work through her frequent travels to Mexico. She also facilitated Orozco's participation in a major international group exhibition in Europe in 1992—*America, Bride of the Sun* at the Royal Museum of Fine Arts, Antwerp— which became a turning point in his early career. The show, which Catherine de Zegher cocurated with colleagues, was designed to mark the five-hundred-year anniversary of Columbus's arrival in the Americas, and organizers hoped to put contemporary Latin American art in dialogue with sixteenth-century works from the Spanish Netherlands and Latin America.

De Zegher was aware of the backlash that *Magiciens de la Terre* had received for its attempts to engage issues surrounding multiculturalism during that period (see chapter 2).[24] As she had previously curated exhibitions by older conceptual artists from Latin America, including Cildo Meireles from Brazil and David Lamelas from Argentina, she aspired to put together a show that would offer a more accurate picture of the artistic developments taking place in Latin America. When Stellweg introduced her to Orozco, she was immediately at-tracted to his conceptual approach and subtlety. In particular, she was drawn to the way his work included allusions to Mexican culture but still showed a clear engagement with the concerns and debates that marked Western conceptual art at the time.[25] For the Antwerp show, she included two pieces of his: *Recaptured Nature* (1990), a large balloon made from the inner tubes of truck tires, which she contextualized with a large sculpture by the Italian painter Lucio Fontana; and *My Hands Are My Heart* (1991), a lump of terra-cotta clay squeezed into the shape of a human heart, which she juxtaposed with a Frida Kahlo paint-ing. Orozco's art was thus presented in between established modern artists from both the West and Mexico.[26] In hindsight, he praised de Zegher's curatorial approach, since it kept his work from being forced into a context that was "pol-luted . . . with cliches about Mexico or Latin America."[27]

The Antwerp show made international headlines as "one of the most impor-tant exhibitions of the year."[28] And Orozco's collaboration with de Zegher—which would continue in 1993 with his first foreign solo show, namely at the Kanaal Art Foundation in Kortrijk—became one of the most consequential networking bridges in his early career. Even as early as the vernissage of *America, Bride of the Sun*, the well-connected de Zegher introduced Orozco to as many of the attending mediators as possible, including Jean Fisher, a progres-sive art critic from England who, at the time, was the editor of *Third Text*, an international art journal focused on multicultural and postcolonial perspec-tives in contemporary art. Another decisive connection that Orozco made in Belgium was Benjamin Buchloh, a German scholar, art historian, and critic based in New York, who would go on to become Orozco's most avid and in-fluential intellectual champion.

Soon after the show in Belgium, Orozco moved to New York. The Mexican art scene did not seem progressive enough for him, and his girlfriend at the time (who later became his wife) was planning to pursue a PhD at NYU. Once he arrived, Buchloh recommended Orozco to Marian Goodman, an interna-tionally influential avant-garde gallerist in New York.[29] Although Goodman says in retrospect that her first encounter with Orozco "was the best meeting" she had ever had "with a young artist" and that he "was very bright, very observant and clearly somebody who had something new to say," she initially hesitated to accept him for her gallery program.[30] In fact, it was over a year before she agreed to officially promote him. In the meantime, she invited Orozco to openings and dinners, put him in contact with other influential art professionals, and sent people to evaluate his work.[31]

In this capacity, Goodman in 1992 introduced Orozco to Francesco Bon-ami, who had been appointed as a curator of the *Aperto* at the 1993 Venice

Biennale, a special show dedicated to showcasing emerging artists. The Italian curator was looking to echo the Venice Biennale's overall theme that year—the art world's opening to multiculturalism—and Orozco's work seemed to be a fitting choice. Although he originated from Mexico, his art was well informed by discourses of "international contemporary art" and offered an original take on the Western conceptual traditions of the 1960s and 1970s, which appealed to the tastes of the Western-trained curatorial team. As Bonami paradoxically explained it, "Everybody was happy to find a Mexican artist who didn't look too Mexican."[32]

THE REBEL FROM ABROAD

In 1993, Orozco's participation at the Venice Biennale was a key event for his breakthrough. It had been a prestigious exhibition platform for decades and thus ensured high-level exposure. And as already described, Orozco used this opportunity in bold ways. Instead of showing work that would submit to the exhibition's guiding theme of multiculturalism, Orozco simply placed an empty shoebox as a readymade in the center of the gallery floor, turning it into a miniature sculpture that commented on the space that he had been allotted (figs. 6.3 and 6.4). As he remembers, "The spaces for the work in the Aperto looked to me like shoeboxes so I said, okay let's neutralize the space, a space inside a space, like a nucleus or atom of a work that implodes the whole space."[33] *Empty Shoe Box* caused annoyance, but Orozco's radical contribution to the show, which also included rising Western stars like Damien Hirst, Matthew Barney, and Maurizio Cattelan, ultimately became one of the *Aperto's* sensations that year. It marked Orozco as a young rebel from abroad and increased the critical attention he received from the art field's international elite.

Shortly after this, Orozco effectively harnessed the momentum he had developed at Venice with exhibitions in Europe and the US. Of particular importance was his solo show in the fall of 1993 at MoMA, which at the time was one of the world's most prestigious art museums. Lynn Zelevansky, an assistant curator, invited him to MoMA's *Projects* exhibition series, a platform dedicated to showcasing work by emerging artists. When the two met for the first time (upon an informal recommendation by Laura Hoptman, whom Orozco knew through a friend in New York), Zelevansky had already developed an interest in Latin American art and had curated shows by Cildo Meireles and Guillermo Kuitca. Just like Stellweg and de Zegher, Zelevansky has noted that it was "refreshing" to encounter an artist who worked with modest artistic means and was seeking to revive the conceptual traditions of the 1970s.[34] Fascinated by the combination of a "minority" artist whose work resonated with larger traditions in Western art history, Zelevansky pushed hard to get the museum's

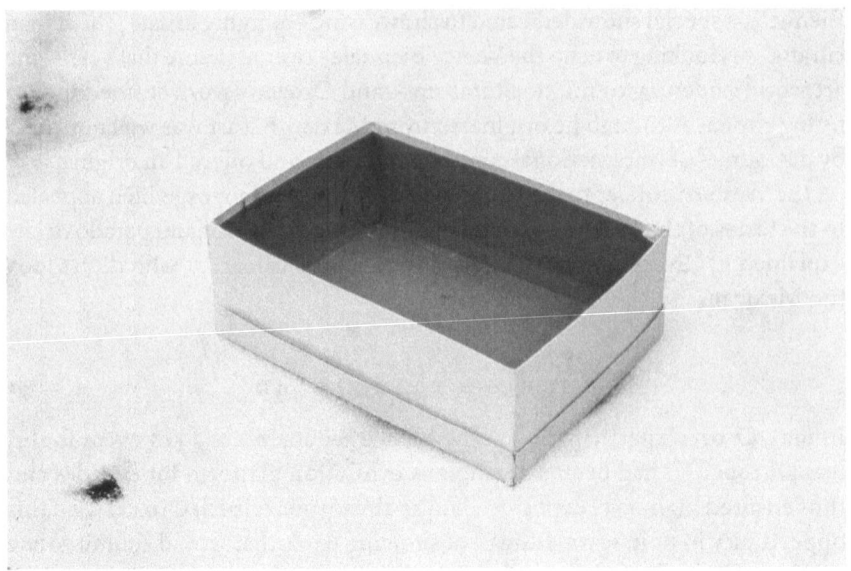

FIGURE 6.3. Gabriel Orozco, *Empty Shoe Box*, 1993. (Courtesy of the artist and Marian Goodman Gallery)

approval for the exhibition. Indeed, it was the "first solo show given to a Mexican artist since Diego Rivera's in 1931."[35]

At MoMA, Orozco once again used an internationally prestigious exhibition context in clever, original ways. Instead of confining himself to the exhibition space that MoMA typically allocated for the *Projects* series, he boldly suggested that he disperse his work—sculptural interventions and photographs that documented "impermenant pieces spontaneously created from found objects and situations"—throughout the museum and garden.[36] As he later explained, "Because I was doing work that was about site specificity, time specificity, interventions into the space of everyday life, with everyday objects, an empty white cube in a museum was not that interesting."[37] Orozco placed his works in interstitial spaces, like corridors, hallways, and public areas where art generally was not found.[38] He also expanded the space of the exhibition to the garden and surrounding neighborhood. In his interactive installation *Home Run*, he asked residents who lived close to MoMA's sculpture garden to put oranges, which would be delivered by the museum and replaced weekly, on their windowsills during the exhibition period (fig. 6.5). Residents became the artist's collaborators, and the seemingly mundane act of placing oranges on windowsills resulted in an eye-catching visual when it was realized at such a scale.

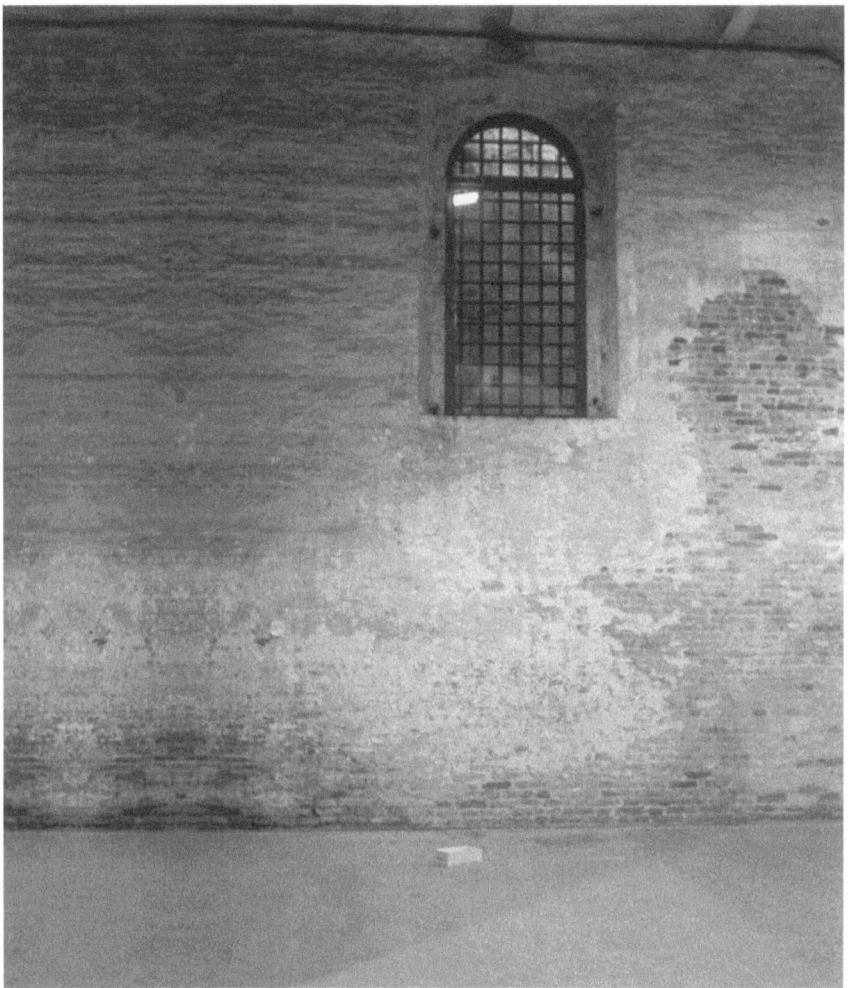

FIGURE 6.4. Gabriel Orozco, *Empty Shoe Box*, installation view, Venice Biennale, 1993.
(Courtesy of the artist and Marian Goodman Gallery)

Orozco created a memorable show that museum members and New York
art circles thought was refreshing in how it departed from the traditional,
object-focused aesthetics that still predominated at MoMA at that time. Holland Cotter, the art critic for the *New York Times*, later noted that this show
was one of the main reasons for Orozco's rising artistic recognition. "Gabriel
Orozco's 1993 solo debut . . . was a barely there, very un-MoMA affair of a few
photographs, a ball of clay, a hammock and some fresh fruit. . . . At least part
of the reason for his continuing appeal can still be traced to the memory of

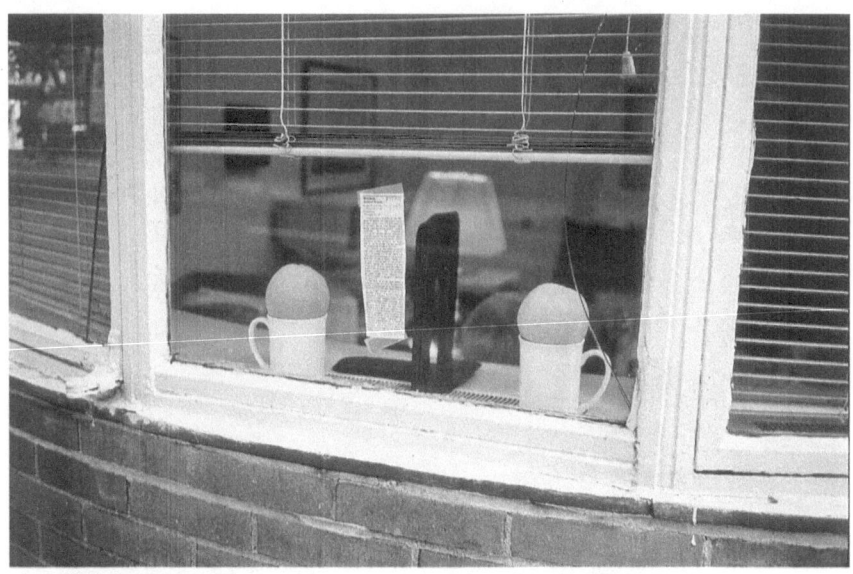

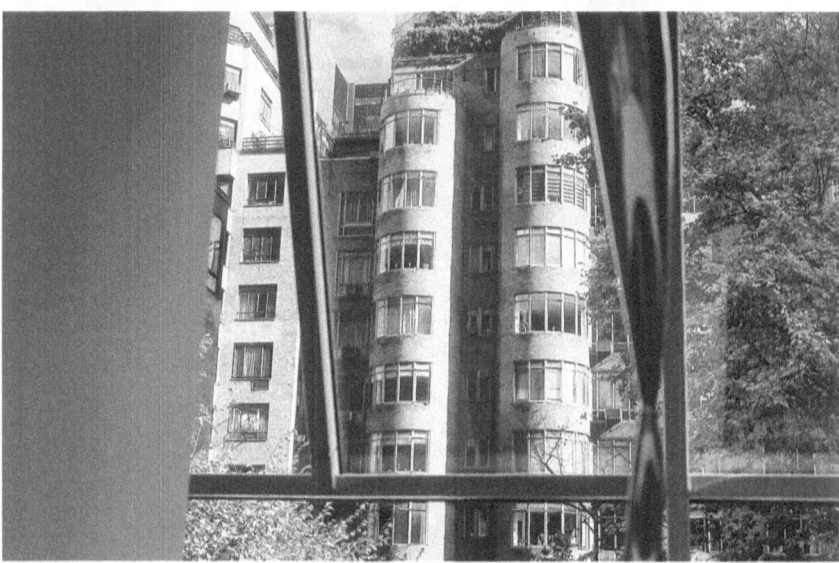

FIGURE 6.5. Gabriel Orozco, *Home Run*, 1993, arrangement of fresh oranges placed on the windowsills across from MoMA, installation for *Projects 41: Gabriel Orozco*, MoMA, 1993. (Courtesy of the artist and Marian Goodman Gallery)

that charmed first MoMA show, and the young, footloose artist who produced it."[39]

As with the Venice Biennale, Orozco avoided directly engaging with his Mexican background. In fact, his conceptual work looked so un-Mexican that Zelevansky felt compelled to stress in the exhibition's brochure that he was a "a thoroughly Mexican artist."[40] In her write-up, Zelevansky portrayed Orozco as a quasi-heroic creator in Mexico's art history, arguing that his work stood in stark contrast to the traditions that had "predominated, both aesthetically and institutionally" in the country for decades.[41] By innovatively engaging with Western conceptual traditions from the 1960s and 1970s, Orozco's "modest objects" managed to "adamantly resist both grandiosity and the overtly political" elements of Muralism.[42] This framing was not well received by art critics in Mexico. Olivier Debroise, for example, argued in a review of the show that Zelevansky had ignored Orozco's roots in a lively experimental 1980s Mexican art scene of its own. Her reading considered his work out of context in rather Eurocentric terms, denying the contemporaneity of conceptual activist models in the country, in which the work could have been situated.[43] Orozco himself became a controversial figure in his home country. He was charged for being complicit with metropolitan misrepresentations that would grant him unwarranted special "Mexican" status, and he would not exhibit in Mexico for several years.

Despite these critiques, Orozco continued to ride the wave of early recognition in the international field. In 1994, a final key event helped further catalyze his international career: he had his first solo show at Marian Goodman's prestigious avant-garde gallery in New York. For this exhibition, he placed four circular yogurt caps on the gallery's four blank walls (fig. 6.6). This gesture was intended to play with viewers' expectations and draw attention to their own interactions with an almost empty gallery room.[44]

Several people who attended the vernissage were annoyed and left quickly. Goodman herself was initially surprised when Orozco proposed the work, but she later perceived it as a kind of "declaration of independence since it was a radical thing to do for a first show."[45] *Yogurt Caps* continued to provoke discussion, and in 2010, the New York critic Jerry Saltz even judged it as "one of the most vexing art works of the past two decades."[46] While some people perceived it as an aggressive gesture, others considered it to be a resolute act in defiance of the market system, which helped Orozco garner respect within the more autonomous circles of New York's influential art scene.[47] The exhibition's most important effect, however, was the critical attention it generated. Orozco once again became an artist whom one had to talk about, a daring figure who rejected and played with institutional conventions after a period in the 1980s when commercial art, pushed by branded dealers, had dominated the international scene (see chapter 3).

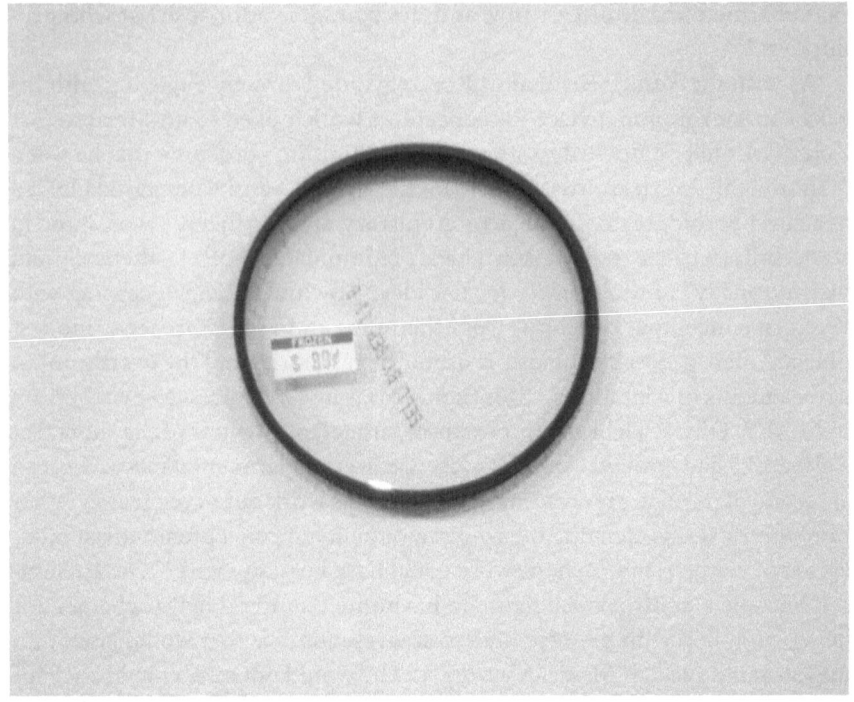

FIGURE 6.6. Gabriel Orozco, *Yogurt Caps*, 1994 (detail). (Courtesy of the artist and Marian Goodman Gallery)

THE RISE OF EXHIBITIONS AND SITE-SPECIFIC ART INTERVENTIONS ACROSS COUNTRIES

Figure 6.7 charts the rise of Orozco's exhibitions at public art institutions, museums, galleries, and biennials following his prestigious shows in 1993 and 1994. After a slight decrease in 1995, when Orozco was completing a residency in Berlin, his visibility nearly doubled from eleven exhibitions in 1994 to twenty in 1996. Until the end of the decade, he maintained a relatively high level of shows, reaching another peak in 1999 with twenty-one. It was evident that the initial interest in his work was not a fad. Rather, it signaled the launch of a steady exhibition career, which, as figure 6.8. illustrates, spread to twenty-four countries on four continents by 1999. The map's darker shades further reveal that Orozco's career trajectory up to the late 1990s was characterized by his highest visibility in traditional Western art centers, especially in the US, Germany, France, the UK, and Italy. Indeed, just four years after making international headlines at the Venice Biennale and MoMA, Orozco received invitations from many of the international field's most prestigious institutions.

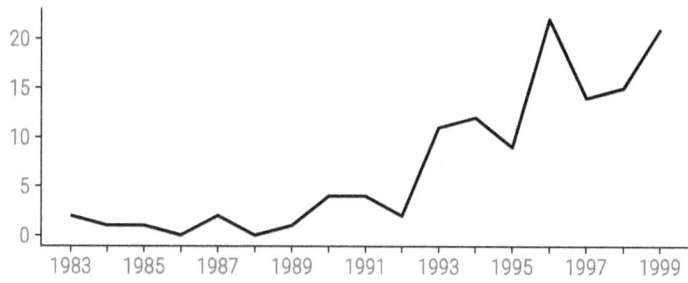

FIGURE 6.7. Orozco's rise of exhibitions, 1983–99.

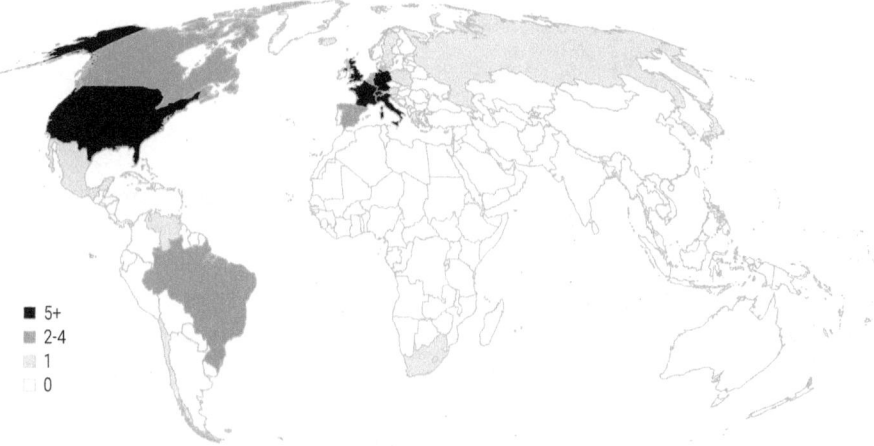

FIGURE 6.8. The geography of Orozco's exhibitions, 1994–99.

They included solo shows at the Musée d'Art Moderne de la Ville de Paris, the Kunsthalle Zurich (which had a reputation for choosing young artists who went on to develop successful careers), the Institute of Contemporary Art in London, the Stedelijk Museum, Amsterdam, and the Portikus in Frankfurt.

Simultaneously, Orozco participated in several group exhibitions in countries outside this traditional power axis, including Venezuela, Chile, Japan, Russia, and Poland. He also was a sought-after artist on the globalizing biennial circuit (see chapter 2). His work appeared at biennials in South Korea, Germany, France, South Africa, and Brazil and at sites in the US. During a period in which the international art field expanded, Orozco became an itinerant artist globe-trotter. For each of his major shows, he traveled to the respective city and spent an extended period preparing his exhibitions partly in situ—that is, by creating work that responded to specific elements of a particular cultural environment. In part, it was because of this roving, site-specific artistic approach that professional critics began to think of Orozco as a paradigmatic "artistic nomad" during these years. It was a label that resonated with advancing ideas of globalization, and as I explain in more detail later in this chapter, it allowed Orozco to become increasingly legitimated in cosmopolitan-universalistic terms in the critical discourse surrounding his work.[48]

Orozco's Consecration as a Global Artist, 2000–2010

In the new millennium's first decade, Orozco's career underwent further consolidation. This process included his symbolic consecration at the art capitals of the globalizing field, the widening circulation of his work across multiple continents, his discursive universalization as a "global artist," and his increasing economic success.

OFFICIAL DEBUT IN MEXICO

In 2000, Orozco's first major midcareer retrospective, which assembled over one hundred works of sculpture, photography, video, installation, and drawing, was initiated at Los Angeles's Museum of Contemporary Art (MOCA). Organizers planned to have the show travel to Mexico in the fall as Orozco's official debut in his home country. Indeed, the idea for this survey originated with Dolores Beistegui, then the director of the Antiguo Colegio de San Ildefonso, who was described as a "cosmopolitan, sophisticated" woman.[49] However, she felt that her institution did not have sufficient resources for the show and thus approached MOCA's director in LA, suggesting that if MOCA organized an exhibition for Orozco, it could then travel to her Mexican institution. MOCA agreed. At that time, it was already seeking to reflect and appeal more to the city's large Hispanic community, and it had also decided "to become more global . . . and started looking towards artists from Latin America." Yet despite this support from a US institution, administrative agencies in Mexico that oversaw the Antiguo Colegio declined the show.[50] To them, Orozco was reportedly "too young" and not established enough, and Beistegui had to search for an alternative venue. She eventually connected with the Museo de Arte Contemporáneo Internacional Rufino Tamayo, which agreed to host the show in collaboration with the Museum de Arte Contemporaneo de Monterrey. Both institutions were located in far less prominent places than the renowned Colegio de San Ildefonso.[51]

The exhibition's massive catalog included writings in both English and Spanish. Along with Benjamin Buchloh and Molly Nesbit, two critics based in New York, three artists from Mexico—Gabriel Kuri, Damián Ortega, and Abraham Cruzvillegas, who all knew Orozco from his workshop in the

1980s—contributed texts. The latter group highlighted especially Orozco's Mexican influences, pointing out, for example, how his conceptual approach could be read as a reaction to the country's dominant traditions of political art or broader existential environments.[52] Such attempts to reinscribe Orozco into the Mexican art field after years of absence did not prevent harsh local reactions. Olivier Debroise—a French citizen who had become an influential figure in Mexico's alternative art scene—continued his earlier claim that Orozco's work was too compliant with Euro-American discourses and their misrepresentations of Mexican contemporary art.[53] Debroise's younger friend and collaborator, Cuauhtémoc Medina—who was completing an art history PhD in the UK and would become associate curator of Latin American Art at London's Tate Modern in 2002—similarly judged Orozco's work as a "metropolitan imposition" that was not "essential in order to understand the history of 'Mexican' art in the nineties."[54] Adverse responses like these, which Orozco's position would provoke over the next decade in Mexico's art field, underline how it operated according to dynamics that were relatively independent of the "centers."

THE GLOBAL ARTIST

Orozco exhibited widely and prominently over the remainder of the decade. Indeed, his public solo shows—the most important format for artistic consecration—rose to twenty-one in this period, and by 2010, his group exhibitions had surged from eighty-one in the 1990s to an impressive 305.[55] While his work attained truly global circulation on six continents in a total of thirty-seven countries, the geography of his exhibitions echoes the more general center-periphery pattern of the careers of the consecrated elite (see chapter 5). Despite a high globality with regard to symbolic recognition (and in contrast to commercial elite artists), his exhibition activities remained strongly concentrated in institutionally powerful Western centers (see figure 6.9).

During this period, Orozco's itinerant trajectory took him again to several biennials, including the Istanbul Biennial, the Yokohama Triennale, and the Taipei Biennial in Asia, as well as the Documenta and Venice Biennale in Europe. After a long history of Eurocentrism, the 2002 Documenta, curated by Okwui Enwezor, and the 2003 Venice Biennale, directed by Francesco Bonami, turned into particularly influential exhibitions that helped further propel global debates about contemporary art at the field's centers (see chapter 2).[56] Orozco's participation at these shows contributed to link his own position with broader discourses concerning artistic globalization.[57] Criticism pertaining to his "artistic nomadism" merged with larger global themes, and he increasingly became labeled as a *global* nomadic artist, as I detail later in this chapter.

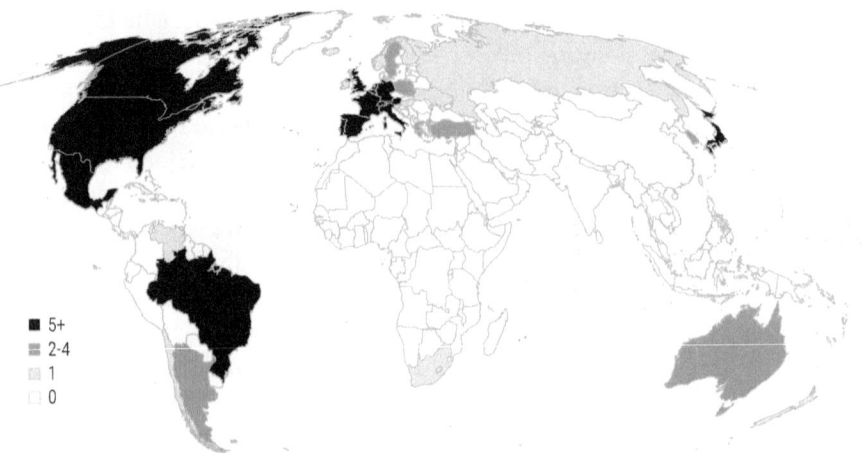

FIGURE 6.9. The geography of Orozco's exhibitions until 2010.

Finally, by the end of the decade, a midcareer retrospective at MoMA between December 2009 and March 2010 solidified Orozco's institutional consecration. The New York exhibition dubbed him one of "the most intriguing and original artists of his generation," and it was conceived as a traveling venture that would move to the Kunstmuseum Basel, the Paris Centre de George Pompidou, and the London Tate Modern in the following two years.[58] With this massive undertaking, Orozco became an established midcareer artist whose work appeared in prestigious museums for contemporary art in three of the globalizing field's biggest capitals: New York, Paris, and London.

The MoMA retrospective, which assembled Orozco's "greatest hits" from the 1990s, including *Empty Shoe Box* (1993), also attracted the fiercest criticism of his career (fig. 6.10). Partly because he also presented newer works in traditional media like printing and painting, one formerly sympathetic art critic reproached him for an "oddly conventional looking survey." "In the context of his earlier art," he wrote, "the prints and paintings come across as the work of a former maverick turned mainstream player."[59] Other critics gave similar assessments, suggesting "that his work feels more ordinary" or that "a once flowing artist now seems frozen" or claiming derisively that Orozco had developed a "blockbuster career."[60]

Orozco's position continued to polarize his home country as well. While some critics in Mexico viewed the MoMA show as further proof that his work merely reflected mainstream Western tastes and aesthetic values, others praised his success abroad.[61]

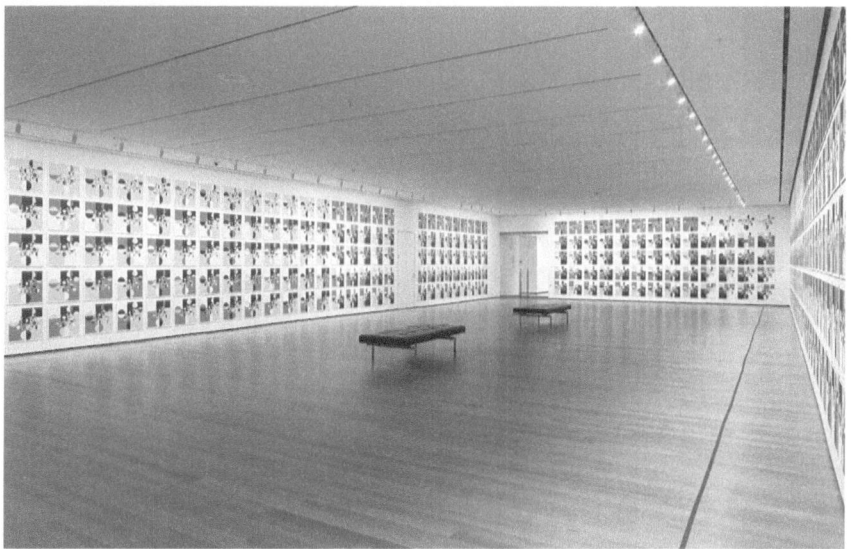

FIGURE 6.10. Installation view of the exhibition *Gabriel Orozco: Samurai Tree Invariants*, December 13, 2009–March 1, 2010, MoMA. (Photo: Jonathan Muzikar; digital image © The Museum of Modern Art, New York, NY/Licensed by SCALA / Art Resource, NY)

CONVERTING CAPITALS AND REPUTATIONS

Finally, Orozco's institutional consecration coincided with increasing economic success. Just as Bourdieu's cycle of consecration suggests, his trajectory allowed him to translate symbolic capital into economic capital (cf. chapter 4).[62] His market rise is indirectly indicated, for instance, by the number of solo exhibitions he had at the Marian Goodman Gallery during this period, which nearly doubled from three to five. And although Sotheby's had previously auctioned his work in London in 1997, it was only during this later stage of his career that his auction sales rose. Out of Orozco's 113 offered lots before 2010, 100 took place in the new millennium. As table 6.1. shows on the next page, his highest ten auction prices occurred during this phase as well, with 50 percent taking place one year after the MoMA show (including the maximum price of $420,000), suggesting a climactic pattern. This surge in the market for his work, of course, was facilitated by his turn to painting, and half of the works that fetched the highest prices were in that more marketable medium.

As indicated, Orozco's heightened market success and his return to painting exposed the artist to accusations that he was selling out, leaving behind his

TABLE 6.1. The Ten Highest Prices for Orozco's Artworks in the Global Auction Market, 1997–2010

Rank	Year of sale	Price	Work, year	Medium	Auction house	Place of sale
1	2010	$420,000	Samurai Tree (Invariant Gold 2), 2005	Painting	Sotheby's	New York
2	2008	$280,000	Samurai Tree 1Q, 2007	Painting	Sotheby's	New York
3	2010	$272,000	Samurai Tree (Invariant 5), 2005	Painting	Sotheby's	London
4	2010	$240,000	Samurai Tree (Invariant #9), 2005	Painting	Sotheby's	New York
5	2010	$196,000	Atomists: Asprilla, 1996	Photography	Sotheby's	London
6	2005	$173,000	Horses running Endlessly, 1995	Sculpture	Christie's	London
7	2008	$149,000	Samurai Tree 3L, 2006	Painting	Phillips de Pury	London
8	2006	$135,000	Atomists: Making Strides, 1996	Print	Christie's	New York
9	2010	$130,000	Atomists: Jump over, 1996	Print	Christie's	London
10	2004	$98,000	Pelotas y platanos/Caballo/dos parejas/ Paleta derretida/Interior, ?	Photography	Phillips de Pury	New York

Source: Artprice.com

days as a daring maverick and opting instead for mainstream appeal. These critiques echo Bourdieu's argument that an artist's greater institutional and economic success and the concessions that success may incite lead to the banalization of their charismatic status. It comes at the cost of a loss of the charisma that accompanies artistic "autonomy," which had been one of the original sources of Orozco's recognition in metropolitan centers.

Gabriel Orozco's Recognition as a "Global Artist" at the Relatively Autonomous Pole

Thus far, this chapter has reconstructed Orozco's career to reveal his development from his beginnings as a Mexican local artist to becoming a "global artist" who exhibited his work around the world. In the following sections, I deconstruct the various macro-, micro-, and meso-level forces that propelled his extraordinary journey. Understanding the interplay of these forces enables us to gain insights into the shifting conditions underlying the recognition of artists from formerly more "peripheral" countries at the relatively autonomous pole of the globalizing field.

The Rise of Multiculturalism as a Macro-Level Precondition

An early milestone for Orozco's career in the early 1990s was his recognition at the Venice Biennale and in New York. And one historical macrosocial precondition that facilitated this initial success was the rise of multiculturalism in the 1980s and the various, contested ways that it was refracted in the international art field. Chapter 2 discussed multiculturalism as a broader social movement that had gained momentum in the wake of rising identity politics and postcolonial independence movements. By the 1990s, multicultural discourses and politics had made their presence increasingly felt in the centers of the international art field, and several exhibitions engaged with them thematically, including the much debated, but nevertheless influential, *Magiciens de la Terre* at the Paris Centre Georges Pompidou and Grande Halle at the Parc de la Villette in 1989 (see chapter 2).

Multiculturalism also began to have stronger repercussions in established intellectual circles in New York, making waves that went beyond culturally specific art organizations and alternative art spaces. For example, in 1991, John Rajchman, a philosopher and art theorist from Columbia University, initiated a symposium in collaboration with *October*, a theory-driven art journal in the US. The outcome was a special issue, "The Identity in Question," in 1992, which interrogated how the rise of identity politics translated into new politics of cultural and artistic representations. One year later, the Whitney Biennial marked the peak of multicultural controversies in New York and beyond. The majority of its participants were members of marginalized populations in the visual arts—women, African American, Latinx, and gay artists—and the organizers placed an emphasis on politically oriented art that explored how marginalized groups could claim the power to define themselves around differences of ethnicity, race, and gender.

The show, at one of the US's foremost art institutions, was widely recognized for the radical way it centered artists of color.[63] But it also attracted a fierce backlash among critics both in the US and abroad.[64] The main tenor of the criticism was that broader social and political questions had overshadowed genuine aesthetic concerns. A review at *Artforum International*, for example, noted, "Taken as a whole, the 1993 Biennial is noteworthy not so much for the quality of art it presents as for the way it mirrors certain disturbing trends.... One such trend is the tendency of artists, curators and art educators to reduce contemporary art to the role of social work or therapy. Much of the work here is numbingly didactic, easily summed up in a sentence or two."[65]

The widespread controversy surrounding the biennial nevertheless demonstrated that multiculturalism and related debates were issues that established art institutions and professionals had to address. Additionally, the severely depressed art market after the 1989 crash fostered a sense that it was time to pursue new directions beyond the Neo-Expressionist celebrity painters who had dominated the previous decade, who were largely white and male (see chapter 3). Yet the pressure on cultural intermediaries to become more inclusive of artists from marginalized and "non Western" populations and their interest in doing so continued to come into conflict with metropolitan norms of artistic autonomy and distinction in the centers of the artistic subfield. Orozco's early career was facilitated precisely by his ability to reflexively navigate these two exigencies.

The Micro-Level of Orozco's Self-Understanding as an Artist

To understand what allowed Orozco to master the "opportunity space" created by multiculturalism, we must of course look more closely at his artistic habitus and approach.[66] Bourdieu suggests that a fundamental sociological precondition for an artist's recognition is the affinity between their practice with the field's dominant norms about what constitutes an "exceptional creator." As outlined in chapter 4, his theory posits two prevailing criteria for the "production of belief" in an artist in (Western) subfields of restricted production: the perception of their autonomy and of their artistic distinction.[67]

Bourdieu's sociological notion of artistic autonomy has negative and positive dimensions. As chapter 4 indicated, he associates it first and foremost with the artist's distance from commercial activities. To gain recognition as a newcomer, an artist must appear to be "pure," meaning they must display an "interest in disinterestedness."[68] At the same time, however, the artist's work needs to be also positively oriented around the relatively autonomous artistic developments that are at stake in the game they are participating in.

Such a twofold autonomy of artistic practice constitutes only a basic precondition for being perceived as a "legitimate producer," however. Bourdieu's second norm of distinction suggests that the art must also be seen as *innovative* in relation to prior and coexisting works in the relevant subfield. In Bourdieu's framework, such distinction is linked to a modernist aesthetics of *l'art pour l'art*. This understanding reduces field-specific innovation to formalist aesthetic strategies that rely on esoteric distance from everyday perception and subject matter, a quality Orozco's case challenges. And Bourdieu's account of distinction also carries a problematically teleological notion of art history as "a progressive discovery of the form" within a given genre.[69]

Nevertheless, the micro-level implications of Bourdieu's arguments are that an artist would need to bring a high level of cultural capital and reflexivity in order to navigate subfields of restricted production. They cannot merely follow their private tastes and bouts of spontaneous creativity, a move that would come across as naive and ignorant. Instead, they must have a solid understanding of the histories and debates of an artistic subfield and develop their practice in distinctive response to it. The informal entry fee is a mastery of the "set of achievements which underly the current problematic," or what Bourdieu calls the "space of possible," which involves a sense of the "problems to resolve, stylistic or thematic possibilities to exploit, contradictions to overcome, even revolutionary ruptures to effect" in the field's given historical state.[70] From the artist's vantage point, therefore, field-specific symbolic recognition depends on both educated assimilation and differentiation.[71]

In this process, an artist's view of a "space of possibles" is never total—as it might appear to a historian looking back at it—but is instead filtered "in fragments" through the "categories of perception constitutive" of their habitus.[72] Moreover, an artist's reflexivity should not be equated with hyperrational strategizing. Rather, it operates both consciously and intuitively through explicit knowledge, acquired practical skills (i.e., cultural capital), and a more tacit, embodied "sense of the game."[73]

As we have seen, Orozco was born into an artistic family in Mexico, which means he acquired a quasi-self-evident sense for becoming an artist himself.[74] Growing up in an intensely cultural environment and the early familiarity with visual art—his early "cultural capital"—also laid a foundation for his confidence and his deft sense of the game later on. In the second half of the 1980s, his studies and travels in Europe and his exchanges in a collaborative circle in Mexico were critical for his secondary socialization. Informed by both national and international artistic developments, Orozco increasingly moved away from painting and adopted more conceptually driven practices. During this early phase, he already began to stand out as an artist with a highly reflexive, distinctive approach. As the curator Guillermo Santamarina recalls, "In the context of that time—in relation to official art and to what was happening in Mexican galleries—[Orozco's] work was totally and utterly different. Few artists had such a broad viewpoint with regard to use of materials, to working models and to their self-image."[75]

Orozco's self-understanding matured further when he moved to New York in the early 1990s and began living for extended periods in various European cities, including Paris, Berlin, London, and Amsterdam. His proximity to places with rich art institutions, along with his extensive informal interactions with their art circles, helped deepen his firsthand understanding of the relative autonomous metropolitan codes and evolving discourses during these years. With this growing metropolitan cultural capital, he progressively refined a self-consciously autonomous working mode while reflexively producing art that gatekeepers in US-European centers could appreciate as meaningfully innovative.

The central tenets that crystallized in Orozco's practice contradict Bourdieu's theory in two fundamental ways. In contrast to a narrow, formalist notion of aesthetic autonomy, Orozco's work became aligned with a broader, contemporary mode involving what one might call "discursive autonomy." More importantly, Bourdieu's theory ignores the long-running Eurocentric exclusion of artists from "non-Western" contexts, which degraded them as merely "ethnic" or "peripheral" in relation to "universal" Western art. For Orozco to master the opportunity space of rising multiculturalism, he also had to find ways to deal with his status as a Mexican artist. Strategically, he gradually developed an alternative position of *cosmopolitan universality*, which he nurtured through his nomadic life and artistic practice. This stance allowed him to escape being exoticized and pigeonholed through discourses of multiculturalism, but it simultaneously meant he could play the game of difference at a time when that difference served as an asset.

AN ANTICOMMERCIAL MODE OF ARTISTIC PRODUCTION

The most fundamental element of Orozco's evolving self-understanding as an artist was his development of a relatively autonomous production mode. This approach was informed by his conscious rejection of national and

international commercial art trends of the 1980s, when there was a boom in
the art market and more heteronomous forces dominated (see chapter 3). As
Orozco states, "When I started to do my work in the early 1990s, my proposition was to deal with production and distribution and perception in a different
way. I did not like mainstream 80s art and I didn't believe in market movements and the way they were producing and distributing work."[76]

Orozco's alternative practice involved three main moves, the first of which
was his abandonment of a studio space. This choice originally grew out of his
gradual experimentation with photography and found objects, "since the materials were in the streets and generally stayed in the street."[77] Later, he associated it with a desire to go beyond conventional modes of circulation: "The fact
that I didn't have a permanent studio, that I didn't want my work to enter the
abstract bubble of formal circulation was part of that. I try to make language
confront reality, the reality of the street and what goes on there."[78]

Orozco also rejected any personality cult that surrounded business artists
like Julian Schnabel and Jeff Koons. He criticized how they ostentatiously
sought public and commercial approval through self-marketing and celebrity.[79] In contrast, he shied away from injecting his presence into his art. As he
explains, "Neither my name nor my portrait is particularly present in my work.
I am for the human identity in my work to be more open and not anecdotally
related to my own person, as that to me would seem like imposing on others."[80]
This strategy stood also in clear contrast to an artist like Damien Hirst, the
rising business artist par excellence of the 1990s who was around Orozco's age:
"Where Hirst is everywhere, Orozco is a spectral shadow artist: here and gone.
One as a pure showman, the other supposedly pure."[81]

A final aspect of Orozco's anticommercial approach was his eclectic way of
working with different artistic media and stylistic elements. By engaging at
once with sculpture, installation, photography, drawing, collage, and other
media, he eschewed a highly recognizable type of work that could be easily
packaged for circulation in gallery exhibitions and sales.[82] He embraced such
artistic eclecticism as a way of preserving an openness toward his work's
unfolding over time, which would be more difficult to achieve if he became
associated with an artistic brand. But Orozco also emphasized that it did not
necessarily lead to work that lacked an inner logic or coherence: "I call this a
'deterritorialization of style.' I mean I do think in terms of a galaxy. A world of
an artist generates planets and different constellations. I also think that the
style or world of an artist can get into establishing a single, fixed territory,
making a certain type of work, a certain style of brand. One artist, one idea.
This style of working becomes a kind of fortress, and I don't believe in that."[83]
Orozco's disposition toward working in a poststudio mode and a postmedium
eclecticism echoes Bourdieu's idea of artistic autonomy as a phenomenon

involving distance from the market. It prioritizes the artist's freedom to choose their own production methods over the commodification requirements of a conventional market system. And it helps the artist avoid cultivating an image that is not markedly different from ones that characterize producers in other commercial cultural industries.

A DISTINCTIVE "REAL" AESTHETIC
AND DISCURSIVE AUTONOMY

Of course, an antimarket stance alone would not have brought Orozco the widespread recognition he received. A second critical element of his reflexive practice was that in the foreign fields he traversed, he was able to carve out distinctive artistic directions that marked a clear departure from the prevailing international aesthetics of the 1980s.

Early on, Orozco and his circle developed a strong distaste toward Neo-Expressionist painting, which had been dominant both in his own country and at the international level.[84] This figurative and symbol-laden style originated in Germany with the work of Georg Baselitz, A. R. Penck, and Anselm Kiefer. It also found followers in the Italian Transavantgardia with such artists as Francesco Clemente and Sandro Chia and in the US, most prominently, with Julian Schnabel. Neo-Expressionism also gained traction in Mexico's art institutions and galleries with the painting movement of "Neomexicanismo," which included artists like Mónica Castillo, Julio Galán, and Javier de la Garza.[85]

Orozco was critical of the aesthetics of these neofigurative movements, which flooded the 1980s. He "did not like . . . the big formats, the German school of neo-expressionist painting, which was very influential in Mexico." As he explains, he "was not so much against painting" but against what he perceived as "noisy, sentimental painting"; for him, "the neo-Mexican tradition . . . was kitsch and empty."[86] Orozco rejected their large and easily readable symbolism as too spectacular and entertaining. In opposition to these prevailing tendencies in Mexico and beyond, he became increasingly "attracted to the spare, idea-driven, Dada-inflected art of older figures like John Cage, Joseph Beuys and Piero Manzoni, and Brazilian conceptualists like Cildo Meireles and Lygia Clark."[87] In the process, he began to refine an alternative vision of art as a tool for everyday awareness that drew upon three aesthetic strategies.[88]

The first involved scale. Orozco deliberately turned to smaller gestures and objects, suggesting, "We have to revise the scale. I don't believe that a bigger object is more powerful than a smaller one. . . . I think the smallest gestures that we make in our lives can have much greater repercussions."[89] Furthermore, he integrated found, everyday objects in his installations, rendering them as signifiers of the quotidian in ways that were simultaneously connected to reality but

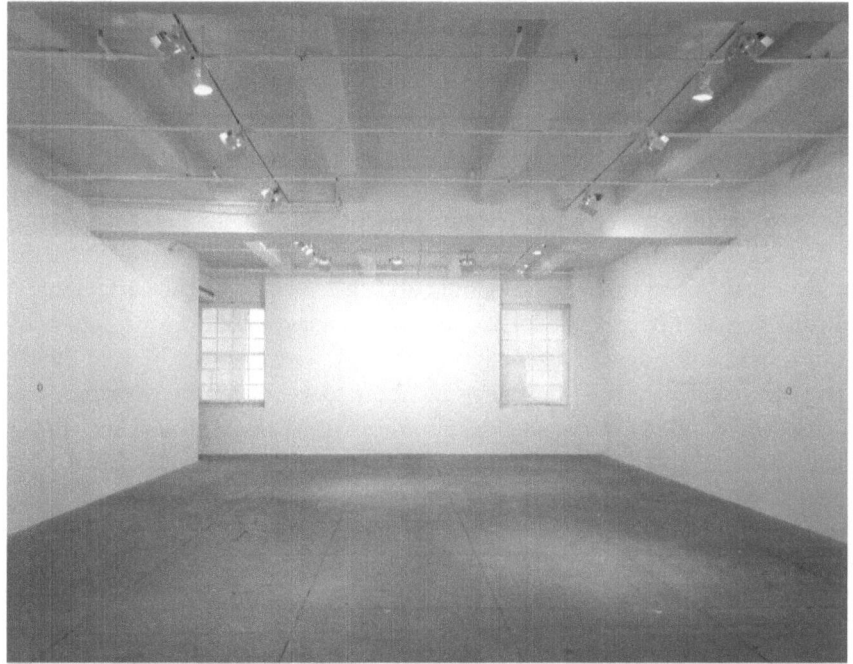

FIGURE 6.11. Gabriel Orozco, Installation *Yogurt Caps,* Marian Goodman Gallery, New York, 1994. (Courtesy of the artist and Marian Goodman Gallery)

still surprising to the viewer: "When I use objects they still work as they are, they still try to be real, . . . [yet] I want to disappoint the expectations of the one who waits to be amazed. . . . It is only then that the poetic can happen."[90] Lastly, he opted for cheap or recycled materials, creating a kind of alternative "spectacle of modesty," an art that emerged from a carefully selected economy of means.[91]

This antispectacular, modest aesthetic is particularly apparent in Orozco's early *Yogurt Caps,* his 1994 installation at the Marian Goodman Gallery (fig. 6.11). The caps were so small against each wall that entering viewers struggled to see them. The work was barely there, and it thus rejected any celebratory notion of the artist as a skilled creator. The installation challenged expectations about grand artistic gestures and instead aimed to sensitize viewers to smaller variations in the room: "One of the things I must say about this work was that I was fascinated with the idea of disappointing the public. I found it interesting to situate people in a void, to neutralize it, and with that power, start from zero to develop my work without expectations of the viewer who, tyrant that he is, begins to demand of the artist what he must be."[92]

Orozco's interest in subtly connecting art to reality diverges from Bourdieu's conception of aesthetic autonomy. His vision of art as a tool for everyday awareness clearly extends beyond a strictly formalist approach that cultivates an esoteric distance from everyday perception. Yet Orozco's practice still remains marked by a quest for artistic independence. That approach is manifest in the way his art rejects commercial spectacle and instead seeks to challenge the audience's established expectations. His reflexive strategies thus underline the need to rethink the narrow, formalistic notion of aesthetic autonomy that Bourdieu develops in *The Rules of Art* so that it can accommodate a broader range of critical engagements with prevailing notions of artistic practice and field-specific discourses.[93] In other words, we should update Bourdieu's framework so that it includes a contemporary understanding of discursive autonomy (or, better yet, a notion of autonomous discursivity). This allows to capture how an artist's assertion of independence can operate in a more conceptual, rather than formalist, mode, while still remaining intelligible within the existing discourses of a field's given state (such as the idea of art as spectacle). In Orozco's case, this shift toward discursive autonomy leads to a seemingly paradoxical position in which it was precisely his turn to the world of everyday life, not his formal detachment from it, that allowed him to assert his artistic independence.

SITE-SPECIFIC PRACTICES AND COSMOPOLITAN UNIVERSALITY

In addition to Orozco's autonomous and reflexive artistic positionings, a third key element of his self-understanding as an artist involved his increasingly cosmopolitan approach. The origins of this approach can be traced back to his critique of paintings in the Neomexicanismo style as well. He rejected the movement's overt use of national symbols and thematization of national identity because he believed that one's individuality, free from delimiting collective categories, should be considered the main source of creative work. As he explained, "I tried to avoid using clichés like 'What does it mean to be Mexican?' or 'What is the nation?' et cetera. Mostly I tried to face myself as an individual, as a person of a determined physique."[94]

Such an emphasis on the artist as the singular individual aligns with the modern tradition of the "individual genius" or, as Bourdieu phrases it, a "charismatic ideology," which admires the artist as an *individual* creator.[95] This ideology implies that the highest recognition an artist can receive is to be seen as an innovative individual who admits "no label other than their own signature," without references to their ethnicity or geography.[96] "After all," as Craig Rawlings writes, "in the 'encyclopedia' of fine art, Picasso and Dali are not referred to as modem 'Spanish' artists."[97]

Such an individualistic position, however, had been unavailable to most artists from "non-Western" countries for decades, and it was not readily available to Orozco when he entered the international field. Coming oftentimes from postcolonial countries that occupied marginalized positions in the postwar art game, such artists were regularly treated as exotic outsiders from artistically "developing" nations.[98] They were subjected to an irreducible principle of cultural difference and were not normally considered part of the international artistic mainstream.[99] Hence, they were positioned not merely *territorially* in an institutional center-periphery macrostructure (e.g., by where they lived) but also in relation to specifically *aesthetic* center-periphery constructs. The cultural status of an artist's origin country functioned like a subconscious national filter through which their work was judged and discriminated against, even after moving to the field's power hubs.[100] By contrast, artists from the West were "naturally" associated with the unmarked centers and thus could operate as *individual* creators capable of producing quasi-*universal*, international work.[101]

With multiculturalism's rise in the 1980s, the "peripheral" difference of "non-Western" artists underwent a positive reevaluation. New exhibition politics symbolically challenged the Western canon and stressed artistic "diversity." But within this new framework, artists still risked being ghettoized in highly particularistic modes of "perception, reception and patronage" that continued to assess the meaning and value of their art primarily with regard to ethnicity or geographic references.[102] A symbolic boundary persisted that made it hard for them to participate under equal aesthetic conditions and reach long-term artistic recognition.[103]

Orozco was reflexive about these symbolic constraints as a "Mexican" (or "Latin American") artist, labels he had to confront from his very first foreign exhibitions.[104] Simply negating his background in that historical context was difficult, and as we have seen, it also earned him fierce attacks from art critics in Mexico who accused him of merely assimilating to metropolitan standards and betraying his national roots. Orozco responded to this double dilemma by embracing a site-specific working mode. As indicated previously, in the 1990s, he developed a propensity for preparing his major shows in situ; he traveled to the location of the exhibition and created new work that reacted to it.[105] These site-specific works did not emerge out of a cultural vacuum but were meant to be dialogical, rooted in Orozco's awareness of his own background: "The idea of a specific place, of a specific intervention, of a contact with a culture and its signifiers that I was interested in exploring and developing, obviously went hand-in-hand in a very natural way with my own identity, my way of being and my awareness of being a Mexican travelling around the world. . . . It was interesting to see what my desire to be mobile, to visit places, to live in different cultures contributed to my work."[106]

One early example for Orozco's site-specific strategy was *La DS*, a modified sculpture of a Citroën DS, a French automobile. He created it in 1993 after spending several weeks in Paris preparing his first solo gallery show at Galerie Chantal

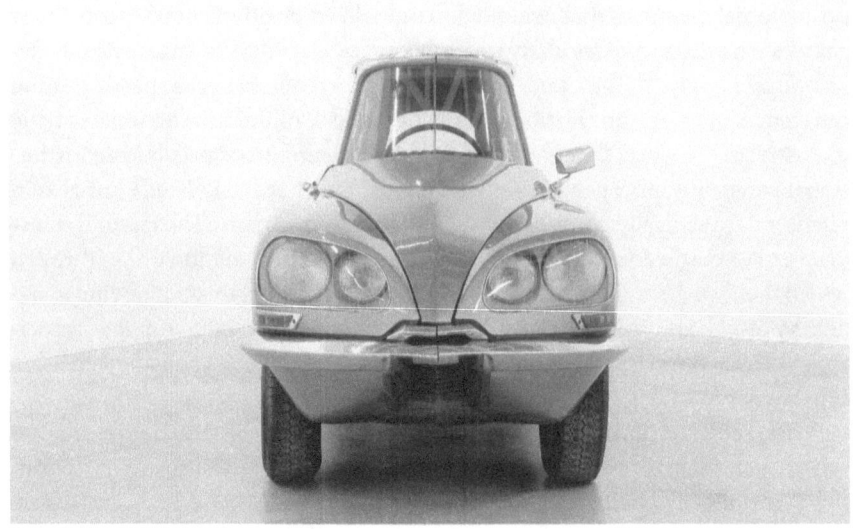

FIGURE 6.12. Gabriel Orozco, *La DS*, 1993. (Courtesy of the artist and
Galerie Chantal Crousel, Paris; photo: Florian Kleinefenn)

Crousel. With the help of an assistant, he cut the car lengthwise into three pieces, and then assembled the two outer pieces together. The narrower car resulting from the gesture hyperbolized the promise of speed made inert without an engine.[107] Orozco chose the Citroën DS deliberately for his Paris exhibition because it represented a "symbol for French ingenuity" when it rolled off the assembly line in the 1950s as the country was still recovering from World War II. It thus held an iconic status in French cultural history, which is signified by Roland Barthes's dedication to it in *Mythologies*.[108] Orozco, however, also associated a personal memory with the automobile from his adolescence in Mexico. As Bonami, the curator, explained, "Orozco drove a Citroën DS, one of very few in Mexico, when he was a teenager. He can still remember its mythical comfort, the sea-sickness, the excitement of vomiting. . . . Orozco transformed that memory into a majestic sculpture, a disturbing vision wherein grandeur, geniality, and culture collapse, crashing full speed against the barrier of their own de-culturalization."[109]

La DS gained widespread acclaim and is emblematic of Orozco's play with difference. It emerged out of his situated encounter with the history and culture of a foreign context and was simultaneously associated with references to his own biography or country. It was this kind of subtle tension that allowed him to circumvent national or ethnic particularisms—which could be a ghettoizing trap—without erasing his national background, which mattered in the cultural politics of the globalizing field. Through a dialogical site-specific approach, he did not have to deny his Mexican roots. But instead of making those roots a central topic in his work, he put them into motion through his artistic negotiations with the surroundings he encountered.

The question of intercultural influences and interpretations soon became a running theme in Orozco's work, in which new locations became "sites for developing specificity that led to generalities and ambiguities."[110] As his work intermingled with multiple places, artistic traditions, and meanings, his oeuvre increasingly assumed a cosmopolitan dimension. And by the new millennium, his artistic self-understanding had shifted from an individualist rejection of nationalist identifiers to a normative conviction that all true art is cosmopolitan at heart: "All art, in every part of the world is made up of different 'international' influences. . . . These kinds of mixtures signal a widespread attitude in any artist who is trying to understand the universe, because it's no longer just one's own country that is interesting."[111]

In sum, for Orozco to navigate his complex predicament as a "non-Western" artist operating within a context of rising multiculturalism and globalization, he developed an intricate aesthetic cosmopolitanism out of site-specific strategies. This approach enabled him to allude to his national background while universalizing his difference at the same time, forging an alternative position that enabled his universal legitimation. In this sense, cosmopolitanism figured not so much as the luxury of a rootless elite class but as a practice of artistic subversion of traditional ascriptions and hierarchies.[112] Ultimately, at the micro-level, it was the combination of Orozco's autonomous, reflexive distinctiveness *and* his cosmopolitan approach that made his cross-border consecration as a "peripheral" artist within the emerging global artistic subfield possible.

The Meso-Level Field Conditions of Orozco's Recognition as a Global Artist

Moving from the micro-level of Orozco's self-understanding as an artist, this section explores the meso-level relations of the most important mediators—galleries, curators, and critics—who supported his career. In my analysis, I pay particular attention to their own trajectories and positions as well as the dispositional and discursive affinities that made their support likely within the broader historical context of the art field's globalization.

THE POWER OF STRONG TIES TO GALLERIES IN THE CENTERS

As chapter 3 made clear, avant-garde galleries are unique gatekeepers in the contemporary visual arts, and they mattered greatly to Orozco's transnational career. These kinds of galleries promote artists to both cultural institutions and collectors, and they stand at the intersection of symbolic and market media-tion.[113] Yet Orozco's case challenges existing views that argue that a broad network of relatively weak gallery ties is most beneficial for cultural produc-ers.[114] Instead, Orozco's worldwide ascendance relied on a small number of particularly powerful avant-garde galleries that were situated at the field's cen-ters. In other words, a few galleries that had both high volumes of capital *and* geographic centrality were able to support Orozco's path toward global success in a way that large numbers of galleries around the world with small amounts of capital might not have been able to.

Orozco's career was primarily involved with four galleries during the period under consideration: the Carla Stellweg Gallery in New York, which he was loosely affiliated with between 1990 and 1993; Chantal Crousel, the Paris gal-lery that he joined in 1993 and where he had five solo shows and seven group exhibitions; the Marian Goodman Gallery in New York, which began promot-ing his work in 1993 and where he participated in eight solo and ten group shows; and the Kurimanzutto gallery in Mexico City, which Orozco inspired and helped to launch in 1999 once his international career was already firmly established.[115] Prior to 2010, Kurimanzutto held two Orozco solo shows and invited him to six group exhibitions.

Carla Stellweg was Orozco's first gallery link outside Mexico. Although he did not have a solo show at her space, Stellweg provided him with crucial early opportunities to make connections in the art scene in New York and internationally. Since the 1970s, Stellweg had worked as a hybrid cultural bro-ker between Latin America and the West, and she had spent her teen years in Mexico when her Dutch parents worked there for the United Nations. She wanted her gallery to be a platform that could heighten the visibility and exposure of both younger and midcareer Latin American artists and provide curators at other exhibition venues with crucial information and firsthand contacts.[116] With this orientation toward artistic promotion rather than commercial motives—which was risky at a time when contemporary art from Latin Amer-ica was still marginal within the field—Stellweg can be considered an avant-garde gallerist.[117]

When Stellweg encountered Orozco during one of her trips to Mexico, she was instantly intrigued by his work's subtle modesty, the ways it relied on the immediacy of small gestures and eschewed the great "sloganeering" or theat-ricality of most Mexican nationalist art.[118] She invited Orozco to visit New York, and when he moved there in 1992, they met regularly. They did not, however, develop a close working relationship. Orozco did not approve of the Latin American concentration of Stellweg's gallery; he did not want to be pre-sented as a Mexican or Latin American artist, nor did he want to be part of a niche market. In fact, Stellweg's pioneering focus, which was far from the

international mainstream at the time, meant that her gallery occupied a relatively weak position.[119] Nevertheless, as outlined earlier, Stellweg helped mediate Orozco's first group exhibitions outside Mexico in the early 1990s. But
perhaps the most consequential aspect of her support was the fact that she
introduced Orozco to Catherine de Zegher during a trip in Mexico, the Belgian curator. It was de Zegher who then promoted Orozco for his first European shows and connected him to other international mediators, including
Benjamin Buchloh, who in turn put Orozco in contact with Marian Goodman.
In this sense, Stellweg's hybrid brokerage played a critical role in Orozco's early
career trajectory because it helped him forge the foreign connections that
would build the foundations of his worldwide career.

After Stellweg, Marian Goodman was the gallerist with whom Orozco developed his strongest working relationship.[120] Goodman's gallery was also the
most powerful one he worked with. Marian Goodman's trajectory and approach establish her as a consecrated avant-garde dealer (see chapter 3). When
she opened her New York gallery in 1977, she was looking to promote contemporary art from Europe; commercial aspirations were secondary. At a time
when US-American artists dominated both the national and international
scene, it was a risky strategy since there was no established market for the art
she represented in the country.[121] But Goodman eventually succeeded in
establishing several of her foreign protégés, including Gerhard Richter, and
she earned recognition for her good eye and pioneering strategies.[122]

Goodman also gained a reputation as a gallerist who represented artists
whose work lent itself to expert discourses and involved a certain level of complexity. This approach earned her the respect—and sometimes friendship—of
intellectuals in the international field, including the art critic and theorist Benjamin Buchloh, who introduced Orozco to her. Thus, by the time Goodman
and Orozco met, she already had a high level of symbolic capital due to her
noncommercial approach and past accomplishments in promoting innovative
artists. Her leading position in New York was intertwined with the symbolic
economy of the relatively autonomous pole.[123]

Goodman made long-term commitments to artists, and Orozco ended up
developing a strong relationship with her gallery that lasted for decades. He
even said that Goodman's gallery felt like "kind of family" to him.[124] From a
sociological perspective, this close bond was facilitated by two kinds of habitus
affinities. On the one hand, Orozco's autonomous approach matched Goodman's relatively autonomous self-understanding as a gallery owner. The two
also had a cosmopolitan sensibility. When she met him, Goodman was already
interested in art from Latin America. As she remembers it, the *Magiciens de la
Terre* exhibition had helped foster her own curiosity about art beyond the
Western canon. Along with the rise of multiculturalism in the US and the

debates that were occurring in the international art field, it piqued her interest in artists from "non-Western" regions. Eventually, her earlier cosmopolitan preference for artists outside the US-American mainstream made it likely that she would include them more and more in her programming, despite the fact that such a move was initially a riskier gallery strategy.[125]

Nevertheless, Goodman emphasized that she did not choose Orozco because he was Mexican. In her eyes, an artist's nationality does not qualify as a valid selection criterion, a stance that is consistent with her autonomous and cosmopolitan outlook. What she appreciated about Orozco was, first and foremost, his art, but she also was drawn to his cosmopolitan orientation. In Goodman's perception, artists from outside traditional art centers could be classified into three types: "indigenous artists," who were dedicated to traditional practices and craft; "local artists," whose work was more modern yet primarily informed by domestic influences; and "truly international" artists, whose work was connected to international (Western) contemporary culture. In her mind, Orozco belonged to the third category, and his work was therefore suitable for her program. As she recalls, he showed a "natural desire to be connected to the international world of culture. He was not somebody who wanted to stay in the past. . . . He was very ambitious, . . . a guy who is eager to present himself, and he wasn't a folkloric figure."[126]

Goodman's considerations reveal the paradox at the root of Orozco's entry into the international art field. Her initial interest was piqued partly because he was an artist from a Latin American country. In a time of heated debates around multiculturalism, such a background mattered greatly. Hence, Orozco's Mexican origin must have played an implicit role in her decision to represent him. She emphasizes, however, that she did not choose him because he was a Mexican artist but because his work reached beyond his national background and inscribed itself within certain international discourses and debates.

Goodman's consistent support played a key mediating role for Orozco's cycle of consecration. Beginning with his solo show at her gallery in 1994, she brought her own high prestige to bear, transferring on the newcomer the credibility of her already-accumulated symbolic capital along with New York's weight as contemporary art's world capital. The sheer fact that Orozco exhibited at her gallery catapulted him into a different artistic league, granting him much-higher visibility among other powerful mediators. But it did not stop there. Over the years, Goodman had also developed a rich network of international intermediaries. Her well-known location in New York facilitated the accumulation of social capital. It was the place that cultural agents from around the world passed through to stay abreast (if they had not moved there already) of new goings-on and gossip in the field, especially in the days before the internet. Goodman, then, was also a critical social liaison, which became all the more important when Orozco pursued a nomadic life and artistic practice in the 1990s. Early on, for example, she helped him establish a relationship with Francesco Bonami, who in turn invited Orozco to the Venice Biennale twice (1993, 2003). And she later brokered several of Orozco's major museum shows in Europe and the US.

Of course, Goodman also played an important role as Orozco's economic gatekeeper. In the US—the country with the strongest collector base in the world—her gallery represented him exclusively. In Europe, she shared her representation of Orozco with the influential Parisian gallery Chantal Crousel. Goodman's monopolistic position in the US and her presence in Europe allowed her to exert control over sales, and she sold works by her artists largely to collectors she trusted rather than to speculators who might resell it at auction for the sole purpose of maximizing profits. That she could choose among well-trusted collectors was itself a by-product of her prestigious position, established networks, and long-standing experience in the market.[127]

In this way, Goodman also affected the *kind* of economic success Orozco had. Since her gallery handled many of his sales, she indirectly influenced his relatively modest presence in the commercial auction sphere. And her approach ensured gradual price increases rather than sudden spikes, which could have damaged Orozco's reputation.[128] Figures 6.13 and 6.14, which include data about Orozco's auction trajectory, illustrate such a climactic pattern, revealing an overall trend of successive peaks with intermittent downturns before finally reaching a zenith in 2010.

Hence, Goodman's strong symbolic position, her rich transnational social capital, and her centrality in New York endowed her with significant power to aid in the launch of Orozco's career across borders, to influence his economic sales, and to sustain her support as he continued on his path toward becoming a consecrated artist. This appraisal counters existing arguments concerning the value of a broad network of weak gallery ties. And it underlines how power in global cultural fields operates both through a mediator's resources and their geographic location within a field's macrostructure.

CURATORS, EXHIBITION VENUES, AND DISCURSIVE AFFINITIES

As we have seen, curators are key mediators for influencing the visibility, meanings, and value of work by contemporary artists. They grant and arrange exhibitions at different venues, and they furthermore contribute to artists' socialization, exposing them "to jargon, norms and modes of conduct."[129] Raymonde Moulin suggests that their importance as cultural mediators has grown so large that the older "dealer-critic" dyad—which Harrison and Cynthia

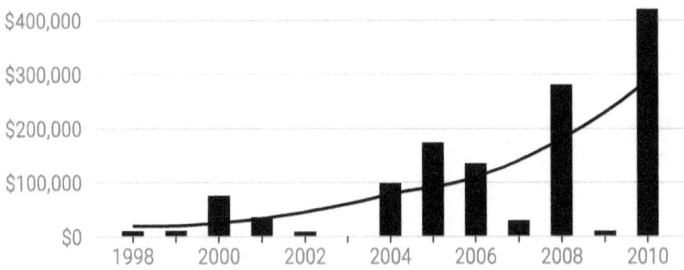

FIGURE 6.13. The evolution of annual top prices for Orozco's work at auction, 1998–2010 (LOESS fitted curve). Source: Artprice.com

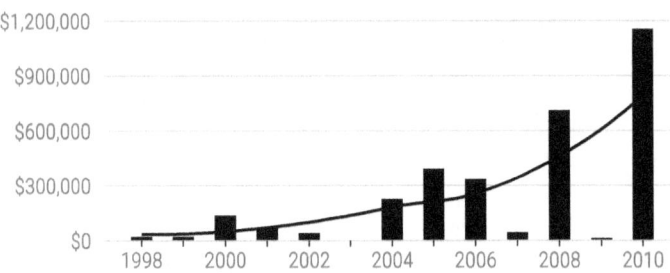

FIGURE 6.14. The evolution of the annual turnover for Orozco's work at auction, 1998–2010 (LOESS fitted curve). Source: Artprice.com

White, in their study on the rise of Impressionism, highlight as crucial for the development of artists' reputations—has been replaced since the 1970s by the "dealer-curator" dyad in the international field.[130] While this characterization risks downplaying the variety of agents and institutions involved in cultural valuation processes, a "curatorial turn" has undoubtedly occurred. The self-understanding and significance of exhibition makers as curator "authors" has increased, and curatorial studies programs have even supplanted art history curricula at some prominent art academies.[131]

Nevertheless, because Orozco had more than three hundred exhibitions before 2010, it would be futile to attempt an exhaustive catalog of all his relations with curators. While his work appeared in many exhibitions around the world, I focus on a few that stood out as critical *turning points* in his career. In doing so, we will see how Orozco's ties with key curators were enabled by aesthetic-discursive affinities between his art and their curatorial agendas and how these relationships were themselves influenced by shifting meso- and macro-level forces. Curators at the relatively autonomous pole are far from autonomous in the literal sense of being completely "free." Like artists, they operate within nested subfields that carry dominant norms for "legitimate" practice.[132] By attending to such norms—including those internalized as habitus—we can understand why these curators promoted Orozco's art at specific historical junctures and how they navigated the tensions between the interests to become more inclusive and the norms of a globalizing game that was still dominated by the "West."

THE DOUBLE BIND AND ITS EXCLUSIONS

This tension is particularly evident in Orozco's early career, when ascending curators from US-European centers gave the nearly unknown artist from Mexico prominent opportunities. In this regard, the Venice Biennale and Orozco's solo show at MoMA in 1993 were particularly influential for his international breakthrough.[133]

In Venice that year, curators opened up the international platform for the first time. Instead of sticking with a more conventional—that is, strictly aesthetic— focus, they aimed to look at issues regarding multiculturalism as well. The organizers wanted to present a new form of artistic internationalism that would overcome national borders and include work from artists who had originated from a broad range of cultural and geographical backgrounds (see chapter 2).

Orozco was invited to take part in the *Aperto* group exhibition in Venice that year. Its chief curator, Francesco Bonami was an Italian in his late thirties who had pursued an international curatorial approach from the outset of his career. Having studied stage design and architecture in Florence, he gradually reoriented himself toward art curation, and he moved to New York in the late 1980s. In 1991, he became the editor of the American edition of *Flash Art,* an international art magazine founded in Italy in 1971. In New York, Bonami established a broad network of art professionals, and he developed a cosmopolitan lifestyle. He could carry both of these with him throughout the rest of his career as he became a globe-trotting curator.

As already indicated, Orozco had gotten to know Bonami in New York a year earlier through Marian Goodman. They happened to be neighbors in the East Village, and the two men developed a strong bond. As Bonami's career advanced, he continued to support Orozco's rising position, writing five critical reviews for international art magazines and collaborating with him on later major exhibitions. Nevertheless, the logic informing Orozco's invitation to Venice should not be reduced to a friendship tie. The invitation was deeply overdetermined by the tension between "external" multicultural pressures and internal "rules" of artistic autonomy and innovation.

Bonami has stated that he invited Orozco to participate in the exhibition primarily because he wanted to feature work from the Latin American region that would adhere to the biennial's overall multicultural programming and he did not have an artist from Mexico yet.[134] The fact that he was an independent curator at the time, and thus not yet fully established institutionally, also might have predisposed Bonami to a more "heterodox" exhibition approach that would be open to considering artists outside established Western centers.

But Bonami was also critical of the so-called multicultural fashion, which he interpreted as a discourse that, rather than judging work by its artistic merits, imposed an external "system ruled by quotas" on the arts.[135] While he wanted to expand the exhibition's traditional Eurocentric focus, he and his curatorial team were also "searching for quality"—that is, work that would not merely cater to a fashionable "exoticism" in his eyes but that had something distinctive to say in relation to prevailing (Western) art historical developments.[136] This latter approach aligned with the *Aperto*'s institutional mission—namely, to identify emerging trends in "international contemporary art." It is in view of this double bind that one must interpret Bonami's statement, "Everybody was happy to find a Mexican artist who didn't look *too* Mexican."[137]

Bonami appreciated Orozco's approach for its art historical depth. He also valued the fact that Orozco self-confidently refused to feature certain ethnic clichés or fulfill multicultural expectations with his work. For Bonami, Orozco had found a way to subtly allude to his difference in background without getting trapped in it. As Bonami later explained,

> Orozco incarnates the dream of all curators, critics, dealers: an *artist capable of handling the language of recent history without giving up his original soul, expanding his roots, not severing them*. . . . What makes Orozco's game so complicated is his deceptive presence in a world of visual, "global" corruption, a Third World masquerade of "interesting" artists. . . . Gabriel Orozco brought his own rules into an old game, which doesn't mean he's cheating or making a different game, but that he's bending the codes to meet his own necessities, and not the other way around. He constantly, simultaneously, both defies and confirms his Mexican roots.[138]

As we have seen, Orozco's work for the Venice Biennale, *Empty Shoe Box*, was particularly daring. This heightened the effect of his foreign debut at this highly prestigious, international venue. Later, Bonami would judge the work as belonging "to the trinity of conceptual art," together with Duchamp's *Fountain* (1917) and Piero Manzoni's *Merda d'artista* (1961).[139]

A similar overdetermined evaluation underpinned Lynn Zelevansky's invitation to Orozco to have a solo show at MoMA. At the same time, her case points us to the way she excluded alternative positions of artists with Latin American roots, which did not fit into her "autonomous" agenda.

Orozco's opportunity to show his work at MoMA, one of the world's most prestigious museums, was again impacted by multicultural discourses, which were exerting increased pressure on established art institutions to become more inclusive. In fact, in the early 1990s, MoMA had already begun organizing exhibitions by Latin American artists, including in the *Projects* series. In 1993, it also hosted a major group show of twentieth-century Latin American art. This show did not garner much approval from the museum's trustees, however, and MoMA remained hesitant to fully pursue such new directions.[140] This reluctance was evident from the fact that these shows had either been organized by assistant curators or people who were not part of the museum's regular staff. More established curators at the museum, who could have used their symbolic power to give novel curatorial directions more authority and force, were not involved.

This generational dynamic is consistent with the idea of a heterodox-orthodox polarity, which implies that agents who are not yet well placed within a field are more likely to pursue innovative strategies (see chapter 1 and part 2). Indeed, in 1992, when Zelevansky met Orozco, she had recently begun her first curatorial position and was frustrated with the New York art scene. She thought it had been too heavily affected by an "era of Wall Street greed" and "garish and overproduced art," a view alluding to the wave of neofigurative painting that had dominated in the 1980s.[141] Her own interest in art from Latin America took root during a trip to the São Paulo Biennial in 1989. And when Zelevansky returned to New York, multicultural debates were becoming increasingly prevalent. She felt encouraged about pursuing her interest further, and she looked for ways to distance her curatorial work from the market-driven art of the 1980s in a way that resonated with emerging historical trends.

However, in Zelevansky's view, most of the artists who produced work within the context of multicultural discourses appeared "not right for the museum," since "these artists were really consumed with identity politics."[142] While she sensed the importance of showcasing "minority" artists, she needed to find artists whose work also resonated with the art historical (Western) discourses that were still at stake at MoMA, artists who would allow her to inscribe her curatorial strategies into the existing aesthetic possibilities.

Given this dilemma, Zelevansky was glad to encounter Orozco's work. She found it "refreshing" that he was working with modest artistic means and was seeking to revive the more conceptual Western traditions of the 1970s. An aesthetic affinity also existed between Orozco's "modest" conceptual orientation and Zelevansky's critical stance toward the "greedy," "big" art of the 1980s. Thus, Orozco allowed Zelevansky to articulate two historical developments at once: the call for giving greater attention to artists with "non-Western" roots and the trend toward conceptual modesty. This important coincidence, in addition to the positive first impression Orozco made with Zelevansky, motivated her to strive to get approval for the show.[143] Because Orozco was still an outsider to the Western art scene—he never had a solo museum show before—it took a considerable amount of effort to secure an invitation for him.[144]

As described earlier, Orozco, with his confident sense for the game, used the exposure in clever, bold ways. Through artistic interventions across the museum, garden, and neighboring apartments, his conceptual, process-oriented works challenged the traditional, object-focused aesthetics then prevailing at MoMA. He created an exhibition that fueled astonishment, discussion, and critical recognition. As MoMA's president at the time, Agnes Gund, remembers, it was a "fairly wonderful show" because it seemed "such a refreshing, different way of dealing with art."[145] Using almost the same perceptual categories as Zelevansky, her words highlight the value of distinction within the institution's more or less implicit aesthetic boundaries.

Indeed, while Orozco's work was selected for inclusion and subsequently praised, other artists with Latin American roots who were more involved in identity and progressive politics were excluded. As Cuauhtémoc Medina later asserted, Orozco served as an alibi "minority" artist, a figure whom Zelevansky and MoMA could use to bypass more politically charged and challenging Latinx artists at the time: "When it seemed possible that artists like Guillermo Gómez-Peña and Daniel J. Martinez could become references for what was understood as 'political art' in the 1990s, certain . . . metropolitan institutions legitimized recently-immigrated artists like Gabriel Orozco when—and only when—their work expressed a tension with the mainstream that was both more hermetic and aesthetic than Chicano, neo-Rican or post-colonial agit-pop. . . . Orozco's neo-conceptualism made him the perfect *Latin American* so that all other American Latinos could be put out to pasture."[146]

Yet if seen through the lens of habitus—with the idea of deeply ingrained dispositions of seeing and evaluating art—we do not have to assume that cynical calculations led Zelevansky to favor Orozco and to celebrate his ephemeral work as offering "odd beauty, . . . pleasure, humor and insight" for what she saw as a "jaded intercontinental art world" at that time.[147]

AFFINITIES WITH CURATORS IN THE BIENNIAL CIRCUIT

In the early 1990s, Orozco had managed to avoid being pigeonholed as a "Mexican" artist, which helped his work maintain its allure even after debates surrounding multiculturalism had waned. On the expanding biennial circuit, as issues surrounding artistic difference and hybridization gained traction in the later 1990s (see chapter 2), Orozco's practice found a natural home. Curators that were involved with biennials saw his increasingly itinerant, site-specific practices as emblematic of a new generation that was constantly circulating to different spaces and places in the world.[148] Many of them emphasized Oroz-co's artistic negotiation of the local and the global, and his status as a Mexican artist with a truly planetary practice.

Within a context of shifting global discourses, curators also began seeing elements in Orozco's work that critiqued Western culture. For example, Yuko Hasegawa, who invited Orozco to the Istanbul Biennial in 2001, asserted that his art challenged Occidental theories about subject and object, associating it with Japanese Zen and the philosophical style of certain Oriental art traditions. What counted for her, however, was how he combined these interests with innovative currents in Western neoconceptualism of the 1990s.[149] Hence, biennial curators valued Orozco's art for its hybridity, a theme that was also echoed, as the next section lays out, in the transnational art criticism of that time.

One of the most influential large-scale shows for Orozco in this later period was the 2002 Documenta 11 in Kassel (see chapter 2). Okwui Enwezor, the Nigerian-born lead curator, had met Orozco at previous exhibitions, and they had worked together for Enwezor's legendary 1997 Johannesburg Biennial. After Enwezor was named curator of the Documenta, he invited Orozco. While En-wezor prominently featured politically engaged contemporary art from African-born artists, Orozco's perpetual wandering between different countries and exhibitions fit with Enwezor's agenda to orient the Documenta around cosmopolitan artistic developments. Likewise, both Enwezor and Orozco rejected the essentialist thematization of certain ethnicities or cultural identi-ties that marked many multicultural discourses, and they favored a more dy-namic, process-oriented understanding of cultural exchange.[150]

Orozco created work for the show that did not match Enwezor's expecta-tions, though it was still related to the exhibition's cosmopolitan focus. Orozco opted to deliver sculptured bowls that he had cocreated in an aleatory fashion with a ceramicist in Burgundy that same year. While the ceramicist sculpted bowls from terra-cotta clay on his wheel, Orozco smashed small clay balls against them to knock them off-center, which resulted in lopsided forms that he titled *Cazuelas (Beginnings*; fig. 6.15).

Orozco later explained his thought process in this way:

They are made in France. It's not the tradition that you can call it Mexican, but I know that they will have this immediate connection with ceramics in Mexico. I don't know why, but in fact, the *cazuelas* came after a travel I did to Mali, and I traveled to Africa to check out the ceramics there, and some-how it came about from that trip. . . . When I participate in the biennials or group shows like this, I try to be specific to do something for the show. . . . They were trying to create a narrative of different things, and I understood that. . . . But it has been always strange the way I take those narratives.[151]

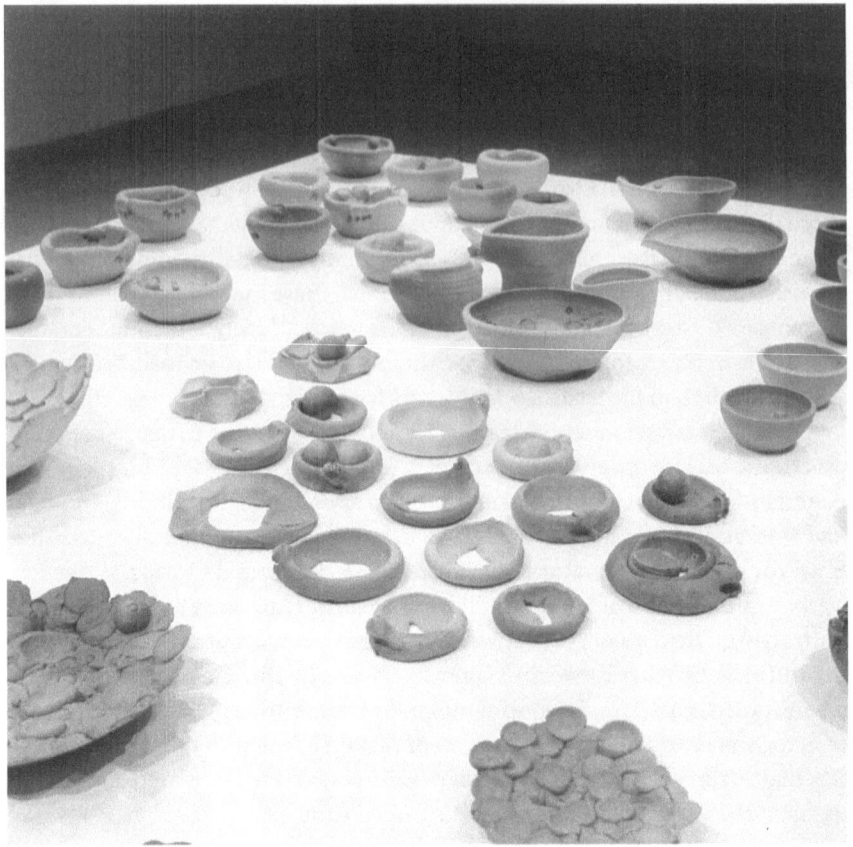

FIGURE 6.15. Gabriel Orozco, *Cazuelas (Beginnings)*, 2002, group of seventy-one terra-cotta elements, installation for Documenta 11, Kassel, 2002. (Courtesy of the artist and Galerie Chantal Crousel, Paris; photo: Florian Kleinefenn)

This statement highlights Orozco's reflexive alignment and artistic differentiation regarding shifting biennial politics and curatorial agendas. His participation at Enwezor's "global exhibition" was critical for Orozco's career because it strengthened the association of his position with rising globalization discourses at the field's centers, and thus was a precondition for his consecration as a "global artist," as we shall see in the section on art critics.

THE MOMA RETROSPECTIVE, 2009

Orozco's MoMA retrospective was arguably another turning point in his institutional consecration before 2010, followed by its traveling to major European art institutions.

Ann Temkin, who curated the MoMA retrospective, was an established senior curator in her midforties when she began preparing Orozco's show. With a BA from Harvard and a PhD in art history from Yale, she had previously been a senior curator at the Philadelphia Museum of Art before transferring to MoMA in 2003, where she became the chief curator of the department of painting and sculpture in 2008. Temkin was renowned for her scholarly approach and expertise in Western postwar art, and she had curated exhibitions or published on such artists as Barnett Newman, Joseph Beuys, and Raymond Pettibon.[152] She was also known for her more scholarly, traditional approach to curation, which, in a manner typical of an art historian, orbited largely around the physical art object and its formal qualities. Temkin's characteristics mark her as a member of the curatorial orthodoxy in the national museum scene. The fact that Orozco's retrospective was organized by a figure with such a strong institutional position and relatively conservative taste indicates how his position had become normalized in mainstream, Western art.

Likewise, Temkin did not learn about Orozco's work through informal networks but instead through his participation at the 1997 Documenta 10, which underlines the important role such major biennials play in exposing artists to international gatekeepers. She was so intrigued by Orozco's contribution to this show—a human skull covered with a painted black and white grid called *Black Kites* (fig. 6.16)—that she decided to acquire it for the Philadelphia Museum of Art and to invite Orozco for a solo show there in 1999. Although this work could have been interpreted in light of the Mexican tradition of the Day of the Dead, her catalog avoided making any such nationalistic references. Instead, Temkin focused on the work's formal characteristics, discussing it as part of Orozco's "autonomous sculptures."[153]

In 2005, after Temkin had become a curator at MoMA, the museum's history with Orozco inspired her to propose a retrospective for him. Partly because of his earlier show and his reputation in the field, Temkin did not have to struggle to convince the board, as Zelevansky had done thirteen years previously. The exhibition also received major funding from institutions in Orozco's home country—the National Council for Culture and the Arts as well as its Fundación Televisa, Mexico—though this support provoked local controversies.[154]

The MoMA retrospective framed Orozco as an artist who was a full-fledged member of the transnational canon of 1990s art, and it celebrated some of the included works—*La DS* and *Black Kites*—as "indisputable classics" of that decade.[155] Temkin's argued that Orozco's practice was distinctive for its versatility and the way it perpetually hopped between materials and styles. Her catalog essay associated this wandering approach with Orozco's poststudio working mode, which challenged the "legacy of modernism."[156] She thereby situated Orozco's distinctive position within a tradition of well-known

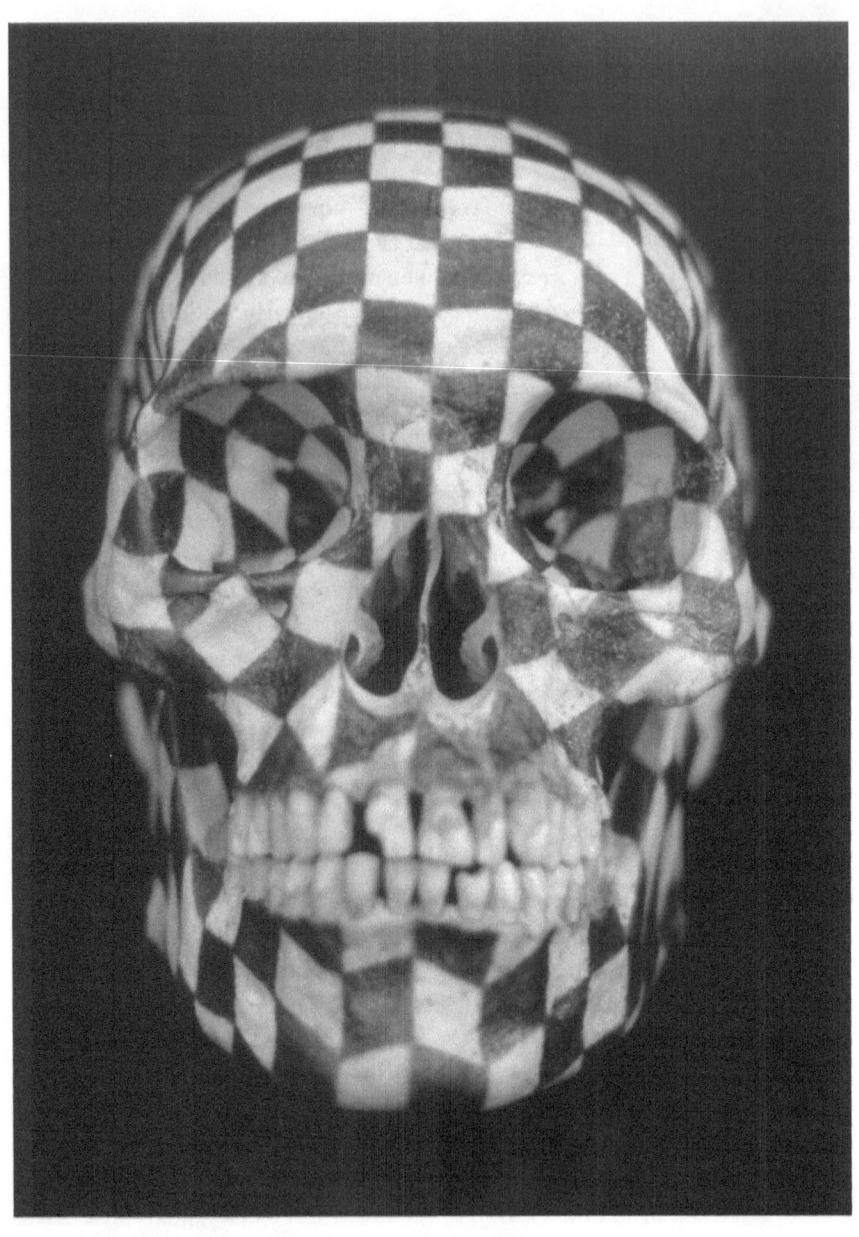

FIGURE 6.16. Gabriel Orozco, *Black Kites*, 1997. (Courtesy of the artist and Marian Goodman Gallery)

"Western" contemporary artists, especially Daniel Buren, Robert Smithson, and Robert Rauschenberg. Thus, Orozco's art was canonized within a traditional linear concept of US-European art history.

The fact that Orozco's Mexican background seemed irrelevant to the way Temkin framed his work may seem surprising in light of the fact that MoMA was by then extremely sensitive to being more receptive to artists from regions beyond the Euro-American axis. The museum had even appointed a specialized curator for Latin American art, though he was not involved in the show. Orozco's consecration in New York thus was accompanied by a tacit universalization of his position, but that happened in a Eurocentric way. In Temkin's orthodox view, his place within a transatlantic art historical narrative credited him with a paradigmatic status among a whole generation of artists, in a decade when the field was actually expanding beyond it. Joaquín Barriendos Rodríguez has decried this type of "universalizing discourse of global contemporary art" as the "apostasy of the colonialist geo-aesthetic representations," referring also to Gerardo Mosquera's critical remarks that the sole alliance with the "elitary production of the centers" automatically grants "universal" status.[157] However, as we will see in the next section, art critics also associated Orozco's universality with newer global meanings that resonated with biennial culture and went beyond the perceptual schemes of institutional orthodoxy.

Art Criticism and the Framing of Orozco from Artistic Nomad to Global Artist

Since the onset of modernity, critics have been a significant force for shaping artistic careers in Western contexts and beyond.[158] The "discourse" surrounding a work of art is "not a simple side effect, designed to encourage its apprehension and appreciation, but a moment, which is part of the production of the work."[159] Whatever an artist's intentions might be, critics play an important role in recognizing and communicating a work's "meaning and its value" within expert-driven subfields of cultural production.[160] As Bourdieu suggests, an artwork is "in fact made not twice, but hundreds of times, thousands of times, by all those who have an interest in it, . . . in classifying it, decoding it, commenting on it, . . . criticizing it."[161]

Indeed, Orozco's work provoked a significant amount of critical discourse in multiple publications and languages. If we focus on those contributions in exhibition catalogues, international art journals as well as international newspapers that appeared in English—contemporary art's global lingua franca—their critics originated from eleven countries on four continents, though at the time they were writing, most of them were situated in Northwestern centers.[162] So once again, we can see how Orozco's career was shaped significantly by agents located in those places with the greatest institutional leverage. We need to keep such inequalities in mind when we analyze the dominant discourses surrounding his position and avoid "naturalizing" them. They reveal recurring evaluative principles that echo selection criteria among key curators: autonomy (in the sense of a distance toward the commercial), artistic distinction, and universality.[163]

Regarding the first two criteria, several critics emphasized how Orozco's conceptual art was a specific response to the spectacular commercial art of the 1980s, by deploying inexpensive and often found materials, using process-based ephemeral artistic strategies, and relying on an unusual economy of means or, as one critic phrased it, a "spectacle of modesty."[164] Orozco's stylistic eclecticism—his deliberate shifts between different styles, media, and even aesthetic paradigms—was also perceived as an original move that echoed innovative tendencies in the contemporary art world.[165] His work thereby went beyond modernist conventions of refining a signature style within a single medium or tradition.[166] After a period marked by the dominance of market-driven and branded art in the international field, critics in institutional centers collectively recognized Orozco's work as being autonomous and distinctive for how it formulated ephemeral conceptual strategies out of an unusual combination of different media and aesthetic traditions.

DIALECTICAL UNIVERSALIZATION

A third evaluative element was significant for Orozco's discursive legitimation, however—namely, the universalization of his artistic position. Along with his exhibition trajectory, it originated within discourses referring to "artistic nomadism," a metaphor that dominated critical writings about the artist. This label then became associated with emerging discourses of globalization, which further highlighted the cosmopolitan aspects of Orozco's nomadic practice, framing it more explicitly in spatialized, global terms.

Benjamin Buchloh's writings offer a particularly clear picture of this gradual yet dialectical universalization of Orozco's work. The US-based German art historian, theorist, and critic was arguably the most influential discursive contributor in Orozco's career. The two men developed a strong bond and had many informal exchanges, and prior to 2010, Buchloh wrote six essays about Orozco and conducted two official interviews with him. As Orozco noted, "to Benjamin Buchloh I owe so many wonderful conversations and an invaluable friendship."[167]

When the two men first met, Buchloh was already a powerful player both in New York and internationally. From 1989 to 1994, he was an associate professor at MIT, and between 1991 and 1993, he directed critical and curatorial studies at the Whitney Museum's Independent Study Program. He had developed further symbolic capital as the coeditor of *October*, an intellectual art journal founded in 1976. It sought to counter conservative, formalist strands in art criticism by championing theoretically informed writing about art, especially using the frameworks of psychoanalysis, deconstruction, poststructuralism, and feminism. In his own work, Buchloh sought to balance the journal's more discursive, intellectual orientations with conservative, formalist traditions in art history, which established museums were still embracing.[168] This inter-mediate approach allowed him to gain cachet with two important audiences at the specific cultural pole. In Buchloh, Orozco found a supporter with high symbolic capital among intellectual avant-garde circles in the US and also among art professionals from more mainstream institutions in international centers.

In Buchloh's earliest catalog essay about Orozco, "Refuse and Refuge" (1993), which Buchloh wrote for Orozco's first solo show in Belgium in 1993, he noted how the artist addressed his Mexican background in critically reflexive ways. In his view, Orozco distanced his work from exoticist projections and instead exposed the mechanisms of "othering" at work in Western art contexts. He also positioned Orozco against the art of the "Neomexicanismos" and "Latinisms" that had gained attention in the art market at the beginning of the 1990s, when multiculturalism was on the rise. Notably, Buchloh's discussion framed these movements' success as heteronomous market fashions, reducing them to fads driven by a "primitivized" longing for an "authentic" other while downplaying the more politically active artists who were engaged with multi-cultural themes as well. Within the frame of this one-sided reading of the field, Buchloh lauded Orozco for exemplifying an alternative, critical position of artistic "refuse and refuge."[169]

In the late 1990s, Buchloh's essays focused more intently on the relationship between Orozco's work and broader North American and western European artistic traditions.[170] Yet the artist's country of origin was still important to the critic, albeit in a different way. Buchloh suggested that Orozco's background gave him a distinct perspective with which to approach established Western traditions. Coming from a country that had not held an important position in the Western contemporary canon predisposed Orozco to shift more freely between different media and to articulate diverse international artistic styles—including Italian Arte Povera, British sculpture, and US-American Post-Minimalism—in heterodox ways.[171] From Buchloh's perspective, Orozco's "alterity" thus cannot be separated from an understanding and appreciation of the "hybrid mixture between geographically and historically separated con-ventions" that his work creates, which transcends their artistic idioms with an unsettling, distinctive eclecticism.[172]

In Buchloh's essay for the catalog of Orozco's 2009 MoMA retrospective, he pushed his interpretation of the conditional "national and historical speci- ficity" of Orozco's work even further and declared him the "sculptor of his generation."[173] He again stressed how Orozco's Mexican background provided him with a different type of access and a distinct sensitivity to dominant West- ern traditions. Simultaneously, Orozco's work eluded simple, reifying identi- tarian claims or attributions, whether they were national, regional, or—as Buchloh explicitly discussed in 2009—global. Instead, his work was sus- pended in a distinctive dialectic that manifested itself in Orozco's site-specific practice. In Orozco's interventions, he mixed context-specific considerations with his awareness of a new globality of the flow of visual signs, creating an unresolved tension between the particular and the universal.[174]

FROM NOMADIC TO GLOBAL ARTIST

Buchloh's arguments concerning Orozco's ephemeral, dynamic, hybrid art, which nevertheless still had specific national roots, resonated with broader discourses that painted him as an artistic nomad. This was one of the most prevalent themes running through criticism about his work, and it combined the main evaluative principles involved in his recognition.[175] It metaphorically captured the innovative distinctiveness of his dynamic approach, or "artistic nomadism," and it also highlighted his resistance to market demands for work with a branded, signature style.[176] Finally, critics linked these two aesthetically "nomadic" characteristics with Orozco's practice of traveling and working in different countries. In this regard, the discourse highlighted how Orozco, as a Mexican artist, had been able to go beyond his national origin by forging a new, more generalized identity as an itinerant artist, which was based on a novel kind of biographical nomadism.

Thus, the idea of the artist as a nomad figure became an interpretative label through which Orozco could escape preconceived artistic categories and dual- isms. By situating himself between "Western" and "non-Western" art in general and between existing artistic categories in particular, he blurred and hybridized these categories in a perpetual, ephemeral movement between forms of aes- thetic expression and various context-specific artistic traditions.[177] This no- madic identity derived its relational meaning and value from the way it spoke to more general transformations and habitus in the contemporary art field of the late 1990s. As discussed in the previous section, during the biennial boom, artists and intermediaries were traveling more broadly, and the era saw a height- ened discursive reflexivity about artistic hybridizations (see also chapter 2).

As the century came to a close, this discourse's cosmopolitan elements be- came associated with rising discourses of globalization. Critics suggested that

Orozco's perpetual displacement reflected a more general "contemporary global state of being" and that he, as a type of artistic wanderer, became himself a "witness and messenger" of global transformations.[178] In a period that saw the emergence of a global vision (see chapter 2), Orozco became portrayed as a global artist, captured in notions like "global flaneur," a "global nomad," or the quintessential "globe-trotter."[179] This discursive transformation from the nomadic to the global implied a subtle shift in emphasis. It no longer foregrounded Orozco's transcendence of his national origin. Rather, it highlighted the novel contemporaneity of his cosmopolitan life and artistic practice, framing it within a broader context of the emerging global biennial circuit and developments in advanced transportation and communication technologies, which, in the new millennium, allowed Orozco to move around easily and sustain workplaces in several cities at once.[180]

However, in line with notions of nomadism from the 1990s, Orozco's itinerant lifestyle was analogically linked with his artistic practice. The global dimension of Orozco's position was discussed as something that was far from topically illustrative or symbolically tagged on. Rather, critics valued it in artistic terms, as a reflexive extension of field-specific aesthetic traditions. This self-referential logic is particularly clear in an appraisal of Orozco by the art historian and critic Margaret Sundell: "Gabriel Orozco practically invented today's genre of globe-trotting artist. But Orozco's at-home-everywhere-and-nowhere persona is *less a stylish pose than an extension of his artistic project*: a fusion of post-Minimalism's concern for site-specificity and Conceptual art's reliance on the portable photographic document."[181] Ultimately, while the discourse of nomadism alluded to Orozco's universality by highlighting how he drew from a range of artistic traditions across art history and geography, the criticism surrounding him as a global artist underscored how his itinerant lifestyle and approach exemplified a novel type of contemporary art practice. In the latter case, critics associated Orozco's universalism with the expansive global transformations that marked the artistic subfield at the dawn of the new millennium.

Conclusion: The Power of Strong Ties, Discursive Autonomy, and Cosmopolitan Universality

This chapter has explored the career of Gabriel Orozco to explain how an artist from a "peripheral" country in the contemporary art field at the end of the 1980s managed to achieve high symbolic recognition at the globalizing field's relatively autonomous pole. Orozco's success was propelled by support from mediators in powerful Western centers. In the late 1980s, as macro-level changes fed the rise of multiculturalism, these agents became more interested in the work of artists with "non-Western" origins. Most of the cultural producers who gained notoriety within the multicultural paradigm, however, were not readily compatible with the histories and aesthetic rules that prevailed in the international art field. Influential Western mediators promoted Orozco's work because it allowed them to reconcile two seemingly contradictory demands: extending the Eurocentric canon and making it more inclusive *and* relating their choices distinctively to the reigning aesthetic discourses and norms of Western art histories and tastes.

Orozco's high cultural capital and autonomous artistic habitus predisposed him to use his first exhibitions at prestigious Western institutions in reflexive, heterodox ways, and he positioned himself as a rebel from abroad who was working against exoticizing attributions and the Neo-Expressionist art that had dominated the 1980s art market. His radical position-takings maximized the initial attention he received and helped him accumulate symbolic capital at dominant centers and eventually at a worldwide scale. Rejecting ethnic labels thereby allowed him to become valorized in field-specific artistic, increasingly universal terms. By making his itinerant lifestyle and site-specific interventions a major focus of his art in the 1990s, he became associated with discourses surrounding artistic nomadism, which further underscored his work's cosmopolitan elements. And as the new millennium began, this critical cultural discourse merged with other ascendant ideas surrounding globalization and global art. Critics universalized his position further, leading to his consecration as a "global artist."

This case study suggests three broader arguments about the theorization of symbolic valuation within a global context. First, Orozco's career confirms that mediators situated in institutional art centers play a critical role for transcontinental artistic careers. But his case challenges existing arguments positing that a wide range of weak network ties is most consequential.[182] A Bourdieusian perspective sensitive to power differentials makes it clear that it is not so much the overall volume of ties that counts but the power that those ties possess. At the relative autonomous pole, the most relevant power resource is field-specific prestige, which, as I suggest, is conferred most effectively through strong network ties rather than weak ones. Additionally, within a global context, mediators' relative influence is not merely related to their individual social position and trajectory but is also derived from their geographic situatedness within the field's larger macro-structure. Taken together, Orozco's case study suggests the importance of strong ties with regard to both close, long-term relationships and mediators' power resources relative to the global field's meso- *and* macro-level configurations.

Second, in several ways, Orozco's career mirrored the traditional conversion path of the consecrated elite, in which an artist's accumulation of symbolic capital occurs before it is translated into economic capital (cf. chapter 5). Along this trajectory, both a critical distance to market demands and field-specific artistic distinction operated as decisive evaluation criteria in a global subfield that continued to be dominated by Western-trained mediators operating out of Northwest centers.[183] Orozco's case, however, requires us to rethink Bourdieu's narrow notion of *aesthetic* autonomy so that it better captures contemporary idioms of discursive autonomy. Such a revised conception—aligned with a logic that one might call "art for art's discursive sake"—involves a broader range of critical engagements with established notions of artistic practice and discursivity that are specific to a particular field. In other words, autonomy in this discursive sense is about much more than just formalist strategies and their aesthetic detachment from the everyday world.[184]

Third, Orozco's cross-border consecration was shaped by the gradual universalization of his artistic position. This dynamic was framed in terms of discourses that mattered to the field's historical states, but it also had an evaluative component that addressed the transcending relevance of Orozco's practice, which moved beyond "particular" questions about his cultural origin or national identity. This finding challenges arguments that suggest the few "non-Western" artists who reached global success at the turn of the new millennium did so through the exoticizing influence of multiculturalism.[185] For Orozco, the exact opposite happened. While multiculturalism served as an indirect historical precondition, his long-term success depended on his critical rejection of overt ethnic or geographic labels and his ability to position himself in the field in more universal parameters. Orozco situated his work in relation to dominant "universal" Western artistic traditions. But his dialogical, site-specific practices likewise had universal implications. Through a practice that crossed geographic and aesthetic borders, he managed to transcend his alterity as a Mexican "peripheral" figure and cultivate a new and distinct kind of cosmopolitan universality.

While the evaluative principles of autonomy and universality are connected, we must be careful not to conflate them. They are only related insofar as certain manifestations of particularism in the arts—such as the specific forms of artistic nationalisms—tend to be heteronomous because they use art to express a broader collective identity or ideal. Universality, however, touches on those aspects that concern an artist's perceived relevance across different countries.[186] In particular—and this idea extends Casanova's findings about the worldwide literary space—we can think about the evaluative principle of universality in three meaningful dimensions. First, there is a universality regarding the artistic traditions of dominant countries that are perceived as being more universal due to the number of internationally canonical works or the range of recognized stylistic innovations a country has previously produced.[187] While such traditions may be nationally framed (e.g., "US-American art"), the field refracts such national categories into aesthetic value judgments, which then credit certain countries with a higher level of universal aesthetic legitimacy in the global field.[188] Consequently, and as Orozco's case illustrates, an artist's association with dominant artistic traditions has a universalizing effect.

Furthermore, during a period of accelerated globalization, universality has come to involve an explicit appreciation of the art historical and geographical scope of the myriad sources an artist's work draws on (see also chapter 2). Lastly, Orozco's implicit ascription of universality was similarly bound up with a new type of artistic practice and position, namely, that of the "global artist" characterized by nomadic, site-specific interventions across multiple continents. In the discourse surrounding his recognition, these latter two dimensions were particularly pronounced. They underscore the fact that the meanings of artistic "universality" have become inextricably linked with the rise of cosmopolitan values in the globalizing artistic subfield (cf. chapter 2). Thus, while "autonomy" corresponds to the sacred value of anti-economism, artistic universality came to imply the additional value of cosmopolitanism in the making of legitimate art and artists across borders.[189]

Ultimately, in artistic terms, Orozco's work could become so successful because it was "multivalent"; it resonated with multiple evaluative principles at once.[190] At the same time, his career is exemplary for how it both reveals and propels a new cosmopolitan universality in the globalizing field, one driven by a vision of art that moves beyond any divisions between "center" and "periphery." As Orozco explains,

> I think it is very important for any artist to go and travel the world. That connectivity does not just apply to peripheral countries but also applies to those at the center. If you are an artist from Chicago or LA, even though you are in a big city, if you don't travel the world and understand what is happening around the globe, you will not understand your own country. But if you travel outside your own bubble to connect with other people and with nature, then you will start to develop your identity as a work in process and not as something prejudiced by what art has to be or what an American or Mexican has to be. You will begin to see what is possible as an artist and as a person, the new ways of expressing what we are living in today. Ultimately, for an artist, it is the same everywhere—you need to get engaged with the planet.[191]

7

The Hype of the Chinese
Market Star Yue Minjun

A GLOBALIZING SPECULATION GAME

The new Chinese art—as a phenomenon—reveals more about the game than
does a string of treatises by Pierre Bourdieu.

—POUL ERIK TOINER, 2007

AS WE SAW IN CHAPTER 5, one of the biggest shifts at the commercial pole
during a period of accelerated globalization involved the dramatic ascent of
contemporary artists from China. Between 2004 and 2008, prices for their
works surged by 2,000 percent, and several fetched multimillion-dollar prices
at globally leading auction houses.[1] This boom surprised many insiders.[2] Just
a decade previously, these artists were rarely part of the international market,
and many of them found themselves at the margins of their own society, considered to be "jobless loafers" who were living illegally in China's underground
artist communities.[3] It was thus puzzling how, against expectations, they could
achieve such an extraordinary economic rise.

This chapter explores some of the factors that contributed to this unique
market "explosion" by focusing on the case of Yue Minjun.[4] His works fetched
breathtaking record prices, and in 2007, he became one of the world's best-
selling contemporary artists, ahead of Richard Prince and a few spots behind
Jeff Koons and Damien Hirst.[5] But what enabled this relative newcomer from
China to become so successful in the globalizing art market? How could an
artist from a country that, back then, was relatively peripheral in the contemporary art field emerge as a global star within a market context that seemed
to favor Eurocentrism and homogenization?

Drawing on abundant empirical sources, this chapter traces how Yue's success involved a global market hype that was fueled by the speculative interests and strategies of mediators from commercial centers and boosted through the nested interplay with regional and national markets.[6] By exploiting future expectations about China's rising wealth and by using cross-border auction price signals, these agents attracted worldwide publicity and speculative buyers from several continents, catapulting Yue to a level in the market that far outpaced his prior symbolic recognition as an artist. Although the valuation of his art did not occur solely through forces at the market-driven pole, they dominated his trajectory toward an elite global position. As such, his case allows us to gain insights into the "rules" governing valorization in the globalizing commercial subfield.

Some of these rules had originated in the international market of the 1970s and 1980s, though they radicalized and expanded in the new millennium (see chapter 3). They include the role that auction prices play as a barometer of artistic value; the force that media publicity exerts as a form of "celebrity capital" for artistic relevance; and, of course, the very notion that contemporary art can be a lucrative, financial asset.[7]

But Yue's meteoric ascent was also facilitated by changes in the globalizing market game. On the one hand, market participants from a broader set of continents came to share these heteronomous principles of evaluation, which allowed the hype to gain global dimensions to begin with. On the other hand, these previously established mechanisms became articulated with newer influences that supported the Chinese newcomer's ability to shatter old hierarchies. At the macro-level, China's economic globalization was a key development. It created the structural basis for the growth of novel collectors and buyers in both the West and East. But it also affected the interpretative valuation of Yue's art since his works became widely appreciated as artistic expressions of China's contradictory transformations. In contrast to Orozco, who dialectically transcended his Mexican background and became a cosmopolitan "universal" artist at the autonomous pole, Yue gained success because of his art's overt national associations. In short, his art became valued for its national referentiality and topicality. These two cultural features could function as currencies at the commercial pole in the 1990s and first decade of the 2000s because they were elevated by broader discourses about China's dynamics and rising global economic status.

A third cultural factor that contributed to Yue's transcontinental economic success was his art's brand-like aesthetic. Yue's artistic style, which involved recurring smiling faces and bright colors, was commonly perceived to resemble Pop art, and many audiences appreciated its "iconic" qualities. Thus, within a global commercial setting—involving buyers from multiple countries with less specialized aesthetic expertise—the art's affinity with a familiar idiom and brand-like aesthetic heightened its accessibility and instant recognizability among broader publics. This ultimately contributed to a universality of legibility, giving Yue's work a distinctive advantage over his Chinese peers.

This chapter unpacks these arguments in two sections. The first describes three main phases in Yue's career before 2010: how he became a contemporary artist and his early experiences with Beijing's artistic underground, the initial symbolic and commercial valorization of his art outside China in the 1990s, and his millennial global market hype. The chapter then moves to a theoretical analysis of Yue's cycle of speculative valuation that looks at the interplay of macro-, micro-, and meso-level factors. This includes an exploration of the macro-level influence of China's economic globalization; a micro-level investigation of Yue's artistic habitus and style; and a meso-level analysis of his cross-border relationships with art market participants, highlighting their evaluative criteria concerning his art's speculative value and its potential as an iconic cultural mirror into China. I conclude by underlining how Yue's case diverges from Orozco's cycle of consecration, further supporting the book's central thesis regarding a dual economy of artistic recognition in the emerging global field.

Yue's Trajectory across Continents

From Worker to Chinese Underground Artist

ART AS AN ALTERNATIVE TO LABOR

Yue Minjun was born in 1962 in Heilongjiang Province in China into a family that one could interpret, in Western terms, as lower-middle class. His father drove trucks for an oil company, and his mother worked as an accountant. Given his parents' backgrounds, it is not surprising that art and cultural practices did not play an important role in Yue's childhood. Unlike Orozco, he was not well acquainted with art at an early age, and he did not acquire the kind of tacit familiarity with high-cultural practices that Bourdieu termed "cultural capital."[8] In fact, his interest in art developed not through his family context but through school. In this period of his life—which coincided with the Cultural Revolution (1966–76)—teaching standards were loose, and Yue began drawing in class to minimize his boredom.[9] These first ventures into drawing, however, did not spark a desire to develop his skills further and become an artist himself.

Indeed, when Yue finished high school in 1979, like his father, he first worked for oil companies in provinces outside Beijing, drilling oil and learning to be an electrician.[10] His experiences on the offshore oil platforms were so miserable, however, that he began to paint in his free time as an escape, creating sea landscapes and portraits of his fellow oil workers as a way to stave off boredom.[11] After five years, the work became so unbearable that he decided to return to school and study art.[12] This decision was not driven by intrinsic dedication to art but by his desire to escape an unhappy existential situation.

To apply to art school, Yue had to get permission from the leader of his Chinese work unit (*danwei*).[13] He then sent applications to three schools and was accepted at Hebei Normal University, where he studied between 1985 and 1989.[14] The provincial university's small art department was primarily designed to train art teachers at the middle-school level, not to educate artists. Therefore, Yue received a less specialized, more diverse training than did artists who attended more prestigious Chinese art academies, which emphasized technical mastery in oil or ink painting. Aside from working in these media, Yue also took courses in calligraphy, folk art, and teaching-related topics.[15]

Nevertheless, while Yue's art education was less specialized than that of his peers in China's established academies, it was similarly conservative. The curriculum emphasized realist paintings, which had been the Chinese art system's dominant mode since the republic's founding. Building on nineteenth-century French academic traditions and Soviet Realism, it was an aesthetic value system that demanded a politicized, collectivist understanding of the artist's role.[16] According to Chairman Mao's "Talk at Yan'an" in 1942, art was, above all, a tool for propaganda, and realism was the only mode capable of sufficiently meeting the demands of "Serving the People."[17] In short, the artist's task was to communicate the system's broader political values to the public.

After Deng Xiaoping opened China in 1979, this doctrine did not go uncontested in the country. With the influx of new information about Western contemporary art and a more relaxed political climate, artists began experimenting with international styles and political themes outside the academic system's strictures.[18] A new avant-garde movement—the "85 Art Movement," which involved more than eighty unofficial art groups and 150 exhibitions— emerged.[19] The official Chinese art academies remained state-oriented and artistically conservative, however, shunning experimental contemporary art forms such as performance, installation, and video art until the 1990s.[20] Indeed, the only other Western styles that Yue encountered in his education were modern Impressionism and abstraction from the turn of the twentieth century.[21]

THE YUANMINGYUAN ARTISTS' VILLAGE AND "CYNICAL REALISM"

After Yue graduated in 1989, his work unit assigned him to teach drawing at the North China Petroleum College, so he remained in Hebei Province. This job left Yue "entirely unfulfilled" again, and when he happened to come across China's first unofficial artists' village, he decided to join and try living as an independent artist.[22]

This community at Yuanmingyuan, west of Beijing, was spread across a large park where young artists from all over China were able to rent relatively cheap housing from local farmers.[23] It had emerged in 1990, after two major events had disillusioned many Chinese artists about their role in a one-party regime. The first was the abrupt closing of the *China/Avant-Garde* exhibition—which surveyed the more innovative contemporary Chinese art practices that had developed outside official art circles in the 1980s—at the National Art Museum of China in February 1989. The exhibition's initial approval seemed to signal the beginning of a public recognition of experimental art in China; unfortunately, the government closed the show mere hours after its opening and tightened censorship activities in the following weeks.[24] A few months later, the Tiananmen Square massacre and the massive prosecutions that followed further destroyed any hope that free expression would have a place in the Chinese state. Many artists either left the country or organized themselves in unofficial structures, such as the one in Yuanmingyuan.

Yue learned about this community by chance when he visited a friend in Beijing. As he recalled, "I immediately noticed the artists who were living in the neighborhood. . . . It was exactly as I had imagined the life of an artist to be, and it all seemed so great that I decided to make the move from Hebei."[25] Yue's decision to join the artistic underground was not largely motivated by a sense of political dissidence toward the events of 1989, although that was how Western critics and mediators would later frame his position. Instead, it was fueled by his personal frustrations with the constricting life and obligations in his Hebei work unit.

Joining such a community was a novel and risky step for an artist at that time. It meant leaving the highly regulated *danwei* system of state support for art professionals while simultaneously being unable to rely on any established infrastructure for independent artists in China.[26] Yue approached the risk pragmatically. In 1991, he did not completely resign from his work unit at first; he instead pretended to take a long sick leave. After skipping a full year of work, however, he was fired, which forced him to continue living in Yuanmingyuan. Thus, almost by coincidence, and for mostly private rather than political motivations, Yue became part of the first group of independent Chinese artists who were willing to try to create self-sufficient careers.[27]

Escaping the official "occupational and household register system," the Yuanmingyuan artists were relegated to the margins of Chinese society, derided in official media as "vagrants," "vagabonds," or "superfluous people."[28] Under impoverished conditions, they lived bohemian lives and found refuge in their creative companionship (fig. 7.1). Indeed, Yue's primary friends at this time were other artists from Yuanmingyuan, indicating the social insularity in which he found himself.[29]

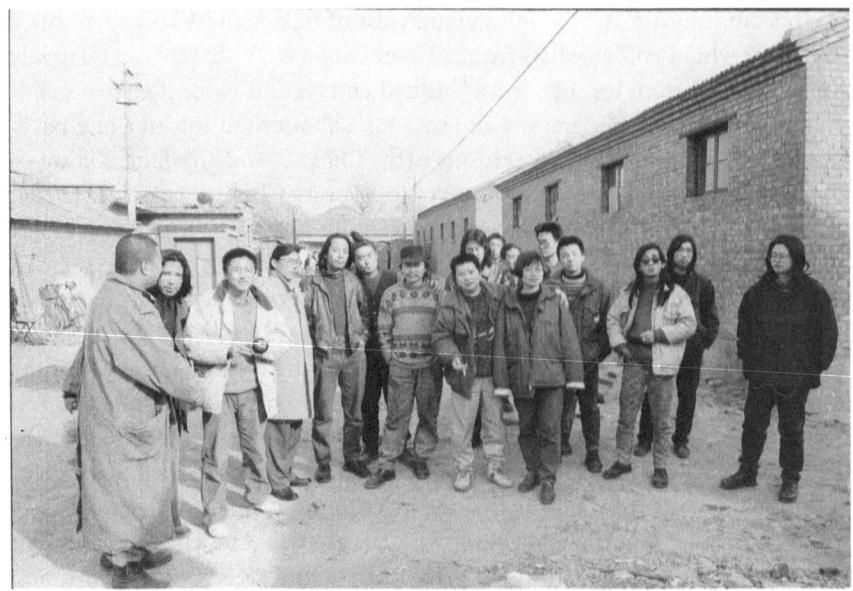

FIGURE 7.1. Artists at the Yuanmingyuan artists' village in 1995. (Photo: Hu Min)

These somewhat closed conditions were conducive for the emergence of a "collaborative circle" that nurtured an oppositional artistic subculture.[30] The close-knit community enabled artists to break away from the Chinese field's orthodox art more easily and develop new directions. Artists in Yuanmingyuan eschewed the big social topics of state-sanctioned art. They instead focused on the human figure and emphasized individual expression, often creating surreal, cynical portraits of subjects at the edges of society.[31] In other words, they converted the politically imposed realism in painting into new, highly subjective forms that expressed a disenchanted worldview.[32]

This subculture influenced Yue's own signature style too, which he would stick with for the rest of his career. When he arrived at the village, he was relatively insecure "to determine" his "own preferences," and he mainly experimented with the styles of fellow artists and made them the subjects of his paintings.[33] Gradually, he gained confidence and started creating self-portraits with laughing faces. A painting by the Chinese artist Geng Jianyi, *The Second State* (1987), which Yue saw in a review of the *China/Avant-Garde* exhibition, inspired his choice of the motif (fig. 7.2). Geng's painting appealed to Yue because it conveyed a profound ambiguity: it was both a parody of Soviet-style realism that featured happy people laughing and a reminder that things could get better in a society that "had frowned upon those who deviated from the norm."[34] As a parody, it resonated with the "mood of bitter frustration that was

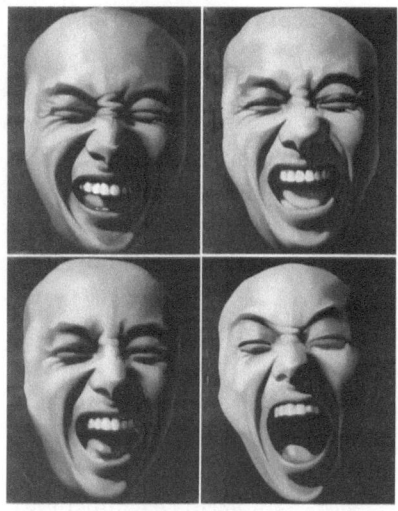

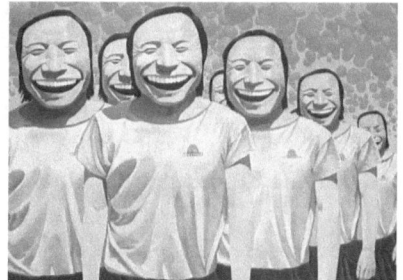

FIGURE 7.2. Geng Jianyi, *The Second State*, 1987, oil on canvas, dimensions variable (each 170 × 130 cm). (M+Sigg Collection, Hong Kong, 20212.2; copyright Geng Jianyi; photo: M+, Hong Kong)

FIGURE 7.3. Yue Minjun, *Happiness*, 1993, oil on canvas. (Courtesy of the Artist and Schoeni Art Gallery, Ltd.)

common amongst our generation."[35] Yue would appropriate this motif in numerous variations, emphasizing the irony by aesthetically stylizing it, furnishing his figures with flamboyant pink skin, toothpaste-white teeth, and a neat crop of black hair. His own laughing self-portraits increasingly came to resemble recognizable cartoon figures (fig. 7.3).[36]

With these portraits, Yue became associated with a style at Yuanmingyuan that the Chinese art critic Li Xianting called "Cynical Realism" and that also included the work of artists like Fang Lijun, Liu Wei, and Yang Shaobin.[37] Li borrowed the term from Aldous Huxley's famous statement, "Cynical realism is the intelligent man's best excuse for doing nothing in an intolerable situation."[38] The poignant label, which positioned Yue within a discourse of political dissidence, facilitated his later success with foreign buyers. For them, Yue's laughing faces often appeared as ironic symbols of disillusionment with the oppression of China's Communist regime.[39] And as I discuss shortly, Yue's accessible aesthetic style, which was perceived as resembling Pop art from the US and Europe, created affinities between his work and an artistic idiom that was already established in the international art market—just as Orozco's link with conceptual art did at the autonomous pole.

From the Artistic Underground to Regional Surfacing, 1992–99

FOREIGN MEDIA ATTENTION AND THE DEVELOPMENT
OF AN UNOFFICIAL LOCAL MARKET

Yue's allegiance to the underground community at Yuanmingyuan was also important for the beginning of his foreign career and initial sales. As the colony's activities attracted foreign media coverage and visitors, its artists became more visible outside China, which contributed to the development of an incipient market for their work.

Specifically, because Yuanmingyuan's artists were banned from official exhibition venues and sales channels, they developed unorthodox art events in unusual locations, including basements, apartments, warehouses, studios, homes, parks, and bars.[40] Such collective gatherings were illegal in China and thus prosecuted by the police, but these regular collisions with authorities attracted increased foreign media coverage.[41] For example, in December 1993, the cover of the *New York Times Magazine* featured work by Fang Lijun.[42] The article, like others at the time, framed Yuanmingyuan as a symbol of dissident art in China. Such portrayals heightened the visibility of the community's artists among foreigners visiting the country, who began frequenting the village to purchase art.

Thus, although Yuanmingyuan's artists were largely ignored by people in China in the early 1990s, many were able to start selling their work due to foreign attention and circulating discourses of political dissidence, as I detail more later. Business professionals, diplomats, or journalists who were working in the country on a temporary basis were the main buyers, and the sales enabled Yue to make a living.[43] Indeed, in 1992, after an American investment banker came to Yuanmingyuan and bought one of his paintings for $5,000, Yue could live entirely off sales of his work.[44] Foreigners "made the market" for Chinese contemporary art in the 1990s, supporting the artists of this heterodox community materially and morally.[45] Thus, their market was a means to remain independent of the official state-controlled art system and its restrictive policing, underlining how important it is to recognize the different ways market dynamics affect artistic practice and value (see chapter 3).

THE ALIGNMENT WITH A REGIONAL SALES GALLERY

Yue's allegiance to Yuanmingyuan also benefited his career because he could forge connections with foreign art intermediaries (i.e., "social capital"). They facilitated his increasing profile in regional and overseas exhibitions from around the mid-1990s. However, unlike some of his peers, the kind of foreign exhibitions Yue appeared in occurred largely at sales galleries. In the 1990s, already, a set of forces of repulsion and attraction had taken shape in the artists' relations with foreigners. These steered Yue in more commercial directions, while they led others from the village toward more symbolic recognition abroad.

This dynamic is particularly clear in Yue's first encounters with gallerists. The Hong Kong gallery owner Johnson Chang visited Yuanmingyuan in 1992 to scout works for an exhibition that was meant to provide an overview of avant-garde currents in China. Chang had the reputation as someone who was driven primarily by artistic rather than economic interests, earning him the nickname "scholar dealer."[46] Indeed, he helped organize several nonprofit initiatives to promote Chinese artists to regional and overseas art audiences. For example, the exhibition *China's New Art, Post-1989*, which he cocurated with Li Xianting, traveled widely to art institutions in Taiwan, Australia, the UK, Canada, and the US after debuting in Hong Kong in 1993. This group show is widely considered to be a milestone for the international reception of Chinese contemporary art.[47] But even though Chang bought one of Yue's paintings for $1,500 during his visit, he did not invite Yue to participate in this show. Nor did he invite Yue to subsequent international projects in which other artists from the village appeared.[48] Chang later explained that he found Yue's artistic approach insufficiently complex.[49] It is no coincidence that Yue's highly accessible painting style, which would later facilitate his success in the global auction market, was not embraced by the avant-garde gallerist.

Yet by 1993, Yue signed a contract with another gallery owner from Hong Kong, the Swiss-born Manfred Schoeni, who was reputed to be more business-oriented than Chang. He would become Yue's strongest gallery tie, offering Yue steady exhibition opportunities and sales outside China for several years. The collaboration started when Schoeni offered Yue his first exhibition outside the mainland in 1994, alongside Yang Shaobin, another artist from the village. Schoeni's motivation seemed guided by personal feelings. As he recalled, "It was a pure chance that I met Yang Shao Bin and Yue Min Jun. . . . Instantly, when I saw their painting, my inner feelings and passion started once again took the better of logical thought—the result is this show."[50]

Yue's foreign debut showcased nearly twenty paintings and was accompanied by a carefully edited catalog, which included a statement by Yue and two texts by art experts from mainland China, the renowned Li Xianting as well as the younger Lu Jie. Li contextualized the artists within Chinese art history as part of a third artistic generation after the Cultural Revolution, hailing Yue and his peer as "undoubtedly among the most promising and individualistic" of a new, post-1989 realist tradition of "Cynical Realism." Yue's repetitive motif of the laughing faces, in "bold, bright colours similar to that of poster design," was framed as more than illustrations of the "humorous and foolish side of social life." They served to "question the ideology of the national propaganda machine" and convey the "absurdity which pervades much of the consumer-oriented society of the 90s" in China. Although Yue's own words in the catalog took more neutral tones, his paintings thus became linked early on with meanings of political dissidence.[51]

This first foreign exhibition was a success with regard to reception and sales, yet it did not make many artistic waves beyond the port city. As a businessman, Schoeni was not as focused on cross-border cultural promotion as Chang was, not least because he worked on multiple ventures, including in the wine and restaurant industry, at once.[52] Indeed, following Yue's debut, most of his foreign exhibitions until 1999 occurred at sales galleries or art fairs. Schoeni initiated eight of them and mediated five. Yue's foreign exhibitions were also predominantly limited to a regional scale (twelve in Hong Kong and one in Bangkok). In short, Yue's association with the foreign dealer was critical for his foreign debut and regional visibility, but that primarily involved market venues.

YUE'S PARTICIPATION AT THE 1999 VENICE BIENNALE

The most important public exhibition in Yue's career during the 1990s was not mediated by Schoeni but by the Swiss entrepreneur and former ambassador to China Uli Sigg. It was the group show *dAPERTutto* at the forty-eighth Venice Biennale where he presented a series of laughing self-portraits in black and white. Sigg was known as the "ambassador of Chinese art in the West"; having become an avid collector of Chinese contemporary art in the mid-1990s, he wanted to introduce Chinese artists to Western audiences.[53] In the time leading up to the Venice Biennale, he had invited the appointed Swiss curator Harald Szeemann to China and introduced him to several artists. By this point, Sigg was already friends with Yue, and he connected him with Szeemann too, thus facilitating the invitation.[54]

The 1999 exhibition, which also included work from seventeen other Chinese artists, was another watershed event for the transnational recognition of contemporary art from China, and it occurred precisely as peripheral biennials and global discourses were beginning to exert more pressure on central Western institutions to open up.[55] Unlike prior iterations at Venice, where Chinese artists had been sequestered within specialized sections, this show included them in the general exhibition, placing them, as Szeemann stated, "on the same level as artists in the West."[56] The high symbolic capital of both the Venice Biennale and its curator contributed to the strong effect this exhibition had on Chinese contemporary art's transnational recognition.[57] While important overviews of the genre had been staged since the early 1990s, they now reached a broader public of international gatekeepers, who were impressed by the spectrum of innovative art coming from China.[58] The show contributed to break "down barriers," establishing Chinese contemporary art "firmly . . . in the international scene."[59]

In the following years, Yue's career benefited from the symbolic surplus of both his participation at the Venice Biennale and his association with "Chinese contemporary art" as a genre with growing legitimacy among foreign art experts. However, when Szeemann curated the Venice Biennale once more in 2001, he did not solicit Yue, even though he included other Chinese artists again.

From Regional Market Success to a
Global Speculative Hype, 2000–2008

The 1999 Venice Biennale marked the beginning of a more global phase in Yue's career. His foreign exhibitions soon multiplied across continents, though, unlike Orozco, he never left his home country to live abroad (figs. 7.4 and 7.5). Between 2000 and 2008, he participated in almost one hundred group shows outside China, a fivefold increase compared to the 1990s. In that same eight-year period, he received opportunities for twelve foreign solo exhibitions; prior to Venice, he had only one solo show. Significantly, most of these exhibitions were now occurring beyond the regional Asian scale that had marked his career in the 1990s; that is, they spread to about thirty countries on four continents (fig. 7.6).

Thus, following Venice, Yue's career trajectory seemed to be on its way toward reaching symbolic recognition on a more globally expanded level as well. What is more, as we shall see, in 2004, his auction sales began rising and extending geographically, culminating with an exponential growth in prices and turnover between 2006 and 2008 that temporarily turned him into a global commercial star. But what seems on the surface to be another example of the cross-border conversion of symbolic to economic capital, as it was in Orozco's case, was driven by quite different actors and processes. Rather than a story of the conversion path, Yue's meteoric rise points to a speculative hype that played out in a globalizing market game.

COMMERCIAL GALLERIES AND COLLECTORS AS DRIVING FORCES BEHIND YUE'S FOREIGN EXHIBITIONS

Among cultural mediators, Yue was in fact unable to garner lasting recognition and support. Most of his shows outside Asia were initiated by commercial galleries, private collectors, and speculators, players who could be considered external to the more autonomous pole of artistic consecration.

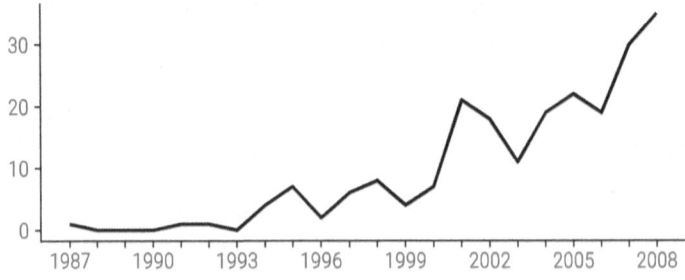

FIGURE 7.4. Yue's frequency of exhibitions, 1987–2008.

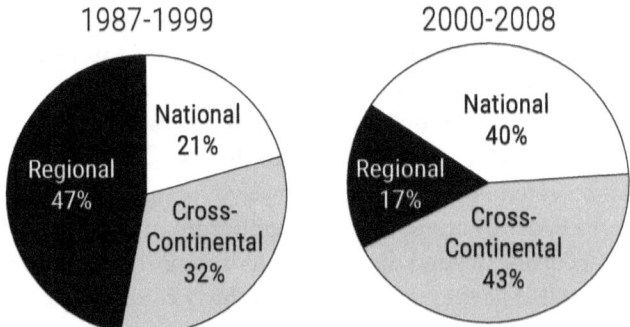

FIGURE 7.5. Yue's exhibition distribution across regional, national, and cross-continental scales.

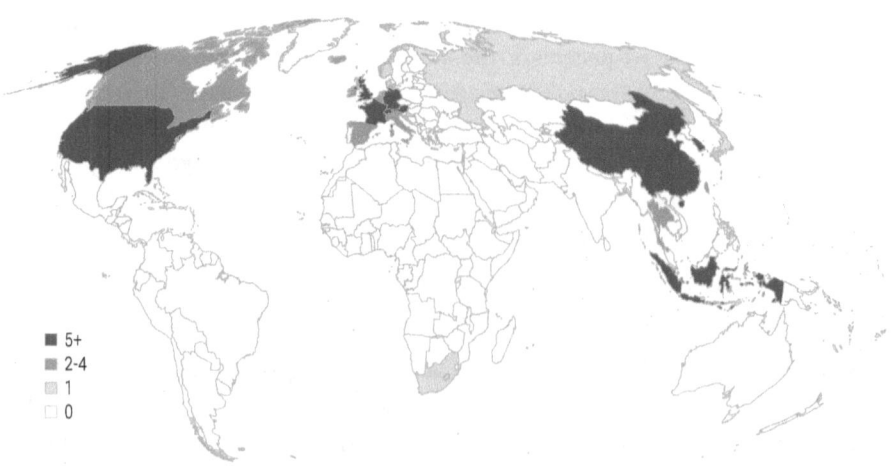

FIGURE 7.6. Geographical distribution of Yue's exhibitions, 2000–2008.

In fact, around half of Yue's foreign exhibitions during these years took place at sales-oriented galleries. Until 2004, Yue expanded his cross-continental dealer network primarily with galleries in Western centers that specialized in Chinese art (i.e., Germany, Switzerland, the UK, and Canada). They sought to extend the momentum that the 1999 Venice Biennale had created for the reception of Chinese contemporary art in the West.

One of Yue's first solo exhibitions beyond Asia, at the gallery *Chinese Contemporary*, was sales driven. Cofounded in 1996 in London by the art historian Julia Coleman and her husband, the former stockbroker Ludovic Bois, the gallery was known for working on a sale-or-return basis, and other galleries reproached it for selecting artists solely for their financial value.[60] Yue was initially hesitant to collaborate with the gallery because he was not convinced by its programming. But he eventually participated in two group shows, starting in 1998, and a solo show in 2000, his first in an international art market capital. For this event, Coleman chose Yue's colorful laughing self-portraits, which had become best sellers in the 1990s, thus following a market-conforming strategy. When Yue attended the London opening, he was disappointed by the simplified way the dealers had presented his work.[61] Though his London debut sold well, unlike Orozco's first New York show at Marian Goodman's gallery, it neither greatly increased the foreign expert attention Yue received nor sparked further invitations for solo exhibitions at other art institutions.

Nevertheless, not all of Yue's gallery ties in these early millennial years were commercial. Two gallerists in particular, Alexander Ochs and Urs Meile, were also pursuing artistic goals that aligned them with an avant-garde strategy. But these galleries did not develop lasting relationships with Yue. Like Chang, they ultimately found Yue's artistic approach insufficiently complex for their agendas, as I explain more later. And after 2004, when Yue's foreign network expanded beyond China-focused galleries, he again largely attracted more commercial dealers. In other words, although Yue enjoyed growing exhibitions at galleries beyond Asia, most of them did not contribute much to heighten his symbolic recognition abroad.

Apart from galleries, the other half of Yue's exhibitions beyond the Asian region from 2000 to 2008 took place at public/noncommercial art institutions, traditionally considered to be more effective at producing "exhibition value" as a form of symbolic capital.[62] Yet these included only two solo showings. And among the group shows, 80 percent were focused on Chinese contemporary art. Rather than being valued as a single artist—as Orozco was—after the 1999 Venice Biennale, Yue was exhibited and seen more readily on the global stage as a representative of a national art genre that he had become associated with.

Moreover, two-thirds of the foreign Chinese shows that Yue participated in were not initiated by professional curators but by collectors. In other words, while his work was also included in group exhibitions at prestigious museums in powerful Western centers, these were largely drawn from private collections instead of being independently curated, demonstrating once again that Yue's expanding exhibition career was not really driven by more autonomous art experts and institutions.[63]

The collectors involved in Yue's career had diverse motives. Some of them wanted to help promote a deeper artistic understanding and appreciation for Chinese contemporary art beyond Asia, while others took a more speculative, instrumental approach, seeing museum shows primarily as an opportunity to symbolically increase the value of the work before its subsequent sale. For example, Yue's only solo museum show during these years, which took place at the Queens Museum of Art between October 14, 2007, and January 6, 2008, was cleverly brokered by the collector-dealer Larry Warsh. Warsh had offered to lend the institution his private holdings of Yue's art for a solo exhibition. The institution agreed, largely for pragmatic reasons. The museum was aiming to have at least 25 percent of its exhibits feature non-American, international artists to better reflect the diversity of Queens's local community. Warsh's offer also meant that the museum would not have to spend as much of its own money to mount an exhibition.[64]

Hitomi Iwasaki, who was asked to curate the show at the museum, was not deeply engaged in its organization. Even though she had previously exhibited Asian art (mainly from Japan), she was not excited about Yue's work. While she knew it had become one of the "hottest commodities in the art market" by then, she generally believed that "the quality of art has nothing to do with the art market."[65] Given her more autonomous approach to curating and her reservations about Yue's art, Iwasaki did not fully identify with her task. She mainly helped prepare the exhibition organizationally, selecting and arranging Yue's laughing self-portraits and twenty life-size terra-cotta soldiers. Yet she did not list her name as the show's curator in publications about the exhibition, and she did not produce an essay or catalog with a curatorial statement about Yue's artistic position. She also did not "engage herself" at the show's opening; instead, a Sotheby's representative spoke at the museum's vernissage.[66] In this sense, Yue's only museum show in a powerful global exhibition center can be considered a staged event by commercial players, designed to heighten the symbolic capital of the private acquisitions of Warsh and of other collectors whose possessions were included in the exhibition before they were resold. By 2009, five paintings featured in Queens were auctioned by Sotheby's in New York, Hong Kong, and London for more than $ 1.5 million combined, and several additional works appeared at auction in the following years.

Unlike Orozco's New York show, Yue's museum debut did not entail a wider critical reception either. It only garnered a single review in a more generalized media outlet, the *New York Times*, rather than a specialized art magazine, and it was written by a book critic, not one of the paper's primary art critics.[67] The show also did not lead to subsequent invitations for solo shows from museums outside Asia until 2010, which contrasts with the careers of other Chinese artists who were part of the earlier Venice Biennale. Yue's work circulated only as part of group exhibitions abroad, and many showcased private collections of Chinese contemporary art as well. Thus, although Yue had a solo show in a museum in *the* center of the globalizing art field, this seemingly crucial step in his consecration cycle did not significantly heighten his recognition at the specific cultural pole.

A GLOBAL HYPE

Parallel with Yue's increasing exhibitions in multiple countries—and despite minimal recognition from conventional consecratory authorities—he experienced increasing success at auctions, which tracked with a broader valorization of the genre of Chinese contemporary art in the global market after 2004. Following an early success in the regional hub of Hong Kong, his auction trajectory was significantly boosted by a sale at Sotheby's New York before reaching auctions across numerous countries and eventually mainland China. Between 2005 and 2008, speculative market dynamics made Yue one of the world's best-selling artists. But as many buyers withdrew from the market after the onset of the global financial crisis, his position fell just as precipitously as it had risen, and his art never reached the same economic value again, suggesting that his extraordinary ascent was largely based on global speculative hype.

Specifically, Yue's works first entered the auction market in 1998 with two paintings that were part of a special sale of the "Asian Avant-Garde" at Christie's London. The house's attempt to commercialize artists from China in an international capital turned out to be premature, however. The sale was a financial "disaster," and Yue's works went either significantly below estimates or unsold altogether.[68] Subsequent attempts to auction his art at Christie's (in Taiwan in 2000, London in 2001, and Hong Kong in 2002) went poorly as well. Indeed, in the millennium's early years, nothing indicated that Yue would ever become a global auction star.

This situation changed in October 2004, when Sotheby's Hong Kong initiated the first stand-alone auction sale for "Chinese Contemporary Art." Henry Howard-Sneyd, the house's managing director for China, Southeast Asia, and Australia, observed a growing gallery market for this genre in the port city and sensed a commercial opportunity. His sense of timing proved prescient.

Although the sale could not attract many mainland Chinese buyers, it was a major financial success with its Hong Kong audience.[69] *Sunflowers*, which sold for $77,100, almost double its estimate, set a personal auction record for Yue. The outstanding sale at a prestigious auction house bolstered the belief in a growth segment that was likely to appreciate further, especially given China's increasing wealth levels. In the following year, as Sotheby's and Christie's competitively expanded their sales of contemporary artists from China in Hong Kong, an investment-driven auction market developed, involving Western expatriates from Hong Kong's financial industry, US and European dealers, and Asian investors. Nobody wanted to miss the train, and buyers began snapping up works.

This speculative dynamic affected the spiraling sales of Yue's works in Hong Kong the following year. In 2005, four out of six lots of his work were bought and resold for higher prices within just two or three years. The new clientele drove prices up quickly. In November of that year, at Christie's Hong Kong, Yue reached a final price of $636,744 for *Gweong-Gweong* (1996; fig. 7.7). The success immediately distinguished his market position from that of his Chinese peers. As Philip Tinari commented, "The sale . . . marked a new era of commercial success for the entire field, breaking a record for a living Chinese artist."[70] It was a Taiwanese, investment-oriented buyer who purchased Yue's painting. Though it seemed like a huge price at the time—especially if one knows that the painting had exchanged hands for $5,000 in 1994 at the Schoeni Gallery—he resold it in 2008 at Christie's Hong Kong for over $6 million.[71] Hence, despite Yue's relatively low symbolic recognition among critics and curators, by 2005, he had emerged as one of the regional auction leaders in Chinese contemporary art, driven by an economic logic in which prior market success and rapid price increases could lead to further gains.

The successful 2004 Chinese contemporary art sale inspired further moves to New York. On March 31, 2006, Sotheby's inaugurated the first specialist auction in New York to establish, as Howard-Sneyd announced in a press release, a "global presence in this exciting and fast developing field."[72] The long-prepared New York sale attracted bidders from four continents. It was a commercial triumph, generating more than $13 million (double the presale estimate) and setting twenty auction records for contemporary artists from China. Yue excelled as well. His featured painting—the same work that could not find a buyer for a tenth of the price at Christie's London in 2001—sold for $564,000. The painting changed hands anonymously, but later it became clear that Diva Fine Arts, a commercial dealer in Geneva, had bid for the work and resold it to a Belgian couple, the business entrepreneur Roland Gillion and his wife, Anne-Marie Crowet, most likely for a substantial profit.[73]

What is more, the New York sale unleashed a global phase in the boom of "Chinese contemporary art" as a market genre, seven years after it had made

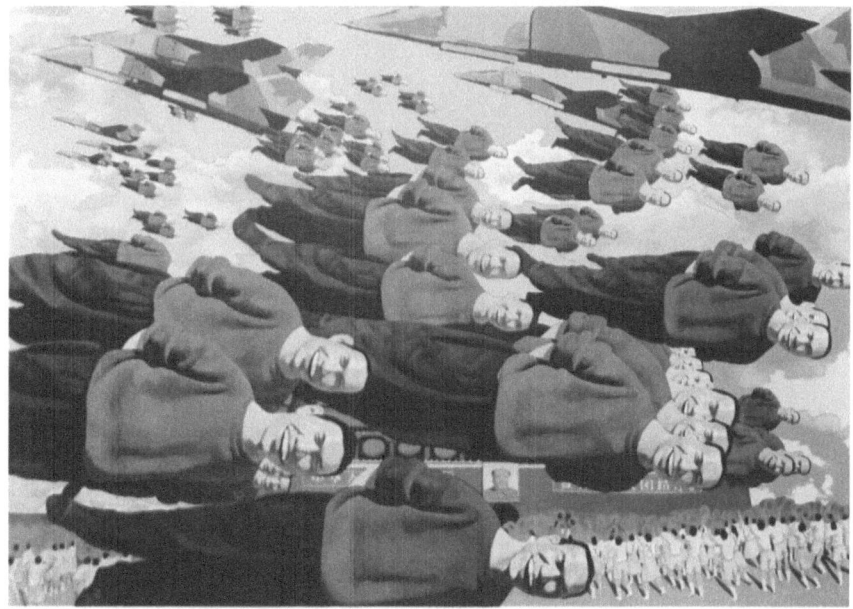

FIGURE 7.7. Yue Minjun, *Gweong-Gweong*, 1996, oil on canvas.
(Courtesy of the artist and Schoeni Art Gallery, Ltd.)

headlines at the Venice Biennale. As the head of worldwide contemporary art and auctioneer for the sale, Tobias Meyer, predicted, "The enormous energy and enthusiasm in the room today validates this collecting area on a global level."[74] Soon, an incredible herding dynamic set in. Within weeks, Christie's and Phillips enlarged their sales of works by Chinese artists in New York and London. Beta houses in Paris, Los Angeles, San Francisco, Cologne, Zurich, and Naples also began auctioning works. At the regional level, Hong Kong experienced an incredible gold rush of buyers from "almost anywhere," including Russia, Australia, the US, and countries in Europe and Latin America.[75] Regional beta houses in Hong Kong, Seoul, Singapore, and Tokyo likewise joined the competition.

Eventually, mainland China bought in too. In the fall of 2006, the country's two major auction houses—Guardian and Poly—initiated their first stand-alone sales for contemporary Chinese art. Thanks to successful sales in a global center—which were widely reported in China and constituted something like a "shock moment"—the long-marginalized artists made their way into China's official auction venues.[76] Just as the 1999 Venice Biennale functioned as a major platform for global symbolic consecration, Sotheby's New York acted as a consecratory institution for the global market, creating a "watershed

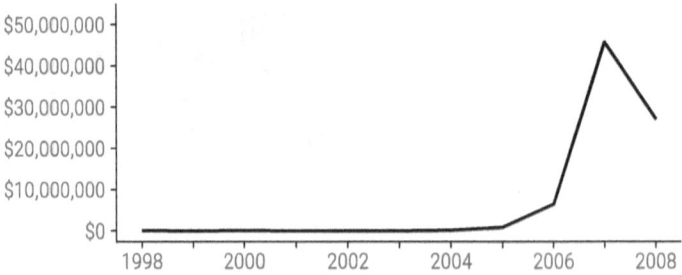

FIGURE 7.8. Yue's auction turnover, 1998–2008. Source: Artprice.com.

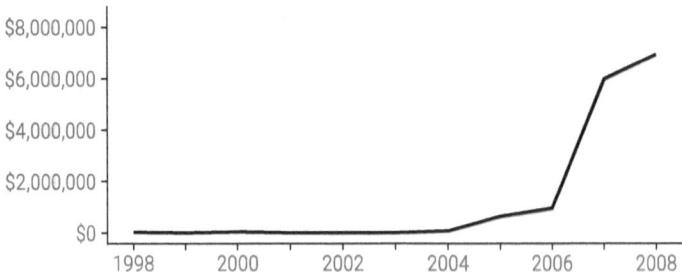

FIGURE 7.9. Yue's maximum prices, 1998–2008. Source: Artprice.com.

event" or "turning point" for the entire genre, which then exerted feedback effects on global, regional, and national market levels.[77]

Amid this market frenzy, auctions involving Yue's art—who had established himself as a foreign market leader in the genre—soared (figs. 7.8 and 7.9). Within just one year, he became one of the top-hundred best-selling artists in this global market. From 2006 to 2007, his annual turnover jumped from $3.6 million to an incredible $44.8 million. That was much higher than figures for the highly recognized Xu Bing, whose annual sales "only" went up to $1.9 million.[78] In 2007, Yue's works could reach those levels with just a single auction, and his prices continued to break new records.

The skyrocketing list hit its first zenith in October 2007 when the painting *Execution* (1995) sold for $5,977,022 at a prestigious evening auction at Sotheby's London (fig. 7.10). It was the highest price a living artist from China had achieved in the foreign auction market up to that point, and it cemented Yue's status as an art star at the commercial pole. The sale also brought much publicity. Western media hailed the work as a critique of the Tiananmen protests and massacre, although Yue publicly denied this association.[79]

The record price occurred just five days *before* the opening of Yue's solo show at the Queen's museum, an incident that the institution's curator called

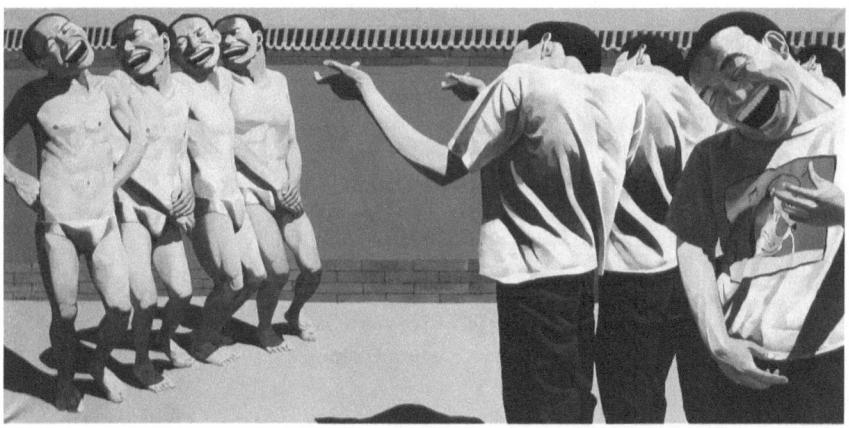

FIGURE 7.10. Yue Minjun, *Execution*, 1995, oil on canvas.
(Courtesy of the artist and Schoeni Art Gallery, Ltd.)

"uncanny."[80] The coincidence of the London sale and the staged museum show in New York further heightened Yue's visibility and added to his "celebrity capital" in the global media.[81] He became even part of *Time* magazine's list of people that mattered in 2007, alongside figures like Angela Merkel, Barack Obama, and Britney Spears.[82] However, it is unknown who bought Yue's painting in London, and market insiders assume that it was probably the result of a speculator's strategic up-bidding. Usually, if a real collector buys a work for such a high price, they will go public to raise their own status. After *Execution*'s expensive sale, however, it entered a "black hole" and has not resurfaced since.[83]

When the financial crisis hit in the fall of 2008, the global economy went into a recession. And just as the heteronomous pole is more directly affected by field-external economic developments, so was Yue's commercial status. Financial elites and investors withdrew, and sales and prices for his works plummeted (figs. 7.11 and 7.12). While other Chinese artists also experienced a decline in sales and while Yue nevertheless could still sell works at a relatively high level, the downward shift was dramatic. His annual auction volume dropped from around $27 million in 2008 to $4.4 million in 2009. In the years after the financial crisis, his work did not attain its previous price or turnover levels. By comparison, sales for works by the consecrated Chinese artist Xu Bing experienced a much less dramatic change, decreasing from about $2.2 million to $960,000; and his position reached higher sales and price levels after the crisis waned. Yue's rise, then, was heavily dependent on hyped promotion. In line with the logic of market bubbles, it was destined to reach a saturation point and drop once speculators spotted the next big opportunity.

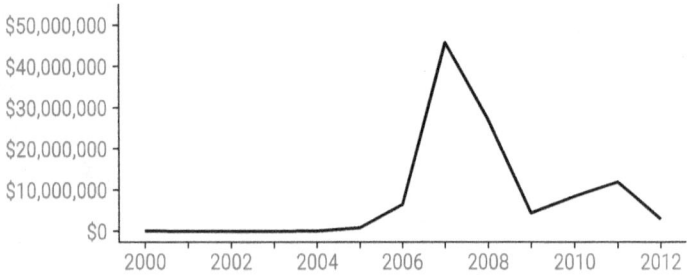

FIGURE 7.11. The rise and fall of Yue's auction turnover, 2000–2012.
Source: Artprice.com.

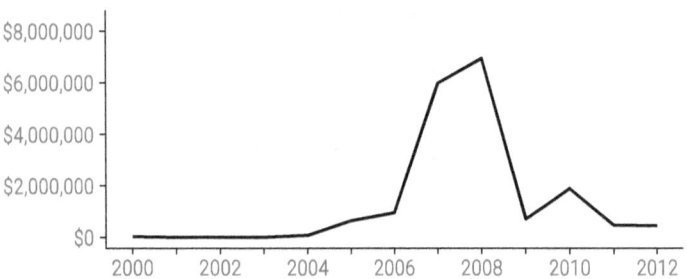

FIGURE 7.12. The rise and fall of Yue's maximum prices, 2000–2012.
Source: Artprice.com.

The Rise of Yue Minjun as a Global Market Star

Thus far, we have followed Yue's trajectory from his early years as an artist to
the onset of a hyped, global cycle of speculative valuation for his work. Yet
what seemed like a rather clear progression of events was the outcome of a
complex interplay between Yue's own habitus, his artistic approach, and the
interpretations and strategies of numerous invested agents. They all operated
within a nested globalizing field and a unique macrohistorical context.

China's Economic Globalization as an External Macro-Level Precondition

The key audiences for Yue's hype in the global market were US-Americans,
Europeans, Asians, and Chinese, apart from a few buyers in Latin America.
The emergence and interest of these constituencies that supported his market
rise need to be understood—in both an objective and interpretative sense—
against the broader historical background of China's accelerated economic
globalization since the 1990s.

China's integration into the global economy began in the wake of increasingly open borders for the free "movement of goods and services, capital, finance, technology and knowledge."[84] Reforms to stimulate foreign investment had been undertaken since 1979, after Deng initiated his "open door" policy.[85] But it was not until the party congress legitimized capitalism as a way to globalize the country, issuing new regulatory changes for foreign direct investment and external trade, that a major wave of investment occurred.[86] Between 1991 and 1992, foreign direct investment (FDI) jumped from $4.37 billion to $11 billion, heralding a period of rapid growth. China became the world's second-largest recipient of FDI by 1996.[87] In the slipstream of trade liberalization, the value of the country's exports increased from $9.8 billion in 1978 to $593.4 billion in 2004.[88] In particular, China's application for World Trade Organization (WTO) membership, which entailed several reforms in its trade sector, led to a dramatic rise in exports.[89]

These changes indirectly affected Yue's career by facilitating an increased interest in Chinese contemporary art among foreign economic elites, especially those from the UK, the US, and western Europe but also from parts of Asia. The rapid rise of FDI in China meant that there was an influx of business professionals who oversaw the establishment of joint ventures in the country. This influx created a novel foreign consumer base for cultural goods in China, including contemporary art. More indirectly, China's economic rise meant that the country also garnered heightened attention from Western mass media. Work by artists who were framed as dissidents in the international media, like those from Yuanmingyuan, could be valued as a unique cultural mirror of the larger political and cultural contradictions marking the country's dramatic transformations.

China's economic globalization also created the preconditions for the growth of Chinese buyers of contemporary art inside the country. As part of the country's application for WTO membership, it initiated significant local market reforms after the mid-1990s. Restrictions regarding wage determination and lifelong employment security underwent liberalization, and financial and housing markets were established, allowing certain individuals to accumulate large amounts of capital in a relatively short time.[90] Wealth rose dramatically, especially in urban China.[91] While there were no billionaires in China in 1997, ten years later, the Forbes list included sixteen, and some sources speak of the growth of a remarkable five hundred new millionaires during the 1990s.[92]

Changes in China's income and wealth distribution in turn established the structural preconditions for the rise of a consumer class for luxury goods in the country, including art.[93] Most of the new collectors, however, were focused on traditional Chinese painting or calligraphy; they perceived contemporary art as being of lower artistic quality. Thus, while China's intensified economic globalization enabled the growth of wealthy audiences within the country and abroad, we also need to understand how market agents, particularly auction houses, were able to attract their interest.

Before turning to those intermediaries and consumers, however, we need to look more closely at Yue's artistic self-understanding at the micro-level to apprehend how he produced an aesthetic style that allowed him to stand out among his peers in the globalizing commercial subfield. Just as the rise of multiculturalism created a macro-level opportunity space for Orozco's career, economic globalization created a favorable context for certain market dynamics, which nevertheless had to be navigated by both the artist and brokers of his work.

Yue's Artistic Self-Understanding and Aesthetic Brand as a Micro-Level Condition

As we saw with Orozco's biography, two key sociological ideas to understand the micro-level dynamics of an artist's career are their habitus and cultural capital in relation to both the national and cross-border fields they traverse.[94] Artists with a large amount of cultural capital are more likely to follow a quasi-intrinsic dedication to art and sense of the game. They tend to have higher intellectual "reflexivity" with regard to the histories and discourses of different art fields.[95] They are also more inclined to take innovative and risky—but thus more symbolically rewarding—artistic positions.[96] All these factors positively impacted Orozco's rise as a global artist as he moved from his Mexican field to cultural centers and then across multiple continents.

In Yue's case, it was his relative lack of early cultural capital and his particular trajectory in the Chinese art field that propelled him into the opposite pole of the globalizing field. This background predisposed him toward a relatively simple aesthetic style and a relationship to artistic production that favored repetition—based on schematic procedures that allowed for quick (re)production—over innovation. In this way, he created an artistic "brand" that gave him significant commercial advantages over his early peers, with whom he shared similar themes and even motifs.[97] Although Yue did not aspire to become a commercial painter and although he spent several years in an avant-garde underground community, his dispositions led him to fashion a style that was ultimately more marketable across borders.

As we have seen, Yue's route to becoming an artist was not as straightforward as Orozco's. Yue grew up in a lower-middle-class family in which art did "not at all" play a role.[98] And his motivation to leave his job in the oil industry was not necessarily driven by a quasi-intrinsic "love of art."[99] He perceived art as a means to a freer lifestyle, a way to liberate himself from his work unit's regimented schedule. Attending art school offered a context with relatively lax social expectations, and the move to Yuanmingyuan promised a more self-determined life:[100] "I didn't want to become resigned to a life as a worker in the way my parents had to be. . . . And then completely by chance I stumbled upon the artists' community of Yuanmingyuan and I knew that this was the opportunity I had been waiting for. . . . It was exactly as I had imagined the life of an artist to be, and . . . I decided to make the move from Hebei."[101]

His longing for personal freedom resonated with Yue's understanding of art as a practice of individual self-expression; that is, the painter's main objective is to portray the world as they see it and deliver their feelings as authentically as possible. Although self-expression and similar concepts related to the subject—and opposed to the collectivist party doctrine—had been important topics in Chinese art discussions since the late 1970s, Yue's ideas did not grow out of a conscious identification with these historical strands in the national art field.[102] Nor did he see his style as a reflexive rejection of alternative aesthetic frameworks. Yue recalled, however, that in line with the Chinese art education he had received, he felt uncomfortable about an autonomous *l'art pour l'art* approach.[103] For him, practices adhering to a pure, abstract aesthetics were a "way to deny reality" and did not resonate with his personality. Avoiding such an approach allowed him "to stay true" to himself.[104] Yue's own understanding of art as a means of self-expression was intimately connected with his image of the artistic life as a means to attain more freedom.

Yuanmingyuan's heterodox subculture was critical for encouraging the development of Yue's hallmark style: Pop-realistic self-portraits with ironically laughing faces. Though Western journalists would frame this motif as a form of political dissidence, Yue at first chose it more for personal reasons. And he embraced it as a symbol with broad appeal, one that even "ordinary folk" could understand.[105] As he recalled,

> For my generation, the expression itself was not entirely alien. . . . Every one of us had a private sense that our existence was not entirely happy. . . . Despite being given an opportunity to assert our independence [in being able to move to the Yuanmingyuan Artists' Village of their own free will], as long as we were marginalized by society for our choice of lifestyle, our desire to explore individual creative impulses, and our inability to conform to social convention, then we could never be entirely happy. . . . I decided that my laughing faces would be my own personal reminder of our situation, and which would be easily understood by people around me, and ordinary folk, too.[106]

In developing his artistic language, rather than deliberately aspiring to innovate, Yue started out with the aesthetic tradition he had been taught and was most familiar with, Soviet Realism. As he explained,

So when I arrived at the Yuanmingyuan, I started thinking, how can I bring my works together with these feelings most meaningfully? So I went back to the realism I had studied and began from there. . . . I didn't think much about painterly language, but more about my present situation, the pressure I felt, my impressions of society, because those things were the strongest for me. I had no time to find a completely different method, so I thought it most effective to use this one directly. To express myself using this most familiar language. . . . In terms of technique, it's all more or less the same.[107]

Although Yue used Soviet Realism as a starting point, he simplified it drastically with regard to composition, the drawing of figures, and coloration. He considered these simplifications not so much as decisions to create something new but as expressions of his "personality" and his taste for an "uncomplicated" style.[108] The fact that Yue entered the Chinese art field through a lower-tier art school—and thus did not endure the rigid technical training of the country's top urban academies—might have contributed to this taste. It predisposed him to break away more easily from state-sponsored oil painting and to embrace a relatively lax, flashy realism. "I never study carefully the composition of my picture. . . . I don't even produce preliminary sketches. . . . I don't care about the proportion at all. That's just my personality. . . . In the beginning, I applied Soviet methods of observing life, like the chiaroscuro . . . from Renaissance painting. Eventually, I totally discarded such techniques because I hate putting in more strokes after having sketched out the composition. It's boring, I prefer simplicity. . . . I can never draw as many times like the teachers and students in art colleges."[109]

Yue's intuitive aesthetic choices thus led him to pursue a drastically pared-down version of the realistic style he had learned. With his taste for simplicity, he created a visual language that was so direct and gaudy that it was not only reminiscent of Soviet propaganda posters but also Western Pop art.[110] Somewhat ironically perhaps, his "lower" cultural capital in the Chinese art field would turn into an advantage, since the resemblance with Pop art appealed to foreign audiences. And just as Orozco's affinity with international conceptual art traditions was a starting point for his success at the autonomous pole, the affinity of Yue's simplified aesthetics with an already established idiom in the international art market was a critical foundation for his commercial success abroad. Although he seemed not to have intended this connection, it served as a crucial cultural precondition for his work's circulation beyond China.

While Yue settled on his style, he perfected his production mode and the motif of the laughing faces through numerous variations. He soon also began integrating more overt political references in his laughing pictures, as in *Gweong-Gweong* and *Execution*. In his artistic self-understanding, Yue did not consider himself to be very political, so these features in some of his paintings could be attributed to the influence of Yuanmingyuan's artistic subculture and the identity it developed among interested foreign reporters and buyers as a place of dissident art. Yue could satisfy their growing demand for his work, and he soon was able to produce paintings quickly according to formulaic steps, sometimes completing them in two sittings.[111] As he has admitted, once he established his signature style, it "subsequently dictated how all aspects" of his art evolved.[112] As a result, he embraced repetition as his preferred mode of production, even when he worked in other media like sculpture and silk-screen prints.[113]

While Yue's production mode tends to violate metropolitan norms at the autonomous pole—which, as we saw in Orozco's case, typically value innovation and artistic risk-taking—it contributed to his commercial success. As almost every intermediary and collector of Yue's work mentioned in interviews, his accessible style, paired with his highly recognizable *and* recurring motif, meant that his work assumed the qualities of a brand. In an emerging market segment in which buyers outside Asia might not even recognize the seemingly exotic names of Chinese artists, Yue's iconic and highly recognizable artistic style gave him an advantage over most of his Chinese peers, even as he shared similar themes with them. He stood out as the "Chinese artist with the laughing faces," and the motif soon figured as a symbol for a mood of frustration and absurdity after the Tiananmen massacre.

In sum, Yue did not aspire to become a commercial artist. Yet his relatively low cultural capital, his kind of educational training, and his early move to Yuanmingyuan instilled in him a taste for a relatively simple artistic style and the use of recurring motifs, which resulted in an aesthetic brand that served as a critical micro-level condition for his success in the globalizing art market. He created an art that a broad, nonspecialized audience across multiple countries could easily distinguish and appreciate for its iconic qualities.

The Meso-Level Conditions of Yue's Market Success in the Globalizing Field

YUE'S WEAK GALLERY TIES ACROSS CONTINENTS

Unlike Orozco, art market agents—sales galleries, collectors, speculators, and dominant Western auction houses—played the most important role in Yue's ascendance to the global stage. Among galleries, Yue developed a broad network across four continents. Between 1994 and 2010, thirty galleries in sixteen countries presented his art outside of China. Most of them were in centers of the globalizing field—eight were in the USA, and five were in Germany. But only three offered him solo shows there, and all of those were one-time events; the remaining ones in these countries displayed his work in group shows just once or twice. These weak, fluctuating connections marked most of his gallery relationships in the other countries as well.[114] Additionally, the majority of Yue's gallery collaborations occurred when he was on the rise as an auction star after 2004 and thus *after* he had already developed a high profile commercially.

Nonetheless, a few galleries were critical as early stepping-stones for Yue's visibility and sales beyond mainland China. The Schoeni Gallery in Hong Kong offered him his foreign debut in 1994 along with Yang Shaobin, and as table 7.1 indicates, it went on to become Yue's strongest gallery tie in the period under consideration, with sixteen shows overall.

When Manfred Schoeni, who was Swiss, established his gallery in 1992, he joined two other dealers in Hong Kong—including the Hanart TZ Gallery, which was founded by Johnson Chang in 1983—to exhibit contemporary artists from China.[115] The backgrounds of the two were markedly different. While Chang had studied philosophy and math at a US university, Schoeni, before establishing his gallery, had earned a degree in hotel management from a professional school, worked for several years in that capacity, and started a business in Chinese antiques.[116] Chang engaged in several nonprofit projects, collaborating with critics and curators on public exhibitions to introduce Chinese contemporary art to an international audience. By contrast, Schoeni pursued various other entrepreneurial activities in the food and wine industries.[117] And while Chang's intellectual interests made him known as the "scholar dealer," Schoeni had a reputation as a "tough businessman."[118]

Given these different trajectories, Schoeni commanded less specific symbolic and social capital to influence the cultural promotion of his artists beyond Hong Kong. After offering Yue his breakthrough show in 1994, Schoeni was able to mediate Yue's work to two foreign exhibitions in the 1990s—a group show he curated at the Gallery Theoremes in Brussels in 1995 and the *China!* exhibition at the Bonner Art Museum in 1996. In the latter case, however, Schoeni was approached by the curator Dieter Ronte. After seeing pictures of Yuanmingyuan by a German journalist, Ronte had planned a show about Chinese contemporary painting and asked Schoeni (as well as Chang) for recommendations.[119] Apart from this one-time connection, Schoeni did not command as many resources to broker Yue's work to major international art institutions.[120]

Schoeni, however, *because* of his Western entrepreneurial habitus, was very important for the development of an initial market for Yue's art outside China. The gallery shows appealed to British finance professionals who flooded Hong Kong before the colony was handed over to China in 1997 and who were looking to acquire a cultural piece of the country.[121] With Schoeni's European roots

TABLE 7.1. Galleries That Exhibited Yue's Work, 1994–2008

Year	Gallery	City	Solo	Group
Regional				
1994	Schoeni Art Gallery	Hong Kong	1	15
2002	Soobin Gallery	Singapore	1	0
2004	Galeri Semarang	Semarang	0	1
2004	Tang Contemporary Art–Bangkok	Bangkok	0	3
2004	Hanart TZ Gallery	Hong Kong	0	1
2005	Soobin Art International	Singapore	0	2
2006	Arario Gallery Cheonan	Cheonan-si	0	2
2008	Gallery Road to the Museum	Seoul	0	1
Cross-Continental				
1995	Galerie Theoremes	Brussels	0	1
1997	Klaus Littmann Gallery	Basel	1	0
1998	Chinese Contemporary	London	1	2
2000	Galerie Skala	Cologne	0	1
2001	Alexander Ochs Gallery	Berlin	1	4
2001	Urs Meile Gallery	Lucerne	1	2
2001	Art Beatus	Vancouver	1	2
2004	Enrico Navarra Gallery	Paris	1	1
2006	Galerie Schrade–Karlsruhe	Karlsruhe	0	2
2006	Anna Kustera Gallery	New York	0	1
2006	Galerie Schrade & Blashofer	Karlsruhe	0	1
2006	Jack Tilton Gallery	New York	0	1
2006	Robischon Gallery	Denver	0	1
2006	Roberts Projects	Culver City	0	1
2007	Arario Gallery	New York	1	2
2007	Max Protech Gallery	New York	1	0
2007	Ethan Cohen Fine Arts	New York City	0	6
2007	34 FineArt	Cape Town	0	1
2008	Burkhard Eikelmann Galerie	Dusseldorf	0	1
2009	Black Cube Gallery	Barcelona	0	1
2009	Goya Contemporary	Baltimore	0	1
2010	Walsh Gallery	Chicago, IL	0	1
National				
2000	Eastlink Gallery	Shanghai	0	1
2001	Yibo Gallery	Shanghai	0	4
2004	Beijing Art Now Gallery	Beijing	0	3
2004	Xin Dong Cheng–Beijing	Beijing	0	2
2004	White Space	Beijing	0	1
2004	L.A. Gallery	Beijing	0	1
2004	Courtyard Gallery	Beijing	0	1
2005	Beijing Commune	Beijing	2	1

(Continued)

TABLE 7.1. (*continued*)

Year	Gallery	City	Solo	Group
National				
2005	Aura Gallery	Shanghai	0	1
2005	Arario Gallery	Beijing	0	1
2006	Pyo Gallery	Beijing	0	1
2008	Triumph Art Space	Beijing	0	2
2008	Pace Gallery	Beijing	0	1
2009	Eastation Gallery	Beijing	0	1
2010	Shanghai Gallery of Art	Shanghai	1	0
2010	Gallery Yang	Beijing	0	1

and tough business approach, he had the habitus to cultivate good relationships with these financial expats. They not only became a lucrative clientele for Yue's paintings in the regional market hub, allowing him to live solely from his art, but also later became a key channel for Yue's art to enter metropolitan auction houses as consignments. *Execution*, for example, whose record price made headlines at Sotheby's London in 2007, was first sold by Schoeni to Trevor Simon, a British investment banker, for $32,000 in 1996. The expat remembered how the two men had already been on "friendly terms" at the time of the transaction.[122] Thus, as someone who could cultivate foreign business audiences, Schoeni was also one indirect link for Yue's art to reach cross-continental economic circulation later on.

Beyond Hong Kong and Asia, the first gallery that featured Yue's work in multiple exhibitions was Chinese Contemporary in London. The gallery had a weak reputation in the gallery market and added little to Yue's symbolic recognition. Peer galleries in other European countries reproached it for not working hard to promote new, innovative positions and deepen their foreign reception. "It was above all about business; it was not about art," as one gallerist put it.[123] Chinese Contemporary's exhibitions were also largely ignored by professional critics. As Bois complained in an internet source, "In ten years, we've done eighty shows, we've never had a write up apart from the *Financial Times*."

However, the dealers were an early stepping-stone for enabling a speculative cycle of valuation. As Bois and Coleman did not seem to discriminate between their buyers, unlike avant-garde gallerists, and as they were themselves consigning Yue's art from the primary market for auction, they contributed to a context where key works could freely circulate and become subject to financial strategies. For example, Yue's *Lions* (1998), which sold at Sotheby's in 2006 for more than $500,000, had been purchased from Chinese Contemporary just a few years earlier by a buyer who remained anonymous when he auctioned it off again for profit.[124] Unlike Marian Goodman's approach, which sought to pro-tect her artists' work from entering auctions at an early career stage (cf. chap-ter 6), the radically sales-oriented gallery opened the floodgates.

Not all of Yue's early gallery connections outside Asia were commercial, and there were two in particular that were more aligned with an avant-garde approach. Yue's relationships with them were relatively brief, however. The Alexander Ochs gallery in Germany, for example, held the second-most exhi-bitions of Yue's work prior to his ascendance as an auction star. Yue had one solo and four group exhibitions there between 2001 and 2004.[125] Ochs, who founded the gallery in 1997, had previously been a producer for "new music" (collaborating with John Cage) and worked as a curator.[126] His promotion of Chinese contemporary art in Germany and Europe quickly earned him a repu-tation as a pioneer in the gallery market.[127] In contrast to Chinese Con-temporary, Ochs invested in developing an international network involving curators and public art institutions, and he was able to mediate Yue's art to group shows in Germany and other European countries in the early 2000s.

Nevertheless, Ochs's working relationship with Yue was looser compared to other Chinese artists he promoted. Eventually, it became clear that the gal-lerist and the artist had different expectations. While Yue wanted the freedom to market his art himself, Ochs felt that this would violate his self-understanding as a gallerist—as someone who cultivated close, long-term relationships with artists—and turn him into a purely commercial dealer.[128] Given these diverg-ing understandings about the "proper" ethos of the gallerist and artist, their working relationship ended before Yue rose in the auction world.

Another of Yue's less commercially driven early supporters was the Gallery Urs Meile, which collaborated with him on two group exhibitions and one solo show between 2001 and 2003. Founded in 1992 in Lucerne, the gallery began specializing in the promotion of Chinese contemporary artists in the mid-1990s. Meile, the son of an art collector, had previously worked as an ar-chitect, an auction salesperson, a restaurateur in a Basel Museum, and a man-ager of a restoration workshop.[129] As a gallerist, he pursued an avant-garde approach in these years, focusing on long production cycles, close relations with artists, artistically ambitions exhibitions, and collaborations with non-profit institutions. By 2006, his gallery gained recognition as one the "world's leading galleries of Chinese contemporary art."[130]

Meile invited Yue to participate in a widely recognized exhibition series in 2001, *Take Part (I and II)*, which he had prepared over several years in conjunc-tion with a catalog to introduce contemporary artists from China to a Western audience. After the 1999 Venice Biennale had created a new level of foreign attention, Meile aimed to assemble a gallery show that provided the artists with a credible and sufficiently complex representation in the West.[131] Two years later, Yue was also offered a solo presentation at Meile's Lucerne show-room. In contrast to Chinese Contemporary, Meile went with Yue's more aty-pical, innovative works that had not yet become mainstream. He chose a series of black-and-white laughing self-portraits, all more focused yet more elemen-tary than his usual, colorful ones. All the paintings sold, and the show attracted some critical coverage.[132] Yet Meile was ultimately more interested in concep-tually driven art that "works on several levels" and was able to make visible "more complex relationships" than he felt Yue's paintings were.[133] The relation-ship ended because the habitus-based taste for complexity of the avant-garde gallerist conflicted with Yue's taste for simplicity.

THE POWER OF AUCTION HOUSES
IN MARKET CENTERS

Judging from Yue's foreign gallery network in his early career, he did not seem positioned to become a successful artist in the traditional "conversion" model. Yue, however, *did* reach the global top of the commercial pole, a rise that was critically fueled by auction houses, the most heteronomous market institu-tions in the art field. To understand Yue's speculative cycle, we must attend to the distinctive norms and strategies that governed auction specialists in the globalizing market game, beyond the merely "parasitic" status vis-à-vis sym-bolic capital that avant-garde gallerists had claimed for them.[134]

In line with the weight of power inequalities in the global commercial sub-field, it is unsurprising that Yue's career was backed by the world's two most powerful auction players, Sotheby's and Christie's. Among the twenty-seven houses that auctioned his art between 1998 and 2010, Sotheby's and Christie's completed the most sales, generated the largest turnover, and garnered the ten highest prices (tables 7.2 and 7.3). As discussed in chapter 3, these enterprises command such high economic and symbolic power as global brands that they basically operate as a global "duopoly," and with this structural position, they can greatly impact the making of commercial stars.[135]

But these houses' powerful position does not sufficiently explain their im-pact on Yue's market valuation. As discussed earlier, Christie's London failed when it tried to sell works by Chinese contemporary artists in 1998. Thus, we also need to attend to the timing of their strategies and the way they framed their sales in relation to the globalizing market environment. Indeed, the fact that another major auction for works by Chinese artists occurred an entire six years later and in Hong Kong is a crucial element to the story, and it speaks to the constraints on auction specialists' strategies. They must calibrate the chal-lenging tensions between constantly expanding their markets and simulta-neously avoiding commercial failures. Unlike galleries, a sales failure at an

TABLE 7.2. The Top Five Auction Houses for Sales of Yue's Art, 1998–2010

Auction house	Total turnover (USD)	Offered lots
Sotheby's	46,952,438	90
Christie's	39,861,896	86
Poly International Auction Co., Ltd.	5,746,800	14
Phillips de Pury & Company	4,715,346	11
Seoul Auction House	3,506,853	11

Source: Artprice.com.

TABLE 7.3. The Top Ten Auction Prices of or for Yue's Artworks, 1998–2010

Rank	Year of sale	Price (millions USD)	Work	Auction house	Place of sale
1	2008	6.9	*Gweong-Gweong*	Christie's	Hong Kong
2	2007	6.0	*Execution*	Sotheby's	London
3	2007	4.3	*The Pope*	Sotheby's	London
4	2007	4.1	*The Massacre at Chios (Diptych)*	Sotheby's	Hong Kong
5	2008	2.8	*"Life"*	Christie's	Hong Kong
6	2008	2.6	*Take the Plunge*	Sotheby's	Hong Kong
7	2007	2.6	*Big Ear*	Christie's	Hong Kong
8	2007	2.6	*Portrait of the Artist and His Friends*	Christie's	Hong Kong
9	2008	2.5	*Big Swans*	Christie's	Hong Kong
10	2007	1.9	*Infanta, The Princess*	Sotheby's	New York

Source: Artprice.com. Note these are final prices, since they include buyer's premium.

auction is public, and it can tarnish both an artist's and a house's reputation in the ongoing competition over consigners and buyers.[136]

Thus, when Howard-Sneyd made the decision to auction Chinese contemporary art in Hong Kong in 2004, it was already a relatively safe bet. By that time, the genre had received a symbolic stamp of approval at the 1999 Venice Biennale. And Western business expatriates in Hong Kong were a profitable audience. They were looking to decorate their homes or get a cultural piece of mainland China at a time when the country's economic boom was becoming constant news.[137] The growth of wealth in mainland China following economic globalization promised another lucrative audience for the work. Howard-Sneyd's choice to market the relatively new auction genre in a location that was close to an existing and a potential market underlines the economic rationality that dictates the strategies of auction managers.

These more commercial rationales also informed the houses' mediation of the Hong Kong sale. Choosing to say that the auction was for "Chinese contemporary art," rather than art from the "Asian Avant-Garde" as Christie's had done before, allowed the new sale to build on a category that had gained broader legitimacy since the 1999 Venice biennale and among audiences in Hong Kong.[138] It simultaneously allowed to appeal to national sentiments among younger buyers from mainland China, whom the auction house sought to attract. Note how Evelyn Lin, the auction specialist responsible for the sale, promoted the art in a Chinese newspaper as a distinctive expression of the artists' contemporary lifestyles in China, contrasting the work with traditional Chinese oil paintings: "Chinese art is no longer traditional landscape paintings. It relates more to the lives of the current generation of collectors—or potential collectors. . . . because the subject matter is closer to our lives these days than the traditional."[139]

Thus, the sale's categorization and framing were informed by commercial considerations in relation to both proximate Western and newer Chinese audiences. This commercial reasoning also explains why the interior cover of Sotheby's auction catalog featured Yue's 2003 painting *Sunflowers* as one of the auction's top lots. Yue's art was already in high demand among Western expatriates at Schoeni's Hong Kong gallery. Moreover, auction specialists often look for iconic art pieces like Yue's when "curating" their sales, knowing they can more easily spark a status competition for iconic trophies, along with the fuel of collective effervescence.[140] Although Yue had relatively lower symbolic capital than some of his Chinese peers did at that time, he was featured in the sale, and that according to market-based criteria.

When the Sotheby's sale succeeded, the house's high standing and the publicly reported auction success instantly raised the economic value of the genre beyond the more opaque gallery market. What developed in the wake of the 2004 auction was a market for professional insiders driven by dealers and the most dedicated speculators from Asia and the West, while buyers from mainland China remained unreached, despite promotional efforts. The sale also had not yet produced any broader hype. The port city's status as a regional market hub did not have the power to catapult the genre, and Yue's art, to a global level. For valuation in the globalizing field, it is crucial to distinguish between the power positions of the mediators and their geographic location.

It was only when Sotheby's moved its auction sales to New York in March 2006, which was *the* global auction capital for contemporary art, that the genre, along with Yue, underwent a bigger commercial breakthrough. But in New York too, structural power had to be articulated with strategic timing and framing to be successful. The stakes were high, and a public failure could jeopardize the future of the entire emerging segment. Indeed, the house took nearly a year to prepare for the sale, which is unusual for the fast-paced world of the auction business.[141] The market strategy aimed to create "cross-pollination" between two larger constituencies. On the one hand, the house hoped to attract more buyers from the established "international contemporary art" segment, which was booming at that time, particularly in New York.[142] On the other, it aimed to raise demand among Asian and mainland Chinese buyers by moving the genre's sale to its most prestigious venue, putting it on "par with American and European work."[143] Indeed, as an market expert commented, "By opening a China-focused shop in New York, Sotheby's will create a more level playing field than it generally obtains in China, thereby attracting a new corps of collectors to this dynamic arena."[144]

To appeal to more Western buyers, the organizers worked to establish meaningful common ground with the established market category "international contemporary art" while simultaneously making claims about valuable differences, a double strategy that operated on multiple levels. For one, Sotheby's hired Xiaoming Zhang as the sale's specialist. As a graduate of the Whitney Museum's curatorial program and a former curator and manager at the Guggenheim, Zhang possessed symbolic capital from her activities at prestigious cultural institutions. When she introduced the foreign genre at the New York auction as the lead specialist, it aligned with a conversion logic. Additionally, in contrast to prior Hong Kong sales, the auction adopted conventions of "international" (i.e., Western contemporary) sales for the first time, including the recruitment of the star auctioneer Tobias Meyer and the layout of the catalog, which included scholarly essays by two US-based art experts.[145] Furthermore, the catalog's opening essay by Britta Erickson—an art critic and curator with a PhD in Chinese art history from Stanford—highlighted how artists from Asia in general, and China in particular, had "emerged into the same international, globalized art space."[146] These measures symbolically placed Chinese contemporary art on the same level as the already booming "international contemporary art" segment at the time.

Against this common frame, Sotheby's could then champion the distinctive cultural and economic values of the up-and-coming market genre and of Yue's art. For the former, the emphasis was put on dynamics in China. The catalog refrained from using traditional "international" art historical frameworks, which valued artworks according to their "'originality' and contribution to the march of the Western artistic tradition."[147] Already in Hong Kong before, auction specialists had realized that some Chinese contemporary artists did not easily fit into such a Western approach to artistic distinction, which might have dismissed their work as being historically derivative.[148] Indeed, Erickson's essay, for example, focused on how the artists innovated artistically *within* their national field's art history or how the artworks, including the style of Cynical Realism, expressed tensions and dramatic changes inside the country. Nevertheless, while Erickson mentioned Fang Lijun as one of Cynical Realism's major representatives, it is notable that her expert discussion did not reference Yue's work.

The sale's economic promotion in turn was pursued through press releases. These highlighted Chinese contemporary art as a distinctive financial growth segment, listing steady sales increases in Hong Kong between 2004 and 2005. The genre's previous regional commercial success thus created an economic context in which the house could advertise the relatively new market segment in a global center, emphasizing that a "dramatic increase" had already occurred elsewhere.[149] The reported price levels also conveyed that the ascendant genre was still less expensive than international contemporary art. By creating first equivalency between Chinese contemporary art and the latter, the new market genre could emerge as a distinctive investment opportunity, a more affordable variant with massive growth potential. As Tobias Meyer emphasized, "The demand we have witnessed for these works in our sales in Hong Kong leads us to anticipate even more widespread interest in New York this March."[150]

Within this market-based logic, in which prior economic triumphs can often lead to further gains, Yue was featured as one of the sale's top artists. Although Erickson's expert essay did not mention him, Yue's best-selling status in Hong Kong counted for Sotheby's press releases. His art was featured among one of the key lots, and the "smiling faces" of his paintings were advertised as "iconic images" of Cynical Realism. His work's easily recognizable quality once again took on positive connotations. The catalog's layout further promoted his work. Out of the more than two hundred offered lots, one of his paintings (*Untitled*, 1996) was selected as the sale's opening work, while a second, *Lions*, was highlighted with a double-page print. A short accompanying text emphasized how the "trademark motif" of Yue's laughing faces spoke to China's broader historical dynamics, signifying "latent political implications,"[151] the country's rising "consumer culture," and the "ideological climate of millennial China." In short, the auction's more straightforward marketing material featured his work by contextualizing its economic value within the genre's overall market growth, and highlighted how the work's iconic quality signified broader historical transformations in China.[152] In contrast to Orozco, the framing and evaluation of Yue's art became closely linked to its national content, a pattern that reappears with collectors, as I detail later.

The carefully orchestrated New York auction attracted bidders from at least three continents and was a major success, both for the genre and for Yue's work.[153] US-European audiences from the established contemporary art market made up the majority of the bidders, showing that the strategy of cross-pollinating with Western contemporary art and its audiences had worked. And in comparison to that established market category and its multimillion-dollar figures, even the high prices of Yue's paintings (around $500,000) could still look financially "undervalued."

With that logic, the New York auction also unleashed a global market hype that lasted the next two years. The combination of a dominant auction house *and* one of the field's global centers *and* the symbolic meaning of widely reported record prices exerted a strong valuation effect amid a broader contemporary art boom.[154] The sale's success further advertised Chinese contemporary art as a genre with high commercial appeal and investment potential; only now it was on a worldwide scale. Sotheby's New York had the visibility and power to influence other houses in global and regional market centers, which soon began to offer Chinese contemporary art as well. At the same time, a broader demand for the genre took hold among (speculative) buyers from five continents, which resulted in an exponential hype in sales and prices and ultimately fed into Yue's ascent.

Importantly, houses in mainland China responded to the New York event too, introducing stand-alone auctions for Chinese contemporary art, including Yue's work, in the fall of 2004.[155] While there had previously been sales in the regional hub of Hong Kong, the genre thus had to move up the subfield's nested power structure to gain higher market legitimacy before it was offered back at the top houses of the domestic auction market. Yet to make sense of this move, we must avoid the trappings of any overly deterministic center-periphery narrative. The way the New York auction fed back into China's art market was mediated by distinctive developments within the national field too. For one, Chinese contemporary art had already gained greater domestic legitimacy in the wake of the 1999 Venice Biennale and other national developments.[156] To appeal to national pride and to project a more contemporary cultural image, the government gradually changed some of its policies, and it no longer stigmatized these artists as being "unofficial."[157] Authorities also allowed more exhibitions at official art institutions within the country. The greater state acceptance created an important cultural precondition for the New York sale's resonance within the domestic market.

Other market-based factors contributing to the success of the first stand-alone auctions for Chinese contemporary art in 2006 included the new class of wealthy Chinese art consumers that had emerged in the country by that time. Their traditionally preferred auction segments—oil paintings and classical Chinese art—underwent a crisis around that same time.[158] Forgeries became more common, and certain works became more scarce, leading to skyrocketing prices.[159] During this national market juncture, Chinese contemporary art's widely publicized auction records at a global center put the genre in the national spotlight as an alternative market segment with commercial potential.[160] And it predisposed investment-oriented Chinese buyers to be open for new opportunities. While initial domestic results for Yue's art were uneven, Poly International, an auction house owned by the Chinese government, soon generated the third-highest auction turnover his work received before 2010 (see table 7.2).[161] In short, though Sotheby's auction in New York boosted national sales for the genre, the global center's influence was mediated by particular historical junctures in the national field.

Eventually, these first successful "official" auctions in mainland China exerted strong feedback effects on regional and global sales. In the fall of 2006, for example, the headline of a *New York Times* article announced, "Chinese Art Is as Hot in the East as It Is in the West."[162] As global media and online price agencies reported results, the idea of the genre's investment potential was bolstered. The "fictional expectation" of an expanding Chinese collector pool amidst the country's growing wealth seemed to become a reality, adding fuel for a speculative buying frenzy.[163] But now it operated on all market levels— global, regional, and national—and it turned Yue into a global auction leader within just one year. The interplay of regional, global, and national auction centers in the speculative valuation process underlines how important it is to go beyond too deterministic and one-directional center-periphery models. Valuation in the global commercial field operated through asymmetric *interdependencies* and within a multiscalar structure (see chapter 3).

THE ACTIVE ROLE OF COLLECTORS

Another central force for Yue's rise as a global star in the market were, of course, the collectors and buyers of his work. It is critical to appreciate the active role that some of these agents played in the valuation of the genre and his art, beyond being mere "consumers." This reflects broader trends of the changing status of collectors in the contemporary art field, which originated in the 1970s and accelerated in the new millennium.[164] According to the market expert Georgina Adam, "the former ways of judging value, . . . what Lucien Karpik called the 'expert-opinion regime' of critics and curators," has been weakened and, instead, "mega-collectors have become the taste-makers of our time."[165] In the traditional expert (or conversion) "regime," art experts, public institutions, and avant-garde galleries first certified symbolic value, and collectors followed their judgments in secondary roles. That situation changed drastically in the twenty-first century, however, as megacollectors exerted unprecedented influence over artistic trends and canons through both public and private museums.[166] In 2009, Diana Crane even suggested, "The importance of contemporary artists is more likely to be measured in terms of their presence in the collections of mega-collectors rather than in prestigious museums."[167]

Yet the rising-power-of-collectors thesis does not sufficiently capture the globalizing field's persisting heterogeneity. Collectors' intentions, just like gallerists', can vary substantially. For example, a field-theoretical typology by Nina Zahner distinguishes between patrons, liberal collectors, and speculators.[168] Patrons, who tend to come from academic or upper-class backgrounds ("old money"), occupy the most autonomous position. These types engage with the arts as connoisseurs and through long-term support, including their donations to institutions. At the opposite, heteronomous pole are speculators, who primarily consider art as a financial asset.[169] Their commitments to certain artists and works are probably brief, oriented around the market's ebbs and flows and the drive for potential profits.[170] In between are "liberal collectors," who tend to originate from the upper-middle class. They are motivated by an interest in the arts but do not necessarily follow field-specific criteria in their artistic choices, and their strategies can be more readily colored by broader economic or political considerations.[171] Zahner developed her typology for the international art field, and in transposing it to a millennial global context, one must be careful not to simply universalize Western class categories or descriptors like "liberal." Yet the framework can serve as a useful heuristic for exploring a spectrum among positions. In this light, semiheteronomous and heteronomous collectors were the most relevant for Yue's career.

SEMIHETERONOMOUS COLLECTORS AND SYMBOLIC VALUATION

Semiheteronomous collectors played an active role, especially with regard to symbolic valorization. As indicated before, the majority of Yue's shows at public/noncommercial institutions were exhibitions of private collections of Chinese contemporary art. Most of the relevant collectors in this regard—including Uli Sigg, Kent Logan, Cees Hendrikse, Karl-Heinz Essl, and Robert Chaney—originated from Europe or the US and thus benefited from social capital in their respective art centers. Budi Tek, who was from Indonesia, also had an important mediating influence in Asia (and in China in particular later on).

Yue's connection with Sigg was especially consequential for his career. Sigg not only bought Yue's works early and connected him with powerful cultural mediators from central locations, such as Harald Szeemann, as we have seen, but also included Yue in a major traveling exhibition of his own collection, *Mahjong*, which toured the Museum of Fine Arts in Berne (2005), the Hamburger Kunsthalle (2005), and the Berkeley Art Museum (2009).

Sigg's involvement with China dated back to 1979. He negotiated the first joint venture of a Swiss company there and later became the Swiss ambassador to China between 1995 and 1998. During that time, he was one of the key brokers for the early introduction of Chinese artists to Western mediators. In 1998, Sigg also established a Chinese contemporary art award (CCAA) and recruited "world famous curators" to serve on its jury. Soon, he could widen his influence with appointments on the international advisory boards of MoMA in New York and London's Tate Museum, among other honors. He thus accumulated the symbolic and social capital to powerfully promote artists and works he had acquired. And while important group exhibitions of Chinese contemporary art had taken place before *Mahjong*, his millennial show earned praise as the most comprehensive survey of the genre to that date. Indeed, the hefty exhibition catalog—which included contributions from several renowned experts and artists—had a profound impact on canon formation, including Yue's position in it.[172]

But what motivated "liberal" Western collectors like Sigg to assume such a supportive role, especially given that contemporary artists from outside Europe or North American had long been rather ignored in the international contemporary art market?

We are arriving at a key cultural element that affected Yue's career: the interest of these collectors was driven by a broader fascination with China, which they had developed as business elites. All of them came from upper-middle-class backgrounds and had amassed wealth as entrepreneurs. For some, like Sigg, economic globalization meant that they became directly involved with China, while others watched it with great interest from afar. In this context, Chinese contemporary art was valued as a cultural window onto the massive changes the country was undergoing around that time. For example, Kent Logan noted, "Well, I think it was more related to the macro picture of China's emerging importance in the world. . . . I have always been interested in societies going through change as I think that is a fertile ground for artists to work. . . . And with China taking its place in the world order, the avant-garde of Chinese contemporary art was emerging, and the changes in Chinese society were compelling to me, as well as artists' works and the strong contextual basis they had to those changes."[173]

Such statements were echoed by Sigg and other active collectors. For example, the Dutch businessman Hendrikse suggested that "the work foretold the coming of a new world order."[174] And the American Robert Chaney made a direct connection with his business activities: "In the mid-nineties, I saw Asia becoming the primary driver of demand for raw materials, particularly energy, which was the focus of my venture capital fund. . . . I concluded that another major impact would be on art. . . . It is a snapshot of what is happening in Asia now and where things are likely to go. . . . This is the rise of an empire—a once-in-a-century occurrence."[175]

Thus, these semiheteronomous collectors embraced the genre mainly for its external topicality, as art that reflected changes in China and its rising status in the broader global economy, especially after the country joined the WTO in 2001. These associations compensated perhaps for the country's still-peripheral status within the artistic subfield at that time. And indeed, their evaluative approach contradicted that subfield's dominant focus on certain expert criteria—that is, as we saw with Orozco, the metropolitan emphasis on self-referential discursive characteristics and related originality. In fact, when Sigg reflected on his motivations, he observed that the art did not necessarily fit into such a Western-based artistic value system: "There is not much self-referential art, but instead there is a lot of art that relates to these enormous changes, whether as social criticism or on the level of human sensitivities. . . . Collecting is ultimately a way of accessing China as well."[176]

The critical implication is that collectors promoted Chinese contemporary art for reasons that bypassed metropolitan expert criteria. With this more het-eronomous approach, they operated as a crucial alternative support network for bringing some of these artists to the globalizing field's centers in ways that evaded the strictures of expert discourse. This channel of collector promotion was critical for Yue in extending his foreign visibility and exhibition credits before the auction market developed its own dynamic. In a time when Western-trained cultural mediators did not fully engage with his work—which did not conform to their evaluative schemes—collectors with a different, en-trepreneurial habitus pushed forward.

For Yue's collectors, what distinguished his work from that of his peers in particular was its aesthetic qualities. His paintings were distinctively appreci-ated for their "iconic" style and visual language that resembled Pop art. As Sigg pointed out, "[Yue's laughing faces] are very good images of the mood after 1989. He had a strong idea about the aftermath of this situation that captures the pervading sense of resignation in a very iconic way. I think one major reason [for his success] is his striking visual image. . . . It has all the characters of a successful brand, which has become so important in today's art market."[177] This sentiment is echoed by Logan's appraisal of Yue's work as well: "I thought it was a striking style: the closed eyes and big smile, which in many ways epito-mizes that period in Chinese society. It was all about society's reaction to the politics at the time. . . . His Pop imagery and the repetition of the same image is reminiscent of what Warhol did in that period in American history. . . . He was matching what was going on in American Pop culture with what was going on in Chinese society at the time."[178]

Overall, Yue's support from semiheteronomous collectors helps explain why he gained recognition as a *Chinese* artist, while Orozco had to transcend his national background to appeal to the "universal" values of more autono-mously operating art experts. Moreover, whereas Yue's art was valued for its iconic, brand-like qualities in reflecting "external" political-economic dynam-ics in China, Orozco's work was praised instead for its field-specific "nomadic" features.

SPECULATORS

Building on the promotion of semiheteronomous collectors, speculative buyers were then critical for Yue's rapid global economic rise since 2004, driving up sales and prices. Approaching contemporary art as a speculative game goes back to at least the 1970s (cf. chapter 3). Yet in the new millennium, the growth of contemporary art auctions, along with the rise of "market-based valuation methods" like online price databases, increased the role that speculative players and logics play.[179] Because speculators often use anonymity strategically, however, my account of their impact on Yue's career relies primarily on interviews with market insiders, supported by multiple secondary sources.

Speculative agents were drawn to "Chinese contemporary art" not only for cultural but also for financial reasons. After the Venice Biennale symbolically legitimated the genre in 1999 and after the success of the 2004 Hong Kong auction, Chinese contemporary art seemed to be an emerging market segment that was still "undervalued," especially compared to the price levels for Western contemporary art. Simultaneously, by that time, it was reasonable to engage in "fictional expectations" about future price increases due to mainland China's growing wealth.[180]

But according to market insiders, two main factors set Yue apart for speculative agents. For one, his iconic style had proved its commercial appeal in the gallery market and at the 2004 Hong Kong auction, which established an economic foundation that could be expanded. What is more, his works were in ample supply. Given Yue's schematic painting procedures, he was very productive; and he often sold work freely out of his studio. His weak ties with sales-oriented galleries also meant that his works could enter auctions without much friction, in contrast to artists who worked with avantgarde galleries that often shunned and blacklisted speculators.[181] Thus, in sheer logistical terms, his work was attractive because it was easy to access, buy, and sell.

Once speculators spot an opportunity, they can employ at least three strategies. The simplest, most straightforward one is called "flipping," which involves buying low and reselling a work at a higher price in a relatively short time. Following the resales of Yue's auctioned works reveals that this strategy occurred in the Asian regional market (especially Hong Kong), in global market capitals (New York and London), and in mainland China, which means that speculation occured at regional, global, and national market centers.

A second, more elaborate strategy involves "shill-bidding," in which speculators first accumulate assets for a low price, preferably in a monopolistic fashion. They then bid up prices for selected works at auction, publicly raising values, which means that they can sell similar assets—for example, work by the same artist—at a higher price afterward. For a layperson, it is crucial to realize that speculators can organize their up-bidding without actually paying the high prices they generate. For example, two agents can collaborate, whereby one party consigns the work for a sale and another party purchases it as a bidder. Then, behind closed doors, the cost of the work is refunded, while publicly, the artist's economic value increases. Because the auction market remains fairly unregulated and grants anonymity to buyers, even a small number of speculators can influence the market by creating virtual prices. Weaponizing special knowledge like this is considered unethical or even illegal in other fields—for example, insider trading with stocks—but it happens regularly in the art market. In Yue's case, we can only hypothesize that some of his works, especially those that disappeared into a "black hole," could have been subjected to this approach.

Finally, an even more complex scheme is to intervene on the side of art's symbolic value, staging exhibitions at public/noncommercial art institutions with the intention of selling the showcased works soon after. In Yue's case, this strategy seems to have been adopted mainly by players from Western centers—like Charles Saatchi (UK), Larry Warsh (US), and Matthias Goedhuis (Netherlands, US). Before entering the Chinese art game, they already had a reputation for actively shaping values and careers in the international market of the 1980s and 1990s.[182] All three engaged in spectacular bidding for works by Chinese contemporary artists. When Saatchi purchased a painting by Zhang Xiaogang in October 2006 for a record of around $1.4 million, Warsh said it was a crucial trendsetting event: "Saatchi is coming late, but he's important, because people will follow him."[183] One year later, Warsh acquired a work by Wang Guangyi for for over half a million USD at Phillips de Pury, a transaction that seemed to be primarily a marketing ploy. Warsh bought the painting from his father-in-law, Howard Farber, and given this family tie, it seems it would be unnecessary to bid for the work at a public auction unless it was serving as a price-advertising event.

These savvy agents also used exhibitions to heighten their acquisitions' symbolic value. In contrast to semiheteronomous collectors, this strategy was connected to short-term financial interests. The most scandalous example involving Yue's art was the Estella Collection, orchestrated by Matthias Goedhuis at the height of the 2007 boom. With a combined background in business and art history, Goedhuis had worked as an "investment advisor" in the arts. He aimed to discover "commercially neglected areas with investment potential and those appropriate for market development" by building major collections and "concurrently stimulating interest."[184] That is exactly what he did with Chinese contemporary art. Goedhuis obtained art on behalf of two US investors at low prices from the artists' studios and their dealers, who believed that the works would become part of a serious collection and later donated to a museum.[185] The Louisiana Museum of Modern Art in Humlebaek, Denmark, and the Israel Museum in Jerusalem were then convinced to exhibit the works as the "Estella Collection"—a fake label. A massive catalog accompanied the shows. Soon after, the collection was auctioned off in April 2008 at Sotheby's Hong Kong for around $18 million.[186] A major scandal ensued when the fraud was uncovered.[187] The involved agents felt misled and instrumentalized for an "investment vehicle" that purely served economic interests rather than primarily cultural ones.[188]

Of course, the most important exhibition for Yue's individual career before 2010 was his only solo museum show in a major cultural center, which was mediated by Warsh, who knew a member of the Queens Museum's board. Publicly, Warsh calls himself a collector, but he has worked in the art field for more than twenty years as a publisher, art adviser, and dealer. Reputedly, he pushed the careers of two commercial art market stars, Jean-Michel Basquiat and Keith Haring, in the 1980s.[189] In 2007, at the height of the boom, Warsh founded AW Asia, a private organization, as a platform for networking with institutions and clients to promote his holdings in Chinese contemporary art.[190] His approach was also informed by financial rationales and the marketing of the genre as an investment opportunity. As he stated,

> Chinese contemporary art is a buying opportunity. It's still *undervalued* relative to painting. . . . Quality works will become *increasingly scarce*, particularly as China develops as a consumer society with its own collector base. The Chinese audience with disposable income is growing, and a consistent percentage of those people will become art advocates and collectors. . . . Also, I think that . . . China will undergo more severe inflation than it's seen recently, making high-quality work a good haven for protecting the yuan. This will also benefit non-Chinese collectors *holding this type of asset*. With its broad acceptance on the international art market—London, New York, Paris, Hong Kong, China—and its performance in Western and Asian auction houses, *high-quality work will be salable around the globe.* . . . With the coming inflation, I predict that art will outperform other non-art investments, as it has done in the past. . . . The Chinese art market has tremendous opportunities yet to be realized.[191]

Warsh's perspective epitomizes a financial logic in dealing with Chinese contemporary art. Framing art as an "asset" that was still "undervalued" but that was becoming "increasingly scarce" emphasized the necessity of timely buying, while the promise about future value increases and art's ability to serve as a hedge against inflation were linked with China's larger political economy. Warsh's insights also reveal a global outlook. He speaks to Chinese and "non-Chinese" collectors alike and foregrounds how works would be "saleable around the globe," adding to their investment appeal. His rhetoric underlines the speculation game's globalization in the new millennium, which was manifested in Warsh's own cross-continental maneuvers for valorizing Yue's art. He initiated a solo show of Yue to heighten symbolic value at a global art center in Fall 2007 before Yue's exhibited works started to appear in 2009 at auction on three continents.

Once a contemporary artist attracts speculators, prices can rise dramatically in a very short time, and they and mediators have little power to resist or stop them. Such a market "hype" characterized Yue's career between 2005 and 2008.[192] In 1994, his paintings sold for around $5,000. In 2004, that figure was less than $100,000. But within a year, his work was auctioned for over $500,000. By 2007, his art could fetch more than $5 million. The fact that this speculative dynamic spanned several continents demonstrates that the logic governing art as a financial asset was operating within an expanding global market game, catapulting Yue Minjun, at least temporarily and without much choice, into the heteronomous pole's upper echelons.

Conclusion: Yue Minjun and the "Rules" of a Globalizing Speculation Game

For the sociologist Alain Quemin, the millennial auction boom of Chinese contemporary art looked like a nationally driven dynamic that was "mostly due to the fact that Chinese collectors and investors" were "eager to buy works by contemporary Chinese artists, especially for reasons of social prestige," while most of their works were "sold at auctions in China," which sent their prices "to record highs."[193]

The career of Yue Minjun—one of the most successful artists during this market upswing—challenges such a nationalistic interpretation, instead suggesting that a global market hype surrounding his art resulted from the historical interplay of at least three developments. At the macro-level, China's economic globalization was a structural *and* cultural precondition for the growth of foreign and national collectors of Chinese contemporary art. At the micro-level, Yue's habitus and early trajectory inclined him toward producing a stylistic brand that resembled Pop art, which was easily accessible to less specialized audiences that appreciated Yue's paintings as a cultural window into China's dramatic transformations. At the meso-level of the commercial subfield, powerful auction houses and speculators—while building on prior promotions by galleries and collectors—propelled Yue's rapid economic rise. By exploiting price signals in market centers and using publicity to define global values, these types of heteronomous players were able to attract investment-oriented buyers from multiple continents and drive up prices for Yue's art. All these forces worked to rapidly turn Yue into a market star, though after the 2008 financial crisis, they also meant that his position declined almost as quickly as it rose.

Yue's trajectory departs from a traditional conversion path from symbolic to economic capital. From the beginning, his career was predominantly driven by market agents and commercial factors. Almost an inversion of Bourdieu's model, Yue's only foreign museum show until 2010 took place after his commercial success had grown. It thus seemed more like a subsequent justification for, rather than a precondition of, his extraordinary market rise. Undoubtedly, Yue's ascent did not take place without building up any symbolic capital, but unlike Orozco, who forged strong ties with autonomous experts, Yue's smaller number of noncommercial exhibitions was primarily associated with a broader interest in Chinese contemporary art. And these shows served as a basic entry point into the market before economic forces took over. In this regard, Yue's incipient regional auction success and the onset of positive price signals set his work apart early on as one of the category's market leaders. And as sales for his works further spiraled in an endogenous market dynamic across four continents, they fed into added media coverage and "celebrity capital," broadly advertising him as a leading contemporary painter from China.

Yue's meteoric rise underlines how the global field's market side follows relatively independent logics of valorization, in which the economic criteria of marketability and the speculative value of artistic positions can develop their own force. In this regard, the meanings concerning contemporary art's status as an asset and the use of price dynamics as a barometer of speculative value were able to attract wide attention because they had become legible in New York, Beijing, London, Hong Kong, and beyond. In other words, the hype surrounding his art reached global dimensions because a shared financial logic had gained traction across a broader range of countries during the art market's globalization process. Yue's case testifies to the global art field's dual economy, in which the "rules" governing the construction of symbolic and economic value across continents can operate relatively independently.

Yue's career offers broader theoretical arguments about the construction of value in a globalizing art market. Structurally, it underlines just how influential mediators situated in market centers can be for the making of global artistic careers. Most importantly, a "landmark" sale at Sotheby's New York launched a hype spanning five continents. Though this underscores the relevance of center-periphery dynamics at the commercial pole (cf. also chapter 3), we must recognize that the power of the center operated only through complex feedback loops with relatively independent regional and national field levels. Put differently the structure that supported Yue's remarkable economic rise worked through a multiscalar configuration, in which global, regional, and national market centers were asymmetrically interdependent in the valuation process.

Moreover, Yue's rise as a "non-Western" artist from a country that was peripheral in the previous international art field suggests three cultural mechanisms at work in the breaking down of old artistic hierarchies and the construction of commercial value across borders. As we saw, the appreciation for Yue's art was affected by market agents' and collectors' broader fascination with China's contradictory transformations and changing political-economic status within the global order. In contrast to Orozco, his art was thus valued for its topicality rather than its discursivity, and for its overt national associations instead of a cosmopolitan universality. Yet these two cultural features only became valuable because they were positively charged with transnational meanings that were circulating in the wider sociohistorical context at that time, in line with the greater heteronomy of the global commercial subfield.

Finally, Yue's career undoubtedly benefited from his association with the collective art labels "Chinese contemporary art" and "Cynical Realism." But what allowed his artistic style to stand out among many peers for economic success was how it aligned with an already successful market idiom and assumed a brand-like quality. This finding might appear obvious, but it is not trivial. Given that a global art market involves less specialized buyers and collectors from very different countries and cultural backgrounds, an artistic brand—something easily accessible, iconic, and instantly recognizable across borders—seems to pay off for producers. Yue's brand of laughing faces in a realist Pop-aesthetic allowed for easier circulation across a space of culturally heterogeneous, less expert-driven publics, establishing a "universal legibility."[194]

8

"Global Art" between Autonomy and Heteronomy

UP UNTIL THE 1980S, the art field was a highly West-centric game. The postwar canon of international contemporary art almost exclusively consisted of artists from the US and western Europe, while, more often than not, artists from other world regions found themselves on the outside looking in. But immense global institutional transformations over the past three decades have led scholars to question whether this discriminatory, quasi-colonial situation has changed. Some have hailed the advent of a more egalitarian global art world community that is eroding old hierarchies. Skeptics, however, who tend to view these global changes through the lens of cultural imperialism, have discredited such an idea as illusory, suggesting instead that art's globalization looks more like the worldwide takeover of Western hegemony.

The Global Rules of Art has carved out a novel, alternative position in this debate, one that avoids the dichotomies of either revolutionary upheaval or outright reproduction, of either increased diversity or a calcifying homogeneity. What has emerged over the past thirty years is a global art field where extended exchange and competition have increasingly subverted West-centric artistic hierarchies, though the old institutional power imbalances have not vanished completely. And while this field has developed new global circuits, practices, and discourses—and, ultimately, some diversity among its most recognized cross-border artists—these processes have not been straightforward, and they have evolved unevenly at its two main poles of mediation.

On the commercial side, the global art market has witnessed rapid changes regarding the rise of artists beyond old Western centers, particularly from China. But it has largely favored producers from countries with growing wealth and art economies. Consequently, the diversity of the global art market's leading artists has remained relatively limited. The autonomous pole, by contrast, has embraced artists from more peripheral world regions—particularly African countries—and its elite ranks have grown much more cosmopolitan overall.

Yet in this expert-driven subfield, in which transformations evolved along generational rhythms of *longue durée*, it took longer for "non-Western" artists to reach global canonization after decades of systemic exclusion.

These divergences are not historically random. They are inextricably linked to the different, sometimes opposing logics of how artistic value gets created at the two poles of "global art." The emerging global field—with its dual cultural world economy—is structured around a fundamental divide between art and money. And grasping that major division allows us to more fully understand the complexities and contradictions at the heart of contemporary art's globalization while avoiding the dichotomic pitfalls that have marked prior debates.

Transformations and Diversity in a Dual Cultural World Economy

Approaching the recognition of artists from a global field perspective means that what rises to elite levels is not just the result of random, individual judgments from aesthetic experts and market players around the world. It is crucially channeled by the unique circuits, structures, and dominant meanings that make up the globalizing field's dual economy—that is, the distinct ways it enables and constrains cross-border valuation processes.

On the market side, broader economic factors heavily influenced global transformations, though these were always refracted through developments specific to that subfield. As the millennium got under way, new wealth, especially in Asia, fueled the growth of national and regional contemporary art markets. These increasingly connected with global commercial centers through extended infrastructures—auction and art fair circuits as well as novel internet platforms—and facilitated the rise of a global field level for art market exchange and competition.

The extended competition transformed the strategies of dominant market brokers in the Northwest. When they saw an opportunity for economic capital, they pounced on work by contemporary artists from promising locations. This meant that the offerings at auctions and other outlets became more diverse. In turn, when "non-Western" artists were promoted at global centers, it boosted their economic value in rising regional and national markets. The transformation of commercial art canons thus evolved within multiscalar power structures and asymmetric interdependencies that go beyond any simple idea of one-way dependencies and flows. Change was invigorated by emerging regional markets and then pushed and solidified by the global centers of art market power. Nowhere is this clearer than in the boom involving certain Chinese contemporary artists in the millennium's first decade.

But these changing power structures and forms of competition cannot fully explain the subfield's diversification. Meso-level logics of valuation mattered of course, too. Of particular importance, auction houses, speculative dealers, risk-oriented collectors, and art investment managers—all agents outside traditional symbolic consecration networks—embraced art as a financial asset. Speculation surrounding contemporary art is not new, but as global auction market infrastructures and online price databases took shape and as investment-driven buyers from around the world entered the market, the practice gained extended traction. Thus, when an artist's fluctuations in "economic capital," along with their "celebrity capital" from broader media channels, became visible on a global scale, it could impact their valorization in ways that were relatively independent of art experts' assessments. These dynamics helped propel the global rise of some "non-Western" artists, including Yue Minjun, who achieved immense commercial success without concomitant levels of symbolic renown. The radicalization of a financial logic is one of the key meso-level factors explaining the stark disparities between money and art in the globalizing field. And it is the main reason why dynamics of artistic diversity have unfolded at the heteronomous pole in much quicker, more volatile ways.

Nationality functioned as an important evaluative filter that enabled some artists to break through the old West-centric hierarchies. Coming from a country with rising wealth provided important advantages, as Yue's case study reveals. For central market agents and speculators to assume risk and promote new artists, they at least needed to sense the potential for a growing national (or regional) market and future profits.

But Yue's story also lays bare nationality's *cultural* relevance—that is, a country's reputation as it is brokered through transnational media and cross-border elites—for market valorization. Before Chinese contemporary art became popular at auctions, it was first appreciated and supported by several collectors who shared a broader cultural fascination with China and its rising status on the world stage.

In this sense, the narratives associated with a country, and the various ways artworks speak to those narratives, created distinctive cultural value that enabled commercial success. This mechanism might explain why "Chinese contemporary art" became such a lucrative genre in the global market while art from other countries that also had a rising millionaire class, like India and Russia, only did so to a lesser extent. The diversification of global commercial canons, then, was filtered through nationality in both economic *and* cultural meanings. For certain artists, the rising status of their country in the wider sociohistorical context made up for that country's still relatively "peripheral" position within the contemporary art field, catapulting them to remarkable heights in the global market also without the imprimatur of experts.

Naturally, the commercial pole was not devoid of any consideration for artistic media and style at the micro-level. Certain forms of aesthetic capital were more valuable than others, and as chapter 5 revealed, this subfield's top levels were overwhelmingly made up of artists who produced paintings or sculptures. Thus, working in easily commodifiable media has been a basic, and perhaps obvious, condition of success. Yet, as Yue's career indicates, there are also advantages to producing work that is analogous to idioms that already have broad market appeal across borders, such as Pop art. Moreover, in a global competitive art market with culturally heterogeneous buyers, the brand-like quality of Yue's art suggests that an aesthetic style with strong recognizability and quasi-"universal" legibility provides an edge. Put differently when an artist's geocultural difference may have added value with regard to an artwork's topicality, that difference had to be packaged within an aesthetic that was easily understandable and marketable across borders. Only then could the work enter the fast-paced world of global consumer mediation.

Of course, Yue's micro-level "formula" was not the only path to global success for "non-Western" artists who were challenging entrenched market hierarchies during this era. But his case clearly demonstrates how commercial valuation followed evaluative criteria that diverged from the autonomous pole's emphasis on experimentation and innovation.

At the relatively autonomous pole, globalizing developments were *less* driven by broader economic forces. Instead, its field-external catalysts were postcolonial independence movements and multicultural politics. In the late 1980s, when these political and intellectual influences converged with a "peripheral" biennial insurgency, new symbolic field struggles proliferated that increasingly challenged the legitimacy of West-centric artistic establishments.

In the wake of this upheaval, expanded infrastructures for contemporary art's symbolic circulation and mediation—the global biennial circuit, global discourses, and global evaluation instances—enabled the gradual, and contested, construction of a more global understanding of the subfield's boundaries and stakes. In social terms, competition over symbolic capital—not economic capital—drove this process, and debates raged concerning how contemporary art could be interpreted and evaluated in ways that went beyond a Western paradigm. In contrast to the art market, where power emanated largely from dominant agents in the field's centers, transformations at the autonomous pole were defined more by a dynamic of give and take, of collaborative competition, between "peripheral" and central players. At metropolitan hubs, diasporic agents also found allies in a younger generation of heterodox Western intermediaries who, in their own quest for innovation and recognition, challenged perennial orthodoxies.

The contested construction of a more global, cosmopolitan vision for contemporary art in turn supported some artists from outside dominant Western countries to gain increasing critical recognition and wider exposure at major exhibitions. However, because these transformations were partly predicated on generational divisions, the diversification of global elite artists unfolded more gradually than it did at the commercial pole.

In macrostructural terms, despite the emergence of a new global logic within the artistic subfield, a few countries and cities in the Northwest still hold most resources for launching transcontinental careers. Its central hubs—New York, Berlin, and Paris—differed somewhat from the heteronomous pole's most powerful centers, however, which consisted of the world's biggest financial hubs: New York, London, and Hong Kong. As chapter 5's discussion of migration flows indicated, autonomous artists also needed to *live in* these cultural centers to succeed. Orozco's case suggests that a key reason for this is that the symbolic economy operates more readily through strong gatekeeper ties, which are facilitated by physical proximity. So in a fundamental way, global artistic canons at the autonomous pole were affected by a partly different set of geographic centers and the distinctive ways they affected migration flows and social capital.

The fact that cultural agents in Western centers were still powerful arbiters for transcontinental careers means that entry into the field's top tier was heavily shaped by their prevailing logics at the meso-level. And those logics remained grounded in self-referential artistic and intellectual values rather than heteronomous ones. That is, expert cultural authorities still approached art as a specialized, essentially noninstrumental sphere of activity. But that approach had shifted from older formalist to discursive parameters, as "art for art's discursive sake."

Orozco's case, along with the career patterns I outlined in chapter 5, suggests that this discursive logic was associated with three dominant evaluative criteria. Two of them had older origins though they became increasingly articulated with newer meanings that emerged in the field's globalization process. In other words, novel discourses and cosmopolitan values for embracing artists from around the world were calibrated with established criteria, dominated by the long shadow of Western art histories and long-specialized dispositions—which again points us to a transformational logic of cultural change.

The first evaluative criterion involves artistic autonomy as distance toward commercial motives. Powerful cultural agents originally hailed Orozco as a rebel who defied market fads, and the most successful artists in the global artistic subfield predominantly engage in media that resist easy commodification and financialization, like installation, video art, and performance. The crucial implication is that the same aesthetic capital that creates a stumbling block in the market can actually feed into one's success at the relatively autonomous pole. The opposite is true as well.

The second criterion of distinction that we saw with Orozco implies that for "non-Western" artists to succeed in the globalizing art game, their work—and, in particular, what I call their work's discursivity—must offer a daring, original engagement with prevailing art histories and discourses. Thus, "peripheral" artists do not succeed through a simple act of assimilation; they can still assert their agency and subvert the dominant frameworks of international contemporary art. But as Orozco's case suggests, that subversion must be contextualized within the latter's dominant tendencies and historical debates to be intelligible and have an impact. In other words, the meso-level principle of distinction underlines how artistic recognition involves *relationally* meaningful artistic interventions, which can then expand the range of the globalizing field's dominant positions and discourses. But that only occurs *from within,* which again shows why the autonomous pole has transformed more slowly than the commercial one.

A third evaluative criterion is related in indirect ways to how national—or, more broadly, geocultural—markers influenced valuation processes, though this worked out very differently than it did at the commercial pole. As global logics took hold in the autonomous subfield, cultural intermediaries and institutions, including those at the field's centers, integrated and featured artists from previously ignored "non-Western" countries to show that they were innovatively moving beyond limited, Eurocentric perspectives (chapters 2, 5). Thus, if an artist originated from a formerly peripheral country, it served as a categorical selection filter that underwent positive reevaluation during this era.

In contrast to the market, however, this national filter was not limited to commercial rationales, and artists were not selected based solely on their home country's wealth level. Artists from less wealthy regions in the Global South even enjoyed slight advantages. This was partly due to the rise of postcolonial discourses in the art field, but it also speaks to structural affinities. As Craig Rawlings has explained regarding African contemporary art, the most heterodox members of the art field often align themselves with marginalized groups because they similarly feel like they are in a "homologously dominated position."[1]

Nevertheless, Orozco's career demonstrates an artist's need to "universalize" his geocultural difference through artistic practice at the autonomous pole. This points to the idea of aesthetic "universality," as the third evaluative principle in the globalizing artistic subfield. To succeed in the long run, "non-Western" artists had to evade being pigeonholed by their national or ethnic difference—that is, being "othered." This is particularly true if their original country lacks artistic prestige. As Orozco's case revealed, this predicament is difficult to navigate and master because it is often precisely a "peripheral" artist's "otherness" that opened doors for them in a period of rising global discourses and exhibition politics.

In light of a long history of exclusion, Orozco could not simply position himself as a universal individual creator who was free of such limiting collective categorizations. His novel solution involved creating a nomadic artistic practice that alluded to his national difference while simultaneously universalizing it. His art's form and discourse forged a new kind of cosmopolitan universality that allowed him to subvert old status hierarchies in the field and ultimately served as an innovative basis for his legitimation as a Mexican-global artist.

At the micro-level, the rules of distinction and universality in Orozco's case required a habitus with an adept sense for the game. In this regard, living in New York and other major art centers was critical for his career. It provided him not only with social capital but also with informal, in-depth knowledge about metropolitan art cultures. The importance of this kind of cultural capital is further revealed by the fact that successful artists at the relatively autonomous pole have typically undergone longer periods of specific arts education (chapter 5) than have successful commercial artists and have more often received it at Western art institutions—yet another key disjuncture in the way the two globalizing economies operate.

Of course, Orozco's specific micro-level strategies, and how they related to dominant evaluative principles, will not work for every artist. This is also because what counts as "distinction" or "universal" is always relational to particular fields and their historically evolving debates. But his case sharply differs from Yue's career trajectory. While Yue's assertion of his Chinese nationality was a key part of his success at the commercial pole, a similar strategy would have collided with the autonomous pole's norms, in which exceptional individual creators were expected to produce field-specific, "universal" art (chapter 6). This dominant norm might also explain why the autonomous subfield did not see a similar upsurge of artists from one particular country. Only one or two artists per formerly "peripheral" national field were able to reach the highest levels of recognition. But that still led to more cosmopolitan diversity in the backgrounds of elite artists overall.

In sum, a dual economy has governed global transformations in contemporary art. It involves, on the one hand, a new cosmopolitan openness and, on the other, a globalization of wealth. And the art field, with its expanding economic role, serves as their zone of confrontation. This twinned structure has affected the recognition and diversity of artists from non-Western countries in systematically different ways. Counter to histories asserting that accelerated globalization and rising market forces have led to a convergence of economic and symbolic expert valuation, we have actually seen increased polarization.[2] Contemporary artists excel in one subfield or another. They rarely do in both.

I am not trying to downplay massive commodification trends in the global art field. Those are real, and they exert strong force. But increasing financial logics and the rise of a new consumer class have meant that the field has further fractured in unexpected ways. And if we do not address the heterogeneity and tensions that are still very much alive, we risk turning the heteronomous market into a measure for artistic value when, in reality, it merely abides by its own discrete machinations and canonization strategies. We would also fail to understand how relative autonomy operates within the emerging global space and how it has facilitated more artistic cosmopolitanism than the commercial sphere has. In short, the rise of "global art," and the conflicts over its expanding canons, has been a divided affair. It is the old story of art versus money, though it is unfolding under different historical and geographic conditions in the twenty-first century. And it continues to serve as an unresolved battleground for the people involved.

New Tools and the Weight of Geography

My book, of course, has primarily explored the global transformations affecting the contemporary visual arts. But its broader theoretical underpinnings hold promise for other fields as well. A global cultural fields approach offers several advantages, allowing us to better understand the interplay between the processes that are internal and external to cross-border cultural realms; to link meso-, macro-, and micro-level factors; to relate structural and interpretive analyses; and to attend to major divisions defining globalizing cultures, such as the autonomous-heteronomous divide and between global, regional, and national levels. It is a demanding integrative framework that is multidimensional, multileveled, and multiscalar at once, but not unnecessarily so. After all, all the factors I have listed contribute to the heterogeneous and manifold layers making up the dynamics of global cultures.

So how might this approach be applied beyond the field of contemporary art? To answer this question, we should emphasize the term "approach." Just as Bourdieu suggests that his national level field analysis is a "mode of construction that has to be rethought anew every time," the book's framework should be thought of as a cross-border mode of construction, not a "ready-made" theory.[3] It suggests, for example, that when analyzing cultural fields in a global context, we should consider macro power structures, which we can grasp through field-specific forms of macro capital that are not reducible to the hierarchies marking the larger capitalist world-system (see chapter 1).[4] But what are the most relevant forms of macro capital in the fields of music or fashion? Is their macrostructure polycentric or monocentric? These are entirely empirical questions, and rather than formulating a static set of propositions, the global fields approach instead offers a dynamic methodology for constructing a "global object."[5] As it finds applications for new domains and historical periods, it needs to be critically interrogated, creatively revised, and dialogically extended as part of global intellectual conversations.

Engaging with global comparative sociology, literatures in the sociology of culture, economic sociology, and valuation studies and building on prior contributions on cross-border fields, my study has proposed ways to extend and revise the conception of the autonomy-heteronomy divisions in a global field. It also has advanced new tools for fields analysis in a global context that could be developed and tested for other realms. For example, I have suggested that there were three field-internal mechanisms for the emergence of a global field level—*global institutional circuits, field-specific global discourse*, and *global institutions of evaluation*—that interacted in refractive ways with external globalization influences. These three mechanisms give Bourdieu's original analysis, which focuses more heavily on individual players and their power relations, a stronger institutional component. Once we move beyond (sub) national studies, we need to think more about organizational, cultural, and technological infrastructures that enable and sustain field relations across vast distances to begin with.

This institutional grounding is also reflected in the way my study has introduced the idea of forms of *institutional macro capital* to map center-periphery inequalities involved in the mediation and valuation of culture across borders, which I have suggested distinguishing from forms of cultural centrality (or commercial centrality). For example, while the US still commands greatest institutional power in the global art field, it has lost in cultural centrality regarding its contemporary artists in the past twenty years—a decline that is most dramatic among younger artistic generations (see chapter 5). To theorize center-periphery hierarchies and their transformations in the global terrain, it is necessary to disaggregate more their different dimensions and types.[6]

My approach has also shown how attending to a *multiscalar* architecture— the coexistence of global, regional, national, and/or subnational levels—can be another effective tool for extending field analysis in the global era.[7] As we saw in Yue's case study, these scales can operate both independently and interdependently as they shape field processes and outcomes across borders. By attending to such a multiscalar configuration, a global cultural fields approach also leaves room for the persisting diversity characterizing various field levels. It does not assume that a global field automatically subsumes everything that has preceded it and thus leads to a simple homogenization. More theoretical work is necessary, however, to fully understand the complex relationships among scalar levels and to explain the strategies that cultural agents employ as they maneuver across (and in between) nested scales.

Lastly, the book's framework contributes to our understanding of geography's unique role in cross-border field processes—something Bourdieu's cultural fields analysis did not address—and to distinguishing between the territorial and symbolic modalities of geographies of valuation. The latter refers to a field's macrostructure, the way certain cities and countries, in institutional center-periphery structures, concentrate the highest levels of field-relevant resources and are thus able to exert genuine "place effects."[8] Pascale Casanova, in her magnificent work on the world literary space, has pointed to this important aspect of geography for global cultural fields.[9] My study has extended this territorial emphasis further, tracing how and why such geographies of power diverge along the autonomy-heteronomy axis and how they are intertwined with unique meso-level logics and relevant forms of micro capital. For example, the fact that successful autonomous artists migrated to geographic centers of mediation more often than their commercial colleagues did is inextricably connected to the greater weight that strong ties with gatekeepers and high cultural capital exert in this sphere.

Perhaps even more interesting is the role that geography plays in global cultural fields involving symbolic modalities. This book's two case studies clearly highlight the importance of geographic labels in valuation processes for global art. It matters if one is a "Chinese" or a "Mexican" or a "global" artist. Of course, geographic classifications have long been ubiquitous in the world of art and art history.[10] They often serve as a shorthand method for bundling artworks and paintings under common rubrics, and in this sense, they only become laden with value when particular meanings are attached to them. But the findings of this book suggest that geographic meanings contribute to the construction of value in cross-border fields in ways that traditional (national) cultural fields theory does not sufficiently account for.

Indeed, if one looks closely at Bourdieu's notion of distinction as innovation within autonomous subfields, it becomes clear that it is firmly underpinned by assumptions that posit a shared art history in a bounded space. In that context, distinction involves introducing something novel into a field that is historically older (that is, traditional, outdated, or out of time: the "classic"). In a global context, though, a unified (Western) history of art—which has proved to be an exclusionary construct for most of the world's art production to begin with—is no longer possible.[11] With that in mind, does the emergence of a global art field foster a shift of emphasis, moving us from a Western paradigm of evaluating innovative cultural goods according to *temporality* (the new versus the traditional; the contemporary and the modern) to a more *spatial* regime in which geography's influence on evaluative processes is more pronounced and explicit?

Naturally, the two case studies in this book cannot conclusively answer such a complex question, also because they are part of one of the first more global generations in the art field. They do, however, provide some conceptual insight into how geographic classifications enter processes of meaning-making and contribute to the construction of value across borders. At the heteronomous pole, the geographic labels of cultural goods are more likely to be associated with field "external" representations (or imaginations), and it is through such associations that respective art categories, or artists, are ascribed value. Yue's career suggests at least two types of heteronomous geographic valuation. The first can be described as "cultural wealth"—a concept that Nina Bandelj and Frederick Wherry introduced to account for the ways meanings that are associated with nations, regions, or communities provide advantages for certain goods in the global marketplace. Such meanings encompass collective narratives, ideas, symbols, or reputations beyond a particular field's boundaries.[12] From this perspective, artworks or artists are valued because of their links to broader geographic meanings—precisely what happened when historical transformations in China impacted Yue's career.

The other type of geographic heteronomous valuation can be called "identarian." This type differs from cultural wealth in that geographically based art categories (e.g., categories, like "Chinese contemporary art," that refer to nation-states, regions, or continents) get framed in terms of cultural identity. Using this logic, a genre is valued as a unique expression of a particular place-bounded cultural identity and its traditions. It is not just the general positive connotations of a geographic place—for example, the rise of China—that confer meaning. More immediately, the most meaningful elements are the identarian associations involved with a country's people (e.g., in the form of Chinese nationalism or the nationalistic cliches associated with Neomexicanismo in the late 1980s).

At the autonomous pole, geographic categorizations affect dynamics of valuation more indirectly, happening primarily through a refractive process. Geographic labels, which are run through the filter of field-specific artistic hierarchies and histories, eventually get translated into value judgments. When Orozco entered the international art field, for instance, Mexico's art production was considered "peripheral" to the standards embodied by "universal" Western contemporary art. This geographic refraction implies that artists are not simply situated territorially. They are also positioned in cultural terms, based on their country's status within a field-specific pecking order. Even for those artists who do not remain in their home country, the symbolic associations of a particular nation can operate like a categorical filter for the judgment of their work. Such a filter may hold certain advantages for artists from dominant Western countries, but it becomes an obstacle when an artist comes from a country that has less specific symbolic capital and thus less "universal" status.

For Orozco, overcoming his peripheral positionality as a Mexican artist did not involve a change in Mexico's broader reputation in the world press. Nor was it related to the rise of multicultural identity politics, which led to increasing favor for certain Mexican artists. His autonomous maneuvering around these geographic constraints was paved by the very language of his art, which aligned him, innovatively, with established "universal" art traditions and created a new nomadic practice that crossed and hybridized the meanings associated with diverse national artistic traditions (e.g., Italian Arte Povera, American conceptual art, British sculpture, Brazilian conceptualists). But the exact same value that was associated with the transgression of such geographic classifications, and the alternative cosmopolitan universality he created, was again tied up with the field-internal meanings that these artistic traditions carried.

Thus, when exclusionary historical genealogies lose credibility as coordinates for the construction of novelty or distinction in globalizing cultures, geographic factors seem to become more valent. My idea of *subfield-specific geographies of valuation* thereby underlines the importance of not taking geographic labels, such as nationality, at face value and rather accounting for their diverse meanings in circulation processes. In this regard, the book advances tools for theorizing how geography—in both its territorial and symbolic dimensions—contributes to the making of artistic careers and canons across borders.

Overall, while these ideas and my global art field framework have sought to critique and open up overly unitary and totalizing approaches, it is necessary to go further to accurately map the field's internal heterogeneity. That is the reason why I have repeatedly written that the global art field is "most fundamentally" structured around the poles of art and money, of a cosmopolitan laboratory and global wealth. In an era that has witnessed the ongoing intellectual deconstruction of binaries, this is a critical point to emphasize. It also returns us to the logic underpinning the development of the book's theoretical framework. I see it as one step toward exploring additional internal differentiations that may exist and further advancing a global cultural fields approach in cumulative research.

In this endeavor of revision and extension, however, let us remind ourselves that *any* theorizing necessarily involves reduction, and any broad claim about a cultural subset does not account for the exceptions. The goal of field analysis would not be to catalog every last element of the (global) art world as it presents itself through daily perceptions on the ground: its endless flux of events, its phenomenological multiplicity, or its seemingly infinite individual stories. Field theory's primary approach is to identify the parameters that most clearly reveal basic structures and prevailing logics beyond the vagaries of everyday common sense. That mode of theorizing is helpful for uncovering a range of impactful patterns, contributing to deepen our grasp of the power mechanisms and dominant meanings at work in the shaping of cross-border cultural spaces—and thus for uncovering possible ways for critical intervention.

Epilogue

COVID-19, GEOPOLITICAL SHIFTS, AND DEGLOBALIZATION?

JUST AS THE FRAMEWORK that I have proposed here remains open to further theoretical refinement and modification, we must remember that it is, essentially, historical. Even in the time I have been writing this book, our world has changed immensely, and often in ways that directly pertain to the arguments I have presented here. Today, nationalist and antiglobalist movements are on the rise. In place of open exchange, we are witnessing the closure of borders and major political crackdowns (e.g., mainland China's strengthening grip on Hong Kong). Nationalizing geopolitical transformations have only been accelerated and aggravated by COVID-19, which brought much of the world, including the global art field, to a virtual standstill. Within weeks, art institutions and market venues around the world shuttered their doors, and artists and mediators lost their traditional means of engaging audiences directly. In the midst of these extraordinary circumstances, new narratives, which suggest the pandemic may portend the end of contemporary art's global era, have already begun to gain ground.

Of course, we are still very much in the middle of these crises, and it would be unwise to try to guess what the future may hold. If anything, the past two years have shown us that making historical predictions is a fool's errand. As I have pointed out earlier, it is also critically important that we do not rely too heavily on anecdotes or small batches of data that seem to say something definitive about larger structures and dominant trends. To truly assess the effects that these macro-level geopolitical events will have on the contemporary art field, we must gather more empirical data. And that will take time.

With that in mind, the framework that I have presented here—and its dynamic, open-ended approach to capturing a field's complexity—may offer useful tools for understanding the trajectories of globalization in the coming years. At its core, the book's approach sees the contemporary art field as a sphere of specialized practice that is relatively independent—albeit at varying degrees and scales—from its external environment. Principally, it asks us to resist the temptation of drawing convenient and direct causal links between the art world and broader geopolitics, a mode of thinking that still has currency among some theorists who posit art's "renationalization," for example. Rather, a global art field approach suggests that we look once again at how broader changes have become refracted through the field's own power structures, main tensions, as well as discourses, and the various players who respond to historical events in diverse ways. Put bluntly, in our historical moment, we should not expect that COVID-19 will have the same consequences for everyone and for the dynamics of "global art."

After being forced to pause the "normal" way of doing things, many mediators in the art field have been reevaluating their approach to the "global." But these reinterpretations have already differed among subfields and positions. For example, though some leading curators from institutional centers have called for a return to the "local" after years of nomadic traveling—almost as if that would be a purifying development for a global system that seemed to be in overdrive—we must remember that such calls largely come from a position of privilege. This type of reset is only a viable option for those who have institutional resources and major audiences at their front door. For agents from more "peripheral" locations, however, conventional cross-border connections may remain much more critical to build up and sustain their local operations and to have the resources to exert influence beyond them.

Likewise, we have certainly not seen agents at the commercial pole voice a similar drive to return to the "local." During the pandemic, global auction houses have aggressively pivoted to more digital offerings to secure their economic profits while further expanding their global audience. These heteronomous players thus seem to be entering a more pronounced (and cost-saving) digital globality that also thrives on a belief in art as an alternative financial asset (which became even more attractive when the pandemic initially sent stocks plummeting).

Nevertheless, among autonomous art circles too, digital forms of global engagement have proliferated in reaction to closed borders and rising nationalist impulses. Such moves have been accompanied by fiercer debates about sustainable approaches to global contemporary art. We might assume that over time, discourses about more sustainability in the artistic subfield will be become more "autonomized" as part of heterodox strategies of art-making and exhibition-making, driving new position-takings, new distinctions, and maybe symbolic revolutions in cross-border cultural circuits.

But recent calls for sustainability at the relatively autonomous pole do not match what is currently happening in the commercial subfield, where the biggest auction houses also have embraced NFTs under the aegis of "demo-cratizing" art. These new types of works carry an incredibly high environmen-tal cost. Yet for commercial players, they promise profits from new and younger audiences; and they seem ready-made for speculation since owner-ship of them can transfer almost instantaneously. In February 2021, Beeple sold a digital NFT work at Christie's for $69.3 million to a Canadian-educated In-dian entrepreneur who operates out of Singapore. Headlines focused on the fact that Mike Winkelmann, the social-media-celebrity-cum-artist, had joined the ranks of Jeff Koons and David Hockney as one of the world's most expen-sive living artists. With this monetary framing of greatness, they avoided men-tioning how he did not even have a single solo exhibition on his résumé. This difference again underlines just how decoupled the global commercial ma-chineries have become from the judgments of art experts.

There is still much to study about the economic challenges and constraints that COVID-19 has placed on individual venues and artists. Initially, we might assume that these transformations will lead to market convergence, where mon-eyed, profit-driven entities will be better positioned to weather the pandemic, snap up bargains, and come out triumphant on the other side, while more autonomous and less commercial entities will have to compromise and make tough choices in order to survive. But on the other hand, if the idea of a divided economy is accurate, a fuller empirical assessment might also reveal in hind-sight the astoundingly innovative ways that agents at the autonomous pole have maintained their resistance to market forces even as they have faced ex-traordinary fiscal challenges. The art field's autonomy was won through more than a century of struggle, and in light of the pandemic and the added threats it has unleashed, this struggle may well continue with new strategies and forms of cross-border solidarity to keep the cosmopolitan laboratory alive and to develop it further in a post-COVID world.

Overall, *The Global Rules of Art* has mapped the history of how the con-temporary art field reached unprecedented global heights. As such, it offers a foundation for exploring how recent historical developments have affected, curbed, or transformed global structures and practices that had emerged over the past thirty years. As sociologists of culture, however, we must always re-main aware that the realms of art and symbolic production are not static enti-ties. We need to come up with dynamic models that can capture this type of constant transformation. Contrary to globalization models that have a more teleological bent, an emerging global field approach can carve out this type of relational space. It sees the art field for what it really is, a power-riven arena where diverse sites, players, and formats are in endless exchange and contesta-tion with one another. It is never fully settled, and therefore, the tools we use to describe it must always remain open-ended as well.

ACKNOWLEDGMENTS

THIS BOOK is the result of a long journey with multiple turns and several new directions. Over the process, I benefited from the help of many generous scholars, colleagues, and art field insiders, as well as friends and family members. First, I would like to thank Ulf Wuggenig and Gil Eyal. Ulf, a preeminent scholar in the sociology of art and culture in Germany, set the standards for a revival of this subfield in this country through his numerous innovative research projects. The discussions I had with him in the uniquely interdisciplinary setting of the Cultural Sciences program at Lueneburg University laid the groundwork for my growing fascination with a sociological approach to art and culture, and he critically challenged my ideas and assumptions when I first began engaging with this topic. I thank him for his demanding feedback, his support as a mentor, and for the intellectual friendship we have developed.

Great thanks are also due to Gil Eyal for his invaluable help as my main advisor at Columbia University. He supported this project when it first took shape as a dissertation and after others had advised me not to pursue it because it was too risky. His penetrating feedback and our numerous conversations helped me think in more nuanced ways about Bourdieu's approach and sharpen my ideas and arguments. Without his commitment and remarkable support, this project would not have gone so smoothly. Yet Gil became more than an advisor to me. He also set an example as a model sociologist and academic who combines great analytical subtlety with a unique sense for intellectual beauty and humanism.

I wish to express my gratitude also to Diane Vaughan and Peter Bearman for their comments on chapters and several inspiring meetings. Some of the ideas for my research design first germinated in a memorable course I took about organizational analysis with Diane Vaughan in the spring of 2008. In hindsight, I can see how much her engaging feedback helped set me on track for this research marathon. With her intellectual curiosity, humble openness, and thorough approach, Diane became a very special mentor at Columbia. Peter Bearman is in a category all his own. With an uncompromising rigor and creativity, he provided important critical feedback when I was pursuing this project, and his analogy of creative sociological research with art came to my mind more than once when I was reflecting and writing about visual artists.

From my time at Columbia, I would also like to express my thanks to Harrison C. White, David Madigan, Fabien Accominotti, Priscilla Ferguson, Victor Corona, and Pierre-Michel Menger, who provided critical comments or suggestions for earlier versions of chapters or aspects of my analysis. Warm thanks are also due to Mustafa Emirbayer. With his deep knowledge about Bourdieu, he provided significant feedback for improving my dissertation's final draft.

I want to thank John Rajchman, who, as a philosopher and art theorist, probed my sociological approach and thinking about art in numerous conversations. He also graciously mediated vital contacts for my first research trip to Beijing in 2010. His course on contemporary Asian art in the spring of 2009 was an exciting interdisciplinary laboratory that made me ask many more questions about the contemporary visual arts in a global context than I had imagined when I first began researching it. I am grateful for the stimulating debates and friendship that we have developed. He also generously agreed to read drafts of this book and provided incredibly stimulating feedback for final revisions. His comments were so rich that they could inform an entirely new book project on the ever-evolving trajectories and struggles surrounding "global contemporary art."

I gratefully acknowledge the funds provided by the Sociology Department at Columbia University for my first research trip to China in the summer of 2010 and thank the Graduate School of Arts and Sciences at Columbia University for awarding me a Lindt Fellowship.

At Stony Brook University, I am grateful for the comments that the wonderful Javier Auyero provided on an earlier paper. His passion for sociology was a source of great intellectual energy, support, and critique. Thanks as well to Diane Barthel-Bouchier, Kiyo Tsutsui, and Herman Lebovics for their insightful and sensitive comments.

As a Junior Fellow at the Harvard Society of Fellows, I had intended to "finish up" my book and get ready for the academic job market. But my interdisciplinary exchanges at the society meetings there were so inspirational and unsettling that they prompted me to rethink the project. Although my dissertation had received awards, I realized that I still had to go deeper into my methodological assumptions as well as my approach to global theorizing, so that the research would avoid overly West-centric results. Consequently, I decided that I had to re-collect all my quantitative data and expand the qualitative research for my case studies with extended field trips to Beijing and Mexico. I gratefully acknowledge the generous backing of the Harvard Society of Fellows as well as a grant from Harvard's William F. Milton Fund. I also especially wish to thank Nur Yalman, Wally Gilbert, Peter Galison, William Todd, and Jerry Green for their kind support as Senior Fellows and greatly stimulating conversations. In the same spirit, I benefited from the weekly exchanges with Junior Fellows, and should particularly highlight Maxim Poz-doorovkin, Rohan Murty, Yvonne Chen, Clay Cordova, William Cheng, Kate Manne, Michaela Bronstein, and Scott Kominers.

At Harvard, I initiated gatherings with junior sociologists, which we called the "Sandwich Club," and I thank the participants—Ya-Wen Lei, Phillipa K. Chong, Bart Bonikowski, Kimberly Hoang, and Maggie Frye—for their most motivating and astute feedback on parts of this project. Furthermore, Michèle Lamont, whose Harvard Culture and Social Analysis Workshop I visited many times, was a crucial intellectual influence for my evolving approach in cultural sociology and qualitative research. I wish to thank Michèle for very inspiring individual meetings and her important support throughout as well. At Harvard, I also met Peggy Levitt, who then invited me to several private meetings and one workshop until 2020. Sparked by questions, I shared freely aspects of my theoretical approach, references, empirical sources, and information on meth-odological strategies regarding my research on the recognition and careers of "non-Western" contemporary artists in the global cultural field.

When I arrived at the School of Communication at Northwestern University, I felt lucky to have entered a department that was incredibly welcoming, inter-disciplinary, intellectually open, and extremely generous. I thank Barbara O'Keefe, Bonnie Martin Harris, and Rick Morris for their fantastic support from the beginning and Ellen Wartella, my first department chair, for how she created an atmosphere of empowerment and excellent support for us junior (female) faculty. I am also very grateful to Leslie Ann DeChurch, my second department chair, who was incredibly helpful in the final phase. Warm thanks as well to Pablo J. Boczkowski, Claudio Benzecry, Bob Hariman, and Dilip Goankar for important conversations about this project and beyond. At Northwestern, I ad-ditionally benefited from proximity to the Sociology Department. Gary Fine has been a huge source of inspiration from the beginning, and I would like to thank him for his wise feedback and significant support. I also appreciated important meetings with Wendy Espeland, Wendy Griswold, and Bruce G. Carruthers.

Furthermore, my extended collections of data for the book were funded by grants from Northwestern's Undergraduate Research Office, which are grate-fully acknowledged. In addition, the type of data work I had done alone over countless hours in prior years now benefited from the support of many under-graduate students, which felt like a veritable "global culture lab." I am grateful to all the students for their wonderful and engaging help. I especially want to thank Patrycja Kaluzynska for her superb assistance on the career data for chapter 5 and new discourse materials for chapter 6; Hanna Anderson for her important help in the filtering of art fairs and in double-checking data for the timeline of Christie's and Sotheby's globalization; Tilly Freedman for her re-search help with the re-collection of the art biennials data; Divya Ramesh for her assistance on extending the bibliography for chapter 5; Kate Salvido for her help on the ranking sections with fact-checks and new sources; and Valerie Gruest Slowing for her enthusiastic support with data on the global exhibition space, among many others. Special thanks also for Yiran Chin's excellent assistance with discourse data as well as to the bright Huy Ho, who worked with me in numerous iterations on the trajectory analyses in chapter 5 with new data. I wish to gratefully acknowledge the important support of Sakhile Matlhare, who, as a PhD alumni of Northwestern's Sociology Department, assisted me in updating parts of the data for chapter 5 as well. Without this multifaceted support from the Northwestern community, I would not have been able to complete the massive work that my expanded and revised book version required.

At Northwestern University in Qatar, several administrative offices and the Qatar Foundation, along with Everette Dennis, Hariclea Zengos, Gregory Ferrell Lowe, and Barry Sexton, provided crucial backing and generous resources for the project's final phase while I was also embarking on new research in the region. Within NUQ's very collegial environment, I would like to highlight especially the meetings with Pamela Erskine-Loftus, Joe F. Khalil, Rana Kazkaz, Scott Curtis, and Jocelyn Mitchell, which provided valuable input and perspective as well. Students in Doha helped with concluding data updates and verifications. Among these, I wish to thank particularly Ena Palaska, who was a fantastic research assistant for final parts of the book; Natasha Das for cross-checking auction house founding dates; Hanmin Kim, who helped with data on shifting global wealth; and Xiahanqing Wu and Teslim Sanna, who assisted with final parts of the quantitative data. Warm thanks also go to the wonderful sisters Rumeysa and Hadice Koç for their engaged help in tracking down last missing data and thus making the final career database as complete as possible.

For the data collection, I am indebted to Jaime Bernice from Christie's for her kind, cooperative help in obtaining information or verifying the data I collected. And I wish to express my appreciation to *ArtFacts.Net* for its important support, especially Marek Claassen, Stine Albertsen, and Susanne Massmann. *Artprice* also generously provided data and facilitated this research. At *Artforum International*, Melissa Mudry assisted me with crucial background data, and at the archive of the Venice Biennale, Marica Gallina provided unwavering (and patient) support over several months.

I would like to thank very much everyone who participated in interviews for sharing their time, thoughts, and unique experiences with me. In Beijing, I am indebted to Jing Yuan Huang for superb help as a translator and insightful guide through this foreign contemporary art scene during my first trip in 2010 and Yi Xie for her and her family's hospitality when I first arrived. Thank you to Lee Ambrozy for mediating the former contact and to Corinne Kirchner for mediating the latter one. During my second trip in 2014, I greatly benefited from the insights, research assistance, and translation help of Yuan Fuca. For my research in China, I also cannot overstate the crucial role of Xiaoming Zhang, whose deep knowledge of the global and Chinese art markets, as well as her contacts, created a crucial foundation for my research as well as hybrid bridges. In Mexico, I am grateful for the illuminating meetings I had with local-global art world insiders during my travels in the fall of 2015 and the winter of 2016. I shall warmly thank Polina Stroganova for helping to locate and mediate my first contacts until the proverbial snowball dynamic set in.

As I was developing this project, I participated in several conferences and benefited from the questions and feedback I received in these settings. I cannot mention all of them, but I want to especially point out the *Practicing Bourdieu* conference at the University of Michigan in the Fall of 2006, whose co-organizer George Steinmetz became a significant mentor and I kindly thank him for all his support. Workshops in Germany in 2011 at the University of Freiburg and the University of Lueneburg, in which Olav Velthuis provided valuable comments, were likewise vital. Very important for the development of the book were furthermore talks at Yale's Sociology Department in 2014 and 2016, and I thank the attendees for their enlightening questions and suggestions, including the engaging feedback by Phil Smith. Moreover, the conversations I had with Phil Gorski about Bourdieu and Critical Realism, in addition to his influential publications, were invaluable inspirations for the historical method and the final elaboration of the manuscript. I wish to thank him for his mentorship as well. Talks at Michele Lamont's and Orlando Patterson's Harvard Workshops in 2013 and 2015 had an impact too, as did the colloquium talks at the Department of Sociology at Brandeis University and at Berkeley in 2015. I thank Marion Fourcade for the kind invitation and the very inspiring meetings with her, Ann Swidler, and John Lie during my visit.

Another very important conference for advancing this project was the international workshop "Crossing Boundaries: Personal Lives and Global Histories," which was convened by Jeremy Adelman and Annie Cohen-Solal at the Center for Advanced Study in the Behavioral Sciences, Stanford University. Annie, whom I met at Harvard, is the embodiment of an ever curious cosmopolitan intellectual. She has been very generous and was a great inspiration in how she dives deep into the materials and lives of her biographical cases, while Jeremy Adelman provided most insightful feedback on the Orozco case. In 2016, I also benefited from the opportunity to participate in Pablo Boczkowski and Claudio Benzecry's Lambert Family conference, "Inventing the New," at Northwestern, were Gary Fine kindly served as a commentator of my talk. I should further mention the 2017 ASA panel titled "The Globalization of Contemporary Art: A Field Perspective," organized by Adrian Favell as influential. Feedback on a keynote at "Analyzing Transnationalism from a Field Perspective" at the Max Planck Institute for the Study of Societies at Cologne, Germany, in 2018 was also very stimulating in the final phases of development and writing, and so where the presentations of the other participants.

As I was working toward finalizing the manuscript, I treasured the engaging and insightful input of multiple readers. For chapter 1, Gary Fine and Phillipa Chong provided important comments that led me to rewrite it multiple times; Ulf Wuggenig also gave very insightful feedback on a later draft. Christoph Behnke made valuable suggestions for chapter 2, and Fabien Accominotti kindly worked his way through the first long draft of chapter 3 and offered very astute comments that helped me shape up the final version. I am most thankful to Clayton Childress and Craig Rawlings for their time and amazing feedback on chapters 4 and 5, which was also crucial for final revisions. Fiona Greenland and Jennifer Josten read an earlier draft of chapter 6 on Gabriel Orozco, and I am grateful for their help as well. Fiona was such an intellectual cheerleader and made invaluable suggestions, while Jennifer's special art historical expertise and prior research was critical for integrating certain Mexican sources and perspectives into the case study. For chapter 7, Birgit Hopfener, a leading expert on Chinese contemporary art and global art methodologies, kindly offered very illuminating feedback and information on sources as well, while the penetrating readings of Hannah Wohl and Linzhi Zhang were also invaluable for developing the final version.

With all these content-related revisions, the editorial help by Michael Jauchen was instrumental for bringing the manuscript to fruition as a more broadly accessible final draft. Michael is the dream of a book editor, very engaged in both developmental and line edits, and I am so thankful for his angelic patience with my tendencies for multiple rounds of revisions and new questions. I could not have wished for a more insightful editor in a time when I had extended periods of health issues and had to work on most of the final revisions while lying in bed.

Moreover, for the book's final stages, I am very thankful to Christina Maimone, from Northwestern's Computing Services Team, who was instrumental in helping develop the ultimate graphs. With over ten years of experience leading and advising on quantitative and computationally intensive social science research projects, she was incredibly knowledgeable, ingenious, and patient as we worked through numerous iterations. I should add that any aspects of the graphs that do not confirm to the expert conventions of data visualization came from me and were benevolently accepted by Christina as graph versions that could speak more to people with no quantitative data background.

Drafts of the chapters were also read and cross-checked for possible "jargon" and reference matchings by a group of fantastic undergraduate students at Northwestern. I would like to especially thank the amazing Lucy Choi Jung, Jessica Chang, Jiyoon Ha, and Autumn Rose for their contributions.

Throughout this entire process, Meagan Levinson at Princeton University Press has been a remarkable and very kind supporter, and her very experienced suggestions were crucial for finalizing the book.

Of course, I also wish to thank special friends who were involved in the book in one way or another, particularly Cornelia Kastellan, Jeremy Estabrooks, Olivia Nicol, Agnes Horvath, and Tanya Piuta for their company and conversations, which added joy, insight, and crucial perspective. And I thank Olivia Barnard for practical help in the final days. My deepest gratitude goes to my family, particularly my mother, Natalie Buchholz, a strong, intelligent, and uniquely generous woman and traveler of the world, to whom I dedicate the work, and my father, whose pioneering spirit as a researcher and explorer had set high standards. Finally, my heartfelt thanks to Wilhelm Pfundner as well as my little Aimy—you continuously inspired me to keep going and kept my spirits up until the end.

Appendix A (Chapter 2)

Sampling of International Art Biennials

To reconstruct a biennial database that is as complete and accurate as possible at the global level, my research assistant Tilly Freedman and I first compiled a "global" database, merging earlier findings on the foundation dynamics of international contemporary art biennials (including triennials and the Documenta) by Buchholz with those of Belting et al. and the dissertation of Joe Martin Lin-Hill, which also sought to reconstruct the history of contemporary art biennials at a global scale.[1] We updated these data with information from additional sources, especially the Biennial Foundation, for years leading up to 2017. The sources that informed my prior sample until 2010 included the following:

- Information on biennials provided by the New York office e-flux (http://www.e-flux.com/about.php, July 20, 2005)
- The Institut für Auslandsbeziehungen's biennial database (http://www.ifa.de/info/biennalen-datenbank/, April 22, 2011)
- The Biennial Foundation website (http://www.biennialfoundation.org/biennial-map/, April 23, 2011)
- The ArtFacts website (http://www.artfacts.net/index.php, April 21, 2011)

We then specified an updated sample of large-scale international contemporary art biennials by subjecting the derived 232 biennials to three criteria aligned with the study's focus:

1. Biennials that featured "contemporary art": We looked at biennials that include "contemporary art" in general. Sticking to one category of art production ensured comparability of the cross-continental diffusion of biennials. Biennials dedicated solely to a particular type of contemporary art (e.g., Asian contemporary art), medium (e.g., photography, sculpture), or production (e.g., craft art, outsider art) were not included. This method follows previously established selection criteria.[2]

2. Biennials that featured artists from at least three continents, based on their country of origin: Though many biennial organizations self-classify as "international" art biennials, existing studies do not sufficiently distinguish between national, regional, and multicontinental biennials, which is important for tracing globalization. To remedy this, we delineated those biennials that include artists from at least three different continents. This ensured that we included biennials with a scope that reached beyond western Europe and North America in principle. This criterion also meant that the selected biennials have played a role in the circulation of art and persons across local and regional contexts. To verify artists' countries of origin, we checked lists published on biennial websites; information provided by the Biennial Foundation; or e-flux's archived announcements (https://www.e-flux.com/announcements/). Importantly, we did not just rely on biennials' broader self-presentation. The Whitney Biennial's mission statement, for example, explains that it features American production from people who live in the US, but those people may come from different countries originally. It is also important to note that the geographic scope of a biennial's artists can have changed over time. Some started out as regional biennials and became more global, or vice versa. We looked at the latest two iterations or oriented ourselves around historical information provided by the Biennial Foundation and e-flux announcements.

3. Biennials that occurred at least twice: As the work of biennials can fluctuate, especially in peripheral locations—which often must overcome insufficient funding or weak institutional infrastructures—this criterion meant that the biennials we considered had achieved a minimal degree of institutionalization in the historical formation of a global artistic subfield.

Through this process, we established a final sample of 130 international contemporary art biennials with at least a tricontinental geographic scope of featured artists. While these numbers are lower than those of some published studies, they are more precise for tracing trends in the multiplication of large-scale exhibitions beyond regional scales and the Euro-American axis toward an increasingly global biennial circuit.

Sampling of Permanent Exhibition Institutions

This data-collection process was extremely labor-intensive. While I had completed research for an extensive world map of art institutions as part of my dissertation, I redid the entire process with a team of undergraduate students in order to employ an even more nuanced sampling strategy across continents. Our sampling strategy was based on a population of 36,552 cultural institutions in 155 countries, which we purchased from ArtFacts.Net. While this source is not perfect, it is the most wide-ranging one that addresses the volume of cultural institutions at such an extensive scope. Our goal was to filter out institutions that are noncommercial exhibition spaces that include contemporary artists from foreign contexts. We ultimately selected only those institutions that fulfill *all* the following criteria:

1. Institutions that are "noncommercial": The institutions had to be dedicated to the exhibition of artworks rather than also their sale for profit. The sample excluded galleries, art fairs, and auction houses. This criterion corresponded to our goal of mapping a space for the mediation of contemporary art that is not directly involved in commercial cross-border exchange.

2. Institutions that exhibit "contemporary art": Obviously, we needed to focus on cultural institutions that engage with contemporary art, though they did not have to exhibit contemporary art exclusively. It could be an art school/academy, so long as it included a space that featured works of contemporary art. We followed an emic strategy for this extensive analysis. We considered either (a) institutions' self-descriptions (if they used the label "contemporary art" on their websites) or (b) the general demarcation criterion of ArtFacts.Net and Artprice, as players in the global art field (see chapters 2 and 3). ArtFacts.Net and Artprice categorize contemporary artists as those born between 1945 and the present. For more about the emic strategy's importance for the sampling of contemporary artists, see appendix C.

3. Institutions that include *foreign*-born contemporary artists in their exhibition programs: This was crucial for distinguishing institutions that engage in cross-border exchange and are open to contributions from artists from different countries than where the institution is located. We analyzed this criterion using their websites that listed current and/or former exhibitions or via email communication with various institutions.

4. Websites that include parts in the English language and are thus accessible to a broader foreign art audience: We chose the criterion of an English-language website component because it is widely acknowledged that English—and especially "international art English"—is the global art space's lingua franca, and the internet is one of its key media for communication.[3]

These last two criteria aimed at a sufficiently valid and feasible operationalization of cross-nationally oriented contemporary art institutions in a global context, which, however, do not necessarily operate at a global scale themselves. One could have also selected those organizations that are actively engaged in exchanges with foreign art institutions (e.g., in the form of traveling exhibitions). However, such a criterion was not feasible for such a large database. The same is true for the tricontinental criterion regarding artists' backgrounds that we applied to art biennials. Based on these criteria, we derived a sample of nearly four thousand art institutions that are noncommercial and *transnational* in their programming, which together form a global exhibition infrastructure for the cross-border circulation of contemporary artists' works across 118 countries on six continents.

The collection and representation of our data per nation-state unit of analysis could be criticized for methodological nationalism (also for analogous data in chapter 3). I should thus add my rationales. For one, it is an inescapable truth that art institutions (noncommercial and commercial) are fundamentally defined by the country in which they are situated, e.g., in terms of legal frameworks, funding structures, as well as core audiences. Location in a particular country often defines the most fundamental structural framework for their operations, while urban level conditions add further layers of context that are important to consider within the book's multiscalar theoretical framework. On the other hand, because we included in our sample only those exhibition institutions that are principally transnational in their arts programming (by exhibiting also foreign artists), we made sure to avoid simply equating national level institutional resources with those that matter for transnational circulation and exchange. In other words, these data represent macro inequalities in the distribution of exhibition institutions across countries that are not simply a reflection of national level hierarchies.

Content and Discourse Analysis, Artforum International, 1987–2017

The first year of analysis, 1987, coincides with the beginning of *Artforum International*'s internet archive, a time when the biennial circuit began to become more global. As figure 2.8 suggests, global discourse increased in the 1990s, so it seemed not mandatory for the analysis to include years before 1987.

We first searched for the terms "global" and "globalization" in the journal's digital archive, counting their appearances in full article publications and excluding smaller, random event announcements. This yielded 1,284 instances of "global" and 270 of "globalization" overall.

For the qualitative analysis, publications referring to "global," the more frequent and relevant term, were subjected to further analysis. Through inductive manual coding of the nearly thirteen hundred text passages, we established four types of usage for "global" at *Artforum*:

1. In relation to field-specific *institutional* and mediation questions (e.g., in debates about biennials, curatorial practices, appointments at institutions, or whether museum collections should become more global)
2. In relation to field-specific *artistic or aesthetic* issues (e.g., writings about artists, art styles, or new kinds of artistic practices, etc.)
3. *External content-related* global references *in artistic practices* (e.g., when an artist's works engage with the subject of global finance)
4. *External broader references* to "the global" not directly related to the art world (e.g., when a cultural theorist's essay refers to global environmentalism).

For the final analysis, we only considered the first two types of text passages, since they fall into what I call "field-specific global discourse" (see chapter 2). Each coded passage was reviewed by at least two readers (myself and a student collaborator) before it entered the final sample of 799 passages.

I then examined these text passages through in-depth discourse analysis. My goal was to identify prevailing substantive foci and meanings associated with global concepts to trace patterns and establish a periodization of different stages in the evolution of global discourse. Specifically, I sought to reconstruct a threefold lens into "subjective" globalization: (1) a historical prism of the events, aesthetic practices, and institutions that the writings associated with global meanings; (2) a cultural lens into the broader debates and meaning patterns that crystallized around "global" concepts at different historical junctures; and (3) a picture of shifting discourse as a constructionist medium that contributed to legitimate global ideas and concepts over time. As such, this part of the examination aimed to understand aspects of "the production of a [global art space] as an object of belief."[4]

Appendix B (Chapter 3)

Sampling of International Contemporary Art Fairs

To reconstruct a database of large-scale "international contemporary art fairs" that is as complete and accurate as possible at the global level, I worked with Hannah Anderson as my research assistant. We first drew on a "global" database from ArtFacts.Net that included 496 art fairs. Since we could not identify other comprehensive lists of art fairs from alternative outlets, we relied on this very comprehensive population as a starting point. Scholarly articles have published aggregated data on art fairs that have included lower numbers, but we are confident that the ArtFacts list is inclusive as a basis for our sampling.

Next, we made sure to sample only those fairs that fulfilled all the following criteria, which are analogous to those we used for biennials (see appendix A) to ensure comparability:

1. Fairs that include "contemporary art": We were interested in fairs that included contemporary art in general in their programming. We did not include analogous types of niche/specialist institutions that were left out of the sampling of biennials as well, as explained in appendix A, cf. criterion 1.

2. Fairs that feature gallery exhibitors from at least three continents, based on their main country of operation: Analog to the biennials sample (see appendix 1, criterion 2), we only included fairs in the final sample that included gallery exhibitors from at least three different continents. To check the galleries' countries of origin, we examined exhibitor lists published on the art fairs' websites or announcements from other sources that contained historical information, including Wikipedia, e-flux newsletters, and blogs. If fairs only published lists of artists, we contacted the art fair organizers via email for more information. For fairs with multiple branches, we checked the background of galleries for past fairs at each separate location. For those fairs that started at national or regional levels with regard to their exhibitors before broadening their participating galleries, we considered the latest two iterations to decide if they matched the criterion.

After researching nearly five hundred art fairs, we identified 153 international contemporary art fairs with a tricontinental scope among their galleries that were founded before 2017, 126 of these were still active in 2017. This number is considerably smaller than those of some previous studies. For example, Christian Morgner counted 315 art fair foundations in his pioneering research.[5] Our sample's more discriminatory number—which does not include local and regional fairs or fairs that do not feature contemporary art—corresponds to the study's goal of identifying globalization tendencies that go beyond the former international scope.

Sampling of Beta Auction Houses

To better understand global inequalities in the auction market regarding the distribution of beta auction houses, the study used the most comprehensive available list that included 1,744 auction houses with fine art sales in 2017, provided by Artnet.[6]

For the final sample, we only selected auction houses that fulfilled the following criteria, analogous to those we used for transnational noncommercial art institutions (see appendix A) to ensure comparability:

1. Auction houses that mediate work by "contemporary artists": We applied the same emic solution we used for exhibition institutions (see appendix A), considering either (a) auction houses' self-descriptions (if they used the label "contemporary art" on their websites or had a special department for that category) or (b) if the institutions auctioned works by artists born in or after 1945. For more discussion on this emic approach to "contemporary art" cf. also appendix C.

2. Auction houses that include works by *foreign*-born contemporary artists in their auction sales: This criterion was again extremely important for distinguishing beta houses that are open to works by artists from other backgrounds than the country where the auction house is situated. This criterion was analyzed based on information provided by auction houses' websites regarding artworks offered at past auction sales or responses that we received via email from respective auction house experts.

3. Auction houses that have an English website (or at least parts in English): This criterion indicated if an auction house was broadly accessible to audiences beyond the country where it is situated.

Overall, this analysis yielded 146 beta auction houses (less than 10 percent of the original population). Given the sampling criteria, this number offers a conservative estimate of beta auction houses around the globe whose sales also offer works by foreign contemporary artists.

Appendix C (Chapter 5)

Sampling of Elite Artists in the Global Auction Market and Global Exhibition Space

To examine whether and how elite contemporary artists diversified at the two main poles of the globalizing field, this study drew on two artist rankings that were then aggregated at the national level with regard to the artists' countries of origins. The first was the Artprice ranking. Artprice assesses the economic success of artists in the global auction market on the basis of their annual sales volume. Auctions tend to differ in price levels from gallery sales.[7] Yet because the auction market represents contemporary art's most commercial arena, Artprice offered a suitable source for the heteronomous spectrum of the global art market.[8]

For the period under consideration, the ranking used information from 2,420 auction houses across six continents. Thus, the database's geographic range was genuinely global. Notwithstanding, the sales data are less complete for auction houses that are farther removed from global art market centers. This limitation particularly applied to the South American region, where some local auction houses—for example, in Brazil or Argentina—refuse to report results. But because we are interested in delineating the commercial "canon" of successful artists at the global field level—those who tend to sell at high-profile alpha or beta auction houses—this shortcoming could at least be put into perspective. Additionally, the sales data referred to hammer prices only; the buyer's premium, which can vary significantly, was excluded, thus ensuring reliability when examining trends over time. For historical accuracy, all hammer prices were converted to US dollars according to the exchange rate on the sale date.

The ArtFacts.Net ranking assesses the visibility and recognition of artists in the global exhibition space. Based on a digital archive of global exhibitions, it ranks more than one hundred thousand artists, though the completeness of coverage also decreases with peripheral venues and locations. Thus, artists who exhibit in more marginal contexts face added disadvantages in the assessment of their positions. Because this study focuses on the global field level of contemporary art, the effects of these limitations can be considered less problematic, too.

The ranking's evaluations operate with a complex index that assigns artists "exhibition points."[9] These are calculated on a multidimensional basis—according to a weighted index for visibility and reputation—by considering (1) the number of artists participating in the exhibition, with the following weighing of points: solo shows > group shows; (2) the type of institution: public institutions with a permanent art collection (usually art museums) > no permanent collection (i.e., contemporary art centers) > galleries; (3) geographic location: capital cities with many museums and galleries > small cities; (4) the relative position of other artists participating in the exhibition; (5) the degree of globality of an artist's exhibition activities: exhibitions in other cultural regions (e.g., Asia, North America, Europe) > exhibitions in other countries > exhibitions in country of birth.

A series of equations then determines the weighed sum of an artist's annual exhibition points, which yields their yearly rank.[10] This study relied on *annual* exhibitions points only; it does not use the cumulative logic that underlies published ArtFacts rankings used in prior studies. This temporal specification is critical for allowing proper comparability with the Artprice ranking, which is exclusively based on annual sales data.

To investigate the evolution of the symbolic recognition of artists from different countries, the ArtFacts ranking offered a fitting source for at least three reasons. First, it most closely approximates specific symbolic capital because it seeks to represent the evaluation of specialists without straightforward commercial orientations. It deliberately excludes information on sales as well as exhibitions at art fairs or auctions. Instead of success in the market, the ranking aims to capture the "curator's point of view."[11] Nevertheless, it should be added that ArtFacts.Net assumes, in line with Bourdieu's conversion model, that over time, positive evaluations by cultural experts can have positive and stable effects on sales in the art market. Second, for examining trends, ArtFacts.Net offers a more reliable source than an alternative ranking of artistic recognition, the Kunstkompass (cf. also chapter 2). Instead of drawing from surveys of subjective judgments by art professionals whose designs may change over time, its data derive from algorithms deployed consistently across all exhibitions and years. Third, the ranking follows a methodology that also aligns with the relational logic of field theory.[12] Its algorithms qualify artists' relative position based on the status of other artists, exhibitions, and cities with which they became associated. This approach implies that the reputational weight of an art institution or city is not assigned "externally" in a quasi-subjective fashion. It results relationally from the association with certain artists, institutions, and cities. Such an interdependent approach to "the dynamics of artistic prestige" has been empirically validated at the national level.[13] At a global level, it has the added advantage of minimizing charges of Eurocentrism, in the sense that certain Western museums or cities would automatically be deemed more important without comprehensive relational data supporting such identifications.

The study's sample encompassed, first, the one hundred worldwide leading living "contemporary" visual artists in ArtFacts and the Artprice rankings in five-year intervals over twenty years (1997, 2002, 2007, 2012, 2017). The year 1997 was the earliest for which valid global data could be obtained for *both* databases. In turn, the top-hundred threshold was important for the Artprice ranking because it differentiated artists who compete in the upper price segment of the auction market from those whose prices are lower and whose turnover is primarily determined by the number of lots sold. Because price level is an important indicator of economic success, this focus was crucial for methodologically justifying the use of the Artprice ranking since it is based on sales volume.[14] Second, to test for the structuring role of cohorts, we sampled the top one hundred living contemporary artists in three cohorts, based on 2017's ranking data. Informed by Bourdieu's approach, we distinguished the cohorts by birth year with a time span of ten years, yielding three cohorts for artists born between 1945 and 1954, 1955 and 1964, and 1965 and 1974.[15] The sample thus relied on data of sixteen hundred ranked positions (one thousand for the upper segments in five selected years and six hundred for the upper segments in three cohorts).[16]

Both ranking databases mix visual artists from various periods and styles. The study devised a sampling strategy to include only those artists belonging to the same category of "contemporary art" in the same global field level of competition. As such, the study departs from prior uses of these databases that draw on journalistic, general rankings.[17] Yet, as already indicated, "contemporary art" is a slippery category. Although its emergence in the West is commonly located in the 1960s, it cannot be easily defined in strictly chronological terms.[18] And while contemporary art tends to be associated with a transgressive approach to art-making, it is notorious for its lack of "stylistic unity."[19] The difficulty of "operationalizing" contemporary art becomes exacerbated at the global level. Different chronologies of "contemporary art" prevail, and the artistic styles to which the label can apply multiply, much like in a kaleidoscope, in ways that do not always correspond to established Western gazes.[20] Likewise, the boundaries of a field—that is, who belongs to global "contemporary art"—are at stake themselves, that is, they are part of classification struggles.

Against this background, we ruled out any attempt to operate with an external, quasi-"objective" definition. Rather, we pursued an emic strategy, following the categorizations that dominant field-internal actors applied. First, for a basic delineation, we drew on the general demarcation criterion of Artprice and ArtFacts: artists born between 1945 and the present. Second, we scrutinized whether artists were part of global art circuits as well as included in sales or exhibitions with the label "contemporary art." We used two criteria for the auction source: (1) having been offered at auctions by one of the market's global players, namely, Christie's or Sotheby's; and (2) having been in a sale whose title included the label "contemporary art." For ArtFacts, the first criterion—being part of global art circuits—applies to the upper thousand positions since globality is integral to the weighting index. However, we also completed an extensive biographical analysis to determine whether artists were exhibited at shows/institutions with the label "contemporary art." This two-step emic approach may be imperfect because it does not attend to aesthetics, but it helps prevent a Western bias in deciding how "contemporary art" should look and which artists should be associated with it.

Finally, to assess the diversity of the artists' backgrounds, we identified each sampled artist's country of origin. We then summarized the percentage shares in exhibition points or sales volume, following Quemin's pioneering methodological approach.[21] Correspondingly, the collective share in the total sum of exhibition points by all included artists from a particular country each year served as an indicator of relative symbolic capital, while the collective share in the annual auction revenue generated by all sampled artists from a particular country in that year assessed relative "economic capital."

For the comparative analysis of symbolic and "economic capital" distributions among artists from diverse countries, the analytic focus was directed to three subquestions: first, we examined the share of artists from "Western" versus "non-Western" countries, corresponding to the question of whether globalization entailed changes in a West-centric order in contemporary art. Our respective classification relied on Johan Galtung's metageographical category of the "Northwest," which encompasses North America and western Europe ("western Europe" being all member states of the European Union before the eastern European expansion in 2004).[22] This categorization corresponds most closely to how the literature on culture and globalization refers to the "West" versus "non-West"/ "Rest" distinction, although it has not provided an explicit definition of it. Second, we investigated whether there had been changes among top positions and, in this sense, in patterns of centrality among countries. Third, we explored transformations in the diversity among the artists' backgrounds by considering their overall countries of origin per year.

Methodology of Quantitative Trajectory Analysis of Transcontinental Elite Careers

In this study, an artist's career was conceptualized as a trajectory through time and a two-dimensional space, defined by the relative position they occupy based on measures of their symbolic and economic capital. For the career study, I worked with Huy Ho—who was a very bright undergraduate student at Northwestern University—as my research assistant. We drew on a sample encompassing the top one hundred artists in the global exhibition space according to ArtFacts (the metric for symbolic capital) *and* the top one hundred artists in the global auction market (the metric for "economic capital") in 2017. This ensured that the artists for the career data were the same as those who were part of the prior analysis on diversity in the final considered year, making it possible to draw empirical and theoretical inferences. Overall, the sample consisted of 179 contemporary artists/artist collectives, indicating an overlap of twenty-one artists.

To reconstruct annual positions for each artist, auction sales data were derived from the Artprice database, while data on exhibition performance came from ArtFacts.Net, based on an artist's *annual* exhibition points. We then constructed career data for all artists between 1997 and 2017. For each year, the artists' positions were defined by their relative "specific symbolic capital" on the one hand and their relative "economic capital" on the other.

To identify the most typical trajectory patterns among the selected artists, the study then used hierarchical clustering analysis. This method employs a machine-learning algorithm to group a set of data points into clusters that are internally coherent yet externally distinct. Artists' career trajectories in the same cluster should be more like each other than those outside it. The clustering algorithms we experimented with are agglomerative, or bottom-up, in nature: they begin the process with each data point as its own distinct cluster and then, through an applied distance matrix, successively merge those "closest"— that is, the most similar clusters—together until a stopping criterion (e.g., maximum cluster limit) is satisfied. This process measures the distance among all pairs of cases, considering their position across the whole set of variables under analysis (e.g., referring to relative ranks of artists at different points in time in this case).

Alternatively, we could use optimal matching, which identifies resemblances in sequence data, to measure similarities in artists' trajectories.[23] However, there are theoretical and methodological reasons why hierarchical clustering analysis seemed more fitting for this study. First, optimal matching requires that trajectories be conceptualized in a one-dimensional scheme where the principal positions an artist can occupy are arrayed in a linear hierarchical order. The field theoretical conception of artistic trajectories, however, defines trajectories as the succession of positions in a space that is at least two-dimensional (symbolic and economic capital). While optimal matching's specific coding would allow us to merge the symbolic and economic dimensions of artists' trajectories in a single sequence, the field theoretical approach suggests considering these two dimensions of artistic careers as analytically separate. Given this, hierarchical clustering analysis appears advisable because it permits examining both dimensions of artistic trajectories separately using one single computation. Second, optimal matching suggests converting continuous data into discrete variables, which would entail a loss of information regarding the available continuous data on artists' exhibition points and sales turnover. The hierarchical clustering method allows us to keep the raw numbers of artists' symbolic and economic success in the analysis. Lastly, optimal matching allows us to determine similarities across trajectories of unequal length.[24] Because the trajectories with which this study deals are all of equal length, if one takes the aforementioned methodological differences into account, optimal matching seems not necessary. All in all, hierarchical clustering appeared to be the procedure that yielded a classification of artists' trajectories that better fits the study's theoretical approach and the structure of the data.

Per standard preferred techniques, several data-processing steps were adopted before the data set was properly clustered. First, to avoid breaking the algorithm, all missing data points were converted to "0"; this is theoretically sound because a missing value in this data set means that an artist failed to generate auction sales or attain exhibition points for some reason that year. Second, we ran the scaled data set through the squared Euclidean distance matrix, which computes the theoretical distance or similarity between any two data points. Squared Euclidean distance is the preferred measure in sociological trajectory studies that draw on hierarchical clustering analysis.[25] This was promising because it is sensitive to greater distances and thus differentiates more clearly between cases whose trajectories demonstrate a high degree of resemblance. Finally, we selected the maximum or complete-linkage algorithm as the main clustering algorithm. This clustering method defines the cluster distance between two clusters to be the maximum distance between their individual components. The complete-linkage algorithm also produced clusters that were more compact and distinct than its alternatives.

Although this methodology thus far has been entirely quantitative, a more mixed-method approach was adopted when it came time to analyze the clusters and identify patterns. Although there is continuing debate about objective procedures to decide the appropriate number of clusters, no agreed rules exist to determine exactly where to stop the agglomeration into ever-larger subsets.[26] Thus, a stopping criterion, and the optimal number of final clusters, was determined through a combination of a statistical test and the visual analysis of a generated dendrogram, supported by background knowledge of the artists at hand.

To determine the optimal number of clusters, we chose one of the most popular testing heuristics: the elbow method. This method produces a graph that lists the sum of the squared errors against a theoretical number of clusters, whereby the "elbow(s) of the curve"—points at which the curve diverges at a different angle—indicate ideal cluster solutions. As seen in graphs displayed on the author's website, a sensible case can be made for a two-cluster, three-cluster, or six-cluster solution.[27] Thorough testing and comparison, however, revealed that a two-cluster solution separates our pool of artists in a way that flattens and eradicates dynamic trajectories in favor of oversimplified patterns, failing to account for the vast range of values in our sample and grouping together one artist who may be five times more "successful" (according to our metrics) than the other.

On the other hand, if a two-cluster solution yielded too few patterns, a six-cluster solution yielded too many. Although these six patterns are more complex, not all of them are fully unique and distinct from one another. For example, depending on the distribution of artists, several clusters in this solution may operate on different success *levels* numerically, though they still display similar *trajectories* over time. Since our ideal goal is to determine fully unique trajectories, grouping these clusters to display one comprehensive trajectory is the better approach. In this regard, a three-cluster solution strikes a good, balanced middle ground.

If the elbow method helped determine the ideal cluster solution, a clustering dendrogram helped determine the corresponding distribution of artists, which is also displayed on the author's website.[28] It revealed that three specific artists (Damien Hirst, Jeff Koons, Richard Prince) are best grouped in their own cluster (the leftmost section of the dendrogram). Tracing this back to the raw data reveals that these three artists have recorded auction sales that are unmatched by those of any other artist in our sample—so much so that they could be considered outliers. For this reason, we chose to keep these artists in their own cluster, bringing the total number of final clusters to four.

With these optimal clusters in hand, we discerned salient patterns—typical trajectories—from our original data by comparing the two main variables through a series of plots over time. However, because auction sales and exhibition points operate on different units and ranges, we had to convert the variables with raw numbers into scaled variables based on the relative distribution of their values. The final scale ranges from 1 (lowest raw value) to 20 (highest raw value) for both variables; this scale is at once parsimonious and capable of capturing the original values' wide variability throughout the years. To generate the final comparison plots for each cluster, we decided to take the median for each year of analysis, which was the optimal measure of central tendency in this case, since the data can often be skewed by things like auctionless or exhibitionless years or outlier years for single artists with regard to especially stellar performances in either of these dimensions.

Appendix D (Chapters 6 and 7)

Comparative Case Selection

Comparative methodology informed the selection of the artist cases for part 3. As Diane Vaughan writes, cases must be "sufficiently analogous to offer us alternative settings in which to explore a particular phenomenon and compare the findings."[29] There has to be commensurability in some of their characteristics in view of the research problem (successful careers of artists from formerly more marginal "non-Western" countries in the globalizing art field). At the same time, relevant differences in the "outcome" have to be explained (commercial versus symbolic worldwide artistic success).[30] For this study, two "non-Western" artists were selected who achieved high recognition at either the relative autonomous or heteronomous poles of the global art field. Specifically, I selected the Mexican-born artist Gabriel Orozco and the Chinese artist Yue Minjun on the basis of four criteria:

1. These artists were among the top one hundred living contemporary visual artists in *either* the global Artprice ranking (Yue Minjun) or the global ArtFacts ranking (Gabriel Orozco) in 2007, which was the original study's last year of analysis.[31] In short, while the "autonomous" Orozco

was represented only in the top league of a symbolic ranking, Yue was only included in the top tier of the auction-based ranking.

2. The countries of origin of both artists were "non-Western" and peripheral in the contemporary art field when they began their careers in the 1990s.[32]
3. The selected artists were born and educated in their countries of origin.
4. The artists were comparable in their biological and artistic age, as both were born in 1962 and entered the international art field in the 1990s. Such generational matching was important to maintain an accurate historical comparison of the trajectories and experiences of individual artists. To find a pair of artists with generational similarity significantly limited the potential artists who could be chosen from the ranking sources.

The artists represent "extreme" comparative cases for worldwide success at either the relative autonomous or heteronomous pole, following the logic of Robert Zussman, who writes, "Successful case studies look at extremes, unusual circumstances, and analytically clear examples, all of which are important not because they are representative, but because they show a process or a problem in particularly clear relief."[33] Yet, although the cases represent opposing positions of autonomous and heteronomous artistic success, there may be many variations between them. Focusing on clear opposing examples should not be taken as a denial of any intermediary variations that may exist (see also chapter 8).

I chose single artists rather than artistic schools or movements for the comparison to keep the "global" qualitative analysis as rigorous as possible. As Wendy Griswold argues, the specification of a particular yet representative cultural object or agent is an important methodological device to avoid analytical indeterminacy.[34] This methodological suggestion is even more important for transnational or global studies, for which it is harder to determine the boundaries of a research object in principle. For examining valuation dynamics in the visual arts, it is also helpful to focus on an artist's career rather than a single artwork because since modernity, the attribution of artistic "quality" and "greatness" has become increasingly centered on perceptions of artists' personalities and careers in art centers.[35] In sum, the case comparison focuses on the transcontinental careers of two "non-Western" artists, seeking to explain their different kinds of global "success" as the "dependent variable."

Qualitative Methodology and Empirical Sources for Case Studies

The comparative analysis was guided by principles of the biographical method.[36] This method has the double advantage of permitting a deep investigation of the details of a single trajectory while not losing sight of the entanglement—which is unfolding in time—of an individual's life with "higher" societal orders and dynamics.[37] Based on the field theoretical framework, and linking the meso-level of specialized art professionals and institutions, the macro-level of larger structures and external changes, and the micro-level of the dispositions and aesthetic evaluations of the two artists as well as the agents involved in their careers, the study thus offers a step toward a multilevel sociological case study of valuation within a global framework.

For my analysis of the artists' careers until 2010, I first examined a broad variety of secondary materials, including published interviews with the artists, art historical essays, reviews in newspapers and art magazines, exhibition catalogs, movie documentaries, and auction results, to offer the most detailed reconstruction possible of each artist's career and its major turning points in the period considered. This analysis became the basis for each career chapter's first part. These turning points then became the center for extensive additional secondary research to illuminate key causal factors along micro-, meso-, and macro-levels. These materials constitute the empirical foundation for the second part of each career chapter, in addition to interviews and fieldwork.

In particular, I supplemented these secondary sources through in-depth interviews with the artists and individuals who were directly or indirectly involved in their careers, including peers, curators, directors of art institutions, art critics, scholars, gallery owners, auction house specialists, collectors, or art investment fund managers. The sampling for the interviewees was thus purposeful and followed a snowball principle in which parts of the sample emerged through personal recommendations during the interview study and fieldwork.

For Orozco, the sample encompassed thirty-six respondents situated in the US, Mexico, Brazil, France, the UK, Japan, France, Belgium, Switzerland, Austria, and Germany. The interviews, which were recorded and transcribed, were semistructured, lasting between forty minutes and two hours. The transcriptions were saved with an anonymous code unless interviewees agreed that they could be quoted directly in the publication. Additionally, Ena Palaska—my fantastic research assistant from Northwestern University Qatar—conducted eight final semistructured interviews on my behalf during a time when I was facing health challenges.

For Yue Minjun, the sample of interviewees was larger. Because the art market, especially speculation, thrives on secrecy, I had to engage with a wider circle of market participants during Yue's career to reconstruct his career from as many perspectives as possible to identify which information and interpretations were most robust. In particular, the interview series encompassed fifty-three interviews in multiple countries, including China, Hong Kong, Indonesia, the US, the UK, Switzerland, Germany, and Austria. To respect some respondents' privacy preferences, eight interviews could not be recorded;

their results are based on handwritten notes taken during the meeting. The interviews were semistructured and lasted between thirty minutes and nearly three hours in one case (with breaks). Forty-five interviews were recorded and transcribed. The transcriptions were saved with an anonymous code unless interviewees agreed that they could be quoted directly in the publication.

For both cases, some interviews took place on the phone or as virtual meetings, but most interviews were conducted in person as part of my extended fieldwork abroad. To capture the full complexity of meanings, simply flying in and out for interviews was not enough. That is why it was important that I immersed myself during longer stays in Western, Southern, and Eastern art cities that were critical for the artists' careers, namely, New York (five months), Berlin (three months), Mexico City (four months), and Beijing (three months). New York is arguably *the* art capital in the contemporary art field and was a key site for catalyzing both artists' transcontinental careers. To understand the role that Western art environments played in the making of artistic success across borders, I wanted to experience a European viewpoint and chose Berlin as a continental art capital that the careers of both artists had crisscrossed in important ways. But of course, it was indispensable for me also to visit the artists' countries of origin for extended periods, unlike globalization scholars who send younger research assistants or advisees abroad to do fieldwork.

During my fieldwork, I visited as many events and exhibitions related to my artists, their peers, and cross-border art topics as possible. I sought to meet with curators and art writers, went to countless gallery openings, and kept detailed notes of my observations and many informal conversations. During my frequent travels, I found myself at spartan international studio openings in Beijing's industrial outskirts, lavish dinners of collectors, hidden experimental art happenings in Mexico, crowded international art fairs, and smaller gatherings of "art world" insiders who argued about the newest exhibitions in the city and shared the latest art world gossip. This fieldwork added meaningful context for the interpretation of the interviews and secondary data. By combining these multifaceted but targeted sources in the biographical analyses, I aimed to understand the experiences, interpretative repertoires, networks, and resources in which the artists' journeys were embedded. Moreover, I sought to tease out how they operated differently for both men—how, ultimately, they navigated different national and cross-border environments in their paths toward global success.

NOTES

Preface

1. Translated from German: *Tal der Ahnungslosen*.
2. Buchholz and Wuggenig 2005.
3. Quemin 2006; cf. also his earliest publication in French, Quemin 2002.
4. Moretti 2013.
5. Connell 2007.
6. Vaughan 2004, 2014.
7. Buchholz 2016.
8. Although I draw upon Pierre Bourdieu's field theory, the orthodox adherents of this approach may find occasions to critique what I have altered in the framework to account for my data.
9. As I am finishing this book, the rise of the COVID-19 pandemic has imposed countless constraints and new material pressures on the art world. But it also has engendered new debates and alternative formats. I say more about this issue and how it relates to the book's theoretical framework in the epilogue.

Chapter 1: A Global Field Approach to Art and Culture

1. Within the extensive publications on the subject, Diane Crane offers a particularly succinct definition, though her qualifier "national" cannot be universalized across historical eras. She writes, "cultural globalization—as opposed to economic, political, or technological globalization—refers to the transmission or diffusion across national borders of various forms of media and the arts" (2002, 1). Regarding the historical periodization of globalization, I do not engage with broader debates as they prevailed in globalization scholarship's first wave (for overviews, cf. Guillén 2001, 252f.; Pieterse 2004, 19–21), which appeared to be conceptually and empirically underdetermined, if not, given the breadth of the phenomenon, unsolvable. Several scholars acknowledge that globalization, involving increasing cross-border flows, is not a recent phenomenon but that it has accelerated since the 1970s (e.g., Hall 1992a, 299; Appadurai 1996; Sassen 2007). Of course, many recent global developments, especially COVID-19, have stalled the trajectories of globalization in new ways. This study is looking at global transformations up until 2017—that is, a period before the pandemic hit.
2. Velthuis 2002, 7. It goes without saying that using examples from Western art history is not intended to ignore the fact that significant cross-border cultural exchanges and innovations

occurred in many other areas of the world (e.g., in trans-Saharan, Arab, or Asian regions). I refer here to Western examples because I am most familiar with them and because they lead up to my case, the West-centric international contemporary art field and its later global transformation.

3. Pieterse 2004, 78.

4. Guilbaut 1983.

5. Crane 1987; Heinich 1998.

6. Moulin 1992; Zahner 2006.

7. Moulin 1995, 46.

8. Moulin 1995; Zahner 2006.

9. While for much of recorded history, flows and cross-fertilizations occurred across a wide variety of art worlds (whereby "art" should be understood broadly in an anthropological sense), most of them remained essentially distinct in their institutions and creative traditions (Carroll 2007, 141).

10. Charting the evolution of a phenomenon as large and intricate as "globalization," of course, is challenging, and it is always subject to the fact that at the moment one tries to describe it, events are occurring that may ultimately force one to revise that description. This is particularly true in our current historical moment, when the rise of new nationalisms, new migration patterns, and, of course, the COVID-19 pandemic have already disrupted our sense of "the global." All of these events are ongoing, and it is difficult to predict the full impact they will have on the global art field. But as I explain later, the theoretical framework I develop in this study is open enough to accommodate the perpetual evolutions and upheavals in a field that will undoubtedly continue to change in the coming years.

11. E.g., Hannerz 1987; Appadurai 1990; R. Robertson 2001; Pieterse 2004; Dowd and Janssen 2011.

12. Of course, the term "diversity" has a complicated and contested history in the art field itself, especially as discourses shifted in the 1990s from multicultural debates to more postcolonial approaches that preferred notions of "difference" and "hybridity" (e.g., Bhabha and Rutherford 1990). I address this further in chapter 2.

13. This issue has long been of interest for sociologists engaging with contemporary art. For a review of early voices in this debate and a sociological approach that argues in favor of reproduction and homogeneity, cf. Buchholz and Wuggenig 2005. A pioneering and persistent sociological contributor in the latter camp has been Alain Quemin (e.g., 2002, 2006, 2012). Other social-scientific accounts have explored this question in relation to biennials (C. Wu 2009), galleries (Velthuis 2013b), or art fairs (Baia Curioni, Forti, and Leone 2015).

14. In this book, the term "West" refers to countries in western Europe and North America, two traditionally strong regions in the international art field. For this reason, I also use the category "Northwest" later on. "Western Europe" was defined as including all member states of the European Union before the eastern European expansion in 2004. This categorization corresponds most closely to how the literature on culture and globalization distinguishes between the "West" and the "non-West," although it has not provided an explicit definition of it. For a critique of the use of this distinction, see the following note.

15. I am aware of Simbao's (2015, 264) lucid critique of characterizing cultural agents from certain world regions world regions with the term "non-Western" as a qualifier that defines them

by "what they are not." However, I use this classification because I believe that this term most accurately captures the emic rhetoric of debates in which the globalization of art has evolved for many years (including by those who have challenged the established system), rather than, say, the more recent concept of the "Global South." But I should emphasize that I use it with a nondiscriminatory intention to accurately map the discursive language in which global transformations unfolded within the field, up until the very critique, and partially even transcendence, of the category of "non-Western" in recent years. To highlight this emic approach, I use the category in quotation marks in the book.

16. For contributions in English, see, for example, Elkins 2007; Belting 2008, 2009; Elkins et al. 2010; Rajchman 2011; Simbao 2015; Dornhof et al. 2018.

17. Luhmann 1993.

18. With the term "global canon," I refer in this book to the groupings of artists who are most successful at a worldwide level with regard to critical recognition and/or market success. This social-scientific take of associating the term with an empirically determinable elite of successful artists in these two dimensions should not be confused with art historical notions of canon formation, which can imply that there is an aesthetic master narrative in which the history of artistic production evolves. Such narrower notions of canon formation have rightly come under attack in recent years as being insufficiently complex and Eurocentric for a global art context (e.g., Gilmore 2003 and his discussion of Hans Belting's work). The association of "success" with levels of critical recognition or market acclaim does not preclude alternative definitions of how artists themselves define success for their practices.

19. For classics in this literature that also apply to the visual arts, cf. White and White's (1993) study of the rise of Impressionist painters; Richard Peterson's (1976) development of the production of culture perspective (for a review, cf. Peterson and Anand 2004); Howard Becker's (1982) influential book on "art worlds"; Bourdieu's (1993, 1996) work on the rise of the modern art field and the cultural fields approach; and Wendy Griswold's (1994) formulation of an integrative cultural diamond model. For a more recent and widely received account on the construction of value in the market of contemporary art, cf. Velthuis 2007.

20. Lamont 2012, 206–7.

21. In sociological work related to valuation, Wendy Griswold ventured out early beyond a West-centric framework when she engaged in a comparative study of literary reception that included not only the US and Great Britain but also the West Indies (1987a) or when she examined the transnational reception of Nigerian novels in Western contexts (1992). More recently, Damon Phillips (2013) has insightfully illuminated early twentieth-century dynamics in the making of a jazz canon across continents. And Alvaro Santana-Acuña (2014, 2020) has offered a rich account on how Gabriel García Márquez's novel *One Hundred Years of Solitude* became a global classic. These contributions on the construction of artistic value across borders engage with "non-Western" cases that rose to prominence before the latest millennial context of globalization. For a comprehensive study of the institutional recognition of authors in the transnational literary field until 2005, cf. Verboord, Kuipers and Janssen 2015, which focuses on elite papers in Euro-American countries, however (France, Germany, the Netherlands, and the US).

22. Regarding local performance, my emphasis is on "tending to," since contemporary art also includes performance works and live happenings as well as site-specific installations and artistic activism.

23. Kramer 2001, 178.

24. E.g., Quemin 2002, 2006, 2012; Buchholz and Wuggenig 2005; Buchholz 2008a; C. Wu 2009. For contributions arguing for strong changes, e.g., Scheps 1999; Belting, Buddensieg, and Weibel 2013.

25. E.g., Stallabrass 2004; Crane 2009; Graw 2010.

26. Buchholz 2013.

27. As I had already begun working on this study (Buchholz 2008b), Malcolm Bull published an insightful contribution, "The Two Economies of World Art" (2011) that shares a similar argumentative direction. His empirical account was based on more confined data, spanning one year only, and it employed different sampling methodologies (cf. chapter 5, Appendix C). And while Bull discussed various possible explanations, which included Bourdieu's theory as one option, he did not elaborate a global theoretical framework in the chapter. Gisèle Sapiro's (2010) work on literary translations has also insightfully shown how globalization impacts commercial and cultural subfields differently in the publishing market, but the study did so at the national level of fields (France and the United States).

28. The term "rules" should not be misunderstood as a set of prescriptive commands on how to thrive in the global art field. Rather, as I elaborate in a later theoretical section, it metaphorically refers to governing principles in the globalizing field that account for clearly discernable patterns in cross-border dynamics.

29. Crane 2002.

30. For early instructive overviews and critical discussions of the social-scientific literature about globalization, see Waters 1995; Held et al. 1999; Guillén 2001; Beck 2000; Lechner 2005; and Sassen 2007. For introductions to central debates and theoretical approaches within the literature on culture and globalization, see Featherstone 1990; Waters 1995; Tomlinson 1999; Mackay 2000; Crane 2002; Pieterse 2004; Lechner and Boli 2005; Adams 2007; and Dowd and Janssen 2011.

31. All these models operate at macro- or meso-levels and seek to provide theoretical frameworks of transnational/global cultural spheres as a whole rather than those models that operate only at micro-levels, such as reception studies.

32. I use the word "scenario" in the sense that Marwan Kraidy has introduced it into the related literature. As he writes, "A scenario is, according to the 1984 edition of Webster's II, 'an outline of a hypothesized or projected chain of events.' More modest than 'paradigm,' less academic than 'thesis,' and less banal than 'perspective,' 'scenario' captures the speculative nature and tentative ontology of theories of global culture" (2006, 16).

33. Launched as a critical reaction against modernization theories in the early 1970s (Tomlinson 1991; M. Griffin 2002), this approach has long represented the most comprehensive macro-model of the globalization of culture (Lizardo 2008). One pioneer was Herbert Schiller (e.g., 1971, 1976, 1989, 1991, 1998). But see also contributions by Jeremy Tunstall (1977), Armand Mattelart (1979), and Chin-Chuan Lee (1979). For a critical dissection of theoretical family resemblances of works in the tradition of cultural or media imperialism, cf. Tomlinson 1991. For a more sympathetic and empirically nuanced review, cf. Crane 2002. Despite the notorious ambiguity that has surrounded the idea of cultural imperialism (cf. Tomlinson 1991; Kraidy 2006), it is justified to speak of it as a model because these approaches formulate converging arguments about how to characterize the formation and structure of global cultures.

34. For reasons of expositional concision, I use the center-periphery terminology as a short-hand for the tripartite classification of center, semiperiphery, and periphery, though center-periphery models operating with a dichotomous logic have rightly been criticized for being oversimplified (cf. Tomlinson 1991).

35. As I explained previously, in this book, the question of cultural homogeneity or diversity refers to asymmetries of recognition among cultural producers from different parts of the world, while the cultural imperialism model includes other interpretations of that distinction as well.

36. Quemin 2012, 70ff (emphasis added).

37. Quemin 2012, 70; cf. also Quemin 2002, 2006.

38. With "global culture" or "globalizing culture" I refer most basically to realms of cultural production with a scope of at least three continents (cf. also Appendix A). The underlying understanding of "culture" can be located in a threefold typology (Reckwitz 2000). It distinguishes between first, a totality-oriented notion of culture as a "whole way of life," in the lineage of Herder and consistent with the interpretation of culture in early anthropology (e.g., Edward Tylor), and second, a meaning-, symbol-, and knowledge-based conception of culture as "signifying practice." This latter notion is represented in research that seeks to elaborate a more theoretically ambitious understanding of "culture" as a genuine analytical perspective for examining or explaining aspects of social process, especially regarding action-theoretical accounts. The third main research tradition relies upon a differentiation-oriented conception of culture, where it figures as a relatively distinct social sphere in which specialized ways of dealing with symbolic interpretations and objectivations in the form of artifacts are institutionalized as being intellectual, artistic, or mass medial in nature. This third conception is central, but not exclusive, to the understanding of culture in this book. The typology is analytical and thus does not preclude overlaps between the second and third use of the term, which also occur in my study. The threefold classification can be interpreted as a refinement of Jeffrey Alexander's and Steven Seidman's classic distinction between "cultural sociology" and the "sociology of culture" (Alexander and Seidman 1990).

39. Quemin likewise assumed such a materialistic position in his early works (2002, 2006), highlighting how a country's economic rank is closely correlated with the cross-border success of its artists. He thereby stressed how his arguments connected with Immanuel Wallerstein's model of a capitalist world-system (e.g., Wallerstein 1979).

40. Buchholz and Wuggenig 2005; Favell 2015.

41. There are other examples that point to such a divergence. For example, the international success of Latin American writers in the twentieth century was at odds with the region's political-economic position at that time (Casanova 2004, 39; Santana-Acuña 2020). Similarly, Johan Heilbron (1999) has insightfully revealed how global patterns of book translation do not map directly onto the structure of the broader world market.

42. Hannerz 1992, 219.

43. Appadurai 1990, 1996. I derive the label for his approach from Diana Crane (2002).

44. The concept of the "scape" suggests that cultural flows are shaped by relatively distinct social spheres that adhere to their own "constraints and incentives" (Appadurai 1990, 298). Apart from an art scape (for flows of artifacts and artistic images) (Appadurai 1999, 236) and a media scape (for flows of broadcasting facilities and images), the framework also includes a finance scape (flows of finance capital), a technoscape (flows of technologies), an ideoscape

(flows of political ideologies), and an ethnoscape (flows of people, i.e., migrants, refugees, tourists; Appadurai 1990).

45. Appadurai 1990, 298f., 295; Crane 2002, 7; cf. also Straubhaar 1991.

46. Appadurai 1990, 296.

47. The model resonates with Hans Belting's interpretation of globalization in contemporary art, which proclaims the end of any "center and periphery scheme" (2013, 184) due to the world-wide multiplication of (sub)national and regional art worlds since the late 1980s.

48. Pieterse 1995, 50.

49. E.g., Carroll 2007; Bielby and Harrington 2008; Crane 2010; and Morgner 2014a, 2014b.

50. Becker 1982, x.

51. Crane 2010.

52. Bielby and Harrington 2008, 12.

53. Crane 2010.

54. The importance of these in-person events has only become clearer over the past two years as many of these events have been canceled, postponed, or held in a digital forum, like Zoom, which many participants find lacking, e.g., Buchholz, Fine, and Wohl 2020.

55. Carroll 2007, 142; cf. also Bydler 2004, 29. Carroll is a philosopher, but he offers one of the earliest and strongest formulations of the idea of a global art world for contemporary art that resonates with the sociological model.

56. Carroll 2007, 140, 142.

57. Carroll 2007, 141.

58. Carroll 2007, 138, 140.

59. E.g., C. Wu 2007b; Dornhof et al. 2018.

60. C. Wu 2007b. To be sure, authors like Carroll caution against assuming too much cultural cohesion. But I am not certain that the term "art world," with its strong connotations of cooperative networks, community, and consensus, provides the right theoretical tools to describe a constellation in contemporary art that appears to be more complex: that of a common global cultural space *and* persistent and contested differences in meanings.

61. Some scholars in this strand have pointed to the relevance of macrostructural inequalities (Bielby and Harrington 2008; Crane 2010). However, because the model focuses on networks of interaction and how they are bound up with shared cultural conventions across borders, the structural side has remained secondary and undertheorized.

62. Buchholz 2006, 2008a, b, 2013, 2016, 2018a, b.

63. While there are several variants of fields theory (cf. Martin 2003), I am focusing on Bourdieu's version because it is particularly geared toward spheres of cultural production.

64. Bourdieu does not deny the relevance of collaboration to art's mediation and valuation. When agents mobilize together to push through and establish an artistic position, it constitutes important "social capital" (Bourdieu 2001a). Cultural agents also collaborate because they want to advance specific professional agendas.

65. Bourdieu defines "illusio" as participants' shared belief in the significance of the "game" and its distinctive stakes. Despite the different agendas that field participants may pursue, the illusio is what makes the game worth playing for all of them (Bourdieu and Wacquant 1992, 117).

66. For a detailed discussion of these four main sorts of capital, cf. Bourdieu 2001a.

67. Bourdieu and Wacquant 1992, 17, 95–97; Bourdieu 1993, 113–15.

68. E.g., Bourdieu, 1993, 115–19; 1996, 142–46.

69. As Rodney Benson (1999) rightly points out, the heteronomous pole does not necessarily consist of market players only but also political and bureaucratic forces, particularly the state. This book, however, focuses primarily on the market side.

70. Bourdieu 1996, 114; 1993, 29–73; 1996, 41.

71. Bourdieu 1996, 154–61, 239–42, 253.

72. Bourdieu 1996, 239.

73. Bourdieu 1977, 56, 95; 1984.

74. Bourdieu 1993, 1996.

75. Buchholz 2006; 2008a, 2016, 33f.

76. Bourdieu did not elaborate a global field analysis in the context of systematic empirical research, but he referred to international or global fields since the 1990s, e.g., in his mention of the "field of world sociology" (1991); the "global media field" (Bourdieu 1999, 41); or the "global economic field" (Bourdieu 2003, 84).

77. While my discussion focuses on spheres of art and cultural production, there have been important contributions theorizing transnational and global fields for other social realms. Particularly pioneering examples would include Dezalay and Garth's (2006) work on international commercial arbitration, Marion Fourcade-Gourinchas' (2006) analysis of the development of the global economics profession, Julian Go's (2008) work on the British and American empires, George Steinmetz's (2008) account of the colonial state, and Monika Krause's (2014) and Shai Dromi's (2016, 2020) insightful studies of a global field of humanitarian intervention. With regard to the broader development of fields theory, "Fielding Transnationalism," a special volume of the *Sociological Review* coedited by Julian Go and Monika Krause (2016), as well as the recent *Charting Transnational Fields*, edited by Christian Schmidt-Wellenburg and Stephan Bernhard (2020), are particularly notable.

78. Casanova 2004.

79. Heilbron 1999; Sapiro 2010, 2015; Regev 1997, 2003, 2007; Adams 2008; Kuipers 2011; Verboord, Kuipers and Janssen 2015.

80. I henceforth do not explicitly distinguish between *transnational* or *global* fields, which define a more extended—that is, transcontinental scope (cf. Appendix A). I believe that the *analytical* operations of transposition from a national level are principally the same (cf. Buchholz 2016 for an explication of analogical theorizing in this regard). What changes at a global level is the more comprehensive and, in this sense, also more inclusive geographical scope, which is one reason why I am using it.

81. C. Wu 2007b.

82. Buchholz 2006, 2008a, 218f.; Kuipers 2011, 542f.

83. It is widely understood that advances in technologies (including transportation) have been crucial for globalization processes over the past few decades. But from a Bourdieusian viewpoint, these advances are facilitating background conditions that need to be realized and adopted by the field's agents. Consequently, they would be ruled out as *direct* causes for a sociological-historical explanation that avoids technological determinism. Shai Dromi (2020) has added a crucial perspective to the external-internal discussion by showing how broader cultural influences can affect the genesis of a global field as well.

84. The higher the degree of autonomy, the higher in turn is the field's refraction effect—that is, its power to absorb and transform external influences or constraints into internal ones (Bourdieu 1996, 220–21).

85. Within sociology, such assumptions that a realm of cultural production merely reflects broader societal processes are now widely regarded as outdated. It thus might be surprising how common such a view still is among some cultural theorists in the humanities, who make direct connections or analogies between contemporary art and global capitalism or global geopolitics (cf. the introduction to part 1).

86. Cf. Casanova 2004; Kuipers 2011.

87. cf. also Buchholz 2006, 44–48.

88. While "discourse" has a broad variety of definitions, one of the main advantages of the concept in the Foucauldian tradition derives from its constructivist stance—that is, Foucault's argument that the very process of writing, debating, or even rejecting a certain concept such as "sexuality" (1988), or in this case "globalization," may contribute to a formation of knowledge that serves as a frame of reference for certain social practices. Ironically, Bourdieu himself (1998, 34) stresses the performative, constructionist nature of discourse in a vehemently critical discussion of the concept of globalization, which he denounces, by focusing on its neoliberal sources as a "power discourse" in the "strongest sense of the word." However, in contrast to Foucault, Bourdieu stresses how power inequalities among players can explain which discourses become particularly influential (cf. Bourdieu 1996, 197–200). In discourse's constructionist capacity and its (symbolic) power potential of worldmaking, it is central to the making of a field (Ferguson 1998; Gorski 2013a). This is true at both the national and global levels.

89. Casanova 2004, 126–63; Buchholz 2013, 2016.

90. In comparison to prior works, the suggested approach to the emergence of global cultural fields has a stronger organizational-infrastructural footing. As discussed elsewhere (Swartz 1997, 215; Buchholz 2016, 38), the importance of a particular "set of specific institutions" (Bourdieu, 1996, 292) in field analysis has often been overlooked, not least because Bourdieu himself only alludes to it.

91. In Critical Realism, a strand in the philosophy of social science, "emergence" designates a state in which a social entity has properties that are not reducible to the sum of their component parts (e.g., M. Archer 1995, 174, 177). For a concise introduction into Critical Realism as well as the concept, cf. Gorski 2013b.

92. For an extended discussion of this idea and the more technical term "relative vertical autonomy," cf. Buchholz 2016. Johan Heilbron (2014) has insightfully discussed the regional scale for global field analysis.

93. National-global divergences regarding the recognition of artists from China may increase as censorship and persecution continue to grow in the country. For a detailed account of OAOs, cf. Kharchenkova, Komarova, and Velthuis 2015.

94. Julian Go's (2008) pioneering article on the British and American Empires early pointed out how a global fields approach allows for the synthesis of material and cultural dimensions with regard to the literature on states within a global context.

95. Casanova 2004, 15, 108, 277; Buchholz 2016, 51. The notion of a continuum of macrostructural positions marks a conceptual difference with Wallerstein's world-systems analysis. In a global field perspective, "the center-periphery distinction does not demarcate functional roles

within a system of a division of labor, as in some versions of world-systems analysis. Instead, it designates a status variable of the continuous type. That means that centers and peripheries are no longer actor entities that fulfill systemic functions, but structural positions within a continuum of inequalities among countries" (Buchholz 2018b , 20).

96. Edward Said (2001) and Amartya Sen (2006), in their critique of Huntington's clash of civilization thesis (1996), lucidly underline that it is not fruitful to think of macro entities as actors.

97. Bourdieu (2003, 91) developed this notion of a multiplier effect regarding the global economic field. Using the logic of Diane Vaughan's approach of analogical theorizing (1992, 2014), this insight could be transposed, as is evident in Casanova's (2004) work on the world literary field.

98. Political macro capital may refer, for instance, to the power a country has in international organizations like UNESCO (Sapiro 2010, 15) or the World Trade Organization (Crane 2002, 15), which influences the legal regulation of cultural flows across national or regional borders. Market macro capital may refer to the size of domestic cultural markets, implying geographical advantages of "economies of scale" for agents to profit from investments and compete in costly global cultural markets, such as in film, publishing, or television (Crane 2002, 5; Sapiro 2010, 424; Kuipers 2011, 546).

99. Casanova 2004, 15–23.

100. Casanova mentions institutional resources (2004, 15) but does not differentiate them as an analytically distinct capital dimension, which is important if one shifts the focus from artistic creation to cultural mediation (cf. Buchholz 2018b, 21–23).

101. Moreover, whether global fields are structured in a monocentric or polycentric way is not a generic reflection of the capitalist world-system. It depends on the historically specific distribution of the relevant macro capitals in a global cultural field.

102. Wei 2013, 482f.

103. This does not exclude the possibility that shared interpretations about contemporary art might emerge. But these features are not inherently included in a global field's definition. By leaving the degree of cultural integration open-ended, it becomes a matter of empirical investigation that can vary. One starts at a lower level of cultural integration and thus can trace varying degrees of unification across countries or different subfields within the same space. In this regard, it is useful to distinguish between the idea of a relatively autonomous field and that of a settled field (Steinmetz 2002, cf. especially 151, 193; 2008, 595). In a settled field, participants agree about the distinctive value of a specialized practice and the type of symbolic capital that dominates it. But they also agree about the specific evaluative criteria that underlie the distribution of that symbolic capital (Steinmetz 2002, 151; 2008, 595). In this sense, they have arrived at a "field settlement," manifested in a "stable consensus regarding rules of conduct and membership criteria" (Fligstein and McAdam 2012, 88–90). Bourdieu (1996, 226) discusses this matter in terms of varying degrees of codification of entry: "A high degree of codification of entry into the game goes along with the existence of explicit rules of the game and a minimum consensus on these rules; by contrast, a weak degree of codification conveys states of the field in which the rules of the game are being played for in the playing of the game."

104. In The Rules of Art, Bourdieu (1996) uses the terms "subfield" and "poles" interchangeably but suggests at one place that he prefers the notion "pole," because it implies less bounded

sub-zones of a field, more fleeting inner boundaries, whose contestation and revision are part of the game, an argument that seems all the more fruitful for theorizing fields at the more ephemeral global level.

105. In fact, even the most commercial global markets, such as television, involve conflicts between cultural and economic logics (Kuipers 2011, 543) and between public and commercial interests (Calhoun 2005).

106. Studies on cultural fields have not fully elaborated the autonomy-heteronomy distinction at the global level yet. Sapiro's (2010) contribution on the impact of globalization on the book market has insightfully demonstrated the usefulness of Bourdieu's dual economy approach, but her comparative study is thereby focused on the national units of France and the US. Kuipers (2011, 543) emphasizes how the transnational TV field is "characterized by a tension between the short-term logic of the market and more long-term striving for quality and artistic innovation." But she ultimately examines what cultural intermediaries across borders share in their practices rather than what divides them across these lines. The only available monograph on a global cultural field, which is by Pascale Casanova, focuses largely on avant-garde literature and thus on more autonomous production. In an impressive book of more than three hundred pages, her discussion of the market is less than ten pages long (Casanova 2004, 164–73). It should be added that Casanova also theorizes heteronomous forces with regard to political constraints—especially national agendas—on writers and thus considers them more at national field levels.

107. Bourdieu 1993, 238–53. The term was introduced in view of the emergence of the French art field.

108. For example, in part 2, the data on the most highly ranked contemporary artists worldwide and their career trajectories refer to the same global institutional spaces that part 1 examines (the global exhibition space and global auction market). In this way, it becomes possible to draw inferences between institutional macro-level configurations and meso-level career dynamics. In turn, the case studies in part 3 focus on individual artists—Gabriel Orozco and Yue Minjun—who were selected from the same sample of artists used in part 2 (cf. appendix D). Thus, my broader findings about meso-level careers can be related to more micro-level, interpretative insights provided by the qualitative cases, and vice versa. Aiming for empirical continuity is preferable for a truly integrative global analysis. In this regard, the focus on careers offered an analytical unit at which macro-, meso-, and micro-level forces intersect (see Zahner 2006) and that is not restricted to territorial boundaries in principle and thus is not susceptible to methodological nationalism (Dezalay and Garth 1996).

Part I: The Emergence of a Global Field in The Contemporary Visual Arts

1. Araeen 1997, 98.
2. Judah 2020.
3. Judah 2020.
4. Judah 2020; Araeen 1997, 103.
5. Moulin 1995, 35.
6. Guilbaut 1983.

7. Moulin 1995, 41; Crane 1987.

8. Quemin 2002; Buchholz and Wuggenig 2005. These "exceptions"—"non-Western" artists who achieved high recognition in the era of the international art field—were usually well integrated in Western art capitals. Because of their rarified status, their recognition did not challenge the boundaries of an overall rather exclusionary North American–European system.

9. Buchholz 2013.

10. Stallabrass 2004, 7. Cf. also Belting 2009, 39.

11. Stallabrass 2004, 7.

12. Bourdieu 1996, 292.

13. Velthuis and Baia Curioni 2015.

Chapter 2: The Genesis of a Global Artistic Subfield

1. This chapter's historical account is far from exhaustive. Consistent with the book's focus, I look only at art institutions that are also particularly important for contemporary art's valuation across borders at the specific cultural pole.

2. Becker 1982; Moulin 1995.

3. For early contributions on the role international biennials played in contemporary art's globalization, e.g., Quemin 2002; Bydler 2004; Stallabrass 2004; Carroll 2007; Buchholz 2008a.

4. In both academic discourse and the art field itself, "biennial" has become a shorthand for any perennial large-scale exhibition that recurs at regular intervals, including triennials, quadrennials, or quinquennials, such as the Documenta in Germany (cf. Wu 2009; Filipovic, van Hal and Øvstebø 2010, 14; Montero 2012).

5. Jones 2010, 70f.

6. Moulin 1995; Thornton 2008.

7. Carroll 2007, 142.

8. Moulin 1995, 45.

9. Morgner 2017, 168 cf. also Moulin 1995, 45.

10. Bydler 2004, 85–97.

11. Cf. the catalog of the first Venice Biennale, quoted in Niemojewski 2010, 92. Despite its rhetoric, Venice was "strongly attached to the conservative taste of the bourgeois public" and did not assume a vanguard position until the 1970s (Niemojewski 2010, 93; cf. also West 1995, 414).

12. Niemojewski 2010, 92f.; Martini 2011, 104f.

13. Jones 2017, 37, 59.

14. West 1995, 415.

15. West 1995, 420.

16. Fleck 2009.

17. I. Robertson 2005a, 29. The categories for prizes shifted over the years, and there were iterations when no prizes were conferred.

18. Ferguson, Greenberg, and Nairne 2005, 52.

19. Sassatelli 2015, 279.

20. Cf. Bydler 2004, 84.

21. Mosquera 2011, 74.

22. There were three biennials founded previous to 1950 in the US: the Carnegie Institute's Pittsburgh International (1896), the Whitney Biennial in New York (1932), and the Corcoran Biennial in New York (1907). According to Monica Sassatelli's (2015, 280) assessment these were initially focused "more on American art only, (Corcoran and Whitney exclusively)," although others would include Carnegie as part of the international biennial's historical timeline (Niemojewski 2010, 93).

23. E.g., Montero 2012, 14. The methodology for the data in fig. 2.2 differs from earlier empirical accounts (Baia Curioni 2012; Belting, Buddensieg, and Weibel 2013; Sassatelli 2015), as specified in appendix A.

24. Figure 2.3 draws from the continental UN classification (UN Statistics Division, n.d.). With the concept of Oceania, it also offers a less "imperial" description of the "Australian" continent. For the category "Northwest," cf. note 25 below.

25. This term relies on Johan Galtung's (2000) metageographical category of the "Northwest," encompassing North America and western Europe. "Western Europe" was defined as including all member states of the European Union before the eastern European expansion in 2004. This categorization corresponds most closely to the way the literature on culture and globalization refers to the "West" versus "non-West" distinction, although it has not provided an explicit definition of it.

26. Buchholz 2006, 2008a.

27. Hoskote 2010.

28. For this notion within the context of global cultural production, cf. Collins 1998, 72ff. For a pioneering scholarly account of such motivations for the establishment of biennials (without explicit reference to "symbolic capital"), cf. Bydler 2004.

29. Boecker 2002, 424.

30. Cf. Bydler 2004; Buchholz 2006, 2008a.

31. Machado 1951, 14; trans. Nelson 2010, 129.

32. Some biennials, like Dakar, started out as international events before the focus became more regional (Fillitz 2011, 385). Others, like the Shanghai Biennale, took the reverse route (Zarobell 2017, 123). Cf. the excellent accounts of biennial historians: Bydler 2004; Ferguson, Greenberg, and Nairne 2005; Martini and Martini 2011; and Jones 2017.

33. E.g., Bydler 2004; Ferguson, Greenberg, and Nairne 2005, 49.

34. Tang 2011, 78.

35. Hoskote 2010.

36. Nelson 2010, 133f.

37. Weiss 2011, 67.

38. The exceptions were foreign-born artists who had long been affiliated with countries in the Latin American region: Annemarie Heinrich, a German-born naturalized Argentine photographer, and Manuel de la Fuente, who was born in Spain and had received Venezuelan citizenship in 1976.

39. Silvia Medina De Miranda, quoted in Rojas-Sotelo 2009, 93.

40. Mosquera 2011, 74.

41. Papastergiadis and Martin 2011, 48f.

42. Mosquera 2011, 74.

43. Weiss 2011, 36.

44. Weiss 2011, 18.

45. Weiss 2011, 63.

46. Weiss 2011, 65.

47. Weiss 2011, 28.

48. Weiss 2011, 61.

49. Weiss 2011, 28.

50. Cf. Block 2013; Gardner and Green 2013; Jones 2017.

51. Niemojewski 2010, 99.

52. Niemojewski 2010, 99; Coates 2014, 117.

53. Cf. Papastergiadis and Martin 2011.

54. Mersmann 2013, 526.

55. Oh 2000, 25ff.

56. Oh 2000, 25ff.

57. Mersmann 2013, 530f.

58. Griffin et al. 2003.

59. Hoskote 2010.

60. Participants represented the biennials of Berlin, Havana, Dakar, Istanbul, Kwangju, Lima, Ljubljana, Lyon, London, São Paulo, Shanghai, Sydney, Taipei, and Werkleitz as well as the Manifesta. A second conference took place in 2002, which already had the title "Exchange or Incest" (trans. from German; see Boecker 2002, 422).

61. Sassatelli 2017, 90.

62. Block 2013, 29.

63. Block 2013, 27.

64. Some regions pooled their biennial openings into shorter periods of time to make it easier for visitors and critics to cover several events in the same trip (Tang 2007).

65. Giddens 1996, 28–33.

66. Bydler 2004, 273–95; Vogel 2010, 120–24.

67. C. Wu 2007a, 384f. Cf. the contentions around the 1998 Dak'Art Biennale, which was criticized for its emphasis on inviting critics and curators from Western centers, including the claim that "the spectre of colonialism cast a sombre shadow" (García-Antón 1998, 87). With the 2004 Taipei Biennial, Chu-Chiun Wei (2013, 474) reports how the cocurator, Amy Huei-Hua Cheng, interpreted the strategy as a form of "aggressive cultural import" that could threaten "Taiwan's cultural identity and ultimately erase its voice."

68. Wei 2013, 483.

69. Bydler 2004, 96f.; Ferguson and Hoegsberg, 2010 , 372.

70. Jones 2017, 171.

71. Van Hest and Vermeylen 2015; Morgner 2017, 180f.; Zarobell 2017, 127.

72. Mersmann 2013, 525.

73. Sassen 2004; Boecker 2002, 424. Yinka Shonibare also speaks of the rise of the "global curator" (in Griffin et al. 2003, 158).

74. Okwui Enwezor, in Griffin et al. 2003, 159.

75. Moulin 1995, 43f.

76. Moulin 1995, 43.

77. The team encompassed Carlos Basualdo, Ute Meta Bauer, Susanne Ghez, Sarat Maharaj, Mark Nash, and Octavio Zaya.

78. C. Wu 2009, 110. By 2013, the share of artists from the US and Germany had dropped to 10 percent (Morgner 2017, 178).

79. Jones 2017.

80. Bydler 2004, 108. Part of the curatorial team consisted of artists and art critics who operated as curators.

81. Quoted in Thornton 2008, 251.

82. Bydler 2004, 105ff.; C. Wu 2009, 110–11; Tang 2011, 81.

83. C. Wu 2007a , 379f.

84. Tang 2011, 81.

85. To be precise, not all national participants are independent nation-states.

86. These data are based on the Venice Biennale's digital archive of national participants. Sometimes it lists a country twice with two different titles when the exhibition was separated into two venues. However, for a proper accounting of the global extension of Venice, I counted each country only once. See ASAC, n.d.

87. Up until the late 1980s, art from this continent was hardly part of the Venice exhibition and was represented mostly by Egypt.

88. Sassatelli 2017, 101.

89. Bydler 2004, 108f. It goes without saying that countries are not homogeneous units. Participants could be financed by the state or by private parties, and decisions about representational politics often involve debates among different factions.

90. Source: Venice Biennale's digital archive of national participations. Cf. also note 86 above.

91. C. Wu 2007a, 385.

92. A wonderful example is Chu-Chiun Wei's case study of Taiwan's changing exhibition politics at Venice toward "critical globalism" (2013), as discussed in chapter 1.

93. Tang 2011, 75. Of course, the higher an institution's symbolic capital is, the more potential influence it will have in shaping the discourse around an artist's work and their recognition. In particular, museums have long been considered as key instances for establishing the symbolic value of artists and their art historical status in the international field (Moulin 1995; Rodner and Thomson 2013).

94. In the following section, I use the term "noncommercial" generically to refer to both public and private exhibiting institutions whose purpose is not the direct economic marketing or sale of art works. Such demarcations can vary for different types of institutions across countries. There are also fleeting boundaries, such as in China, where "noncommercial" art institutions rent out exhibition spaces for profit (cf. Wong 2015).

95. Crane 2002, 14; Levitt 2015, 9, 8.

96. For an insightful essay on China's recent museum boom, cf. Wong 2015. Yet many newer sites privilege classical or modern Asian artistic traditions. If they showcase contemporary art, they tend to be more nationalistic in programming. Yet China is still stronger than many other "non-Western" countries in the world exhibition structure.

97. Quemin 2002, 2012.

98. For the use of the term in relation to global media production, cf. Straubhaar 1991. For an earlier application for the globalization of contemporary art, cf. Buchholz 2006, 2008a.

99. Buchholz 2016, 46.

100. Ferguson 1998; Gorski 2013, 334f.

101. Thornton 2008, 124.

102. Thornton 2008, 150.

103. I thank Melissa Mudry from *Artforum* for providing this information.

104. Given field theory's attention to power inequalities, we can assume that dominant positions potentially exert more discursive power (for a critical discussion of Foucault's work in this regard, cf. Bourdieu 1996, 197–99). This assumption is bolstered by *Artforum*'s linguistic power—that is, the fact that the magazine is published in English, which operates as the global lingua franca of contemporary art (Bydler 2004; Rule and Levine 2013).

105. Moretti 2013.

106. Bydler 2004, 17. For a notable exception, see especially Jones 2017.

107. All passages contained the word "global" in two field-specific ways: (1) in view of institutional aspects of contemporary art—that is, in view of biennials, museums, curatorial mediating practices, or the art market; or (2) regarding artistic aspects, such as critical reviews of artists or aesthetic and art historical debates. For more methodology, cf. appendix A.

108. Bourdieu previously theorized the emergence of the modern art field in France in phenomenological terms by pointing to the "progressive invention" of a "pure gaze," a new mode of seeing and believing in art as a relatively autonomous practice (1996, 299). What he did not discuss was how this embodied gaze was profoundly Eurocentric and exclusionary. A focus on *Artforum International* reveals the gradual and contested undoing of this apparently pure Western gaze, which occurred at a geographic center that grew increasingly globalized "from within," as Ulrich Beck would put it (Beck 2002, 17).

109. Lippard 1984. Multicultural politics were of course also influenced by anti-imperialist discourses of the preceding decades and independence movements in former colonies (Bell 1999).

110. Jary and Jary 1991.

111. A. Johnson 1995.

112. Overall, between 1990 and 1994, there were thirty-five occurrences of "global" in *Artforum* publications, but only twelve were related to contemporary art. The majority of the latter referred to themes associated with multiculturalism.

113. For example, the mainstream art journal *Art in America* and the more critical art magazine *Third Text* in the UK devoted special issues to the discussion of the show. For a comparative discourse analysis, cf. Guasch 2017.

114. As Martin stated, "Pendant une demi-douzaine d'années, j'ai été marginalisé dans le milieu de l'art, j'étais regardé comme un animal un peu bizarre." (Transl. "For half a dozen years, I was marginalized in the art world, I was looked at as a bit of a weird animal.") Martin 2014.

115. McEvilley 1990.

116. McEvilley 1990.

117. E.g., Stallabrass 2004; Belting 2009; Weiss 2011, 35.

118. Another landmark show around that time was curated by Rasheed Araeen from Pakistan in London: *The Other Story* at the Hayward Gallery (November 29, 1989–February 4, 1990). It provided a prominent forum for artists of African, Caribbean, and Asian ancestry who had been overlooked and excluded from mainstream art institutions in the UK.

119. McEvilley 1993b; cf. also Verzotti 1993.

120. McEvilley 1993b.

121. They include a collection of papers delivered at the Smithsonian Institute, in Washington, DC, in 1988 and 1990, which sought to chart new directions in museological discourse and praxis: *Exhibiting Cultures: The Poetics and Politics of Museum Display*, edited by Ivan Karp and Steven Lavine (1991); and *Museums and Communities: The Politics of Public Culture*, edited by Ivan Karp, Christine Mullen Kreamer, and Steven Lavine, 1992.

122. Karp and Lavine 1991, as quoted in McEvilley 1993c, n.p.

123. Green 1993.

124. Green 1993.

125. Storr 1997.

126. Plagens 1999 (emphasis added); Cameron 1997 (emphasis added).

127. McEvilley 1993a.

128. Cameron 1997; Staniszewski 1997; Benson 1999, 465.

129. Staniszewski 1997.

130. Staniszewski 1997.

131. Cameron 1997.

132. Cameron 1997; cf. also Madeleine Grynsztejn quoted in Brenson 1999; Birnbaum 2004.

133. Cameron 1997.

134. Cameron 1997.

135. Melo 1997.

136. Basualdo 1997.

137. Basualdo 1997

138. Bhabha and Rutherford 1990; Cameron 1997.

139. Or its own "taken for granted" reality, as Bourdieu would say (in Bourdieu and Wacquant 1992, 238).

140. P. Lee 2003. Of course, in sociology, it was Howard S. Becker (1982) who advanced the concept of the "art world," highlighting the role of shared conventions among actors who participate in the collective activities of the making of art. As I am interested in unpacking and tracing emic understandings, I am basing my discussion on Pamela Lee's (2003) distinctions in *Artforum*.

141. Lagnado 2006.

142. Pelizzari 2013.

143. Joselit 2013 (emphasis added).

144. Dimendberg and Rose 2015.

145. Meissen 2008. Cf. also Buchloh and Bois 1997; Armstrong 2006; Enwezor 2011. In the next decade, other articles in the journal referred to the Museum de Arte do Rio, the planning of the M+ museum in Hong Kong, and museums in Singapore as examples of how museums beyond the Euro-American axis were striving to become global players.

146. Other new strategies that were discussed included attention to "global branding" through prestigious architecture or large-scale, spectacular artworks and a growing global isomorphism involving trendy museum features, such as shops and cafés.

147. Quart 1999.

148. Quiles 2009.

149. Godfrey 2007. Other critics were Katy Siegel, Jessica Morgan, Francesco Bonami.

150. Storr 2008.

151. E.g., Cameron 1999; Meyer 2005; Haidu 2011.

152. Morgan 2013.

153. Morgan 2013.

154. Joselit 2016.

155. Cras 2015.

156. Following the practice of the Venice Biennale's own accounting of awards, these numbers include special or honorable mentions. Cf. ASAC, n.d.-b. Furthermore, from 1970 until 1984, no awards were conferred. Thus, this comparison is based on biennials that took place between 1938 and 1968, which together amount to the same number of fourteen biennials.

157. Cras 2015.

158. Spoerhase 2014.

159. Bongard 1974.

160. Verger 1987, 106, 117.

161. Rohr-Bongard 2001, 13ff.

162. For a historical discussion of the ranking and critique, e.g., Tabor 2010. For the recognition by these and other players, cf. author interview with Linde Rohr-Bongard, March 2012 (phone).

163. Verger 1987, 106, 117.

164. Rohr-Bongard 2001, 11Cf. Verger 1987, 117.

165. ArtFacts.Net 2003.

166. Gottwald 2008. By 2010, 230,000 exhibitions were registered, and in 2014, ArtFacts claimed an archive of 600,000 exhibitions.

167. Rudolph and Wuggenig 2012, 328.

168. Author interview with Marek Claassen, Berlin, February 2012.

169. Tabor 2010.

170. Boxer 2005.

171. Boxer 2005. The immediate publicity was so enormous that the website broke down for several days.

172. Information provided by the ArtFacts leadership, after the interview meeting with Marek Claassen in Berlin, February 2012.

173. Graw 2010, 41.

174. Boltanski and Esquerre 2016, 47.

175. Moulin 1994.

Chapter 3: From an International Avant-Garde Market to a Global Commercial Subfield

1. E.g., Fillitz 2014; Velthuis and Baia Curioni 2015; Zarobell 2017.

2. Zarobell 2017.

3. Chong 2011, 436; McAndrew 2018, 262–316.

4. Horowitz 2011a, 203; Velthuis 2015.

5. E.g., Renneboog and Spaenjers 2015; Yogev and Ertug 2015.

6. For auction houses, see Moulin 2003. For art fairs, see Schultheiss et al., 2015, 2016. For art investment funds, see Coslor and Spaenjers 2016.

7. E.g., Crane 2009; and K. Lee 2018, 78.

8. "Grobalization" refers to "the imperialistic ambitions of nations, corporations, organizations, and other entities and their desire—indeed, their need—to impose themselves on various geographic areas. Their main interest is in seeing their power, influence, and . . . profits *grow* (hence the term *grobalization*)." (Ritzer 2003, 194).

9. Crane 2009, 333; Velthuis and Baia Curioni 2015.

10. Guilbaut 1983; Moulin 1995, 40–41.

11. Each of these dealers—to convince collectors and ensure that artists are placed in exhibitions, art journals, and public collections they are most closely connected to—mobilized local knowledge and social capital from their national market turf (Moulin 1995).

12. Nonetheless, gallery branches had already existed in the late nineteenth century (e.g., Zarobell 2017, 114).

13. E.g., I. Robertson 2005a, 24; Thompson 2008.

14. Bourdieu 1996. Following Bourdieu (1996, 386f.), I use the term "avant-garde" not in any essentialist way but as a relational marker of a position that can assume different historical manifestations, depending on the state of the cultural field. This usage differs from that of sociologists who have discarded the concept as outdated.

15. Guilbaut 1983; Moulin 1995.

16. Zahner 2006, 256.

17. Velthuis 2007.

18. Velthuis 2007, 5, 41; Beckert and Rössel 2013, 184.

19. Moulin 2003, 43.

20. Velthuis 2007, 21, 27.

21. Paradoxically, by engaging in antieconomic self-representations that emphasize symbolic credibility, these galleries can foster their sales. Avant-garde galleries, however, do not simply sell art; ideally, they "place it" in the hands of dedicated art lovers (Velthuis and Coslor 2012, 474). Mere "status seekers" or "speculators"—buyers who approach art mainly as a project of social or economic maximization—are to be avoided because they violate the code of noninstrumentalist dedication to art (Velthuis 2007, 7, 42).

22. Bourdieu 1996, 145.

23. Zahner 2006, 256.

24. Zahner 2006, 256.

25. Moulin 1995; K. Peterson 1997, 257; Moulin 2003, 42f.

26. K. Peterson 1997, 257.

27. Chong 2011, 437. Often, consecrated galleries represent younger artists to avoid appearing too commercial and outdated, since "longevity" at the market's "elite level" includes "the cultivation of new artists" (Chong 2011, 445).

28. Zahner 2006, 257–259.

29. Crane 1987, 111; Zahner 2006, 259.

30. Quoted in Freeman 2019.

31. Moulin 1995, 52.

32. Janelle Reiring, quoted in Shnayerson 2019.

33. For the term "branded dealers" cf. Thompson 2008, 27–40.

34. Crane 1987; Tomkins 2007a.

35. Tomkins 2007a .

36. Zahner 2006, 258–259.

37. Freeman 2019.

38. Velthuis 2013a , 377.

39. Velthuis 2007, 37.

40. Michael Shnayerson, quoted in Sayej 2019; Velthuis 2007, 37.

41. "International contemporary art fair" is a term used by art professionals from the field. I use the abbreviation "ICAF," as coined by Quemin (2013).

42. Moulin 1995, 39.

43. Mehring 2008.

44. Morgner 2014b, 327.

45. Morgner 2014b, 327.

46. Mehring 2008, 322.

47. Mehring 2008, 328.

48. Schultheis et al. 2015, 82.

49. Morgner 2014b, 331.

50. Morgner 2014b, 331.

51. Morgner 2014a, 36

52. E.g., *Ghurka Blog* 2021.

53. Baia Curioni 2012, 118–119.

54. Zarobell 2017, 154; McAndrew 2008, 80f.

55. As chapter 1 discussed, one should not reduce globalization in cultural fields to a *direct* reflection of the global political economy. External influences impacted the art market to the extent that they were taken up and "refracted" into its own historically specific constellations (Buchholz 2013; cf. also Velthuis and Baia Curioni 2015, 7–11). This also applies to the global diffusion of art fairs, as I specify in the following paragraphs.

56. Baia Curioni 2012, 123.

57. Horowitz 2011a, 131.

58. Marc Spiegler, in Von Benningsen, Gludowacz, and Van Hagen 2009, 276.

59. Ma 2018.

60. Thompson 2014, 237.

61. For a sociological account of the rise of the international art fair as a global institution, cf. Morgner 2014a,b.

62. The first iteration of Art Dubai was called "Gulf Art Fair." Adam 2014, 105; Sindelar 2016, 3.

63. Vermeylen 2015, 35, 49.

64. Vermeylen 2015, 49f.; cf. also Zarobell 2017, 140.

65. In 2016, for example, the enterprise that owns Art Basel bought a majority stake of the India Art Fair (Zarobell 2017, 155).

66. As chapter 2 indicated, the foundation of art biennials is not completely independent of economic interests, especially regarding tourism or urban regeneration. In addition, until 1968, the Venice Biennale enabled the sale of artworks and was also a marketplace in this sense. However, the dominant impulse for the biennial boom since the 1980s involved heightening the recognition for the art of a country or region within a broader international/global context, and as such, biennialization was primarily driven by the quest for foreign symbolic capital.

67. E.g., Bowley 2013.

68. Schultheis et al. 2015, 76.

69. Yogev and Ertug 2015, 203f.

70. Anonymous gallerist from Berlin, quoted in Schultheis et al. 2015, 78.

71. Thompson 2014, 240.

72. Thompson 2014, 240; cf. also Baia Curioni 2012, 136. Since April 2016, Endeavor Group Holdings, the US media and entertainment corporation, holds a controlling share.

73. Baia Curioni, Forti, and Leone 2015; Zarobell 2017.

74. Spiegler, in Von Bennigsen, Gludowacz, and Van Hagen 2009, 275.

75. Quoted in Vogel 2006a.

76. Horowitz 2011a, 152.

77. Adam 2014, 116.

78. Morgner 2014b, 333.

79. E.g., Vermeylen 2015; Schultheis et al. 2016. Fair organizers also leverage favorable tax conditions or direct invitations to prestigious foreign galleries; if they attend, it can raise a newer fair's own status (Thompson 2014).

80. Cf. data on the geographic diversity of gallery participations for ten art fairs in 2014 in Zarobell 2017, 157f.

81. Fillitz 2014, 90; Baia Curioni, Forti, and Leone 2015; Morgner 2014a.

82. Morgner 2014b, 319; Horowitz 2014.

83. Bowley 2013.

84. Baia Curioni 2012, 136.

85. Author interview with a consecrated avant-garde gallerist in New York City, June 2008.

86. McAndrew 2013a, 54; cited also in Horowitz 2014.

87. McAndrew 2018, 47.

88. Schultheis et al. 2015, 88.

89. Joost Bosland, quoted in Adam 2014, 103.

90. Quemin 2013, 166.

91. Yogev and Grund 2012, 24.

92. Graw 2010, 74.

93. Graw 2010, 75.

94. After all, admittance to top fairs is also based on the program's cultural strength. At the level of ideology, it could even be "dangerous" to be perceived as too commercial at an art fair (Spiegler, in Von Bennigsen, Gludowacz, and Van Hagen 2009, 282), an admission by Art Basel's director that supports Bourdieu's notion that orientations toward economic profit should not be too obvious in cultural markets, even in a field's more heteronomous regions (Bourdieu 1993).

95. Spiegeler, in Von Bennigsen, Gludowacz, and Van Hagen 2009, 275.

96. E.g., Vermeylen 2015; Schultheis et al. 2016, 221.

97. Velthuis 2012, 19; cf. also Zarobell 2017, 152.

98. McAndrew 2018, 222. The data published in Clare McAndrew's market report were generated by the online platform Artsy; cf. McAndrew 2018, 346.

99. Carroll 2007, 138; cf. also Jones 2010, 68.

100. Horowitz 2011a, 139–40; Fillitz 2014.

101. Horowitz 2011a, 139.

102. To be sure, small booths at crowded fairs have always contrasted with the austere white cubes of the gallery space, which allow for more contemplation and discursive interaction.

103. Bankowsky 2005, 229.

104. Several contributions have emphasized art ICAFs' strong similarities to biennials when it comes to the globalization of contemporary art's mediation activities. They portray ICAFs' worldwide proliferation as a parallel development (Baia Curioni 2012) or subsume them into the same global "exhibitionary complex" (Zarobell 2017, 99–104). Others observe increasing overlaps in the setup of biennials and art fairs (C. Wu 2010) and their modes of operation (Barragán 2020), including the coordination of opening times or the use of cultural programming, e.g., scholarly panels, discussion forums, and curators for special fair sections or gallery shows. Such arguments imply strong interdependencies, if not a growing convergence, between the cultural and market-based mediation of contemporary art within a global context.

105. Spiegler, in Von Bennigsen, Gludowacz, and Van Hagen 2009.

106. Fillitz 2014, 91.

107. Velthuis 2007, 86.

108. Velthuis 2007, 88.

109. Thompson 2008, 104.

110. Smith 1989.

111. Veblen (1899) 2017.

112. Plattner 1996, 45, 166; Velthuis 2007, 89.

113. Velthuis 2007, 80–81. An artist's career can be negatively affected by a poor performance at an auction or by declines in prices. Artworks, for example, are said to be "burned" when they remain unsold at auctions (Ashenfelter and Graddy 2006, 933).

114. Barbara Rose, interview in Kahn 2018.

115. Crane 2009, 333.

116. Lisa Dennison, in Von Bennigsen, Gludowacz, and Van Hagen 2009, 258.

117. Data from Artprice as quoted in Horowitz 2011a, 8.

118. McAndrew 2015, 70. The reported sum in euros is €5.9 billion.

119. E.g., Moulin 2003; Crane 2009; Velthuis and Baia Curioni 2015.

120. Adam 2014, 31.

121. Author interview with a specialist from Sotheby's, September 2014.

122. Van den Bosch 2005.

123. E.g., Fourcade-Gourinchas and Babb, 2002.

124. Van den Bosch 2005, 11, 13.

125. Watson 1992, 318ff.; van den Bosch 2005, 28. In 1964, Sotheby's acquired Parke-Bernet, which was the biggest US fine art auction house (Horowitz 2011a, 10). In 1977, Christie's began to hold regular auctions in New York as well.

126. The Swiss locations tended not to involve contemporary art sales, however.

127. "Japanese buying power nearly doubled following the appreciation of the yen after 1985. . . . Impressionist and modern art appeared as bargains to many Japanese. By 1988, 53% of all worldwide auction sales went to Japan" (Goodwin 2008, 11).

128. The relationship between Sotheby's and Russia has a longer history. In 1988, for example, Sotheby's held a major sale of avant-garde and Soviet art in Moscow. Elton John and David Bowie were reportedly among the buyers.

129. The sale was dedicated to modern and contemporary Indian art and fetched $15.5 million, which was double the presale estimate (Adam 2014, 31).

130. Thompson 2014, 217.

131. Thompson 2014, 217.

132. Cf. Velthuis 2015. In a coauthored contribution, Velthuis and Baia Curioni likewise suggest that a "single, unified, integrated global market for contemporary is not in sight" (Velthius and Baia Curioni 2015, 25).

133. Clare McAndrew, cited in Belting 2013, 139.

134. Thompson 2008, 106f.

135. Thompson 2014, 133.

136. The "global status" of some sales was underscored through the installment of large screens that converted each bid simultaneously into several currencies, such as US dollars, euros, British pounds, Swiss francs, Hong Kong dollars, Japanese yen, or Russian rubles (Thompson 2014, 133).

137. Thornton and Ruiz 2008. At Hirst's spectacular auction, "Beautiful Inside My Head Forever," with Sotheby's London in September one year later, the royal family again made headlines by purchasing his *Golden Calf* for a record price of £10.3 million (about US$18 million).

138. Artprice 2018 (emphasis added).

139. Thompson 2014, 138.

140. Johansson and Ronkainen 2005.

141. Thompson 2014, 126. The internet and social media enhance this global reach. One example is new price databases, which I discuss in the next section.

142. Thompson 2014, 126.

143. Thompson 2014, 126.

144. Velthuis 2007, 83ff.

145. The idea of *transcontinental valuation chains* should not be confounded with the idea of arbitrage. The latter means that specialists sell at the location that promises the highest prices for certain works (Moulin 2003, 89f.; Herrero 2011, 140), which can function without greater market integration. In the former strategy, by contrast, auction houses exploit strategic movements between locations as a *processual* approach for expanding the appeal of genres or artists across borders.

146. Archer 2018, 3.

147. Henry Howard-Sneyd in a Sotheby's press release prior to the sale on March 31, 2006. The title of the auction was "Contemporary Art Asia."

148. Sotheby's presale press release.

149. Cf. Buchholz 2017.

150. Some market analysts interpreted galleries' gravitation toward fairs "as a conscious reaction to the rising power of auction houses . . . to replicate some of the dynamics of auctions, . . . [such as] the competitive atmosphere and 'one-room excitement' of an auction" (e.g., McAndrew 2018, 190).

151. Adam 2014, 28.

152. Kharchenkova and Velthuis 2018; Buchholz 2013. I thank Lee Ambrozy, who was a China correspondent for *Artforum International*, for drawing my attention to this aspect with regard to the art market in that country, which was confirmed in several conversations during fieldwork

there in 2010 and 2014. The case study in chapter 7 exemplifies how much auction sales, far from being "objective," are vulnerable to short-term manipulation and speculative intervention.

153. I. Robertson 2005a, 26.

154. McAndrew 2008, 19f.; Buchholz 2013.

155. I. Robertson 2005a, 33; McAndrew 2008, 18.

156. Nevertheless, beta houses offer works that often have more affordable price points or are perceived to be of a lower "quality"—there is, after all, competition from Christie's and Sotheby's for consignments.

157. Zarobell 2017, 219.

158. Thompson 2008, 48.

159. Favorable legislative conditions played a part in Hong Kong's ascent. More liberal regulations, tax breaks on importing and exporting artworks, and the ability to broker confidential bank transactions made it an attractive location for the auction business, especially in comparison to mainland China (Artprice 2018).

160. "In practice, HNWIs [high-net-worth individuals] are primary consumers of fine and decorative art" (Hwang 2009, 11).

161. Stallabrass 2006, 4f.; Taylor 2011, 11.

162. Horowitz 2012, 88. It was spearheaded by the German dealer Hans Neuendorf, who also had played a supporting role in founding the world's first contemporary art fair, Art Cologne (formerly Kunstmarkt Köln).

163. Kräussl 2012, 69f.

164. Kräussl 2012, 70. The number of auction houses is based on information by an economist who worked for Artprice in 2017.

165. Plattner 1996, 45, 166; Velthuis 2007.

166. Artprice defines "contemporary art" by an artist's age, and the category covers those who were born in or after 1945.

167. Ehrmann 2011.

168. K. Lee 2018, 72f.

169. Cf. Olav Velthuis' excellent account on the symbolic meaning of prices. Velthuis 2007.

170. Bourdieu 1996, 217.

171. Schultheis et al. 2015, 89.

172. Velthuis and Coslor 2012, 475.

173. Velthuis 2007, 95.

174. Velthuis and Coslor 2012, 478.

175. A development that had previously originated with analog art prices services in the late 1980s and early 1990s; cf. Velthuis and Coslor 2012, 476–77.

176. Horowitz 2011a; Coslor 2016; K. Lee 2018. This is not to say that all financial elites merely pursue financial interests with their purchases. However, if one accounts for Bourdieu's idea of a hysteresis of the habitus—which suggests an inertia of schemes of appreciation and evaluation acquired during secondary socialization in professional fields—then we can assume that such buyers transpose a certain calculative rationality to the art market in their practices.

177. Velthuis 2015; Renneboog and Spaenjers 2015.

178. E.g., Velthuis and Baia Curioni 2015.

179. E.g., Zarobell 2017; K. Lee 2018, 86.

Part II: Dynamics of Artistic Recognition in the Globalizing Field

1. For the use of the term "non-Western," cf. notes 14 and 15 in chapter 1.

2. Dziewor 1999, 345; Scheps 1999, 16ff.; Hanrou 1994, 79; Hanrou and Minglu 1998, 183.

3. Araeen 2001, 23. Nevertheless, Araeen also suggested that these younger, postcolonial artists would remain subjected to unequal cultural norms, being required to "express or reference" their "own supposed culture" in their work: "The white/European artist has no obligation to the multicultural society and he does not require any sign of identity for the work to be recognized; the 'other' artists must carry the burden of the culture they have originated from, and they must indicate this in their art works before they can be recognized and legitimated" (23).

4. E.g., Schoellhammer 1999; Mosquera 2003.

5. Oguibe 2004, xiv.

6. Oguibe 2004, xiif.

7. E.g., Quemin 2002, 2006, 2012; Quemin and Van Hest 2015.

Chapter 4: Cross-Border Valuation between Art Experts and the Market

1. E.g., Regev 1994; Baumann 2001; Khaire and Wadhwani 2010.

2. Rawlings 2001; Baumann 2007.

3. Lamont 1987; Heise and Tudor 2007; Rodner and Preece 2016.

4. Bromberg and Fine 2002; Kapsis 1989; DeNora 1995.

5. Lamont 2012, 206–7.

6. Gartman 2002. Regarding meso-level relations among field participants, agents' micro-level dispositions, and macro-level inequalities and broader influences, cf. Zahner 2006.

7. Moulin 1995; Van den Bosch 2005; Zahner 2006; Crane 2009; Graw 2010, 2012.

8. Bourdieu 1996, 169f.

9. Bourdieu 1996, 168.

10. Bourdieu 1996, 297, 81.

11. Bourdieu 1996; cf. also Wijnberg and Gemser 2000.

12. Bourdieu 1996, 162.

13. Bourdieu extends Weber's conception of charisma ([1922]1980, chap. 3) and Durkheim's differentiation of the sacred and the profane ([1912] 2001) while also recognizing the historical influence that Romanticism and bohemian artistic culture had on modern art's ascendance (Graña 1964).

14. For an account that aligns with Bourdieu but specifies the "exceptional economy of the arts," see Hans Abbing's (2002) insightful study.

15. Bourdieu 1993, 169.

16. Bourdieu 1993, 164.

17. Bourdieu 1996, 83.

18. Bourdieu 1996, 253f.

19. Bourdieu 1996, 142.

20. Heinich 1997.

21. Bourdieu 1993, 169.

22. Bourdieu 1996, 239f.

23. Bourdieu 1996, 154–61, 239–42, 253.

24. Bourdieu 1993.

25. Moulin 1992, 1995; McCarthy et al. 2005; Van den Bosch 2005; Zahner 2006; Crane 2009; Graw 2010, 2012.

26. McCarthy et al. 2005, xvii.

27. Crane 2009, 337f.; Graw 2010, 48. While such cases occurred earlier in history—the Neo-Expressionist painter Julian Schnabel is a particularly notorious example from the 1980s (Moulin 1995, 51)—now they would no longer be exceptions but rather the new normal.

28. Cf. Crane 2009; K. Lee 2018, 71.

29. Boltanski and Esquerre 2020.

30. Crane 2009, 349; cf. also Moulin 2003.

31. Graw 2012, 188.

32. Graw 2010, 39.

33. Zorloni and Ardizzone 2016.

34. Here, Crane (2009, 337) quotes a statement by an American art critic (Tomkins 2007a, 71).

35. Warhol 1975.

36. Zahner 2006.

37. Crane 2009; Graw 2010; Taylor 2011.

38. McCarthy et al. 2005, xvii; Graw 2010.

39. Philipsen 2010, 182, 181.

40. McCarthy et al. 2005, xvii.

41. I use the word "world" rather than "global" for the dual cultural economy model to keep it open for the interplay of different scales (sub)national, regional, global as another source for heterogeneity in valuation dynamics across borders, as we will see in Part III.

42. Buchholz 2013; cf. also Schultheis et al. 2015, 214–20, regarding the impact of art fairs on the field.

43. Schultheis et al. 2015, 219.

44. As chapter 3 discussed, these logics have existed before the new millennium but have grown and become more radicalized in the past twenty years.

45. Cf. Rovers 2009.

46. "Relative" suggests a spectrum of artistic, curatorial, or discursive freedom that varies according to institutional demands, funding sources, or geographic locations within the subfield and over time.

47. Bourdieu 1996, 154.

48. This is consistent with Bourdieu's notion of longer production cycles in relatively autonomous subfields.

49. Bourdieu, 1996, 149–53. I borrow the concept of *longue durée* from Fernand Braudel and Immanuel Wallerstein (2009), who pioneered a plural conception of social times for examining historical patterns. As Richard E. Lee (2012, 3) summarizes, *longue durée* designates a mode of structural time that pertains to the duration of a historical system as a whole whose changes are less perceptible. It is distinguished from "the short term of events or episodic history (for instance political history)" or "the medium term of conjunctures," such as economic booms and busts.

50. Schultheis et al. 2016, 19.

Chapter 5: Diversity and Careers in a Dual Cultural World Economy

1. For a methodological explanation of the database, cf. Appendix C.

2. For a detailed discussion of the methodology (including questions regarding Eurocentrism), please consult appendix C.

3. Boxer 2005. Marek Claassen, the platform's German cofounder, describes it this way: "The more international artists a gallery or museum has, the more its exhibition value" (Claassen 2008).

4. For a discussion of the advantages and limitations of the ranking's approach for this study, see appendix C.

5. Author interview with Marek Claassen, 2012.

6. As outlined in note 18 of chapter 1, with "global canon," I am talking about an empirically determinable tier of top artists with regard to their relative symbolic acclaim and/or sales success at a global level. This approach also helps avoid traditional notions of canon formation in visual art that are overly Eurocentric.

7. In Von Bennigsen, Gludowacz, and Van Hagen 2009, 259.

8. Note that auction sales do not represent an artist's "economic capital" exactly because artists usually do not see a cent from auctions, which has long been a point of heated contention in the art field. So I use the term in quotation marks. Auction sales, however, are perceived as a public barometer of economic success, or market position, as discussed in chapter 3. Cf. also Shin et al. 2014.

9. Hall 1992b, 276–80: "It [the discourse of 'the West and the Rest'] represents what are in fact very differentiated (the differentiated European cultures) as homogenous (the West). And it asserts, that these different cultures are united by one thing: the fact that they are all different from the Rest. Similarly, the Rest, though different among themselves, are represented as the same in the sense that they are all different from the West. In short, the discourse, as a 'system of representation,' represents the world as divided according to a simple dichotomy—the West / the Rest." Hall's terminology corresponds to the way I have used the "Northwest" category, while I have placed the notion of the "Rest" in quotation marks to underscore his critical discussion of the pejorative and Eurocentric connotations.

10. This finding on the ascent of Chinese artists in the auction market extends earlier studies by using a broader time frame and a more differentiated methodological basis (cf. Buchholz 2008b, 2013; Bull 2011; Quemin and Van Hest 2015). As these results are derived from an especially discriminating sampling strategy, China's rise cannot be discounted as merely a local phenomenon in global disguise (Quemin 2012, 63). The sampling also safeguarded against an overly loose application of the label "contemporary art." The Artprice rankings that had been used in prior publications mix contemporary (Chinese) artworks with other stylistic orientations, including ink art, calligraphy, or traditional oil painting. This can distort the results because traditional Chinese art tends to achieve higher auction price levels than its contemporary counterpart. Please see appendix C for details.

11. Rawlings 2001, 42.

12. Cf. chapter 4.

13. At the same time, these findings indicate that any transformations in terms of artistic centrality are not necessarily related with changes regarding *institutional* centers, and thus need

to be distinguished. As we shall see later as well, despite the declining status of its artists, the US has remained a key node for the making of global art careers.

14. Bull 2011, 182–85.

15. Cf. appendix C.

16. Taking the top one hundred artists from each dimension yielded 179 artists overall. Twenty-one artists appeared in both rankings.

17. Cf. Buchholz 2013. I presented the idea for this longitudinal approach toward symbolic and economic recognition, which moves away from a more static, variable-centered way of studying contemporary art careers, first at a workshop in November 2011 at Leuphana University. Olav Velthuis was a commentator on the paper and I thank him for his feedback.

18. Crane 2009; Graw 2010, 2012.

19. Kräussl, Lehnert, and Martelin 2016.

20. Art world members typically refer to noncommercial art institutions as "public" institutions. However, the database also encompassed "private" noncommercial exhibition spaces and therefore I added the two terms here. See also note 94 in chapter 2. Additionally, while galleries are market actors that sell artworks, not all are commercial to the same extent, as explained in chapter 3.

21. A binary categorical division was applied since no transgender case could be identified.

22. A predilection that was certainly ushered in by the influence of various feminisms on developments in the international artistic subfield since the 1960s (cf. Lippard 1976).

23. Artistic styles or the content of artworks were not considered in this broader analysis because they are more difficult to quantify. In addition, it is challenging to determine clear style attributions among contemporary artists since their "postmodern" artistic practices tend to be more eclectic.

24. Note that the percentages do not total 100 because artists can engage with multiple media over the course of their career.

25. Strikingly, digital art—which some people might guess would be a dominant global medium because it can be quickly disseminated over the internet to a worldwide audience— only appears at the fringes. It clearly is not a leading medium in the globalizing field, though this might change over the next generational cycle.

26. Stallabrass 2006, 16.

27. Crane 2009, 336.

28. Stallabrass 2006, 16–17.

29. Cf. Bishop 2005.

30. Stallabrass 2006, 17.

31. Stallabrass 2006, 16.

32. Jones 2010; cf. also Jones 2017.

33. Stallabrass 2006, 17.

34. Moulin 2003, 155–76; Horowitz 2011a.

35. Globe-trotting biennial curators may be also drawn to it for the fact that it embodies a technology that deftly represents the communication density of an increasingly connected world. Video art is relatively easy (and cheap) to transport across borders, too. Carroll 2007, 139; cf. also Jones 2010, 2017.

36. Belting 2012, 22; cf. also Carroll 2007.

37. Scheps 1999, 16ff.

38. As discussed in chapter 1, Bourdieu's term "cultural capital" refers to the degree of cultural competencies or one's familiarity with field-relevant practices, in addition to the possession of cultural goods (e.g., books, paintings) and educational credentials or academic titles (Bourdieu 2001a). For a critical engagement of the concept's multiple meanings, see Lamont and Lareau 1988.

39. The notion of "prevailing subcultures" is also meant to avoid a reifying understanding of cross-border patterns of aesthetic evaluation. As we shall see in the "Geographies of Circulation and Migration" section in this chapter, the uncovered aesthetic and cultural norms are associated with the persisting dominance of Western institutional centers for mediation.

40. Quoted in Taylor 2011, 14.

41. Zahner 2006.

42. For the idea of the business artist, cf. Warhol 1975.

43. Graw 2010, 47–49.

44. Crane 2009, 344; Taylor 2011, 3.

45. Horowitz 2011b, 2.

46. Crane 2009, 343.

47. Koons quoted in Tomkins 2007b, 67.

48. For discussion of the meanings of the material value of the work, cf. Graw 2010, 35–38.

49. Taylor 2011, 15.

50. Stallabrass 2017.

51. Stallabrass 2022.

52. Concannon 2005.

53. Rosenberg 2008, as quoted in Crane 2009, 334.

54. McAndrew 2018, 187.

55. This also applies to other countries in this group: 61 percent of the commercial artists who had most of their solo shows in the US are born there, and 64 percent of those with Germany as their top exhibition location are from that country. These numbers flip for the most autonomous group. Only 12 percent of the artists who have the US as their top country are from there originally. That percentage is 25 percent for artists exhibiting in Germany and 40 percent for France. These distributions confirm a stronger home bias among heteronomous artists with regard to where artists get their highest level of exhibition exposure.

56. This is another example that illustrates why a political-economy model, which would point to countries' socioeconomic position in the capitalist world-system to map power structures in global cultural production, would be too simplistic.

57. In the autonomous cluster, these figures are 88 percent for the US, 75 percent for Germany.

58. Cf. Quemin 2002, 2006; Buchholz 2008a; C. Wu 2009, 112–14; Velthuis and Baia Curioni 2015.

59. A finding that confirms, on the basis of extended career data, arguments on the continuing weight of institutional centers in contemporary art, e.g., Quemin 2002, 2006, 2012; Buchholz and Wuggenig 2005; Velthuis and Baia Curioni 2015.

60. Of artists in this cluster, 30 percent reach four continents in auctions, and 12 percent among them reach five. One artist has had sales on six.

61. Twenty-one percent reach four continents, 3 percent reach five.

62. Velthuis, in his insightful work (2013b), first focused on galleries before he included a discussion of auction sales in his critical analysis of globalization.

63. Cf. also chapter 7.

64. If one disaggregates the percentage of autonomous types of elite artists who stayed and left , the figures hardly change from the older Consecrated Elite (85 percent) to the younger Mid-Garde (with 88 percent of migrants from "non-Western" regions), which means there is no decrease across generations.

65. This is most pronounced with Hong Kong, since none of the artists who received their greatest exposure in this market hub lived there.

66. The distinction of globalist, skeptical, and transformational positions in the "great globalization debate" was suggested by the British social scientists David Held and Andrew McGrew (eds. 2003). In their usage, globalists believe in the reality of globalization, while sceptics consider globalization as a myth or at least an exaggeration. Transformationalists, by contrast, underline the contractions and openness of globalization as a historical process, which would be more in line with my study's position.

67. Cf. note 66 above, on how an emphasis on "transformations" aligns with an intermediate perspective.

68. This point was made early and forcefully by Quemin (2002, 2006). Yet the analyses in this chapter disaggregate the picture with data that also consider circulation patterns, not only the relative success of artists. In addition, they point to a multidimensional geography of power, aligned with the distribution of field-specific macro capitals rather than the broader capitalist world-system.

Part III: Creative Lives: from the "Periphery" to Global Recognition

1. Mosquera 2003, 146.

2. For the methodology about case selection, see appendix D.

3. Bourdieu 1977, 53, 56, 95.

4. Bourdieu (1984) famously elaborates this concept as part of his social class theory. However, one should be wary of universalizing the class construct for primary socialization because other social categories might be more apt globally (cf. Neubert 2022). Though a full discussion of this idea goes beyond the focus of this book, I plan to return to it in a follow-up project on collectors.

5. Bourdieu 1977, 56, 95; Bourdieu 1967, 161f.

6. Bourdieu 1977, 53.

7. This distinction also helps underline how Bourdieu's approach is more intricate than certain critiques have suggested, which reproach him for utility-maximizing pictures of action. Yet I agree with Rogers Brubaker (1993, 214) that one should not limit habitus to "non-rational" social practices. To be sure, Bourdieu seeks to counter overly rationalistic (and, from his point of view, "scholastic") accounts of action, and he correctly highlights traditional, intuitive, and affective modes of conduct. But the true challenge in making sense of certain "strategies" involves finding a way to avoid thinking about them as either overly calculating or totally subconscious and quasi-innocent. Social life is far too complex to be forced into such neat categories.

8. Regev 2007, 127f.

9. Dezalay 2006.

10. For insightful contributions on studying meanings in global circulation processes, cf. Hopfener 2018; Jijon 2019.

11. For the rise of global mediators in contemporary art, cf. Griffin et al. 2003. For pioneering accounts of the role of hybrid brokers in global cultural production, cf. Bielby and Harrington 2008; Kuipers 2011.

12. Bourdieu 1996, 127–28, 239–41.

13. For an excellent case study on Andy Warhol that uses a multileveled field approach, cf. Zahner 2006.

Chapter 6: Becoming a Global Artist at the Relatively Autonomous Pole

1. Story based on Gabriel Orozco, author interview, December 2020.

2. Kovac 2019, 91.

3. Jennifer Josten, a specialist on Mexican art history, conversation with the author.

4. For an excellent account of the Mexican art field and its complex international relations in these years, cf. Josten 2018.

5. For insightful critical discussions, cf. Belting 2009; Khaire and Wadhwani 2010.

6. Quoted in Pinchbeck 1998, 22.

7. The main journals were *Art in America* and *Artforum International*.

8. Springer 1997, 90.

9. Springer 1997, 90.

10. Springer 1997, 90.

11. Schjeldahl 2009, 146.

12. Orozco in Santamarina 2005, 136.

13. Santamarina 2005, 135–136.

14. Schjeldahl 2009, 146.

15. Orozco in Santamarina 2005, 136.

16. Some of the participants in these meetings included Abraham Cruxvillegas, Damian Ortega, Gabriel Kuri, José Kuri (now director of Kurimanzutto gallery, Mexico City), Tatiana Parcero, Laureana Toledo, Jerónimo (Dr. Lakra) López, Mauricio Rocha Iturbide (architect, photographer), Manuel Rocha Iturbide (musician, sound artist, photographer), and Flavia Gonzalez Rosetti (art historian). Guillermo Santamarina, author interview, March 2010.

17. Author interviews in 2010, 2015, 2016; cf. also Kovac 2019, 193.

18. The concept of "collaborative circle" designates a "primary group consisting of peers who share similar occupational goals and who, through long periods of dialogue and collaboration, negotiate a common vision that guides their work" (Farrell 2003 , 11).

19. Author interviews in 2010, 2015, and 2016.

20. It is critical to note that since at least the 1970s, the Mexican field also had a more unofficial history of experimental art collectives and conceptually driven practices, which probably influenced Orozco's development too. For an excellent genealogy, cf. Medina and Debroise 2007.

21. Translation: "In context. 14 artists around Joseph Beuys."

22. Santamarina interview.

23. Springer 1997, 90.

24. Josten 2006, 4; De Zegher interview February 2010.

25. Josten 2006, 4; De Zegher interview February 2010.

26. It should be noted that Fontana was born in Argentina to Italian parents.

27. Quoted in Josten 2006, 5.

28. Cameron 1999.

29. Schjeldahl 2004.

30. Quoted in Sontag 2009.

31. Marian Goodman, author interview, February 2010.

32. Francesco Bonami, author interview, March 2010.

33. Orozco interview.

34. Lynn Zelevansky, author interview, February 2010.

35. Josten 2006, 9.

36. Zelevansky 1993.

37. Quoted in Temkin et al. 2009, 81f.

38. Temkin et al. 2009, 82.

39. Cotter 2009.

40. Zelevansky 1993.

41. Zelevansky 1993, quoted in Josten 2006, 9.

42. Zelevansky 1993. See also Josten 2006, 9.

43. Debroise 1993, quoted and discussed in Josten 2006, 9–10.

44. Kimmelman 1998, E37.

45. Goodman interview.

46. Saltz 2010.

47. De Zegher 1996, 55.

48. Gell 2009.

49. Alma Ruiz, interview conducted by Ena Palaska, May 2021.

50. Ruiz interview. The administrative bodies involved in the decision-making process were related to the National University of Mexico, the CONACULTA, and the government of Mexico City.

51. Account and quotes based on Ruiz interview.

52. Kuri 2000; Ortega 2000; Josten 2004, 86ff.

53. Review by Debroise in *Reforma*, October 2, 2000, quoted and discussed in Josten 2004, 88–89.

54. Review by Medina in *Reforma*, October 25, 2000, quoted and discussed in Josten 2004, 89–90.

55. Becker 1982; Bourdieu 1991.

56. The Documenta 10 in 1997, curated by Catherine David, in which Orozco participated too, was also a pioneering exhibition with regard to opening up debates around globalization, as discussed in chapter 2.

57. For Venice, Orozco acted as a curator.

58. MoMA 2009. Announcement of the exhibition on the museum's website.

59. Cotter 2009.

60. Viveros-Fauné 2009; Haidu 2010.

61. For an in-depth discussion, cf. Kovac 2019.

62. Bourdieu 1996, 141–53.

63. Als 1993; Fox 1993; Heartney 1993; Camnitzer 1993.

64. Cf. Sussman 2005; cf. Camnitzer 1993.

65. Heartney 1993.

66. Baumann 2007, 48.

67. Bourdieu 1993, 74.

68. Bourdieu 1996, 216.

69. Bourdieu 1996, 138f. This argument, of course, recalls Clement Greenberg's (1961) philosophy of formalist modernism as a movement toward defining the essential, formal nature of each artistic medium while excluding external subject matters.

70. Bourdieu 1996, 243, 102, 235.

71. For an in-depth insightful account of artistic production in this dual mode, cf. Wohl 2021.

72. Bourdieu 1996 , 93, 235.

73. Bourdieu 1996, 275.

74. Boullosa 2007, 67.

75. Santamarina 2005, 134.

76. Fer 2006, 157.

77. Fer 2006.

78. Boullosa 2007, 67.

79. Santamarina 2005.

80. Santamarina 2005, 144.

81. Saltz 1999, 111.

82. Nesbit 2003.

83. Fer 2006, 180.

84. Moulin 1992, 70–75.

85. It remains a matter of discussion as to whether it can justifiably be called a "movement."

86. Orozco in Fer 2006, 158.

87. Cotter 2009.

88. Gell 2009.

89. Boullosa 2007, 71.

90. Fer 2006.

91. Camnitzer 1997, 86.

92. Fer 2006.

93. In the mid-1990s, in a conversation with the artist Hans Haacke, Bourdieu conceded that a purely formalist understanding of artistic autonomy is no longer sufficient. While the process of "autonomization" in the nineteenth century entailed the "renunciation of certain functions, particularly political functions," Haacke's work would point to the reintroduction of a "critical function" (Bourdieu in Bourdieu and Haacke 1995, 84f.). Haacke would do so, however, with an "aesthetic language" that says things in a "form" that is "necessary" and "esoteric"; that is, it is informed by "art history" and a subversive engagement with it (Bourdieu in Bourdieu and

Haacke 1995, 85f.). Bourdieu thus still adheres to a formalist approach and sees such newer critical art practices in a more additive fashion.

94. Boullosa 2007.

95. Becker 1982, 14–15; Bourdieu 1996, 246.

96. Moulin 1995, 34.

97. Rawlings 2001, 50.

98. Araeen 1997.

99. Oguibe 2004; Belting 2009; Khaire and Wadhwani 2010.

100. Quemin 2006.

101. Buchholz 2018a.

102. Oguibe 2004, 21; Kravanga 2002, 105, 108.

103. Rawlings 2001.

104. Josten 2006.

105. Fer 2006.

106. Orozco in Santamarina 2005, 134.

107. Temkin et al. 2009, 86.

108. Temkin et al. 2009, 86.

109. Bonami 1994, 95.

110. Miles 2001, 47.

111. Boullosa 2007, 69.

112. For a critical discussion of the former manifestation of "cosmopolitanism," cf. Calhoun 2002.

113. E.g., Becker 1982; Bourdieu 1993.

114. Guiffre 1999.

115. Jose Kuri, author interview, January 2016.

116. Carla Stellweg, author interview, April 2010.

117. In fact, Stellweg's was the first gallery for Latin American contemporary art in New York.

118. Stellweg interview.

119. For example, in 1994, Stellweg's gallery was denied entry at the US Special Section and Projects at the ARCO Art Fair in Madrid, on the basis of the rationale that it fell outside the scope of contemporary American (US) art, even though it showcased work by artists who lived and worked in New York, among others.

120. Compared to the other important galleries mentioned, Goodman's gallery organized nearly twice as many solo shows and the largest number of group exhibitions of Orozco's work until 2010.

121. Belcove 2007, 379.

122. Belcove 2007, 379.

123. Cf. Schjeldahl 2004; Belcove 2007.

124. Orozco interview.

125. By 2010, Goodman had established an expanded program with artists coming from China, Albania, India, and Russia. In fact, only three of her thirty-six artists were US-American.

126. Goodman interview.

127. Schjeldahl 2004, 36.

128. Cf. Velthuis 2007; and chapter 4.

129. Yogev 2010, 517.

130. White and White 1993; Moulin 1995.

131. Heinich and Pollak 1996; Sassatelli 2015, 279; Belting 2013, 184.

132. Apart, of course, from budget and logistical constraints as well as institutional hierarchies.

133. Catherine de Zheger was also extremely influential in discovering Orozco, as discussed in the chapter's first section.

134. Bonami interview.

135. Bonami 1998, 26.

136. Bonami interview.

137. Bonami interview (emphasis added).

138. Bonami 1998, 26 (emphasis added).

139. Bonami 2011, 92.

140. Agnes Gund, author interview, February 2010.

141. Zelevansky interview.

142. Zelevansky interview.

143. Zelevansky was intrigued, for example, by her first verbal exchange with Orozco. When she called the artist to ask for a studio visit, he responded, "I don't have a studio, but we can take a walk." Zelevansky interview.

144. Zelevansky interview.

145. Gund interview.

146. Medina 2002, 43, quoted and discussed in Josten 2004, 65–66.

147. Zelevansky 1993.

148. Interviews by Ena Palaska with curators who were involved in the biennial circuit and worked with Orozco.

149. Yuko Hasegawa, interview by Ena Palaska, June 2021.

150. Enwezor 2002.

151. Orozco interview.

152. As a longtime MoMA board member and the chairman of the trustee's painting and sculpture committee, Leon D. Black commented at the occasion of Temkin's appointment to the chief curator, for example: "One of the big advantages is that we've had the benefit of seeing how scholarly Ann is" (Vogel 2008).

153. Temkin 1999, 175.

154. Kovac 2019.

155. MoMA 2009.

156. Temkin 2009.

157. Barriendos Rodríguez 2011, 362–363; Mosquera 1994.

158. White and White 1993; Shrum 1991; Wijnberg and Gemser 2000. The US-American sociological literature refers to US-European countries, which does not preclude their relevance in other settings, of course.

159. Bourdieu 1996, 170f.

160. Bourdieu 1996, 170f.

161. Bourdieu 1996, 170f.

162. Bydler 2004; Rule and Levine 2013 2. Critics who wrote about Orozco's work in English in such outlets had backgrounds in: Algeria, Chile, France, Germany, Italy, Mexico, South Korea, Sweden, Switzerland, the UK, and the US. It is additionally noteworthy that 50 percent of them hold a PhD in art history or a related field, mostly from US or European universities.

163. As I am interested in valuation across borders, I focus on discursive patterns that were published in a dominant language with the widest possible audience. This does not preclude the fact that other meanings and criteria revolved around Orozco's work before 2010, as previous sections indicated.

164. This expression is from Camnitzer 1997. For other critical discourse contributions that share this aesthetic interpretation, e.g., Zelevansky 1993; Cotter 1993; Kwon 1995; Volk 1995; Ritchie 1995; Lingwood 1996; Fisher 1996; Bürgi 1996; Bonami 1996; Criqui 1996; de Zegher 1996; Springer 1997; Turner 1998; Bonami 2005; Cotter 2009; Pohlenz 2009.

165. The theme was shared by critical discourse in the 1990s and new millennium, e.g. Volk 1995; Papastergiadis 1996; Fisher 1996; Haworth-Both 1996; Brett 1996; Buchloh 1996; Springer 1997; T. Griffin 2000; Nesbit 2000; K. Johnson 2001; Miles 2001; Nesbit 2003; Steiner 2004; Saltz 2009; Temkin et al. 2009.

166. Nesbit 2003; Schuster 2008.

167. Orozco 2004.

168. Bradt 2005; Scott 2005.

169. Buchloh 1993, 49.

170. Buchloh 1996, 2000, 2004.

171. Buchloh 1996, 2004, 2009.

172. Buchloh 1996, 18.

173. Buchloh 2009, 37.

174. Buchloh 1996, 19; 2004, 86; 2009, 42.

175. Criqui 1996; Bürgi 1996; Turner 1998; Frerot 1999; Saltz 1999; Birnbaum 1999; Nesbit 2000; Miles 2001; Dixon 2004; Bois 2006.

176. Bois 2006; Criqui 1996, 91; Frerot 1999; Birnbaum 1999; Nesbit 2000; Dixon 2004.

177. Frerot 1999; Bois 2006.

178. Fisher 1996; cf. also Miles 2001; Buchloh 2004; Criqui 1996.

179. Schjeldahl 2001; Hoare 2006; Dixon 2004; Sundell 2004 ; Viveros-Fauné 2009.

180. Schjeldahl 2009; Hoare 2006; Dixon 2004.

181. Sundell 2004 (emphasis added). Cf. also Hoare 2006.

182. Guiffre 1999.

183. Bourdieu 1996, 231–34, 242–49.

184. For a fascinating ethnographic account of how a more discursive approach is taught at MFA programs in US universities, cf. Fine 2018.

185. Quemin 2002, 2006; cf. also Oguibe 2004 for background on such cases.

186. Santana-Acuña 2014, 2020.

187. Casanova 2004, 135f., 169.

188. Buchholz 2018a.

189. Embedded in a field framework, we must think of the discussed evaluative principles and underlying values as *dominant*, not general, ones, and their relevance to other global careers awaits further research.

190. Wendy Griswold (1987a, 1108) has argued in her seminal contribution that an artwork's "ambiguity"—its capacity to evoke "multiple interpretations"—enhances its cultural power and diffusiveness across countries. In comparison, for the cultural power of a "multivalent" artwork, the diversity of meanings operates not so much at the level of content but at the level of evaluative principles.

191. Orozco interview.

Chapter 7: The Hype of the Chinese Market Star Yue Minjun

1. Pollack 2008, 118.

2. Zhan 2007; as well as statements by art market insiders in semistructured interviews I conducted in 2008 in New York.

3. Zhan 2007.

4. Pollack 2008, 118.

5. According to Artprice's 2007 ranking of best-selling artists, Yue was twenty-fifth. Prince was thirty-fifth, Koons twenty-fourth, and Hirst fifteenth.

6. Cf. appendix D.

7. Olivier Driessens (2013, 543) has suggested to conceptualize "Celebrity capital, or broadly recognizability . . . as accumulated media visibility that results from recurrent media representations."

8. Bourdieu 2001.

9. Yue Minjun, author interview, Beijing, July 2010.

10. Huang 2009, 48.

11. Huang 2009, 48.

12. Yue interview.

13. A *danwei* was an organizational unit that figured as the first level in a multitiered hierarchy linking an individual with the central Communist power structure. The work unit assigned individuals to living quarters, gave them work, and provided food. Its influence was substantial, and permission had to be obtained before undertaking travel, marriage, or having children (cf. Bray 2005).

14. Yue applied to the China Academy of Art in Hangzhou, the Beijing Film Academy, and the art department at Hebei Normal University (Yue interview). None were top-tier art academies (Vine 2008, 12).

15. Yue interview.

16. Huang 2006; cf. also Li Xianting 2005, 25.

17. Li Pi 2005, 35.

18. Erickson 2007, 15. Foreign loan exhibitions were instrumental. Robert Rauschenberg's show at the National Art Gallery Beijing in 1985 was particularly pathbreaking, and more than three hundred thousand people attended.

19. Erickson 2007, 16.

20. Sigg 2005, 15; Chumley 2016.

21. Yue interview.

22. Yue interview; Yue 2006, 20.

23. Smith 2008, 25.

24. Dal Lago 2008, 22; Erickson 2007, 17.

25. Huang 2009, 49; cf. also Smith 2008.

26. Feng 2006a, 49f.

27. Smith 2008, 29.

28. Feng 2006a, 49f.; Dal Lago 2008, 25.

29. Yue 2006, 18.

30. Farrell 2003.

31. Hopfener 2007; Albertini 2008, 9; Dal Lago 2008, 27f.

32. Li Xianting 2005, 26. For an excellent sociological interpretation of the meaning of styles in Chinese art history, cf. J. Zhang 2011.

33. Yue 2006, 20.

34. Yue 2006, 16.

35. Yue 2006, 16.

36. Smith 2008, 30.

37. Li played a pioneering role for promoting the artists' work to foreign curators, media, and collectors, earning him the reputation as the "Godfather" of Chinese contemporary art (Tinari 2007a, 425).

38. Huxley, Aldous. 1993. *Time Must Have a Stop*. London: Chatto & Windus.

39. Li fostered this interpretation in his writings.

40. Erickson 2007, 17; Feng 2006a, 48.

41. Feng 2006a, 48f.

42. Solomon 1993.

43. Sigg 2005, 16.

44. Yue interview.

45. Sigg 2005, 16; cf. also Vine 2008, 14; DeBevoise 2014.

46. Vine 2008, 9.

47. Vine 2008, 9.

48. E.g., the Chinese Exhibition of the 1995 Venice Biennale and an exhibition of Chinese contemporary art at the 1994 São Paulo Biennial.

49. Johnson Chang, author interview, November 2010.

50. Schoeni 1994, 3.

51. E.g., "I hope my laughing character will be seen everywhere, whether through mass-communications or the interaction of our daily lives. If everybody would laugh from their hearts, then the world would be nicer for us." Yue, quoted in Schoeni 1994, 11.

52. Tromans 2000.

53. Harald Szeemann, quoted in Spiegler 2004, 100.

54. Uli Sigg, author interview, June 2010.

55. Vine 2008; Fibicher 2005; Sigg 2005.

56. Storr 1999.

57. Author interviews with experts involved with Chinese contemporary art in 2008, 2010, 2014.

58. Vine 2008, 8.

59. Sigg 2005, 19; Fibicher 2005; cf. also Vine 2008, 8. Another crucial show around that time for deepening and broadening the reception of contemporary art from China was *Inside/Out:*

New Chinese Art. It was curated by Gao Minglu and toured New York, San Francisco, Monterrey (Mexico), Seattle, and Hong Kong from 1998 to 2000. It did not include Yue's work.

60. Author interviews with market intermediaries in 2010 (cf. appendix D).

61. Yue interview.

62. Tang 2011, 75.

63. E.g., Museum of Fine Arts in Bern (2005), Hamburger Kunsthalle (2006), Denver Art Museum (2006), Houston Museum of Fine Arts (2007), and Museum of Modern Art Ludwig in Vienna (2007).

64. Hitomi Iwasaki, author interview, June 2010.

65. Iwasaki interview.

66. Iwasaki interview.

67. Bernstein 2007.

68. Author interview with an involved art market agent, 2010.

69. Archer 2018, 14.

70. Tinari 2007b.

71. Thompson 2014.

72. Sotheby's press release to announce the sale on March 31, 2006. The sale, titled "Contemporary Art Asia," involved artists from other Asian countries, although Chinese artists were featured.

73. Provenance information from Contemporary Art Day Sale, Sotheby's Hong Kong, October 7, 2020.

74. Rangarajan 2006.

75. Eric Chang, Christie's lead specialist, author interview, September 2014.

76. Author interview with an auction specialist in Beijing, September 2014; the statement was echoed in interviews with other Chinese art market agents.

77. Vogel 2006b; Cohn 2006; author interviews.

78. Xu Bing was a 1999 MacArthur Fellow and had eight solo shows at foreign museums by 2006.

79. CNN Edition, October 11, 2007, world news.

80. Interview with Iwasaki, op. cit.

81. Thorpe 2007; Davis 2007; Yuan 2007.

82. Von Drehle 2007.

83. Author interview with an auction expert, July 2010; the statement about "real collectors" going public was confirmed in interviews with other art market agents.

84. Siddique 2006, 215.

85. The first step to attract foreign direct investment was the "Chinese-Foreign-Joint Venture Law" in 1979 (Siddique 2006, 221; K. Zhang 2006, 31). China, however, did not immediately become a destination for investors due to the low quality of its infrastructure and the country's regulations and tariffs. To combat these problems, China first established special economic zones with infrastructural incentives in the 1980s, including favorable tax rates (Siddique 2006, 221).

86. Siddique 2006, 216; D. Smith 2007, 59f.

87. Siddique 2006, 223. Additionally, by 1999, FDI in joint ventures and wholly foreign-owned companies exceeded $250 billion, several times larger than the FDI since World War II in Japan, Korea, and Taiwan combined (Guthrie 2006, 136f.).

88. Y. Wu 2006, 5. Between 1978 and 2002, China's trade to gross domestic product ratio increased by 200 percent. While China ranked thirty-second in the world with regard to its international trade in 1978, it was ranked fifteenth in 1989, tenth in 1997, and sixth in 2001 (Wan, Lu, and Chen 2006, 3; Siddique 2006, 222).

89. By 1991, almost all exports were deregulated, and by 1994, almost all planning on exports was abolished. In the same year, the foreign-trade law significantly liberalized the country's trading sector (Siddique 2006, 219).

90. Deng and Li 2009; cf. Meng 2007.

91. Deng and Li 2009. My discussion focuses on inequality in urban areas (distinguishing further between income/earnings inequality and wealth inequality) since it is associated most strongly with the rise of a consumer class that, given infrastructural opportunities, is concentrated in those locations.

92. Davies et al. 2007; Elegant 2006.

93. Cf. D. Davis 2000; Wang 2006; Melikian 2007.

94. Bourdieu 1996, 231–51.

95. Bourdieu 1996, 242–48.

96. Bourdieu 1996, 262.

97. Aaker 1991. The word "brand" is derived from *brandr*, meaning "to burn," which refers to the burning of a mark onto products as a tool of mass marketing that originated in the nineteenth century. A brand can take many forms (e.g., sign, symbol, color combination, or slogan), but it always signifies specific qualities that distinguish a product and make it easy to remember.

98. Yue interview.

99. Bourdieu et al. 1990.

100. Sans 2009, 169.

101. Yue 2006, 20.

102. Hopfener 2014.

103. Yue interview.

104. Yue interview.

105. Smith 2008, 30f.

106. Smith 2008, 27.

107. Sans 2009, 170.

108. Li and Yue 2005, 19.

109. Li and Yue 2005, 18ff.

110. Feng 2006b.

111. Li and Yue 2005, 19.

112. Yue 2006, 20.

113. Sans 2009, 172.

114. Only 33 percent showed his work more than twice, and 90 percent of his solo exhibitions were singular showings.

115. The other was Plum Blossoms Gallery, which also opened in the 1980s.

116. Koch 2008; Tromans 2000.

117. Tromans 2000.

118. Vine 2008; author interview with an art market agent, 2010.

119. Dieter Ronte, author interview, July 2010.

120. For example, in 1993 Chang was able to broker the first participation of mainland Chinese artists—including Fang Lijun, Wang Guangyi, and Zhang Peili—at the Venice Biennale in addition to co-curating the touring exhibition "China's New Art, Post-1989."

121. Author interviews with mediators in Hong Kong and mainland China, 2010; see also Archer 2018, 3f.

122. Yuan 2007.

123. Author interview of a gallerist in 2010.

124. Cf. provenance information from a Sotheby's Hong Kong sale, October 7, 2020: "Chinese Contemporary, London; Private Collection; Sotheby's, New York, 31 March 2006, Lot 25."

125. In the early 2000s, the gallery was called "Prüss & Ochs Gallery" and was a collaborative venture.

126. Nippe 2006.

127. Muenter 2005 ; Nehb 2010.

128. Alexander Ochs, author interview, July 2010.

129. Barboza 2006b.

130. Barboza 2006b.

131. Urs Meile, author interview, 2010.

132. Meile interview.

133. Meile interview.

134. Velthuis 2007, quoted in Archer 2018, 7.

135. Thompson 2008, 103.

136. Author interviews with auction specialists, 2010, 2014, and 2015.

137. Henry Howard-Sneyd, author interview, 2014; Archer 2018, 3.

138. This contrasted also with strategies by Christie's Hong Kong, which promoted them as part of "Asian contemporary art" auctions in 2005.

139. Evelyn Lin quoted in SCMP Reporter 2004.

140. Author interviews with auction specialists 2010, 2014 and 2015.

141. The official start was the opening of Sotheby's New York's Department for Asian Contemporary Art in May 2005.

142. In Hong Kong, Howard-Sneyd observed that it was Western, not Asian, buyers who were primarily interested in contemporary Chinese works. Howard-Sneyd interview; Archer 2018, 14.

143. Vogel 2006b.

144. Cohn 2006. Sotheby's also scheduled the auction during Asia Week, which draws specialized dealers and collectors from all over the world but especially from Asia (Vogel 2006b).

145. Xiaoming Zhang, author interviews, August and October 2014.

146. Erickson in Sotheby's 2006. This statement could resonate with an emerging global vision in the art field around that time (cf. part 1).

147. Khaire and Wadhwani 2010, 1290.

148. Eric Chang, auction specialist at Christie's, follow up author interviews in May and June 2015. Chang had started to include works by Chinese contemporary artists into mixed China sales in 2000 in Taipei and since 2002 in Hong Kong.

149. E. Chang interview.

150. Sotheby's press release to announce the sale on March 31, 2006.

151. Sotheby's 2006.

152. It needs to be emphasized that the auction's promotion was not merely about a market-based logic. Xiaoming Zhang, a leading expert, thoughtfully involved aesthetic experts and connoisseurs who were deeply familiar with the genre in the auction's preparation, and she also prominently featured artists who were critically recognized. An art installation by Xu Bing, for example, appeared on the catalog's cover. But for Yue's work, with its lower symbolic pedigree, it was primarily a market logic, based on his previous regional sales success, that distinguished him as a hot artist for this event.

153. The bidders' geographic locations included the US (49 percent), Europe (12 percent), mainland China (12 percent), Hong Kong (8 percent), Taiwan (6 percent), the rest of Southeast Asia (9 percent), and other countries (5 percent). Sotheby's press office.

154. Velthuis 2007.

155. Author interviews with directors and specialists of three leading auction houses in China—Guardian, Poly Auction, and Beijing International—2014.

156. The third Shanghai Biennale in 2000, the first to go truly international, is often seen as a turning point for the increasing acceptance of Chinese contemporary art by the government (Vine 2008, 14f.).

157. Hopfener 2007; Feng 2006a, 58; author interviews with Chinese artists and mediators in Beijing in 2010 and 2014.

158. Pollack 2008, 121; Hopfener 2007.

159. Hopfener 2007; Pollack 2008, 118f.

160. Author interviews with art market agents in Beijing in 2014; Vogel 2006b; Cohn 2006.

161. At Poly, Yue's work achieved auction results of over $500,000 and over $100,000 in November 2006, and the works were auctioned off later, though one lot remained unsold. At the Guardian auction, the country's more traditional house, sales were not successful. My interviewees attributed these uneven results to the fact that Yue's less technically rigorous style and his lack of credentials from a prestigious national art academy still mattered in the Chinese field for traditional art buyers and their (long-embodied) tastes.

162. Barboza 2006a.

163. For the term fictional expectations and their role for market dynamics, cf. Beckert 2016.

164. Moulin 1995.

165. Adam 2014, 85.

166. Fraser 1995, 37; Fraser 2016; Larry's List 2016.

167. Crane 2009, 338f.

168. Zahner 2006.

169. Zahner 2006, 252.

170. Crane 1987, 38–39.

171. For example, in view of tax regulations or artworks' political connotations (Zahner 2006, 184f., 252).

172. Author interviews with mediators that were involved with Chinese contemporary art, 2010 and 2014.

173. Kent Logan, author interview, June 2010.

174. Hendrikse 2008, 9.

175. French 2007.

176. Sigg 2005, 16, 18.

177. Sigg interview.

178. Logan interview.

179. K. Lee 2018, 68.

180. Beckert 2016.

181. Velthuis 2007.

182. Cf. Moulin 2003; Zahner 2006. Saatchi, for example—the former owner of the world's largest advertising agency—had been the chief driver of the rise of the Young British Artists in the 1990s, and many sociologists consider him to be an archetype of the speculative collector.

183. Elegant 2006.

184. ArtSpeak China. http://www.artspeakchina.org/mediawiki/index.php/Michael _Goedhuis (October 12, 2010).

185. The investors included Ray Debbane, the chief executive of the Invus Group, a private equity firm in New York and Sacha Lainovic, who was the co-founder and managing partner at the firm (Barboza 2008a).

186. Adam 2008.

187. Barboza 2008a.

188. Barboza 2008a . According to the Louisiana Museum curator Anders Kold, the museum would not have exhibited the collection if it had known that it would be sold afterward. Representatives of the Israel Museum complained that they had not been informed about any intention to sell. Furthermore, Britta Erickson, who edited the catalog, felt misled because she "believed it was to be a personal collection being assembled for the long term" (Barboza 2008a).

189. Elegant 2006.

190. In 2008, for example, he sold twenty-eight photographs by eleven contemporary Chinese artists to MoMA.

191. Petterson 2009 (emphasis added).

192. Moulin 1992, 73f.

193. Quemin 2012, 63.

194. The expression stems from Michelle Kuo in a roundtable discussion of *Artforum*'s summer 2016 issue, where it was unrelated to the case.

Chapter 8: "Global Art" between Autonomy and Heteronomy

1. Rawlings 2001, 42.

2. Crane 2009; Graw 2010.

3. Bourdieu and Wacquant 1992, 110.

4. Cf. also Buchholz 2018b.

5. Buchholz 2016.

6. Cf. also Buchholz 2018b.

7. Cf. also Heilbron 2014; Buchholz 2016.

8. Oberlin and Gieryn 2015, 21.

9. Casanova 2004.

10. Rooms at the major classical art museums, for example, tend to be categorized according to geographic space (e.g., American or European painting, Dutch or Italian painting, etc.).

11. Belting 2009, 55.

12. Bandelj and Wherry 2011, 1f.

Appendices

1. Buchholz 2008a, 2013; Belting, Buddensieg, and Weibel 2013; Lin-Hill 2013.

2. Cf. Buchholz 2008a, 2013; Lin-Hill 2013, 639–40.

3. Bydler 2004; Rule and Levine 2013.

4. Bourdieu 1996, 304. The word "art object" has been replaced here with "global art space," in line with analogical theorizing.

5. Morgner 2014b, 329.

6. Note that Artprice, an alternative data firm, does not provide (or sell) a database of auction houses to researchers. Otherwise, we would have merged and cross-checked the data.

7. Hutter et al. 2007.

8. Velthuis 2007.

9. ArtFacts.Net 2003.

10. ArtFacts.Net 2003.

11. Marek Claassen, ArtFacts.Net director, author interview, February 2012. To be sure, the ranking includes gallery exhibitions because it considers galleries as hybrid brokers between art institutions and commercial ones like auction houses. However, it decidedly weighs these the lowest in comparison to exhibitions at public art institutions. As Susanne Massmann from ArtFacts.Net explains, "We see the gallery (especially the mass of small and middle-sized galleries) as an institution that is definitively part of the market, but also acting like a 'meta-artist' in the sense that they are investing in hope and the future with a high risk-taking endeavor, very often accepting the precariat before being called 'commercial.' A renowned example of this is Betty Parsons Gallery in New York." Email to the author, November 16, 2017.

12. Cf. Bourdieu 1996, 166–73.

13. DeNooy 2002.

14. Velthuis 2007.

15. Bourdieu 1996, 155.

16. Note that having sixteen hundred ranked positions of artists does not mean that the sample contained sixteen hundred artists; there can be overlap between the selected years and cohorts.

17. For example, the regularly published Artprice list of the top five hundred contemporary artists discriminates only by birth year of the artists. It does not consider artistic styles or the kind of auction houses (global or national) at which work is being sold. However, for Chinese artists, for example, a specification whether they work traditionally or are considered more contemporary is crucial to avoid distortions in the results, since traditional Chinese oil paintings tend to achieve higher auction results, especially in China itself.

18. Crane 1987; Danto 1997, 9; Heinich 2012, 700.

19. Danto 1997, 11.

Carroll, Nöel. 2007. "Art and Globalization: Then and Now." *Journal of Aesthetics and Art Criticism* 65 (1): 131–43.

Casanova, Pascale. 2004. *The World Republic of Letters*. Cambridge, MA: Harvard University Press. Originally published 1999.

Chong, Derrick. 2011. "The Emergence of Powerhouse Dealers in Contemporary Art." In *Globalization and Contemporary Art*, edited by Jonathan Harris, 431–62. London: Wiley.

Chumley, Lily. 2016. *Creativity Class: Art School and Culture Work in Postsocialist China*. Princeton, NJ: Princeton University Press.

Claassen, Marek. 2008. "Interview with Marek Claassen, the Director of Artfacts.net." Interview by Zsuzsa Laszlo. *Periferic 8, Biennal for Contemporary Art. Art as Gift*, October 20, 2008. https://perifericbiennial.wordpress.com/2008/10/20/interview-with-with-marek -claassen-the-director-of-artfactsnet/.

Coates, Rebecca. 2014. "From the Margins to the Center: The São Paulo Biennial, the Biennale of Sydney, and the Istanbul Biennial." *Museum Worlds* 2 (1): 113–32.

Cohn, Don. 2006. "Cultural Imports: Sotheby's Brings Chinese Contemporary Art to New York." *Art AsiaPacific* 48 (2006): 56–57.

Collins, Randall. 1998. *The Sociology of Philosophies: A Global Theory of Intellectual Change*. Cambridge, MA: Harvard University Press.

Concannon, Molly. 2005. "Collecting Richard Prince: Strategies of a New Type of Investor in the Contemporary Market." Master's thesis, Courtauld Institute of Art.

Connell, Raewyn. 2007. "The Northern Theory of Globalization." *Sociological Theory* 25(4): 368–385.

Coslor, Erica. 2016. "Transparency in an Opaque Market: Evaluative Frictions between 'Thick' Valuation and 'Thin' Price Data in the Art Market." *Accounting, Organizations, and Society* 50: 13–26.

Coslor, Erica, and Christophe Spaenjers. 2016. "Organizational and Epistemic Change: The Growth of the Art Investment Field." *Accounting, Organizations, and Society* 55: 48–62.

Cotter, Holland. 1993. "Projects: Gabriel Orozco" *New York Times*, September 10, 1993. http://www.nytimes.com/1993/09/10/arts/art-in-review-463093.html.

Cotter, Holland. 2009. "Slicing a Car, Fusing Bicycles and Turning Ideas into Art." *New York Times*, December 14, 2009.

Crane, Diana. 1987. *The Transformation of the Avant-Garde: The New York Art World, 1940–1985*. Chicago: University of Chicago Press.

———. 2002. "Culture and Globalization: Theoretical Models and Emerging Trends." In *Global Culture. Media, Arts, Policy and Globalization*, edited by Diana Crane, Nobuko Kawashima, and Ken'ichi Kawasaki, 1–25. London: Routledge.

———. 2009. "Reflections on the Global Art Market: Implications for the Sociology of Culture." *Sociedade e Estado* 24 (2): 331–62.

———. 2010. "Culture Worlds: From Urban Worlds to Global Worlds." Paper presented at the ESA Research Network Sociology of Culture Midterm Conference: Culture and the Making of Worlds, October 14, 2010.

Cras, Sophie. 2015. "Prizes and Awards in Contemporary Art: Evaluation and Promotion in a Competitive System." *Critique d'Art: Actualité Internationale de la Littérature Critique sur l'Art Contemporain* 45 (Fall–Winter): 1–5.

20. Belting, Buddensieg, and Weibel 2013.

21. Quemin 2002.

22. Galtung 2000, 14.

23. E.g., Abbott and Hrycak 1990; Stovel, Savage, and Bearman 1996; Abbott and Tsay 2000; Accominotti 2009.

24. Hollister 2009, 242.

25. E.g., Stovel and Bolan 2004; Accominotti 2009.

26. Cf. Milligan and Cooper 1985.

27. The graph is listed on this website: https://larissabuchholz.soc.northwestern.edu /research/.

28. The dendogram is accessible on this website: https://larissabuchholz.soc.northwestern .edu/research/.

29. Vaughan 1992, 180.

30. Cf. Vaughan 1992, 178–84.

31. Buchholz 2013. The methodological logic of both rankings is specified in appendix C.

32. The positions of the countries pertain to "contemporary art" specifically, rather than modern art or other art forms. In addition, the case studies begin at the end of the 1980s, and there have been important changes in both countries since the new millennium as rising contexts for the cross-border mediation of *contemporary* art. Area specialists on Mexico might question the label "non-Western" for that country. In this regard, I should point out that the distinction of "West" vs. "non-West" is based on Galtung's meta-geography, as quoted in note 22. For background about the use of this distinction in this book, rather than global north/south, cf. also the note 15 in chapter 1.

33. Zussman 2004, 362.

34. Griswold 1987b, 14ff.

35. Cf. White and White 1993, 76–110.

36. Cf. Baur 2003, 2005; Zahner 2006.

37. Baur 2005, 255ff., 261.

Aaker, David. 1991. *Managing Brand Equity*. New York: Free Press.

Abbing, Hans. 2002. *Why Are Artists Poor? The Exceptional Economy of the Arts*. Amsterdam: Amsterdam University Press.

Abbott, Andrew, and Alexandra Hrycak. 1990. "Measuring Resemblance in Sequence Data: An Optimal Matching Analysis of Musicians' Careers." *American Journal of Sociology* 96 (1): 144–85.

Abbott, Andrew, and Angela Tsay. 2000. "Sequence Analysis and Optimal Matching Methods in Sociology." *Sociological Methods and Research* 29 (1): 3–33.

Accominotti, Fabien. 2009. "Creativity from Interaction: Artistic Movements and the Creativity Careers of Modern Painters." *Poetics* 37 (3): 267–94.

Adam, Georgina. 2008. "Estella Collection Pushes Chinese Contemporary Total to US$51.7m." *Art Newspaper* 17 (191): 69.

———. 2014. *Big Bucks: The Explosion of the Art Market in the 21st Century*. Farnham, UK: Ashgate.

Adams, Laura L. 2007. "Globalization of Culture and the Arts." *Sociology Compass* 1 (1): 127–42.

———. 2008. "Globalization, Universalism, and Cultural Form." *Comparative Studies in Society and History* 50 (3): 614–40.

Albertini, Claudia. 2008. *Avatars and Antiheroes: A Guide to Contemporary Chinese Artists*. New York: Kodansha.

Alexander, Jeffrey C., and Steven Seidman, eds. 1990. *Culture and Society: Contemporary Debates*. Cambridge: Cambridge University Press.

Als, Hilton. 1993. "Whitney Biennial 1993." *Artforum International* 31 (9): 7.

Appadurai, Arjun. 1990. "Disjuncture and Difference in the Global Cultural Economy." *Theory, Culture & Society* 7 (2–3): 295–310.

———. 1996. *Modernity at Large. Cultural Dimensions of Globalization*. Minneapolis: University of Minnesota Press.

———. 1999. "Traditionsängste in globalisierten Kunstkontexten." In *Widerstände. Kunst-Cultural Studies-Neue Medien*, edited by Christian Hoeller, 233–44. Vienna: Folio.

Araeen, Rasheed. 1997. "Westliche Kunst kontra Dritte Welt." In *Inklusion: Exklusion*, edited by Peter Weibel, 98–103. Cologne: DuMont Verlag. Originally published 1978.

———. 2001. "Art & Post-colonial Society." In *Remarks on Interventive Tendencies: Meetings Between Different Economies in Contemporary Art*, edited by Lars Bang Larson, Henrik P. Jakobsen, and Superflex, 19–25. Copenhagen: Danish Contemporary Art Foundation.

Archer, Anita. 2018. "Genesis of an Auction Sale Category: Sotheby's Inaugural Auction of 'Contemporary Chinese Art.'" *Journal for Art Market Studies* 2 (3): 1–15.

Archer, Margaret. 1995. *Realist Social Theory: The Morphogenetic Approach.* Cambridge: Cambridge University Press.

Armstrong, Carol. 2006. "Canon Fodder: Carol Armstrong on the Whitney Museum and Tate Modern Collections." *Artforum International* 45 (3): 113–14.

ArtFacts. 2003. "Artist Ranking. Explanation of the System." Accessed December 4, 2021. https://artfacts.net/lists/global_top_100_artists.

Artprice. 2018. *The Contemporary Art Market Report 2018.* https://www.artprice.com/artprice-reports/the-contemporary-art-market-report-2018/the-contemporary-art-market-report-2018.

ASAC. n.d.-a. "57. Esposizione Internazionale d'Arte: Viva arte viva: Eventi." http://asac.labiennale.org/it/passpres/artivisive/annali.php?m=399&c=e.

ASAC. n.d.-b. "57. Esposizione Internazionale d'Arte: Viva arte viva: Premi." http://asac.labiennale.org/it/passpres/artivisive/annali.php?m=399&c=p.

Ashenfelter, Orlev, and Kathryn Graddy. 2006. "Art Auctions." In *Handbook of the Economics of Art and Culture,* edited by Victor Ginsburgh and David Throsby, 910–45. Amsterdam: Elsevier.

Baia Curioni, Stefano. 2012. "A Fairy Tale: The Art System, Globalization, and the Fair Movement." In *Contemporary Art and Its Commercial Markets: A Report on Current Conditions and Future Scenarios,* edited by Maria Lind and Olav Velthuis, 115–51. Berlin: Sternberg.

Baia Curioni, Stefano, Laura Forti, and Ludovica Leone. 2015. "Making Visible: Artists and Galleries in the Global Art System." In *Cosmopolitan Canvases: The Globalization of Markets for Contemporary Art,* edited by Olav Velthuis and Stefano Baia Curioni, 55–77. Oxford: Oxford University Press.

Bandelj, Nina, and Frederick F. Wherry. 2011. "An Inquiry into the Cultural Wealth of Nations." In *The Cultural Wealth of Nations,* edited Nina Bandelj and Frederick F. Wherry, 1–20. Stanford, CA: Stanford University Press.

Bankowsky, Jack. 2005. "Tent Community: Jack Bankowsky on Art Fair Art." *Artforum International* 44 (2): 228–32.

Barboza, David. 2006a. "Chinese Art Is as Hot in the East as It Is in the West." *New York Times.* https://www.nytimes.com/2006/11/29/arts/design/chinese-art-is-as-hot-in-the-east-as-it-is-in-the-west.html.

———. 2006b. "Urs Meile's Long March into China." *Artzine,* October 10, 2010.

———. 2008a. "An Auction of New Chinese Art Leaves Disjointed Noses in Its Wake." *New York Times,* May 7, 2008.

———. 2008b. "The Many Faces of Yue Minjun." *Artzine,* October 25, 2008.

Barragán, Paco. 2020. *From Roman Feria to Global Art Fair / From Olympia Festival to Neo-Liberal Biennial.* Miami: Artium.

Barriendos Rodríguez, Joaquín. 2011. "Global Art and Politics of Mobility: (Trans) Cultural Shifts in the International Contemporary Art-system." In *Arts and Visibility in Migratory Culture,* edited by Mieke Bal and Miguel Hernandez-Navarro, 341–381. Amsterdam, Netherlands: Rodopi.

Basualdo, Carlos. 1997. "Maxima Moralia." *Artforum International* 35 (6): 58–63.

Baumann, Shyon. 2001. "Intellectualization and Art World Development: Film in the United States." *American Sociological Review* 66 (3): 404–26.

———. 2007. "A General Theory of Artistic Legitimation: How Art Worlds Are like Social Movements." *Poetics* 35 (1): 47–65.

Baur, Nina. 2003. *Die biografische Methode. Ein Verfahren zur Qualitativen Analyse Individueller Verlaufsmuster in den Sozialwissenschaften. Reihe: Bamberger Beiträge zur empirischen Sozialforschung* 3. Bamberg: Otto-Friedrich-Universität Bamberg.

———. 2005. *Verlaufsmusteranalyse. Methodologische Konsequenzen der Zeitlichkeit Sozialen Handelns.* Wiesbaden: VS Verlag für Sozialwissenschaften.

Beck, Ulrich. 2000. *What Is Globalization?* Hoboken, NJ: Wiley.

———. 2002. "The Cosmopolitan Society and Its Enemies." *Theory, Culture & Society* 19 (1–2): 17–44.

Becker, Howard S. 1982. *Art Worlds.* Berkeley: University of California Press.

Beckert, Jens. 2016. *Imagined Futures: Fictional Expectations and Capitalist Dynamics.* Cambridge, MA: Harvard University Press.

Beckert, Jens, and Jörg Rössel. 2013. "The Price of Art: Uncertainty and Reputation in the Art Field." *European Societies* 15 (2): 178–95.

Belcove, Julie L. 2007. "Marian Goodman: Tiny in Stature but with a Commanding Presence in the Art World." *W*, November 11, 2007.

Bell, Daniel. 1999. "The End of Ideology in the West." In *Social Theory: The Multicultural and Classic Readings*, edited by Charles C. Lemert, 409–47. Boulder, CO: Westview.

Belting, Hans. 2008. "The Question of Global Art." In *Contemporary Art and the Museum: A Global Perspective*, edited by Andrea Buddensieg and Peter Weibel. Ostfildern, Germany: Hatje Cantz.

———. 2009. "Contemporary Art as Global Art: A Critical Estimate." In *The Global Art World: Audiences, Markets, and Museums*, edited by Hans Belting, Andrea Buddensieg, and Peter Weibel, 38–73. Ostfildern, Germany: Hatje Cantz.

———. 2012. "Contemporary Art and the Museum in the Global Age." *Disputatio. Philosophical Research Bulletin* 1 (2): 16–30

———. 2013. "From World Art to Global Art: View on a New Panorama." In *The Global Contemporary and the Rise of New Art Worlds*, edited by Hans Beltin, Andrea Buddensieg, and Peter Weibel, 178–85. Cambridge, MA: MIT Press.

Belting, Hans, Andrea Buddensieg, and Peter Weibel, eds. 2013. *The Global Contemporary and the Rise of New Art Worlds.* Cambridge, MA: MIT Press.

Benson, Rodney. 1999. "Field Theory in Comparative Context: A New Paradigm for Media Studies." *Theory and Society* 28 (3): 463–98.

Bernstein, Richard. 2007. "An Artist's Famous Smile: What Lies Behind It?" *New York Times*, November 13, 2007.

Bhabha, Homi K., and Jonathan Rutherford. 1990. "Third Space. Interview with Homi Bhabha" in *Identity: Community, Culture, Difference*, edited by Rutherford, Jonathan, 207–221, London: Lawrence and Wishart, 207–221.

Bielby, Denise D., and C. Lee Harrington. 2008. *Global TV: Exporting Television and Culture in the World Market.* New York: New York University Press.

Bishop, Claire. 2005. *Installation Art: A Critical History.* London: Routledge.

Birnbaum, Daniel. 1999. "Carte Blanche: Orozco on the Beach." In *Gabriel Orozco: Chacahua*, edited by Gabriel Orozco and Daniel Birnbaum, 72–75. Frankfurt am Main: Portikus.

———. 2004. "Sampling the Globe." *Artforum International* 43 (2): 240–44.

Block, René. 2013. "We Hop On, We Hop Off: The Ever-Faster Spinning Carousel of Biennials." *Yishu. Journal of Contemporary Chinese Art* 12 (3): 26–36.

Boecker, Susanne. 2002. "Austausch oder globaler Inzest? 2. Konferenz Biennalen im Dialog in Frankfurt." *Kunstforum International* 29 (161): 422–26.

Bois, Yves-Alain. 2006. "The Tree and the Knight." In *Gabriel Orozco*, edited by Gabriel Orozco, Yves-Alain Bois, Benjamin H. D. Buchloh, and Briony Fer, 42–65. Mexico City: Museo del Palacio de Bellas Artes.

Boltanski, Luc, and Arnaud Esquerre. 2016. "The Economic Life of Things. Commodities, Collectibles, Assets." *New Left Review* 98: 31–54.

Boltanski, Luc, and Arnaud Esquerre. 2020. *Enrichment: A Critique of Commodities*. Hoboken, NJ: Wiley.

Bonami, Francesco. 1993. "Gabriel Orozco." *Flash Art* 26 (171): 93.

———. 1994. "Gabriel Orozco." *Flash Art International* March/April (175): 95.

———. 1996. "Gabriel Orozco: Back in Five Minutes." *Parkett* 18 (48): 40–53.

———. 1998. "Sudden Death: Roughs, Fairways, and the Game of Awareness—Gabriel Orozco." *Parachute* 90 (April–June): 26–32.

———. 2005. "Francesco Bonami on Joseph Beuys." *Tate Etc.* 3: 88–93.

———. 2011. "The Early Adventures: Gabriel Orozco." *Tate Etc.* 21: 92–95.

Bongard, Willi. 1974. "Zu Fragen des Geschmacks in der Rezeption Bildender Kunst der Gegenwart." *Künstler und Gesellschaft. Kölner Zeitschrift für Soziologie und Sozialpsychologie, Sonderheft* 17 (26): 250–64.

Bourdieu, Pierre. 1977. *Outline of a Theory of Practice*. Cambridge: Cambridge University Press. Originally published 1972.

———. 1984. *Distinction: A Social Critique of the Judgement of Taste*. Cambridge, MA: Harvard University Press. Originally published 1979.

———. 1991. "Epilogue: On the Possibility of a Field of World Sociology." In *Social Theory for a Changing Society*, edited by Pierre Bourdieu and James Coleman, 373–87. Boulder, CO: Westview.

———. 1993. *The Field of Cultural Production*. New York: Columbia University Press.

———. 1996. *The Rules of Art: Genesis and Structure of the Literary Field*. Cambridge, UK: Polity. Originally published 1992.

———. 1998. *Countre-Feux. Propos pour servir à la résistance contre l'invasion Néo-Libérale*. Paris: Liber-Raisons d'Agir.

———. 1999. *On Television*. New York: New Press.

———. 2001. "The Forms of Capital." In *The Sociology of Economic Life*, edited by Mark Granovetter and Richard Swedberg, 96–111. Boulder, CO: Westview.

———. 2003. "Unite and Rule." In *Firing Back: Against the Tyranny of the Market* 2, edited by Pierre Bourdieu, 82–96. New York: New Press.

Bourdieu, Pierre, Alain Darbel, and Dominique Schnapper. 1990. *The Love of Art. European Art Museums and their Public*. Stanford: Stanford University Press.

Bourdieu, Pierre, and Loïc Wacquant. 1992. *An Invitation to Reflexive Sociology*. Chicago: University of Chicago Press.

Bourdieu, Pierre, and Hans Haacke. 1995. *Free Exchange*. Cambridge, UK: Polity Press.

Bowley, Graham. 2013. "For Art Dealers, a New Life on the Fair Circuit." *New York Times*, August 22, 2013. https://www.nytimes.com/2013/08/22/arts/for-art-dealers-a-new-life-on-the-fair-circuit.html.

Boxer, Sarah. 2005. "Picasso and Warhol. Neck and Neck." *New York Times*, January 22, 2005. https://www.nytimes.com/2005/01/22/arts/design/picasso-and-warhol-neck-and-neck.html.

Bradt, Steve. 2005. "Buchloh Named Rosenblatt Professor of Modern Art." *Harvard University Gazette*, June 16, 2005. http://news.harvard.edu/gazette/2005/06.16/07-buchloh.html.

Braudel, Fernand. 2009. "History and the Social Sciences: The Longue Durée." *Review* 32 (2): 171–203.

Bray, David. 2005. *Social Space and Governance in Urban China: The Danwei System from Origins to Reform*. Stanford, CA: Stanford University Press.

Brenson, Michael. 1999. "Michael Brenson talks with Madeleine Grynsztejn. *Artforum International* 38 (1).

Brett, Guy. 1996. "The Light Touch." In *Empty Club*, edited by Gabriel Orozco, James Lingwood, Jean Fisher, Mark Haworth-Booth, and Guy Brett, 100–106. London: Artangel.

Bromberg, Minna, and Gary Alan Fine. 2002. "Resurrecting the Red: Pete Seeger and the Purification of Difficult Reputations." *Social Forces* 80 (4): 1135–55.

Brubaker, Rogers. 1993. "Social Theory as Habitus." in *Bourdieu: Critical Perspectives*, edited by Craig J. Calhoun, Edward Lipuma and Moishe Postpone, 212–34. Cambridge: Cambridge University Press.

Buchholz, Larissa. 2006. "Field Theory and the Globalization of Art: Rethinking 'Interdependency.'" Paper presented at the conference "Field Theory and the Globalization of Art: Rethinking 'Interdependency': Practicing Bourdieu, in the Field & across the Disciplines, an International and Interdisciplinary Conference," University of Michigan, Ann Arbor, September 28–30, 2006.

———. 2008a. "Feldtheorie und Globalisierung." In *Nach Bourdieu: Kunst, Visualität, und Politik*, edited by Beatrice von Bismarck, Therese Kaufmann, and Ulf Wuggenig, 211–38. Vienna: Turia + Kant.

———. 2008b. "Field Theory and Cultural Globalization: The Case of the Contemporary Visual Arts." Working paper, Department of Sociology, Columbia University.

———. 2013. "The Global Rules of Art." PhD diss., Columbia University.

———. 2016. "What Is a Global Field? Theorizing Fields Beyond the Nation-State." *Sociological Review* 64 (2): 31–60.

———. 2017. "The Nested Structure of a Global Status Market: The Rise of Chinese Contemporary Art." Working paper, presented at the Department of Sociology, April 12 2018, Northwestern University.

———. 2018a. "Beyond Reproduction: Asymmetrical Interdependencies and the Transformation of Centers and Peripheries in the Globalizing Visual Arts." In *Art and the Challenge of Markets*, vol. 1, edited by Victoria D. Alexander, Samuli Hägg, Simo Häyrynen, and Erkki Sevänen, 277–304. Cham, Switzerland: Palgrave Macmillan.

———. 2018b. "Rethinking the Center-Periphery Model: Dimensions and Temporalities of Macro-Structure in a Global Field of Cultural Production." *Poetics* 71 (December): 18–32.

Buchholz, Larissa, Gary A. Fine, and Hannah Wohl. 2020. "Art Markets in Crisis: How Personal Bonds and Market Subcultures Mediate the Effects of COVID-19." *American Journal of Cultural Sociology* 8 (3): 462–76.

Buchholz, Larissa, and Ulf Wuggenig. 2005. "Cultural Globalisation between Myth and Reality: The Case of the Contemporary Visual Arts." *Glocalogue* 4. http://artefact.mi2.hr/_a04/lang_en/theory_buchholz_en.htm.

Buchloh, Benjamin H. D. 1993. "Refuse and Refuge." In *Gabriel Orozco*, exhibition catalogue, edited by Catherine de Zegher, 38–51. Kortrijk, Belgium: Kanaal Art Foundation.

———. 1996. "Gabriel Orozco: Die Skulptur des Alltagslebens." In *Gabriel Orozco*, edited by Gabriel Orozco, Bernhard Bürgi, Bettina Marbach, and Benjamin H. D. Buchloh, 11–36. Zurich: Kunsthalle Zurich.

———. 2000. "Gabriel Orozco: The Sculpture of Everyday Life." In *Gabriel Orozco*, edited by Alma Ruiz, Gabriel Kuri, Benjamin H. D. Buchloh, Damian Ortega, Molly Nesbit, and Abraham Cruzvillegas, 66–102. Los Angeles: Museum of Contemporary Art.

———. 2004. "Cosmic Reification: Gabriel Orozco's Photographs." In *Gabriel Orozco*, edited by Gabriel Orozco, Briony Fer, Benjamin H. D. Buchloh, and Rochelle Steiner, 75–96. London: Serpentine Gallery.

———. 2009. "Sculpture between Nation-States and Global Commodity Production." In *Gabriel Orozco*, edited by Ann Temkin, Anne Byrd, Benjamin H. D. Buchloh, Briony Fer, and Paulina Pobocha, 34–43. New York: Museum of Modern Art.

Buchloh, Benjamin H. D., and Yve-Alain Bois. 1997. "Critical Reflections." *Artforum International* 35 (5): 68–69.

Buckermann, Paul. 2021. "Ranking Art: Paradigmatic Worldviews in the Quantification and Evaluation of Contemporary Art." *Theory, Culture & Society* 38 (4): 89–109.

Bull, Malcolm. 2011. "The Two Economies of World Art." In *Globalization and Contemporary Art*, edited by Jonathan Harris, 179–90. Malden, MA: Wiley-Blackwell.

Bürgi, Bernhard. 1996. "Die Ausdehnung der Reflexion." In *Gabriel Orozco*, edited by Gabriel Orozco, Bernhard Bürgi, Bettina Marbach, and Benjamin H. D. Buchloh, 5–6. Zurich: Kunsthalle Zurich.

Bydler, Charlotte. 2004. *The Global Art World, Inc.: On the Globalization of Contemporary Art.* Uppsala, Sweden: Uppsala University Press.

Calhoun, Craig. "Cosmopolitanism: The Class-Consciousness of Frequent Flyers." *South Atlantic Quarterly* 101: 869–97.

Calhoun, Craig J. 2005. "Informationstechnologie und die Internationale öffentliche Sphäre." In *Publicum. Theorien der Öffentlichkeit*, edited by Gerald Raunig and Ulf Wuggenig, 164–75. Vienna: Turia + Kant.

Cameron, Dan. 1997. "Glocal Warming." *Artforum International* 36 (4): 17.

———. 1999. "Best of the 90s: 10 Top Tens." *Artforum International* 38 (4): 132.

Camnitzer, Luis. 1993. "The Whitney Biennial." *Third Text* 7 (23): 128–30.

———. 1997. "The 1997 Whitney Biennial, Meta-Spectacle." *Art Nexus* 11 (25): 84–88.

Criqui, Jean-Pierre. 1996. "Like a Rolling Stone: Gabriel Orozco." *Artforum International* 34 (8): 88–93.

Dal Lago, Francesca. 2008. "The Voice of the 'Superfluous People': Painting in China in the Late 1980s and Early 1990s." In *Writing on the Wall: Chinese New Realism and Avant-Garde in the Eighties and Nineties*, edited by Cees Hendrikse, 21–32. Rotterdam: Nai.

Danto, Arthur C. 1997. *After the End of Art: Contemporary Art and the Pale of History*. Princeton, NJ: Princeton University Press.

Davies, James B., Susanna Sandstrom, Anthony Shorrocks, and Edward N. Wolff. 2007. "The World Distribution of Household Wealth." Paper presented at the Conference on Mapping Global Inequalities, Center for Global, International and Regional Studies, University of California at Santa Cruz, December 13, 2007.

Davis, Ben. 2007. "Guy Smiley." *Artnet Magazine*, November 11, 2007. http://www.artnet.com /magazineus/reviews/davis/davis11-12-07.asp.

Davis, Deborah, ed. 2000. *Consumer Revolution in Urban China*. Berkeley: University of California Press.

DeBevoise, Jane. 2014. *Between State and Market: Chinese Contemporary Art in the Post-Mao Era*. Leiden, Netherlands: Brill.

Debroise, Olivier. 1993. "Gabriel Orozco en el MoMA." *La Jornada*, September 21, 1993. http:// www.arte-mexico.com/critica/od38.htm.

Medina, Cuauhtémoc, and Olivier Debroise. 2007. *The Age of Discrepancies: Art and Visual Culture in Mexico 1968–1997*. Nashville: Turner.

Deng, Quheng, and Shi Li. 2009. "What Lies behind Rising Earnings Inequality in Urban China? Regression-Based Decompositions." *CESifo Economic Studies* 55 (3–4): 598–623.

DeNooy, Wouter. 2002. "The Dynamics of Artistic Prestige." *Poetics* 30 (3): 147–67.

DeNora, Tia. 1995. *Beethoven and the Construction of Genius*. Berkeley: University of California Press.

Dezalay, Yves, and Bryant Garth. 1996. *Dealing in Virtue: International Commercial Arbitration and the Construction of a Transnational Legal Order*. Chicago: University of Chicago Press.

Dezalay, Yves. 2006. "State Expertise on the International Market: Professional rivalries between lawyers and economists." Paper presented at the Conference: Field Theory and the Globalization of Art: Rethinking 'Interdependency.'" *Practicing Bourdieu, In the Field & Across the Disciplines. An International and Interdisciplinary Conference*. University of Michigan, Ann Arbor, September 28–30, 2006.

de Zegher, Catherine. 1996. "The Os of Orozco." *Parkett* 18 (48): 55–67.

Dimendberg, Edward, and Julian Rose. 2015. "Bright Lights, Big City: Julian Rose and Edward Dimendberg on the Broad Museum and Urban Development in LA." *Artforum International* 54 (2): 139–50.

Dornhof, Sarah, Nanne Buurman, Birgit Hopfener, and Barbara Lutz, eds. 2018. *Situating Global Art: Topologies-Temporalities-Trajectories*. Bielefeld, Germany: Transcript Verlag.

Dowd, Timothy J., and Susanne Janssen. 2011. "Globalization and Diversity in Cultural Fields: Comparative Perspectives on Television, Music and Literature." *American Behavioral Scientist* 55 (5): 519–24.

Driessens, Olivier. 2013. "Celebrity Capital: Redefining Celebrity Using Field Theory." *Theory and Society* 42 (5): 543–60.

Dromi, Shai M. 2016. "Soldiers of the Cross: Calvinism, Humanitarianism, and the Genesis of Social Fields." *Sociological Theory* 34 (3): 196–219.

———. 2020. *Above the Fray: The Red Cross and The Making of the Humanitarian NGO Sector.* Chicago: University of Chicago Press.

Durkheim, Émile. (1912) 2001. *Elementary Forms of Religious Life.* New York: Oxford University Press.

Dziewior, Yilmaz. 1999. "On the Move. Interkulturelle Tendenzen in der aktuellen Kunst." In *Kunstwelten im Dialog—von Gauguin zur Globalen Gegenwart,* edited by Marc Scheps, Yilmaz Dziewor, and Barbara Thiemann, 345–50. Cologne: DuMont.

Ehrmann, Thierry. 2011. "Exclusive Interview with Thierry Ehrmann, the Founder and CEO of Artprice.com." *Art Market Insight,* June 11, 2011. http://web.artprice.com/AMI/AMI.aspx?id =NzU3OTY4MjE3MDM4NDk=.

Elegant, Simon. 2006. "The Great China Sale." *Time,* November 19, 2006.

Elkins, James, ed. 2007. *Is Art History Global?* Vol. 3. Abingdon, UK: Taylor and Francis.

Elkins, James, Zhivka Valiavicharska, and Alice Kim, eds. 2010. *Art and Globalization.* University Park: Pennsylvania State University Press.

Enwezor, Okwui. 2002. "The Black Box, 2002." in *Documenta 11, Platform 5: Exhibition Catalogue,* 42–55. Ostfildern, Germany: Hatje Cantz.

Enwezor, Okwui. 2011. "Spring Rain." *Artforum International* 49 (10): 75–76.

Erickson, Britta. 2007. "An Explosion of Possibilities." In *China Onward: The Estella Collection: Chinese Contemporary Art, 1966–2006,* edited by Frances Bowles, 12–19. Humlebæk, Denmark: Louisiana Museum of Modern Art.

Farrell, Michael P. 2003. *Collaborative Circles: Friendship Dynamics and Creative Work.* Chicago: University of Chicago Press.

Favell, Adrian. 2015. "The Contemporary Art Market in Galapagos: Japan and the Global Art World." In *Cosmopolitan Canvases: The Globalization of Markets for Contemporary Art,* edited by Olav Velthuis and Stefano B. Curioni, 238–63. Oxford: Oxford University Press.

Fraser, Andrea. 1995. "Es ist Kunst, wenn ich sage, dass es das ist, oder . . ." *Texte zur Kunst* 5 (20): 35–40.

Fraser, Andrea. 2016. in *Museums, Money, and Politics.* Cambridge, MA: MIT Press.

Featherstone, Mike, ed. 1990. *Global Culture: Nationalism, Globalization and Modernity.* London: Sage.

Feng Boyi. 2006a. "A Single Spark Can Start a Prairie Fire—Chinese Avant-Garde since the 1990s." In *China Now,* edited by Günther Oberhollenzer, S. Zein, Anna Szöke, M. Maresch, 44–65. Klosterneuburg, Austria: Edition Sammlung Essl Privatstiftung.

———. 2006b. "To Be Is Just Absurd: The Art of Yue Minjun." In *Reproduction Icons: Yue Minjun Works, 2004–2006,* edited by Minjun Yue, 6–15. Shenzhen, China: Museum Collection Services.

Fer, Briony. 2006. "Crazy About Saturn: Gabriel Orozco Interviewed by Briony Fer." in *Gabriel Orozco. October Files,* edited by Yves Alain Bois, 157–180. Cambridge: MIT Press.

Ferguson, Bruce, Reesa Greenberg, and Sandy Nairne. 2005. "Mapping International Exhibitions." In *The Manifesta Decade. Contemporary Art Exhibitions and Biennials in Post-Wall Europe,* edited by Barbara Vanderlinden and Elena Filipovic, 47–56. Cambridge, MA: MIT Press.

Ferguson, Bruce W. and Milena M. Hoegsberg. 2010. "Talking and Thinking about Biennials: The Potential of Discursivity." In *The Biennale Reader*, edited by Filipovic, Elena, Solveig C. Øvstebø, and Marieke van Hal. 360–373. Bergen, Norway: Bergen Kunsthall.

Ferguson, Priscilla P. 1998. "A Cultural Field in the Making: Gastronomy in 19th Century France." *American Journal of Sociology* 104 (3): 597–641.

Fibicher, Bernhard. 2005. "Cultural Partnerships, Maybe More: On the Reception of Contemporary Chinese Art in the West." In *Mahjong: Contemporary Chinese Art from the Sigg Collection*, edited Bernhard Fibicher, 41–49. New York: Art Publishers.

Filipovic, Elena, Solveig C. Øvstebø, and Marieke van Hal, eds. 2010. *The Biennial Reader: An Anthology on Large-Scale Perennial Exhibitions of Contemporary Art: The Bergen Biennial Conference*. Bergen, Norway: Bergen Kunsthall.

Filipovic, Elena, Marieke van Hal, and Solveig Øvstebø. 2010. "Biennialogy." in *The Biennale Reader*, edited by Filipovic, Elena, Solveig C. Øvstebø, and Marieke van Hal, 12–27. Bergen, Norway: Bergen Kunsthall.

Fillitz, Thomas. 2011. "Worldmaking: The Cosmopolitanization of Dak'Art, the Art Biennial of Dakar." In *Global Studies: Mapping Contemporary Art and Culture*, edited by Hans Belting, Jacob Birken, and Andrea Buddensieg 382–401. Ostfildern, Germany: Hatje Cantz.

Fillitz, Thomas. 2014. "The Booming Global Market of Contemporary Art." *Focaal* 69: 84–96.

Fine, Gary A. 2018. *Talking Art*. Chicago: University of Chicago Press.

Fisher, Jean. 1996. "The Play of the World." In *Empty Club*, edited by Gabriel Orozco, James Lingwood, Jean Fisher, Mark Haworth-Booth, and Guy Brett, 16–25. London: Artangel.

Fleck, Robert. 2009. *Die Biennale von Venedig: Eine Geschichte des 20. Jahrhunderts*. Hamburg: Philo Fine Arts.

Fligstein, Neil, and Doug McAdam. 2012. *A Theory of Fields*. Oxford: Oxford University Press.

Foucault, Michel. 1988. *The History of Sexuality. Vol I: An Introduction*. New York: Vintage Books. Originally published 1976.

Fourcade-Gourinchas, Marion. 2006. "The Construction of a Global Profession: The Transnationalization of Economics." *American Journal of Sociology* 112 (1): 145–94.

Fourcade-Gourinchas, Marion, and Sarah Babb. 2002. "The Rebirth of the Liberal Creed: Paths to Neoliberalism in Four Countries." *American Journal of Sociology* 108 (3): 533–79.

Fox, Catherine. 1993. "Surveying the Whitney Biennial: Angry Show Scans Politics of Race and Sex." *Atlanta Journal-Constitution*.

Freeman, Nate. 2019. "The Rise and Fall of Mary Boone." *Artsy*, February 14, 2019. https://www.artsy.net/article/artsy-editorial-rise-fall-mary-boone-revolutionary-art-dealer-going-prison-tax-fraud.

French, Christopher. 2007. "Interview with Robert Chaney." *Glasstire*. July 20, 2007. https://glasstire.com/2007/07/20/interview-with-robert-chaney/.

Frerot, Christine. 1999. "Gabriel Orozco: Museum of Modern Art of the City of Paris." *Art Nexus* 13 (31): 111–12.

Galtung, Johan. 2000. "Globale Migration." In *Zuwanderung im Zeichen der Globalisierung*, edited by Christoph Butterwegge and Gudrun Hentges, 9–19. Opladen, Germany: VS Verlag für Sozialwissenschaften.

García-Antón, Katya. 1998. "Dak'art 98." *Third Text* 12 (44): 87–92.

Gardner, Anthony, and Charles Green. 2013. "Biennials of the South on the Edges of the Global." *Third Text* 27 (4): 442–55.

Gartman, David. 2002. "Bourdieu's Theory of Cultural Change: Explication, Application, Critique." *Sociological Theory* 20 (2): 255–77.

Gell, Aaron. 2009. "Crazy Tourist: Conceptual Artist Gabriel Orozco Travels the World, Finding Art in the Most Unusual Places." *United Hemispheres,* December 2009. http://www .hemispheresmagazine.com/2009/12/01/crazy-tourist/.

Ghurka Blog. 2021. "Art Basel's Art World Domination." October 6, 2021. https://ghurka.com /blogs/journal/art-basel-s-art-world-domination.

Giddens, Anthony. 1996. *Konsequenzen der Moderne.* Frankfurt am Main: Suhrkamp.

Gilmore, Jonathan. 2003. "Discipline Problem." *Artforum International* 42 (2): 35–36.

Go, Julian. 2008. "Global Fields and Imperial Forms: Field Theory and the British and American Empires." *Sociological Theory* 26 (3): 201–29.

Go, Julian, and Monika Krause. 2016. "Fielding Transnationalism: An Introduction." *Sociological Review* 64 (2): 6–30.

Goodwin, James. 2008. Introduction to *The International Art Markets: The Essential Guide for Collectors and Investors,* edited by James Goodwin, 1–32. London: Kogan Page.

Gorski, Philip S. E. 2013a. "Bourdieu as a Theorist of Change." in *Bourdieu and Historical Analysis,* edited by Philip Gorski, 1–18. Durham, NC: Duke University Press.

———. 2013b. "What is Critical Realism? And Why Should You Care?" *Contemporary Sociology* 45 (2): 658–70.

Gottwald, Sandra. 2008. "Capital Kunstmarkt-Kompass. Nach Art des Hauses." *Capital,* November 6, 2008. http://www.capital.de/guide/kunstmarkt-kompass/:Kunstmarkt-Kompass --Nach-Art-des-Hauses/100016268.html.

Graña, César. 1964. *Bohemian versus Bourgeois: French Society and the French Man of Letters in the Nineteenth century.* New York: Basic Books.

Graw, Isabelle. 2010. *High Price: Art Between the Market and Celebrity Culture.* Berlin: Lukas and Sternberg.

Graw, Isabelle. 2012. "In the Grip of the Market? On the Relative Heteronomy of Art, the Art World, and Art Criticism." In *Contemporary Art and Its Commercial Markets: A Report on Current Conditions and Future Scenarios,* edited by Maria Lind and Olav Velthuis, 183–207. Berlin: Sternberg.

Green, Charles. 1993. "Biennale." *Artforum International* 31 (8): 110.

Greenberg, Clement. 1961. *Art and Culture.* Boston: Beacon.

Griffin, Michael. 2002. "From Cultural Imperialism to Transnational Commercialization: Shifting Paradigms in International Media Studies." *Global Media Journal* 1 (1): 1–27.

Griffin, Tim. 2000. "Gabriel Orozco's Game Gets Real." *Art on Paper* 4 (3): 51–55.

Griffin, Tim, James Meyer, Francesco Bonami, Catherine David, Okwui Enwezor, Hans Ulrich Obrist, Marta Rosler, and Yinka Shonibare. 2003. "Global Tendencies: Globalism and the Large-Scale Exhibition." *Artforum International* 42 (3): 152–63.

Griswold, Wendy. 1987a. "The Fabrication of Meaning: Literary Interpretation in the United States, Great Britain, and the West Indies." *American Journal of Sociology* 92 (1): 1077–1117.

———. 1987b. "A Methodological Framework for the Sociology of Culture." *Sociological Methodology* 17 (1): 1–35.

———. 1992. "The Writing on the Mud Wall: Nigerian Novels and the Imaginary Village." *American Sociological Review* 57 (6): 709–24.

———. 1994. *Cultures and Societies in a Changing World.* Thousand Oaks, CA: Sage.

Guasch, Anna Maria. 2017. "Art and Globalisation: The Beginnings: Third Text versus Art in America." *MODOS: Revista de História da Arte* 1 (2): 22–28.

Guiffre, Katherine. 1999. "Sandpiles of Opportunity: Success in the Art World." *Social Forces* 77 (3): 815–32.

Guilbaut, Serge. 1983. *How New York Stole the Idea of Modern Art*. Chicago: University of Chicago Press.

Guillén, Mauro F. 2001. "Is Globalization Civilizing, Destructive or Feeble? A Critique of Five Key Debates in the Social Science Literature." *Annual Review of Sociology* 27 (August): 235–60.

Guthrie, Doug. 2006. *China and Globalization: The Social, Economic and Political Transformation of Chinese Society*. New York: Routledge.

Haidu, Rachel. 2011. "Luis Camnitzer." *Artforum International* 49 (9): 272.

———. 2010. "Faux Terrain. On Gabriel Orozco at the Museum of Modern Art, New York." *Texte zur Kunst* 77: 240–247.

Hall, Stuart. 1992a. "The Question of Cultural Identity." In *Modernity and its Futures*, edited by Stuart Hall, David Held, and Anthony McGrew, 274–325. Cambridge: Polity Press.

———. 1992b. "The West and the Rest: Discourse and Power." In *Formations of Modernity*, edited by Stuart Hall and Bam Gieben, 275–332. Cambridge, UK: Polity.

Hannerz, Ulf. 1987. "The World in Creolization." *Africa* 57 (4): 546–59.

———. 1992. *Cultural Complexity: Studies in the Social Organization of Meaning*. New York: Columbia University Press.

Hanrou, Hou. 1994. "Entropy: Chinese Artists, Western Art Institutions: A New Internationalism." In *Global Visions: Towards a New Internationalism in the Visual Arts*, edited by Jean Fisher, 79–88. London: Kala.

Hanrou, Hou, and Gao Minglu. 1998. "Strategies of Survival in the Third Space: A Conversation on the Overseas Chinese Artists in the 1990s." In *Inside Out: New Chinese Art*, edited by Gao Minglu, 183–89. Berkeley: University of California Press.

Haworth-Booth, Mark. 1996. "The Atomists." In *Empty Club*, edited by Gabriel Orozco, James Lingwood, Jean Fisher, Mark Haworth-Booth, and Guy Brett, 52–57. London: Artangel.

Heartney, Eleanor. 1993. "Report from New York: Identity Politics at the Whitney." *Art in America* 81 (5): 42–47.

Heilbron, Johan. 1999. "Toward a Sociology of Translation: Book Translations as a Cultural World-System." *European Journal of Social Theory* 2 (4): 429–44.

Heilbron, Johan. 2014. "The Social Sciences as an Emerging Global Field." *Current Sociology* 62 (5): 685–703.

Heinich, Nathalie. 1997. *The Glory of Van Gogh: An Anthropology of Admiration*. Princeton, NJ: Princeton University Press.

———. 1998. *Le triple jeu de l'art contemporain: Sociologie des arts plastiques*. Paris: Minuit.

———. 2012. "Mapping Intermediaries in Contemporary Art According to Pragmatic Sociology." *European Journal of Cultural Studies* 15 (6): 695–702.

Heinich, Natalie, and Michel Pollak (1996 [1989]) "From Museum Curator to Exhibition Auteur: Inventing a Singular Position." In *Thinking about Exhibitions*, edited by Bruce W. Ferguson, Reesa Greenberg, and Sandy Nairne, 166–179. London: Routledge.

Heise, Tatiana, and Andrew Tudor. 2007. "Constructing (Film) Art: Bourdieu's Field Model in a Comparative Context." *Cultural Sociology* 1 (2): 165–87.

Held, David, Anthony McGrew, David Goldblatt, and Jonathan Perraton. 1999. "Globalization, Culture and the Fate of Nations." In *Global Transformations*, edited by David Held, Anthony McGrew, David Goldblatt, and Jonathan Perraton, 327–75. Stanford, CA: Stanford University Press.

Held, David and Andrew McGrew. "The Great Globalization Debate: An Introduction." In *The Global Transformation Reader*, edited by David Held and Andrew McGrew, 67–86. London: Polity Press.

Hendrikse, Cees. 2008. "A Word from the Curator." In *Writing on the Wall: Chinese New Realism and Avant-Garde in the Eighties and Nineties*, edited by Cees Hendrikse, 8–9. Rotterdam: Nai.

Herrero, Marta. 2011. "Selling National Value at the Auction Market: The London and Dublin Markets for Irish Art." *Cultural Sociology* 5 (1): 139–53.

Hoare, Philip. 2006. "Tattooed Leviathan: Gabriel Orozco's Inscribed Andalusian Whale." *Modern Painters*, October 2006, 68–75.

Hollister, Matissa. 2009. "Is Optimal Matching Suboptimal?" *Sociological Methods & Research* 38 (2): 235–64.

Holte, Michael N. 2016. "System of Belief: Michael Ned Holte on Public Fiction." *Artforum International* 54 (6): 176.

Hopfener, Birgit. 2007. "In the Middle of the Goldrush." In *China Art Book*, edited by Uta Grosenick and Caspar H. Schübbe, 9–16. Cologne: Dumont.

———. 2014. *Installationskunst in China: Transkulturelle Reflexionsräume einer Genealogie des Performativen*. Bielefeld, Germany: Transcript Verlag.

———. 2018. "What Do You Think What I Am Doing Here? A Transcultural Analysis of Ai Weiwei's 'Iconoclastic' Works." In *Global Art History: Transkulturelle Verortungen von Kunst und Kunstwissenschaft*, edited by Julia Allerstorfer and Monika Leisch-Kiesl, 169–92. Bielefeld, Germany: Transcript Verlag.

Horowitz, Noah. 2011a. *Art of the Deal: Contemporary Art in a Global Financial Market*. Princeton, NJ: Princeton University Press.

———. 2011b. "Comment on 'Financialization of Art' (by Mark C. Taylor)." *Capitalism and Society* 6 (2): 1–9.

———. 2012. "Internet and Commerce." In *Contemporary Art and Its Commercial Markets: A Report on Current Conditions and Future Scenarios*, edited by Maria Lind and Olav Velthuis, 85–114. Berlin: Sternberg.

———. 2014. "Postscript to the Paperback Edition." In *Art of the Deal*, 215–28. Princeton, NJ: Princeton University Press.

Hoskote, Ranjit. 2010. "Biennials of Resistance: Reflections on the Seventh Gwangju Biennial." In *The Biennial Reader*, edited by Elena Filipovic, Solveig C. Øvstebø and Marieke van Hal, 306–21. Ostfildern, Germany: Hatje Cantz.

Huang Du. 2009. "Interview with Yue Minjun." In *Yue Minjun: The Archeological Discovery in A.D. 3009*, edited by Aier Chen, 48–57. Beijing: Today Art Museum.

Huntington, Samuel P. 1996. *The Clash of Civilizations and the Remaking of World Order*. New York: Simon and Schuster.

Hutter, Michael, Christian Knebel, Gunnar Pietzner, and Maren Schäfer. 2007. "Two Games in Town: A Comparison of Dealer and Auction Prices in Contemporary Visual Arts Markets." *Journal of Cultural Economics* 31 (4): 247–61.

Huxley, Aldous. 1993. *Time Must Have a Stop*. London: Chatto & Windus.

Hwang, Hsiang-Chih. 2009. *International Trade in Unique Artworks: A Panel Data Analysis*. Hong Kong: Lingnan University Hong Kong Department of Economics. http://www.jace.gr.jp/ACEI2012/usb_program/pdf/7.7.4.pdf.

Jary, David, and Julia Jary. 1991. *The HarperCollins Dictionary: Sociology*. New York: Harper Collins.

Jijon, Isabel. 2019. "Toward a Hermeneutic Model of Cultural Globalization: Four Lessons from Translation Studies." *Sociological Theory* 37 (2): 142–61.

Johansson, Johny, and Illka Ronkainen. 2005. "The Esteem of Global Brands." *Journal of Brand Management* 12: 339–54.

Johnson, Allan. 1995. "Multiculturalism." In *The Blackwell Dictionary of Sociology*, edited by Allan G. Johnson, 185. Cambridge, MA: Blackwell.

Johnson, Ken. 2001. "Gabriel Orozco at Marian Goodman." *New York Times*, December 21, 2001. http://www.nytimes.com/2001/12/21/arts/art-in-review-gabriel-orozco-fear-not.html.

Jones, Caroline A. 2010. "Biennial Culture: A Longer History." In *The Biennial Reader*, edited by Elena Filipovic, Solveig C. Øvstebø, and Marieke van Hal, 66–87. Ostfildern: Hatje Cantz.

———. 2017. *The Global Work of Art: World's Fairs, Biennials, and the Aesthetics of Experience*. Chicago: University of Chicago Press.

Joselit, David. 2013. "Categorical Measures." *Artforum International* 51 (9): 296–301.

———. 2016. "'International Pop' and 'The World Goes Pop': Walker Art Center, Minneapolis, and Tate Modern, London." *Artforum International* 54 (5): 230–31.

Josten, Jennifer. 2004. "'La Nacion del arte': Gabriel Orozco and the Image of Mexico in International Contemporary Art." Master's thesis, University of Essex, Department of Art History and Theory.

———. 2006. "From Local to Global: Recapturing Gabriel Orozco's *Naturaleza recuperada*." Paper presented at the graduate symposium *World Art/Art World: Changing Perspectives on Modern and Contemporary Art*, Museum of Modern Art, New York, April 29.

———. 2018. *Mathias Goeritz*. New Haven, CT: Yale University Press.

Judah, Hettie. 2020. "'My Life Has Been a Struggle against the Establishment': Artist Rasheed Araeen." *The Guardian*, January 16, 2020. https://www.theguardian.com/artanddesign/2020/jan/16/rasheed-araeen-interview-restaurant-shamiyaana-stoke-newington.

Kahn, Nathaniel, dir. 2018. *The Price of Everything*. HBO.

Kapsis, Robert E. 1989. "Reputation Building and the Film Art World: The Case of Alfred Hitchcock." *Sociological Quarterly* 30 (1): 15–30.

Karp, Ivan, and Steven D. Levine, eds. 1991. *Exhibiting Cultures: The Poetics and Politics of Museum Display*. Washington, DC: Smithsonian Institution Press.

Karp, Ivan, Christine Mullen Kreamer and Steven D. Levine, eds. 1992. *Museums and Communities: The Politics of Public Culture*. Washington DC: Smithsonian Institution Press.

Khaire, Mukti, and R. Daniel Wadhwani. 2010. "Changing Landscapes: The Construction of Meaning and Value in a New Market Category—Modern Indian Art." *Academy of Management Journal* 53 (6): 1281–1304.

Kharchenkova, Svetlana, Nataliya Komarova, and Olav Velthuis. 2015. "Official Art Organizations in the Emerging Markets of China and Russia." In *Cosmopolitan Canvases: The Globalization of Markets for Contemporary Art*, edited by Olav Velthuis and Stefano Baia Curioni, 78–101. Oxford: Oxford University Press.

Kharchenkova, Svetlana, and Olav Velthuis. 2018. "How to Become a Judgment Device: Valuation Practices and the Role of Auctions in the Emerging Chinese Art Market." *Socio-Economic Review* 16 (3): 459–77.

Kimmelman, Michael. 1998. "When Meaning Emerges Slowly from Missing Parts." *New York Times,* December 11, 1998. http://www.nytimes.com/1998/12/11/arts/art-review-when -meaning-emerges-slowly-from-missing-parts.html?pagewanted=all&src=pm.

Koch, Barbara. 2008. "In Search of Johnson Chang." *Artzine China,* October 3, 2008.

Kovach, Jodi. 2019. "Remotely Mexican: The Critical Reception of Gabriel Orozco's Mobile Matrix, at Home and Abroad." *Art Journal* 78 (1): 88–106.

Kraidy, Marwan M. 2006. *Hybridity, or the Cultural Logic of Globalization.* Philadelphia: Temple University Press.

Kramer, Dieter. 2004. "Willkommen im System." *Zeitschrift für Kulturaustausch* 53 (1): 69–72.

———. 2001. "Andere Lebenswelten der Kunst. Kuenstler aus dem Sueden in der 'Galerie 37' des Museums fuer Voelkerkunde in Frankfurt am Main." In *Kulturelle Globalisierung. Zwischen Weltkultur und kultureller Fragmentierung,* edited by Bernd Wagner, 178–183, Essen: Klartext.

Krause, Monika. 2014. *The Good Project.* Chicago: University of Chicago Press.

Kräussl, Roman. 2012. "Art Price Indices." In *Fine Art and High Finance: Expert Advice on the Economics of Ownership,* edited by Clare McAndrew, 63–86. Hoboken, NJ: Wiley.

Kräussl, Roman, Thorsten Lehnert, and Nicolas Martelin. 2016. "Is There a Bubble in the Art Market?" *Journal of Empirical Finance* 35 (C): 99–109.

Kravagna, Christian. 2002. "Das dichte Jahrzehnt. Positionsverschiebungen Afrikanischer Kunst 1989–2002." In *Kunst und Politik. Jahrbuch der Guernica Gesellschaft,* edited by Viktoria Schmidt-Linsenhoff, 99–112. Osnabrück, Germany: Rasch.

Kuipers, Giselinde. 2011. "Cultural Globalization as the Emergence of a Transnational Cultural Field: Transnational Television and National Media Landscapes in Four European Countries." *American Behavioral Scientist* 55 (5): 541–57.

Kuri, Gabriel. 2000. "General Orozco: By Way of Introduction" In *Gabriel Orozco,* edited by Alma Ruiz, Gabriel Kuri, Benjamin H. D. Buchloh, Damian Ortega, Molly Nesbit, and Abraham Cruzvillegas, 34–65. Los Angeles: Museum of Contemporary Art.

Kwon, Miwon. 1995. "The Fullness of Empty Containers." *Frieze* 4 (24): 54–57.

Lamont, Michèle. 1987. "How to Become a Dominant French Philosopher: The Case of Jacques Derrida." *American Journal of Sociology* 93 (3): 584–622.

———. 2012. "Toward a Comparative Sociology of Valuation and Evaluation." *Annual Review of Sociology* 38 (August): 201–21.

Lamont, Michèle, and Annette Lareau. 1988. "Cultural Capital: Allusions, Gaps and Glissandos in Recent Theoretical Developments." *Sociological Theory* 6 (2): 153–168.

Larry's List. 2016. *Private Art Museum Report.* Manchester: Cornerhouse Publications.

Lechner, Frank. 2005. "Globalization." In *Encyclopedia of Social Theory,* edited by George Ritzer, 330–33. Thousand Oaks, CA: Sage.

Lechner, Frank J. and John Boli. 2005. *World Culture: Origins and Consequences.* Malden, MA: Blackwell.

Lee, Chin-Chuan. 1979. *Media Imperialism Reconsidered: The Homogenizing of Television Culture.* Beverly Hills, CA: Sage.

Lee, Kangsan. 2018. "Neoliberal Marketization of Global Contemporary Visual Art Worlds: Changes in Valuations and the Scope of Local and Global Markets." In *Art and the Challenge of Markets*, edited by Victoria D. Alexander, Samuli Hägg, Simo Häyrynen, and Erkki Sevänen, 65–97. London: Palgrave Macmillan.

Lee, Pamela M. 2003. "Boundary Issues: The Art World under the Sign of Globalism." *Artforum International* 42 (3): 164–67.

Lee, Richard E., 2012. "Fernand Braudel, the Longue Durée, and World-Systems Analysis." in *The Longue Durée and World-Systems Analysis*, edited by Richard E. Lee, 1–7. Albany: SUNY Press.

Levitt, Peggy. 2015. *Artifacts and Allegiances*. Oakland: University of California Press.

Li Pi. 2005. "Between Scylla and Charybdis: The New Context of Chinese Contemporary Art since 2000." In *Mahjong: Contemporary Chinese Art from the Sigg Collection*, edited by Bernhard Fibicher, 35–36. New York: Art Publishers.

Li Xianting. 2005. "Contemporary Chinese Art and a Declining Culture." In *Mahjong: Contemporary Chinese Art from the Sigg Collection*, edited by Bernhard Fibicher, 25–28. New York: Art Publishers.

Li Xianting, and Yue Minjun. 2005. "Creation of a Superficial Idol: Dialogue about Yue's Art." In *Yue Minjun: The Lost Self*, edited by Yue Minjun, 16–25. Hebei, China: Hebei Educational.

Lingwood, James. 1996. "Circulation System." In *Empty Club*, edited by Gabriel Orozco, James Lingwood, Jean Fisher, Mark Haworth-Booth, and Guy Brett, 8–10. London: Artangel.

Lin-Hill, Joe Martin. 2013. "Becoming Global: Contemporary Art Worlds in the Age of the Biennials Boom." PhD diss., New York University.

Lippard, Lucy R. 1976. *From the Center: Feminist Essays on Women's Art*. New York: Dutton.

———. 1984. *Mixed Blessings: New Art in a Multicultural America*. New York: Pantheon.

Lizardo, Omar. 2008. "Understanding the Flow of Symbolic Goods in the Global Cultural Economy." *International Journal of Contemporary Sociology* 45 (1): 13–34.

Luhmann, Niklas. 1993. "Deconstruction as Second-Order Observing." *New Literary History* 24 (4): 763–82.

Ma, William. 2018. "Art Fairs and Biennials in Asia." *Grove Art Online*, July 31, 2018. https://doi .org/10.1093/oao/9781884446054.013.2000000140.

Machado, Lourival Gomez. 1951. Introduction to *I Bienal do Museu de Arte Modern de São Paulo: Catálogo*, 2nd ed.14–22. São Paulo: MAM-SP.

Mackay, Hugh. 2000. "The Globalization of Culture?" In *A Globalizing World? Culture, Economics, Politics*, edited by David Held, 47–85. London: Routledge.

Madsen, Mikael. 2006. "Transnational Fields: Elements of a Reflexive Sociology of the Internationalisation of Law." *Retfærd. Nordisk Juridisk Tidsskrift* 114 (3): 34–41.

Martin, Hubert. 2014. "Les Magiciens de la Terre fut une expérience totale, un pari." Interview with Emmanuelle Jardonnet. *Le Monde*, March 28. https://www.lemonde.fr/culture/article /2014/03/28/les-magiciens-de-la-terre-a-marque-un-tournant-dans-la-facon-d-apprehender -l-art-contemporain_4391438_3246.html.

Martin, John L. 2003. "What Is Field Theory?" *American Journal of Sociology* 109 (1): 1–49.

Martini, Federica. 2011. "One Biennale, Many Biennials." In *Just Another Exhibition: Storie e Politiche delle Biennali*, edited by Federica Martini and Vittoria Martini, 99–116. Milan: Postmedia Srl.

Martini, Federica, and Vittoria Martini, 2011. eds. *Just Another Exhibition: Storie e Politiche delle Biennali*. Milan: Postmedia Srl.

Mattelart, Armand. 1979. *Multinational Corporations and the Control of Culture: The Ideological Apparatuses of Imperialism*. Atlantic Highlands, NJ: Harvester.

McAndrew, Clare. 2008. *The International Art Market: A Survey of Europe in a Global Context*. Helvoirt, Netherlands: European Fine Art Foundation (TEFAF).

———. 2009. *Globalisation and the Art Market: Emerging Economies and the Art Trade in 2008*. Helvoirt, Netherlands: European Fine Art Foundation (TEFAF).

———. 2013a. *TEFAF Art Market Report 2013*. Helvoirt, Netherlands: European Fine Art Foundation (TEFAF).

———. 2013b. "The Art Market (Conversation with Hans Belting)." In *The Global Contemporary and the Rise of New Art Worlds*, edited by Hans Belting, Andrea Buddensieg, and Peter Weibel, 261–65. Cambridge, MA: MIT Press.

———. 2015. *TEFAF Art Market Report 2016*. Helvoirt, Netherlands: European Fine Art Foundation.

———. 2018. *The Art Basel and UBS Global Art Market Report*. Basel: Art Basel. https://artbasel.com/stories/art-market-report-1.

McCarthy, Kevin. F., Elizabeth H. Ondaatje, Arthur Brooks, and András Szántó. 2005. *A Portrait of the Visual Arts: Meeting the Challenges of a New Era*. Santa Monica, CA: RAND.

McEvilley, Thomas. 1990. "Marginalia: The Global Issue." *Artforum International* 28 (7): 19–21.

———. 1993a. "Arrivederci Venice: The Third World Biennials." *Artforum International* 32 (3): 114–15.

———. 1993b. "Venice the Menace." *Artforum International* 32 (2): 102–3.

———. 1993c. "Exhibiting Cultures and Museums and Communities." *Artforum International* 31 (7).

Medina, Cuauhtémoc. 2002. "Mutual Abuse." In *Mexico City: An Exhibition about the Exchange Rates of Bodies and Values*, edited by Klaus Biesenbach et al., 38–48. New York: PS1.

Mehring, Christine. 2008. "Emerging Market: The Birth of the Contemporary Art Fair." *Artforum* 46 (8): 322–28.

Meissen, Markus. 2008. "Eastern Promises: Markus Miessen on OMA/AMO at the Hermitage." *Artforum International* 47 (2): 179–80.

Melikian, Souren. 2007. "Chinese Works Elicit Surprise at Christie's and Sotheby's Contemporary Sales." *New York Times*, October 15, 2007.

Melo, Alexandre. 1997. "Border Crossing." *Artforum International* 35 (6): 33–35.

Meng, Xin. 2007. "Wealth Accumulation and Distribution in Urban China." IZA Discussion Papers, Institute for the Study of Labor, Bonn.

Mersmann, Birgit. 2013. "Global Dawning: The Gwangju Biennial Factor in the Making and Marketing of Contemporary Asian Art." *Third Text* 27 (4): 525–35.

Meyer, James. 2005. "'Open Systems': Tate Modern." *Artforum International* 44 (2): 271.

Miles, Christopher. 2001. "Gabriel Orozco." *Art Nexus* 15 (36): 44–48.

Milligan, Glenn W., and Martha C. Cooper. 1985. "An Examination of Procedures for Determining the Number of Clusters in a Data Set." *Psychometrika* 50 (2): 159–79.

Montero, Gustavo G. 2012. "Biennalization? What Biennalization? The Documentation of Biennials and Other Recurrent Exhibitions." *Art Libraries Journal* 37 (1): 13–23.

Moretti, Franco. 2013. *Distant Reading*. London: Verso Books.

Morgan, Jessica. 2013. "Intercontinental Drift." *Artforum International* 51 (6): 222–29.

Morgner, Christian. 2014a. "The Art Fair as Network." *Journal of Arts Management, Law, and Society* 44 (1): 33–46.

———. 2014b. "The Evolution of the Art Fair." *Historical Social Research* 39 (3): 318–36.

———. 2017. "Diversity and (In)equality in the Global Art World: Global Development and Structure of Field-Configuring Events." *New Global Studies* 11: 165–96.

Mosquera, Gerardo. 1994, "Some Problems in Transcultural Curating" in *Global Visions: A New Internationalism in the Visual Art*, edited by Jean Fisher, 133–139. London: Kala Press.

———. 2003. "From." In *Creolité and Creolization: Documenta11_Platform3*, edited by Okwui Enwezor, Petrine Archer-Straw, Jean Bernabe, Robert Chaudenson, Isaac Julien, Carlos Basualdo, Susanne Ghez, Sarat Maharaj, Mark Nash, Octavio Zaya, and Ute Meta Bauer, 145–48. Ostfildern, Germany: Hatje Cantz.

———. 2011. "The Third Bienal de La Habana in Its Global and Local Contexts." In *Making Art Global (Part 1): The Third Havana Biennial 1989*, edited by Rachel Weiss, Charles Esche, Luis Camnitzer, Coco Fusco, Llilian Llanes Godoy, Geeta Kapur, Mirko Lauer, and Lucy Steeds, 70–79. London: Afterall Books.

Moulin, Raymonde. 1992. *L'artiste, l'institution et le marché*. Paris: Flammarion.

———. 1994. "The Construction of Art Values." *International Sociology* 9 (1): 5–12.

———. 1995. "The Museum and the Marketplace: The Constitution of Value in Contemporary Art." *International Journal of Political Economy* 25 (2): 33–62.

———. 2003. *Le marché de l'art: Mondialisation et nouvelles technologies*. Paris: Flammarion. Originally published 2001.

Muenter, Ulrike. 2005. "Porträt: Galerie Urs Meile, Luzern." *Artzine*, October 7, 2005.

Museum of Modern Art. 2009. "Gabriel Orozco. Dec 13, 2009-Mar 1, 2010." https://www.moma .org/calendar/exhibitions/323.

Nelson, Adele. 2010. "Monumental and Ephemeral: The Early Sao Paulo Bienais." In *Constructive Spirit: Abstract Art in South and North America, 1920s-1950s*, edited by Mary Kate O'Hare, Karen A. Bearor, Tricia Laughlin Boom, Aliza Edelman, Adele Nelson, 127–139. Petaluma: Pomegranate Communications, Inc.

Nesbit, Molly. 2000. "The Tempest." In *Gabriel Orozco*, edited by Benjamin H. D. Buchloh, Alma Ruiz, and Gabriel Orozco, 22–45. Los Angeles: Museum of Contemporary Art.

Nesbit, Molly. 2003. "Walking to Work." In *Gabriel Orozco: Trabajo*, edited by Gabriel Orozco, 3–25. Paris: Galerie Chantal Croussel.

Neubert, Dieter. 2022. "Do Western Sociological Concepts Apply Globally? Towards a Global Sociology." *Sociology*, January 2022, 1–16.

Niemojewski, Rafael. 2010. "Venice or Havana: A Polemic on the Genesis of the Contemporary Biennial." In *The Biennial Reader*, edited by Elena Filipovic, Solveig C. Øvstebø, and Marieke van Hal, 88–103. Ostfildern, Germany: Hatje Cantz.

Nippe, Christine. 2006. *Kunst der Verbindung—Transnationale Netzwerke, Kunst und Globalisierung*. Münster, Germany: Lit Verlag.

Oberlin, Kathleen C., and Thomas F. Gieryn. 2015. "Place and Culture-Making: Geographic Clumping in the Emergence of Artistic Schools." *Poetics* 50: 20–43.

Oguibe, Olu. 2004. *The Culture Game*. Minneapolis: University of Minnesota Press.

Oh Kwang-su. 2000. *Kwangju Biennale 2000: Man + Space*. Kwangju, South Korea: Kwangju Biennale Press.

Ortega, Damian. 2000. "The Bird: For Beginners." In *Gabriel Orozco*, edited by Alma Ruiz, Gabriel Kuri, Benjamin H. D. Buchloh, Damian Ortega, Molly Nesbit, and Abraham Cruzvillegas. Los Angeles: Museum of Contemporary Art.

Papastergiadis, Nikos. 1996. "Gabriel Orozco." *Third Text* 10 (36): 94–95.

Papastergiadis, Nikos, and Meredith Martin. 2011. "Art Biennales and Cities as Platforms for Global Dialogue." In *Festivals and the Cultural Public Sphere*, edited by Gerard Delanty, Liana Giorgi, and Monica Sassatelli, 45–62. Abingdon, UK: Routledge.

Pelizzari, Maria A. 2013. "Between Two Worlds: Maria Antonella Pelizzari on the Art of Luigi Ghirri." *Artforum International* 51 (8): 206–11.

Peterson, Karin. 1997. "The Distribution and Dynamics of Uncertainty in Art Galleries: A Case Study of New Dealerships in the Parisian Art Market, 1985–1990." *Poetics* 25 (4): 241–63.

Peterson, Richard A. 1976. "The Production of Culture: A Prolegomenon." *American Behavioral Scientist* 19 (6): 669–84.

Peterson, Richard A., and Narasimhan Anand. 2004. "The Production of Culture Perspective." *Annual Review of Sociology* 30 (August): 311–34.

Petterson, Anders. 2009. "Chinese Art Market Outlook: Q&A with Larry Warsh." *ArtTactic*, May 22, 2009.

Philipsen, Lotte. 2010. *Globalizing Contemporary Art: The Art World's New Internationalism*. Aarhus, Denmark: Aarhus University Press.

Phillips, Damon J. 2013. *Shaping Jazz: Cities, Labels, and the Global Emergence of an Art Form*. Princeton, NJ: Princeton University Press.

Pieterse, Jan N. 1995. "Globalization as Hybridization." In *Global Modernities*, edited by Mike Featherstone, Scott Lash, and Roland Robertson, 45–68. Newbury Park, CA: Sage.

———. 2004. *Globalization and Culture: Global Mélange*. Lanham, MD: Rowman and Littlefield.

Pinchbeck, Daniel. 1998. "Gabriel Orozco." *Art Newspaper* 17 (87).

Plagens, Peter. 1999. "Manhattan Transfer." *Artforum International* 38 (3): 43.

Plattner, Stuart. 1996. *High Art Down Home: An Economic Ethnography of a Local Art Market*. Chicago: University of Chicago Press.

Pohlenz, Ricardo. 2009. "Gabriel Orozco." *Flash Art* 42 (267): 94.

Pollack, Barbara. 2008. "The Chinese Art Explosion." *Artnews* 107 (8): 118–27.

Nehb, Hannah. 2010. "Gallery Profile: Alexander Ochs Galleries Berlin / Beijing." *Kunst* 1002: 20–23.

Quart, Alissa. 1999. "Hunger Artist." *Artforum International* 38 (3): 48.

Quemin, Alain. 2002. *L'art contemporain international: Entre les institutions et le marché*. Nîmes, France: Jacqueline Chambon / Artprice.

———. 2006. "Globalization and Mixing in the Visual Arts: An Empirical Survey of 'High Culture' and Globalization." *International Sociology* 21 (4): 522–50.

———. 2012. "The Internationalization of the Contemporary Art World and Market: The Role of Nationality and Territory in a Supposedly 'Globalized' Sector." In *Contemporary Art and Its Commercial Markets: A Report on Current Conditions and Future Scenarios*, edited by Maria Lind and Olav Velthuis, 53–83. Berlin: Sternberg.

———. 2013. "International Contemporary Art Fairs in a 'Globalized' Art Market." *European Societies* 15 (2): 162–77.

Quemin, Alain, and Femke Van Hest. 2015. "The Impact of Nationality and Territory on Fame and Success in the Visual Arts Sector: Artists, Experts, and the Market." In *Cosmopolitan Canvases: The Globalization of Markets for Contemporary Art*, edited by Olav Velthuis and Stefano Baia Curioni, 170–92. Oxford: Oxford University Press.

Quiles, Daniel. 2009. "Leon Ferrari and Mira Schendel: Museum of Modern Art, New York." *Artforum International* 47 (10): 328.

Rajchman, John. 2011. "The Contemporary: A New Idea?" In *Aesthetics and Contemporary Art*, edited by Armen Avanessian and Luke Skrebowski, 125–44. Berlin: Sternberg.

Rangarajan, Raj. 2006. "Asia Week Roundup: Buying Is Strong in All Sectors." *Artnews*, April 25, 2006.

Rawlings, Craig M. 2001. "'Making Names': The Cutting-Edge Renewal of African Art in New York City, 1985–1996." *Poetics* 29 (1): 25–54.

Reckwitz, Andreas. 2000. *Die Transformation der Kulturtheorien. Zur Entwicklung eines Theorieprogramms*. Weilerswist, Germany: Velbrueck.

Regev, Motti. 1994. "Producing Artistic Value: The Case of Rock Music." *Sociological Quarterly* 35 (1): 85–102.

———. 1997. "Rock Aesthetics and Musics of the World." *Theory, Culture & Society* 14 (3): 125–42.

———. 2003. "'Rockization': Diversity within Similarity in World Popular Music." In *Global America? The Cultural Consequences of Globalization*, edited by Ulrich Beck, Natan Sznaider, and Rainer Winter, 222–34. Liverpool: Liverpool University Press.

———. 2007. "Cultural Uniqueness and Aesthetic Cosmopolitanism." *European Journal of Social Theory* 10 (1): 123–38.

Renneboog, Luc and Christophe Spaenjers. 2015. "Investment Returns and Economic Fundamentals in International Art Markets." In *Cosmopolitan Canvases: The Globalization of Markets for Contemporary Art*, edited by Olav Velthuis and Stefano Baia Curioni, 129–146. Oxford: Oxford University Press.

Ritchie, Matthew. 1995. "Gabriel Orozco." *Flash Art* 28 (180): 86.

Ritzer, George. 2003. "Rethinking Globalization: Glocalization/Grobalization and Something/Nothing." *Sociological Theory* 21(3): 193–209.

Robertson, Iain. 2005a. "The International Art Market." In *Understanding International Art Markets and Management*, edited by Iain Robertson, 13–36. London: Routledge.

Robertson, Iain, ed. 2005b. *Understanding International Art Markets and Management*. London: Routledge.

Robertson, Roland. 2001. "Globalization Theory 2000+: Major Problematics." In *Social Theory*, edited by George Ritzer, 458–69. London: Sage.

Rodner, Victoria L., and Elaine Thomson. 2013. "The Art Machine: Dynamics of a Value Generating Mechanism for Contemporary Art." *Arts Marketing: An International Journal* 3 (1): 58–72.

Rodner, Victoria L., and Chloe Preece. 2016. "Painting the Nation: Examining the Intersection between Politics and the Visual Arts Market in Emerging Economies." *Journal of Macromarketing* 36 (2): 128–48.

Rohr-Bongard, Linde. 2001. *Kunst = Kapital. Der Capital Kunstkompass von 1970 bis heute*. Cologne: Salon.

Rojas-Sotelo, Miguel Leonardo 2009. *Cultural Maps, Networks and Flows: The History and Impact of the Havana Biennale 1984 to the Present*. (Doctoral dissertation, University of Pittsburgh).

Rosenberg, Karen. 2008. "New York Cool: a Transitional Generation is Given its Due." *New York Times*, April 25, 2008.

Rovers, Eva. 2009. "Special Issue: The Art Collector—Between Philanthropy and Self-Glorification." *Journal of the History of Collections* 21 (2): 157–61.

Rudolph, Steffen, and Ulf Wuggenig. 2012. "Symbolischer Wert und Warenwert." In *Das Kunstfeld: Eine Studie über Akteure und Institutionen der zeitgenössischen Kunst am Beispiel von Zürich, Wien, Hamburg und Paris*, edited by Heike Munder and Ulf Wuggenig, 325–42. Zürich: JRP Ringier.

Rule, Alix, and David Levine. 2013. "International Art English." *MERKUR* 67: 516–27.

Said, Edward. 2001. "The Clash of Ignorance." *Nation*, October 22, 2001.

Saltz, Jerry. 1999. "Here and Gone." *Village Voice*, January 5, 1999. http://www.villagevoice.com /1999-01-05/art/here-and-gone/.

———. 2009. "Picking over the Bones." *New York Magazine*, December 18, 2009.

Sans, Jérôme. 2009. "Yue Minjun: Forever Young with a Big Smile." In *China Talks: Interviews with 32 Contemporary Artists*, edited by Jérôme Sans, 168–72. Hong Kong: Timezone 8.

Santamarina, Guillermo. 2005. *Gabriel Orozco*. (Exhibition Catalogue). Madrid: Museo Nacional Centro de Arte Reina Sofía.

Santana-Acuña, Álvaro. 2014. "How a Literary Work Becomes a Classic: The Case of *One Hundred Years of Solitude*." *American Journal of Cultural Sociology* 2 (1): 97–149.

Santana-Acuña, Álvaro. 2020. *Ascent to Glory*. New York: Columbia University Press.

Sapiro, Gisèle. 2010. "Globalization and Cultural Diversity in the Book Market: The Case of Translations in the US and in France." *Poetics* 38 (4): 419–39.

———. 2015. "Translation and Symbolic Capital in the Era of Globalization: French Literature in the United States." *Cultural Sociology* 9 (3): 320–346.

Sassatelli, Monica. 2015. "The Biennalization of Art Worlds." In *Routledge International Handbook of the Sociology of Art and Culture*, 277–89. London: Routledge.

———. 2017. "Symbolic Production in the Art Biennial: Making Worlds." *Theory, Culture & Society* 34 (4): 89–113.

Sassen, Saskia. 2004. "Countergeography of Globalization." Web Journal *Absolute One*, http:// absoluteone.ljudmila.org/globalisation.php.

———. 2007. *A Sociology of Globalization*. New York: Norton.

Sayej, Nadja. 2019. "This New Book Rounds Up All the Most Explosive Art-World Gossip." *Vice Garage*, June 5, 2019. https://garage.vice.com/en_us/article/j5wbb3/boom-art-world-gossip.

Scheps, Marc. 1999. "Kunstwelten im Dialog." In *Kunstwelten im Dialog—von Gauguin zur globalen Gegenwart*, edited by Marc Scheps, Yilmaz Dziewor, and Barbara Thiemann, 16–20. Cologne: DuMont.

Schiller, Herbert I. 1971. *Mass Communications and American Empire*. Boston: Beacon.

———. 1976. *Communication and Cultural Domination*. New York: International Arts and Sciences.

———. 1989. *Culture Inc.: The Corporate Takeover of Public Expression*. New York: Oxford University Press.

———. 1991. "Not Yet the Post-Imperialist Era." *Critical Studies in Mass Communication* 8 (1): 13–28.

———. 1998. "American Pop Culture Sweeps the World." In *Approaches to Audiences: A Reader*, edited by Roger Dickinson, Ramaswami Harindranath, and Olga Linné, 2–13. London: Arnold.

Schjeldahl, Peter. 2001. "Exquisite Debris: The Transforming Eye of Gabriel Orozco." *New Yorker* 77 (38): 102.

———. 2004. "Dealership: How Marian Goodman Quietly Changed the Contemporary-Art Market." *New Yorker* 79 (45): 36–41.

———. 2009. "Man of the World: A Gabriel Orozco Retrospective." *New Yorker* 85 (42): 146–47.

Schmidt-Wellenburg, Christian, and Stefan Bernhard, eds. 2020. *Charting Transnational Fields: Methodology for a Political Sociology of Knowledge*. New York: Routledge.

Schoellhammer, Georg. 1999. "Art in the Era of Globalization." In *The Global 500*, edited by Oliver Ressler, 23–34. Vienna: Selene.

Schoeni, Manfred. 1994. "Foreword." In *Faces Behind the Bamboo Curtain. Works by Yue Min Jun and Yang Shao Bin*, edited by Manfred Schoeni, 3, Hong Kong: Schoeni Art Gallery LTD.

Schultheis, Franz, Stephan Egger, Thomas Mazzurana, and Erwin Single. 2015. *When Art Meets Money: Encounters at the Art Basel*. London: König.

Schultheis, Franz, Raphaela Köfeler, Erwin Single, and Thomas Mazzurana. 2016. *Art Unlimited? Dynamics and Paradoxes of a Globalizing Art World*. Bielefeld, Germany: Transcript Verlag.

Schuster, Aaron. 2008. "Gabriel Orozco." *Frieze* 17 (123): 194–95.

Scott, Samuel C. 2005. "Buchloh Joins Art History Faculty." *Harvard Crimson*, July 8, 2005. http://www.thecrimson.com/article/2005/7/8/buchloh-joins-art-history-faculty-harvards/.

Sen, Amartya. 2006. *Identity and Violence: The Illusion of Destiny*. New York: Norton.

Shin, Dongyoub, Kangsan Lee, and Hakbae Lee. 2014. "Neoliberal Marketization of Art Worlds and Status Multiplexity: Price Formation in a Korean Art Auction, 1998–2007." *Poetics* 43: 120–48.

Shnayerson, Michael. 2019. "Mary Boone is Taking a Break." *Town and Country Magazine*, April 18, 2019. https://www.townandcountrymag.com/society/money-and-power/a26932490/what-happened-to-mary-boone/.

Shrum, Wesley M., Jr. 1991. "Critics and Publics: Cultural Mediation in Highbrow and Popular Performing Arts." *American Journal of Sociology* 97 (2): 347–75.

Siddique, Abu. 2006. "Globalization and Economic Development." In *Economic Growth, Transition and Globalization in China*, edited by Yanrui Wu, 214–38. Bodmin, UK: MPG Books.

Sigg, Uli. 2005. "Access to China." In *Mahjong: Contemporary Chinese Art from the Sigg Collection*, edited by Bernhard Fibicher, 15–21. New York: Art Publishers.

Simbao, Ruth. 2015. "What 'Global Art' and Current (Re)turns Fail to See: A Modest Counternarrative of 'Not-Another-Biennial.'" *Image and Text* 25 (1): 261–86.

Sindelar, Melanie. 2016. "Local, Regional, Global: An Investigation of Art Dubai's Transnational Strategies." *Arabian Humanities International Journal of Archaeology and Social Sciences in the Arabian Peninsula* 7: 1–18.

Smith, Charles. 1989. *Auctions: The Social Construction of Value*. Berkeley: University of California Press.

Smith, David. 2007. *The Dragon and the Elephant: China, India and the New World Order*. London: Profile Books.

Smith, Karen. 2008. "Interview with Yue Minjun." *Yishu: Journal of Contemporary Chinese Art* 7 (2): 25–36.

Solomon, Andrew. 1993. "Their Irony, Humor (and Art) Can Save China." *New York Times Magazine*, December 19, 1993.

Sontag, Debora. 2009. "A Whale of a Return to MoMA." *New York Times*. December 11, 2009.

Sotheby's. 2006. *Sotheby's March 2006 Contemporary Art Asia - China, Japan, Korea*. (Auction Catalogue). New York: Sotheby's.

Spiegler, Marc. 2004. "Treasure Island." *Art Review*, November 1, 2004. http://www.marcspiegler .com/Articles/ArtReview/ArtReview_2004_11_Sigg.PDF.

Spoerhase, Carlos. 2014. "Das Maß der Potsdamer Garde. Die ästhetische Vorgeschichte des Rankings in der europäischen Literatur- und Kunstkritik des 18." *Jahrbuch der Deutschen Schillergesellschaft* 58: 90–126.

Springer, Jose Manuel. 1997. "Gabriel Orozco: Placement, Displacement." *Art Nexus* 11 (25): 90–91.

Stallabrass, Julian. 2004. *Art Incorporated. The Story of Contemporary Art*. New York: Oxford University Press.

———. 2006. *Contemporary Art: A Very Short Introduction*. New York: Oxford University Press.

———. 2017. "Elite Art, Populism and Critique." *e-skop*, November 19, 2017. https://www.e-skop .com/skopbulten/elite-art-populism-and-critique/3587.

———. 2022, in press. "Art and the Condition of Criticism." in *Judgement Practices in the Artistic Field*, edited by Beate Söntgen, Stephanie Marchal and Hubert Locher. Munich, Germany: Verlag Silke Schreiber.

Staniszewski, Mary Anne. 1997. "Charting of Course." *Artforum International* 36 (1): 79–80.

Steiner, Rochelle. 2004. "Path of Thought." In *Gabriel Orozco*, edited by Gabriel Orozco, Briony Fer, Benjamin H. D. Buchloh, and Rochelle Steiner, 65–89. London: Serpentine Gallery.

Steinmetz, George. 2002. "Precoloniality and Colonial Subjectivity: Ethnographic Discourse and Native Policy in German Overseas Imperialism, 1780s–1914." *Political Power and Social Theory* 15 (November): 135–228.

Steinmetz, George. 2008. "The Colonial State as a Social Field: Ethnographic Capital and Native Policy in the German Overseas Empire before 1914." *American Sociological Review* 73 (4): 589–612.

Storr, Robert. 1997. "Kassel Rock." *Artforum International* 35 (9): 79–80.

———. 1999. "Prince of Tides: Interview with 1999 Venice Biennale Visual Arts Director Harald Szeemann." *Artforum International* 37 (9): 160–65.

Storr, Robert. 2008. "Venice Revisited: Robert Storr Responds to His Critics." *Artforum International* 46 (5): 48.

Stovel, Katherine, and Marc Bolan. 2004. "Residential Trajectories: Using Optimal Alignment to Reveal the Structure of Residential Mobility." *Sociological Methods Research* 32 (4): 559–98.

Stovel, Katherine, Michael Savage, and Peter S. Bearman. 1996. "Ascription into Achievement: Models of Career Systems at Lloyds Bank, 1890–1970." *American Journal of Sociology* 102 (2): 358–99.

Straubhaar, Joseph D. 1991. "Beyond Media Imperialism: Asymmetrical Interdependence and Cultural Proximity." *Critical Studies in Mass Communication* 8 (1): 39–59.

Sussman, Elizabeth. 2005. "Then and Now: Whitney Biennial 1993." *Art Journal* 64 (1): 74–79.

Margaret Sundell. 2004. "Gabriel Orozco." *Artforum International* 42 (9).

Swartz, David. 1997. Culture and Power: The Sociology of Pierre Bourdieu. University of Chicago Press.

Tabor, Jürgen. 2010. "Zur sozialen Logik der Kunstindustrie." *Kunstgeschichte. Texte zur Diskussion* 9.

Tang, Jeannine. 2007. "Of Biennials and Biennialists: Venice, Documenta, Münster." *Theory, Culture & Society* 24 (7–8): 247–60.

Tang, Jeannine. 2011. "Biennalization and Its Discontents." In *Negotiating Values in the Creative Industries: Fairs, Festivals, and Competitive Events*, edited by Brian Moeran and Jesper Strandgaard Pedersen, 73–93. Cambridge: Cambridge University Press.

Taylor, Mark C. 2011. "Financialization of Art." *Capitalism and Society* 6 (2): 1–19. https://doi.org/10.2202/1932-0213.1091.

Temkin, Ann. 1999. "Afterword." In *Gabriel Orozco Photogravity*. Exhibition Catalogue edited by Ann Temkin, Gabriel Orozco, and David Sylvester, 173–177. Philadelphia: Philadelphia Museum of Art.

Temkin, Ann. 2009. "Open Studio." in *Gabriel Orozco*. edited by Ann Temkin, Anne Byrd, Benjamin H. D. Buchloh, Briony Fer, and Paulina Pobocha, 11–21. New York: Museum of Modern Art.

Temkin, Ann, Anne Byrd, Benjamin H. D. Buchloh, Briony Fer, and Paulina Pobocha. 2009. *Gabriel Orozco*. New York: Museum of Modern Art.

Thompson, Don. 2008. *The $12 Million Stuffed Shark: The Curious Economics of Contemporary Art*. Basingstoke, UK: Palgrave Macmillan.

Thompson, Don. 2014. *The Supermodel and the Brillo Box: Back Stories and Peculiar Economics from the World of Contemporary Art*. New York: St. Martin's.

Thornton, Sarah. 2008. *Seven Days in the Art World*. New York: Norton.

Thornton, Sarah, and Cristina Ruiz. 2008. "Revealed: Royal Family of Qatar Is Buyer of World's Most Expensive Hirst." *Art Newspaper*, April 30, 2008. https://www.theartnewspaper.com/2008/05/01/revealed-royal-family-of-qatar-is-buyer-of-worlds-most-expensive-hirst.

Thorpe, Vanessa. 2007. "Chinese Work Leads Boom in Art Sales." *The Guardian*, October 14, 2007.

Tinari Philip. 2007a. "Li Xianting." In *Artists in China*, edited by Mario Ciampi, 425. London: Verba Volant.

Tinari Philip. 2007b. "Yue Minjun." In *Artists in China*, edited by Mario Ciampi, 40–45. London: Verba Volant.

Tomkins, Calvin. 2007a. "A Fool for Art: Jeffrey Deitch and the Exuberance of the Art Market." *New Yorker*, November 4, 2007, 64–75.

Tomkins, Calvin. 2007b. "The Turnaround Artist: Jeff Koons, Up from Banality." *New Yorker*. April 16, 2007, 58–67.

Tomlinson, John. 1991. *Cultural Imperialism: A Critical Introduction*. Baltimore: John Hopkins University Press.

———. 1999. *Globalization and Culture*. Chicago: University of Chicago Press.

Tromans, Peter. 2000. "South Africa Goes East and West: Sanctions Lift Boosts Red Wine Production to Compete Worldwide." *Wine Business Monthly*, June 1, 2000.

Tunstall, Jeremy. 1977. *The Media Are American: Anglo-American Media in the World*. Vol. 1. London: Constable.

Turner, Grady T. 1998. "Gabriel Orozco." *Contemporary Visual Arts* 22 (17): 25–26.

UN Statistics Division. n.d. "Methodology: Standard Country or Area Codes for Statistical Use (M49). Department of Economic and Social Affairs. http://unstats.un.org/unsd/methods/m49/m49regin.htm.

Van den Bosch, Anette. 2005. *The Australian Art World. Aesthetics in a Global Market*. Sydney: Allen and Unwin.

Van Hest, Femke, and Filip Vermeylen. 2015. "Has the Art Market Become Truly Global? Evidence from China and India." In *Crossroads in New Media, Identity and Law*, edited by Wouter de Been, Payal Arora, and Mireille Hildebrandt, 179–96. London: Macmillan.

Vaughan, Diane. 1992. "Theory Elaboration: The Heuristics of Case Analysis." In *What Is a Case? Exploring the Foundations of Social Inquiry*, edited by Charles C. Ragin and Howard S. Becker, 173–202. Cambridge: Cambridge University Press.

———. 2004. "Theorizing Disaster: Analogy, Historical Ethnography, and the Challenger Accident." *Ethnograph* 5 (3): 313–45.

———. 2014. "Analogy, Cases and Comparative Social Organization", in *Theorizing in Social Science: The Context of Discovery*, edited by Richard Swedberg, 61–84, Stanford, CA: Stanford University

Veblen, Thorstein. (1899) 2017. *The Theory of the Leisure Class*. Milton Park, UK: Routledge.

Velthuis, Olav. 2002. "Globalization and the Visual Arts." *Newsletter of the Sociology of Culture, Section of the American Sociological Association* 17 (1): 7–9.

———. 2007. *Talking Prices: Symbolic Meanings of Prices on the Market for Contemporary Art*. Princeton, NJ: Princeton University Press. Originally published 2005.

———. 2012. "The Contemporary Art Market between Stasis and Flux." In *Contemporary Art and Its Commercial Markets: A Report on Current Conditions and Future Scenarios*, edited by Maria Lind and Olav Velthuis, 17–52. London: Sternberg.

———. 2013a. "Globalization and Commercialization of the Art Market." In *Contemporary Art: 1989 to the Present*, edited by Alexander Dumbadze and Suzanne Hudson, 369–78. Chichester, UK: Wiley-Blackwell.

———. 2013b. "Globalization of Markets for Contemporary Art: Why Local Ties Remain Dominant in Amsterdam and Berlin." *European Societies* 15 (2): 290–308.

———. 2015. "There Is No Single, Global Art Market." *Art Newspaper*, June 22, 2015. https://www.theartnewspaper.com/2015/06/22/there-is-no-single-global-art-market.

Velthuis, Olav, and Erica Coslor. 2012. "The Financialization of Art." In *The Oxford Handbook of the Sociology of Finance*, edited by Karin Cetina and Alex Preda, 471–87. Oxford: Oxford University Press.

Velthuis, Olav, and Stefano Baia Curioni. 2015. "Making Markets Global." In *Cosmopolitan Canvases: The Globalization of Markets for Contemporary Art*, edited by Olav Velthuis and Stefano Baia Curioni, 1–30. Oxford: Oxford University Press.

Verboord, Marc, Giselinde Kuipers, and Susanne Janssen. 2015. "Institutional recognition in the transnational literary field, 1955–2005." *Cultural Sociology*, 9 (3): 447–465.

Verger, Anne. 1987. "L'art d'estimer l'art: Comment classer l'incomparable." *Actes de la Recherche en Science Sociales* 12 (66–67): 105–21.

Vermeylen, Filip. 2015. "The India Art Fair and the Market for Visual Arts in the Global South." In *Cosmopolitan Canvases: The Globalization of Markets for Contemporary Art*, edited by Olav Velthuis and Stefano Baia Curioni, 31–54. Oxford: Oxford University Press.

Verzotti, Giorgio. 1993. "'Aperto 93': The Better Biennale." *Artforum International* 32 (2): 104.

Vine, Richard. 2008. *New China, New Art*. London: Prestel.

Viveros-Fauné, Christian. 2009. "Globetrotting Gabriel Orozco Alights at MOMA." *Village Voice*, December 29, 2009. http://www.villagevoice.com/2009-12-29/art/globetrotting -gabriel-orozco-alights-at-moma/.

Vogel, Carol. 2006a. "High Rollers and Blue-Chip Artists at Basel Fair." *New York Times*, June 15, 2006

———. 2006b. "Sotheby's Bets on a Windfall for Today's Chinese Art." *New York Times*, March 29, 2006.

———. 2008. "Contemporary Chinese on Sale in Hong Kong." *New York Times*, March 28, 2008.

Vogel, Sabine. 2010. *Biennials. Art on a Global Scale*. Vienna: Springer.

Volk, Gregory. 1995. "Orozco: Circumstantial Evidence." *World Art* 3: 54–58.

Von Bennigsen, Silvia, Irene Gludowacz, and Susanne Van Hagen. 2009. *Global Art*. Berlin: Hatje Cantz.

Von Drehle, David. 2007. "People Who Mattered." *Time*. December 19, 2007.

Wallerstein, Immanuel. 1979. *The Capitalist World-Economy*. Vol. 2. Cambridge: Cambridge University Press.

Wan, Guanghua, Ming Lu, and Zhao Chen. 2006. "Globalization and Regional Income Inequality: Empirical Evidence from within China." WIDER Research Paper, World Institute for Development, United Nations University, Helsinki.

Wang, Jian. 2006. "The Politics of Goods: A Case Study of Consumer Nationalism and Media Discourse in Contemporary China." *Asian Journal of Communication* 16 (2):187–206.

Warhol, Andy. 1975. *The Philosophy of Andy Warhol: From A to B and Back Again*. New York: Harcourt Brace Jovanovich.

Waters, Malcolm. 1995. *Globalization*. London: Routledge.

Watson, Peter. 1992. *From Manet to Manhattan*. London: Hutchinson.

Weber, Max. (1922) 1980. *Wirtschaft und Gesellschaft*. Tübingen, Germany: Mohr.

Wei, Chu-Chiun. 2013. "From National Art to Critical Globalism: The Politics and Curatorial Strategies of the Taiwan Pavilion at the Venice Biennale." *Third Text* 27 (4): 470–84.

Weiss, Rachel. 2011. "A Certain Place and a Certain Time: The Third Bienal de La Habana and the Origins of the Global Exhibition." In *Making Art Global (Part 1): The Third Havana Biennial 1989*, edited by Rachel Weiss, Charles Esche, Luis Camnitzer, Coco Fusco, Lilian Llanes Godoy, Geeta Kapur, and Mirko Lauer, 14–69. London: Afterall Books.

West, Shearer. 1995. "National Desires and Regional Realities in the Venice Biennale." *Art History* 18 (3): 404–34.

White, Harrison C., and Cynthia A. White. 1993. *Canvases and Careers: Institutional Change in the French Painting World*. Chicago: University of Chicago Press. Originally published 1965.

Wijnberg, Nachoem M., and Gerda Gemser. 2000. "Adding Value to Innovation: Impressionism and the Transformation of the Selection System in Visual Arts." *Organization Science* 11 (3): 323–29.

Wohl, Hannah. 2021. *Bound by Creativity: How Contemporary Art Is Created and Judged*. Chicago: University of Chicago Press.

Wong, Winnie. 2015. "Arresting Development: Winnie Wong on China's Museum Boom." *Artforum International* 54 (3): 123–26.

Wu, Chin-Tao. 2007a. "Occupation by Absence, Preoccupation with Presence: A Worm's-Eye View of Art Biennials." *Journal of Visual Culture* 6 (3): 379–86.

———. 2007b. "Worlds Apart: Problems of Interpreting Globalised Art." *Third Text* 21 (6): 719–31.

———. 2009. "Biennials without Borders?" *New Left Review* 57 (3): 107–15.

———. 2010. "Biennials and Art Fairs." *Grove Art Online*, February 24, 2010.

Wu, Yanrui. 2006. Introduction to *Economic Growth, Transition and Globalization in China*, edited by Yanrui Wu, 1–12. Bodmin, UK: MPG Books.

Yogev, Tamar. 2010. "The Social Construction of Quality: Status Dynamics in the Market for Contemporary Art." *Socio-Economic Review* 8(3): 511–536.

Yogev, Tamar, and Gokhan Ertug. 2015. "Global and Local Flows in the Contemporary Art Market: The Growing Prevalence of Asia." In *Cosmopolitan Canvases: The Globalization of Markets for Contemporary Art*, edited by Olav Velthuis and Stefano Baia Curioni, 193–212. New York: Oxford University Press.

Yogev, Tamar, and Thomas Grund. 2012. "Network Dynamics and Market Structure: The Case of Art Fairs." *Sociological Focus* 45 (1): 23–40.

Yuan, Elizabeth. 2007. "Painting's Owner 'Un-Executed.'" *CNN*, October 12, 2007. http://edition.cnn.com/2007/WORLD/asiapcf/10/12/china.artist/index.html.

Yue, Minjun. 2006. *Reproduction Icons: Yue Minjun Works, 2004–2006*. Shenzhen, China: Museum Collection Services.

Zahner, Nina. 2006. *Die neuen Regeln der Kunst. Andy Warhol und der Umbau des Kunstbetriebs im 20. Jahrhundert*. Frankfurt am Main: Campus Verlag.

Zarobell, John. 2017. *Art and the Global Economy*. Oakland: University of California Press.

Zelevansky, Lynn. 1993. *Gabriel Orozco: Projects 41*. New York: Museum of Modern Art.

Zhan, Yan. 2007. "Chinese Contemporary Art Comes out of the Shadow." *People's Daily Online*, September 20, 2007. http://eg.china-embassy.org/eng/xinwen/t364715.htm.

Zhang, Julia C. 2011. "The Meaning of Style: Postmodernism, Demystification, and Dissonance in Post-Tiananmen Chinese Avant-Garde." *Sociologie de l'Art* 16 (1): 99–142.

Zhang, Kevin H. 2006. "Foreign Direct Investment: Opportunity or Challenge for China after WTO Membership?" In *China and the Challenge of Economic Globalization: The Impact of WTO Membership*, edited by Hung-Gay Fung, Changhong Pei, and Kevin H. Zhang, 23–36. Farnham, UK: Ashgate.

Zorloni, Alessia, and Antonella Ardizzone. 2016. "Celebrity Effect in the Contemporary Art Market." In *Art Wealth Management*, edited by Alessia Zorloni, 67–79. Cham, Switzerland: Springer.

Zussman, Robert. 2004. "People in Places." *Qualitative Sociology* 27 (4): 351–63.

INDEX

Note: Page numbers in italic type indicate illustrations.

Adam, Georgina, 252

African contemporary artists, symbolic capital of, 128

Alÿs, Francis, 170

America, Bride of the Sun (exhibition, 1992), 171–72

analogical theorizing, xix

anticommercial conversion model, 112–14, 117–18, *117*, 131, 134–35, 142, 183, 186–87, 214–15, 246, 260

Appadurai, Arjun, 8–9, 16, 45–47, 151, 158

A propósito (exhibition), 171

Araeen, Rasheed, 23–24, 107, 128, 317n118, 326n3

Art Basel, 74, 77, 79, 81

art criticism. *See* discourse

Art Dubai, 78

Arte Povera, 169, 211, 273

ArtFacts, 64–65, 121–22, 132

art fairs: aesthetic focus of, 82–84; biennial circuit compared to, 74–75, *75*, 82–84, 323n104; corporate interventions in, 77–79; gallery competition in, 80–82; global character of, 78–80; global fair circuit, 73–84; government support for, 77–78; hierarchy in, 79; rise and growth of, 73–78, 95; role of, in constituting global commercial subfield, 14, 69

art for art's discursive sake, 215, 266

art for art's sake, 71, 113–14, 142, 187, 239

Artforum International (journal), 47–62, 83, 186

art industry, xx, 116–18, 142

artistic prestige: *Artforum* as means to, 47; artists' careers in relation to, 132–37; Bourdieu's conversion model of, 112–14; market-convergence model of, 115–16; market success vs., xviii, 5; Orozco and, 182. *See also* symbolic capital; symbolic recognition; valuation

art market: art fairs, 69, 73–84; auction houses, 69, 84–99; commercialization and financialization of, 68–69, 84, 102, 104, 143–46; effect on, of globalization in the arts, 122–25; external wealth as factor in, 75, 76, 77, 98, 104, 115; galleries in, 70–73; global, regional, and national aspects of, 67, 69, 83, 87, 92–94, 97–98, 103–4, 151–52, 270; global developments in, 68–69; hierarchy in, 103; international, of 1990s, 70–73; online price databases, 69, 99–102; other cultural markets compared to, 101; price escalation in, 133, 145, 231–35; primary vs. secondary, 71. *See also* collectors; global art field; market-convergence model; market success; prices

Artnet, 99–102

l'art pour l'art. See art for art's sake

Artprice, 100–102, 121, 132

art prizes. *See* symbolic recognition

asymmetric interdependencies, 46, 66, 252, 261, 263

A NOTE ON THE TYPE

This book has been composed in Arno, an Old-style serif typeface in the classic Venetian tradition, designed by Robert Slimbach at Adobe.

GPSR Authorized Representative: Easy Access System Europe - Mustamäe tee 50, 10621 Tallinn, Estonia, gpsr.requests@easproject.com

www.ingramcontent.com/pod-product-compliance
Lightning Source LLC
Chambersburg PA
CBHW020852180526
45163CB00007B/2481